CHICAGO PUBLIC LIBRARY

SOCIAL SCIENCES DIVISION
CHICAGO PUBLIC LIBRARY
400 SOUTH STATE STREET
CHICAGO, IL 60605

FORM 19

DEMCO

VALUE
and the
Good Life

VALUE
and the
Good Life

Thomas L. Carson

University of Notre Dame Press
Notre Dame, Indiana

Manufactured in the United States of America

Library of Congress Cataloging-in-Publication Data

Carson, Thomas L., 1950–
    Value and the good life / Thomas L. Carson.
        p. cm.
    Includes bibliographical references and index.
    ISBN 0-268-04352-3 (alk. paper) — ISBN 0-268-04353-1 (pbk. : alk. paper)
    1. Ethics. 2. Values. 3. Conduct of life. I. Title.

BJ1012.C334 2000
170—dc21

                                                        00-027542

for
Nora & Danny

WITH LOVE FROM DAD

Contents

Acknowledgments

My general plan for this book developed as a result of a long series of conversations with Paul Moser. His advice has helped me greatly throughout the writing of this book. I am also indebted to him for reading parts of the manuscript and for his collaboration on our paper "Relativism and Normative Nonrealism: Basing Morality on Rationality," which is the basis for the first four sections of chapter 8.

Harry Gensler did a very careful reading of several drafts of the entire manuscript and has given me many helpful criticisms and suggestions. My graduate assistants, Dwayne Mulder, Jason Beyer, Patrick Stone, and especially Chris Meyers, have read many drafts of the book and saved me from errors of both substance and style. Connie Rosati read the final chapter of the book and offered many helpful criticisms. Her criticisms and published work have influenced the conclusions I reach at the end of the book.

Others who have helped me in various ways (by reading part of the manuscript, discussion, or correspondence) include Julie Ward, J. D. Trout, Richard Kraut, Thomas Hurka, Brad Hooker, Robert Adams, Noah Lemos, Charles Taliaferro, James Sterba, Richard Brandt, Tom Wren, and Victoria Wike. Adams, Kraut, and Hurka have also helped through their own published work, which figures importantly in this book. I would also like to thank Rebecca DeBoer, Ingrid Muller, and James Langford of the University of Notre Dame Press for their fine editorial assistance and help in bringing this to press.

My work on this book was supported by a paid leave of absence from Loyola University, two Loyola summer research grants, and a Loyola research support grant.

My children, Nora and Danny, have waited most of their lives for me to finish this book. I thank them and my wife, Judy, for their love, patience, and help.

Introduction

The nature of goodness is one of the central issues of philosophy. The question of how best to live a good life is one of the most important practical questions any human being can ask. Any suggestions about how to live a good life (implicitly or explicitly) rest on assumptions about the nature of the good life. Questions about good and bad are also important for determining what is right and wrong or just and unjust. Utilitarians hold that right actions and just laws and institutions are those that result in the best consequences (of all possible alternatives). Most moral theories take the good and bad consequences of actions or social policies to be relevant to their moral assessment. Moral theories that deny this are, on their face, implausible.

This book addresses both first-order questions about what things are good and bad and metaethical questions about the meaning and status of value judgments. The first half of the book examines a number of important first-order theories of value. I argue that many familiar arguments for and against these theories rest on undefended assumptions about the answers to certain metaethical questions. The second part of the book addresses these metaethical questions and offers a qualified defense of the desire- or preference-satisfaction theory of value. I argue that the most plausible version of the preference-satisfaction theory is a divine-preference theory of value.

Chapters 1–5. Chapter 1 reconstructs and criticizes two classic arguments for the hedonistic theory of value (HTV): Mill's "proof" of hedonism in *Utilitarianism* and Sidgwick's arguments in *The Methods of Ethics*. Mill argues that the HTV is true because psychological hedonism is true. I argue that at least some versions of psychological hedonism would (if true) provide strong reasons for accepting the HTV (or at least for rejecting any non-hedonistic

1

theory of value). However, Mill does not adequately defend psychological hedonism (among other things, his defense of psychological hedonism involves an equivocation on the meaning of the word "happiness"), and the very strong version of psychological hedonism his argument presupposes is almost certainly false. I also note difficulties created by Mill's sharp distinction between "desire" and "will" that have been overlooked by most commentators. Mill construes the term "desire" very narrowly; he says that to desire something is to take pleasure in the thought of it and that desiring something does not imply that one has any kind of preference for it. To "will" something is to be disposed to pursue it or bring it about. In light of what Mill says about the meaning of the words "desire" and "will," his claim that to be good is to be worthy of desire is implausible; "good" means something more like "worthy of being desired *and* willed." Unless we accept this, we cannot account for the practical, action-guiding significance of value judgments. I sketch and criticize a revised version of the proof that employs the assumption that "good" means "worthy of being desired and willed." Chapter 1 also presents a reconstruction of Sidgwick's main arguments for the HTV. I argue that Sidgwick fails to give adequate reasons for accepting the HTV.

Chapter 2 discusses several standard objections to the HTV: Mill's "contented-pig" objection, the objection that the HTV implies that being attached to an electronic pleasure machine would be preferable to living an ordinary human life, the objection that malicious pleasures are intrinsically bad, Nietzsche's objection that the HTV is an unduly pessimistic theory, and objections to the HTV's temporal neutrality. I argue that Mill's contented-pig objection and his qualitative HTV presuppose certain (controversial) views about the nature of pleasure/pain (they presuppose the falsity of the "motivational" theory of pleasure/pain). Given the motivational theory (which I take to be a plausible view about the nature of pleasure/pain), the contented-pig objection and Mill's qualitative HTV are both incoherent. The objections considered in chapter 2 appeal to allegedly false or absurd consequences of the HTV. However, the falsity or absurdity of these consequences is disputed by some. Therefore, these objections must be regarded as inconclusive in the absence of a defense of the intuitive judgments to which they appeal. Those who attack hedonism by appealing to intuitive judgments about controversial cases need to show why their intuitions are correct and the hedonist's mistaken. However, these standard objections suggest a different and much stronger objection to the HTV. The thought experiments employed in these arguments reveal that many apparently rational and well-informed people have preferences contrary to those that the HTV would endorse. For example, many ostensibly rational people would prefer to live a "normal" human life to being attached to an electronic pleasure machine, even though the life they would have while attached to the pleasure machine would afford them much more pleasure and much less pain. Proponents of the HTV need to show that these preferences are incorrect or mistaken. I argue that this claim is plausible only if axiological realism is true; proponents of the HTV are committed to endorsing axiological realism.

My very lengthy discussion of the HTV (one of the longest discussions by a non-hedonist) is part of the broader argument of the book. Chapter 2 includes numerous thought experiments in which we are asked to choose between different kinds of lives. These thought experiments help to reveal and clarify our own considered preferences and thus form part of the elaboration of the desire- or preference-satisfaction theory of value I defend later in the book.

Chapter 3 discusses the desire- or preference-satisfaction theory of value. (I use the terms "desire" and "preference" interchangeably.) I distinguish between the desire-satisfaction theory as a theory of value and as a theory of personal welfare. (I defend the desire-satisfaction theory of value, but I am not certain that the desire-satisfaction theory of welfare is defensible.) I sketch a number of different formulations of the preference-satisfaction theory of value and make some distinctions that have been overlooked in the literature. (One of these distinctions, the distinction between what I call the "welfarist" and "non-welfarist" versions of the desire-satisfaction theory of value, is particularly important for the issue of relativism.) I argue that the most plausible versions of the preference-satisfaction theory of value hold that what is good is determined not by our actual desires but, rather, by the desires we *would have* if we were rational. I also argue that "global" versions of the desire-satisfaction theory are more plausible than "summative" versions. The global version claims that the goodness or badness of one's life depends on the satisfaction of one's (rational) desires about one's life as a whole; it is not determined by summing the satisfaction or non-satisfaction of one's individual desires about particular things. I address the issue of posthumous harms and benefits and argue that events that happen after one ceases to exist can be logically relevant to determining the goodness or badness of one's life (or one's welfare).

Chapter 3 also considers objections to the desire-satisfaction theory. I pay particular attention to five important objections that haven't been discussed or adequately dealt with elsewhere: analogues of the contented-pig objection to the HTV, Richard Kraut's objection that it might be rational to desire to harm or punish oneself, Brandt's objection about changing desires, Charles Taylor's objection that preference-satisfaction theories of value are atomistic theories that cannot adequately account for the existence of "irreducibly social goods," and objections to the effect that the desire-satisfaction theory commits us to relativism about good and bad. Some objections to the desire-satisfaction theory presuppose the truth of moral/axiological realism and, therefore, cannot be assessed adequately apart from an examination of realism. I argue that the other objections, those that don't presuppose the truth of realism, can be answered. Chapter 3 defends the desire-satisfaction theory against objections but does not give any positive arguments in favor of it. I give a qualified argument for the rational-desire-satisfaction theory of value later on in the book (Interlude 2). This argument rests on assumptions defended in chapters 6 and 7.

In chapter 4, I argue that Nietzsche's *Übermensch* ideal constitutes a distinctive theory of value and the good life. Nietzsche takes strength or power to be the ultimate standard of value; strong people have good lives and weak people have bad lives. I present a detailed reconstruction of Nietzsche's theory of value and defend it against the objection that an *Übermensch* must be (or might be) immoral. I agree with many of the standard criticisms of Nietzsche's moral theory, but (what I take to be) the glaring faults of Nietzsche's views about questions of right and wrong and justice are not reasons to reject his theory of the good life. One could accept Nietzsche's theory of the good life even if one rejects the other aspects of his moral theory. Nietzsche claims that strength or power is the ultimate standard of value, because the "will to power" explains all human behavior. This argument is a rough analogue of Mill's argument for hedonism: power is the only thing we pursue as an end; therefore, power is the only thing that is good as an end. I argue that Nietzsche's theory of the will to power would (if true) provide strong reasons for accepting his theory of value (or, at least, for rejecting any alternative theory of value). However, Nietzsche doesn't do nearly enough to explain or defend his theory of the will to power.

In contemporary moral philosophy, topical discussions of first-order theories of value generally overlook Nietzsche's theory altogether. It needs to be taken seriously as an alternative to other standard theories of value. At least some Nietzsche scholars credit him with having a theory or standard of value. Chapter 4 is a more detailed reconstruction and critical assessment of Nietzsche's theory of value than others have offered. Nietzsche scholars have done surprisingly little by way of assessing the truth or plausibility of Nietzsche's theory of value.

Chapter 5 discusses Aristotle's theory of the good life. Aristotle holds that to have a good life is to fulfill one's purpose or function as a human being. According to Aristotle, one's function or purpose consists in the development and exercise of capacities or abilities unique to human beings or essential for being human. I argue that we should not attach special normative significance to those abilities and characteristics that are unique to human beings or essential for being human. I also criticize recent versions of the Aristotelian theory of value proposed by Peter Geach and Thomas Hurka.

Although I am critical of Nietzsche and Aristotle, I believe that their ideals of the good life have considerable importance within the context of a rational-desire-satisfaction theory of value. An ideally rational person must be able to vividly imagine the kinds of lives envisaged in such ideals (being fully informed would require understanding all the various kinds of lives one might lead). The process of imagining these lives is likely to alter the preferences that a person has for her own life. Many of us find, upon due consideration, that we want our lives to possess some of the features described in these very concrete ideals.

A large number of the arguments discussed in chapters 1–5 appeal to disputed intuitions; others appeal to our informed preferences for certain kinds of lives over others. Before we can assess these arguments, we need to determine the evidential status of disputed intuitions and informed preferences for first-order standards of value. Yet other arguments considered in chapters 1–5 presuppose either the truth or falsity of axiological realism. These arguments must be considered inconclusive apart from reasons to accept or reject realism. The work of historical philosophers on first-order questions of value is often methodologically and metaethically naive. Many of their arguments rest on undefended assumptions about controversial metaethical questions. On the other hand, twentieth-century work on metaethical questions is often narrow and often has little to say about first-order standards of value. It is important that these first-order normative questions be addressed in connection with foundational or metaethical questions.

Chapters 6–8. The second part of the book discusses foundational or metaethical questions. Chapter 6 examines the concept of goodness. I argue that conceptual questions about the proper analysis of "good" cannot be settled by appeal to the meaning of "good" in ordinary language. Even if "good" in the sense of "good life" has a determinate meaning in English, it might still be advisable for us to wield an alternative concept of value. We have a *choice* between alternative concepts of value. I defend pragmatic criteria for the choice of a concept of value (good). These criteria favor the view that to call something good (in the sense of "good life") implies that it is desirable or worthy of being desired. To say that X is better than Y implies that it is "correct" (in a sense that is opposed to mistaken) to prefer X to Y. This view affords a more adequate analysis of the concept of goodness than any of the standard analyses: naturalism, non-naturalism, emotivism, and prescriptivism. It is necessary to accept something like this view in order to account for the fact that value judgments are practical or action guiding. It is impossible to explain the practical import of value judgments unless we assume that being desirable is at least *part* of what we mean when we say that something is good.

Many of the arguments for and against particular theories of value discussed in chapters 1–5 presuppose either the truth or falsity of moral/axiological realism.

For example, arguments that take people's informed preferences about different kinds of lives to be the ultimate basis for answering normative questions presuppose the falsity of axiological realism (axiological realism implies that our informed rational preferences can be incorrect or mistaken). Chapter 7 addresses the issue of realism. Axiological realism (AR) is the view that value judgments are true or false in virtue of facts that exist independently of our actual (or possible) beliefs or attitudes about them. Realists hold that certain things are good independently of whether anyone desires them or believes that they are good (and independently of whether anyone *would* desire them or believe that they are good if she were rational and fully informed). By contrast, some non-realist theories of value (including the version of the desire-satisfaction theory that I favor) hold that things are good *because it is rational to desire or pursue them.*

I examine what I take to be the most important versions of realism, paying particular attention to recent formulations of the theory. I argue that there are no compelling reasons to accept realism or any particular version of moral/axiological realism; I do not attempt to show that AR is false. I argue that recent versions of AR are not stated or developed in sufficient detail for us to be able to determine whether they are true or false. Proponents of what I call "Cornell realism" claim that the kinds of moral facts they posit enter into the best explanations we can give of certain human beliefs and behaviors. But this is, at best, a conjecture. At the present stage of the development of psychology we are so far from having an adequate theory to explain human beliefs and actions that we cannot be sure what features an adequate theory would have. Since we don't know what the best possible psychological theory would look like, we cannot be sure that the best theory to explain human beliefs and human actions would make reference to moral facts. Several recent versions of British realism claim that moral properties can be directly perceived. Defenders of this kind of perceptual realism have not given an adequate explanation of the difference between veridical and non-veridical perceptions of moral qualities. I argue that, in the absence of such an explanation, there is no reason to accept the claim that ostensible moral perception involves the apprehension of independent moral facts about what is good and bad. Although my own sympathies are strongly anti-realist and I think that my arguments weaken the case for realism, I don't attempt to show that AR is false. There are so many possible versions of AR that it's doubtful that any argument could show that they are all false. The truth or falsity of AR may not be rationally decidable at the present stage of philosophical discussion.

In Interlude 2, I offer a qualified argument for the rational-desire-satisfaction theory of value that rests on assumptions defended in chapters 6 and 7. I argue that questions about first-order standards of value cannot be settled as long as questions about the truth of AR remain open. For any given first-order theory of value that we may propose or defend, it is possible that AR is true and that the true or correct version of AR commits us to a different first-order theory of value. On the assumption that AR is false, however, we can make a strong case for accepting the rational-desire-satisfaction theory of value. If AR is false and there are no independent axiological facts, we can still say that things are good or bad in virtue of its being correct or incorrect to desire them. The only theories of correct and incorrect preferences consistent with non-realism that have been developed to date are theories of rationality. Rational-desire-satisfaction theories of value seem to be the main option for non-realists at present.

Almost all non-realist normative theories (including the theories of Kant, Hare, Firth, Brandt, Rawls, Gauthier, and Gibbard) are based on theories of rationality. The content of non-realist normative theories is, in large measure, determined by the kinds of theories of rationality they employ. What things are actually good and bad according to the rational-desire-satisfaction theory of value depends on the view of rationality the theory employs. Things that it is rational to desire according to one theory of rationality may not be rational to desire according to other theories of rationality. Non-realists haven't paid nearly enough attention to questions about how to justify theories of rationality.

Chapter 8 attempts to determine what kind of theory of rationality is most suitable for use in the rational-desire-satisfaction theory of value. Full-information theories of rationality/value/welfare have been very prominent of late. I argue that full-information theories of rationality are untenable. The most serious objection to the full-information theory is that full information so greatly exceeds the capacities of human beings that counterfactual statements about what human beings would desire or prefer if they were fully informed lack determinate meaning or truth value. I formulate an informed-preference theory of rationality that requires less than full information. This theory, which is modeled on Crispin Wright's concept of "superassertability," has many attractive features and avoids the main objections to the full-information theory.

I also formulate a "divine-preference" theory of rationality and argue that it is the most plausible theory of rationality consistent with non-realism. Given the rational-preference theory of value, the divine-preference theory of rationality commits us to a divine-preference theory of value. The divine-command theory is widely discussed as a theory of right and wrong. But there has been very little discussion of divine-command or divine-preference theories of *value*. Such theories are, on their face, much more problematic than divine-command theories of right and wrong, which often allow that what is good and bad is independent of God's will. I argue that, in order to be plausible, the divine-preference theory of rationality/value needs a requirement similar to

Robert Adams's requirement that God be loving (this is a feature of Adams's divine command theory of right and wrong). If God is cruel and malicious, God's preferences cannot constitute the basis for a plausible theory of rationality/ value. However, Adams's requirement that God be loving cannot be incorporated into the divine-preference theory of value, because the concept of love presupposes an independent notion of good and bad. (To say that God is loving entails that God desires our good or what is good for us, where what is good or good for us is good independently of God's will.) We can formulate an alternative requirement about God's nature for the divine-preference theory that does not presuppose that things are good and bad independently of God's preferences but still serves roughly the same function as Adams's requirement that God be loving. This requirement is incorporated in the following version of the divine-preference theory of rationality/value that I defend in chapter 8:

> If there is an omniscient God who designed and created the universe and human beings for certain purposes/reasons, cares deeply about human beings, and is kind, sympathetic, and unselfish, then God's preferences are the ultimate standard for the correctness/rationality of human preferences and for the goodness or badness of things. (If such a God exists, it is rational (correct) for person S to have a certain preference, p, if, and only if, God prefers that S have p.) If such a God does not exist, then the correctness or rationality of human preferences (and the goodness or badness of things) is determined in some other way.

If there is no God of the sort described by this theory, then my informed-preference theory of rationality is a plausible alternative or "fall-back" theory of rationality that can be incorporated into the preference-satisfaction theory of value.

I conclude the book by discussing the implications of the desire-satisfaction theory of value for first-order questions of value (what things are good or bad), paying special attention to the question of whether the theory commits us to relativism. I argue that, when combined with the divine-preference theory of rationality, the rational-preference-satisfaction theory of value allows us to endorse a robust version of normative objectivism, according to which value judgments (or most value judgments) are objectively true or false. On the other hand, when combined with the informed-preference theory of rationality, at least some versions of the preference-satisfaction theory of value commit us to relativism about good and bad, i.e., the view that judgments about the goodness and badness of things aren't objectively true or false. What things are good or bad? Given our ignorance of God's ultimate aims and preferences, the divine-preference version of the preference-satisfaction theory leaves us with considerable uncertainty about first-order standards of value. I offer some conjectures about this, most notably that God values moral virtue or moral goodness as an end in itself. To the extent that people have ostensibly rational desires for many different kinds of things, the informed-preference version of the desire-satisfaction theory supports the view that a number of different kinds of things such as pleasure, pain, moral goodness, and the full development of one's artistic and intellectual abilities are good or bad as ends.

Arguments for Hedonism

I. Introduction

1. Terminological Preliminaries: Intrinsic Value versus Non-Instrumental Value

The hedonistic theory of value (HTV) is the view that pleasure is the only thing that is good for its own sake (or good as an end) and that pain is the only thing that is bad for its own sake (or bad as an end). According to the HTV, pleasure and the absence of pain are the only things that ultimately constitute a good life; other things make for a good life only insofar as they promote pleasure or prevent pain. Many philosophers describe the HTV as a theory of intrinsic value, and, when they do, they generally take "intrinsically good/bad" to mean "good/bad as an end" or "good/bad for its own sake." Things that are good as ends are good independently of their consequences. There is an alternative concept of intrinsic goodness that also has wide currency among philosophers. Moore takes intrinsically good to mean "good in itself" or "good in isolation." According to Moore, to say that something is intrinsically good is to say that a universe in which it is the only thing that ever exists would be better than a universe in which nothing ever exists.[1] In this second sense, the intrinsic value of something is the value it possesses apart from its relations to other things. A thing's extrinsic value is the value that it possesses in virtue of its relations (both causal and non-causal) to other things. Something might be valuable as an end or valuable apart from its consequences, even if it is not good in isolation. Similarly, it is possible that something that is good in isolation is not good as an end when it occurs as part of a larger situation. Many philosophers use the term "intrinsically good" rather indiscriminately to mean both good as an end and good in isolation. In order to avoid confusion on this point, I will use the terms "non-instrumentally good/bad" and "instrumentally good/bad" to mark the distinction between things that are good/bad as ends and things that are only good/bad as means to other things. I will use the term "intrinsically good/bad" in Moore's sense. I discuss the difference between intrinsic value and non-instrumental value at greater length in chapter 6 (6.I).

2. The Hedonistic Theory of Value

The HTV makes the following four claims: (1) pleasures or pleasant experiences are the only things that are non-instrumentally good; (2) pains or unpleasant experiences are the only things that are non-instrumentally bad; (3) all pleasant experiences are non-instrumentally good; and (4) all unpleasant experiences are non-instrumentally bad. Mill gives a different but equivalent statement of the HTV. He says that happiness (which he defines as "pleasure and the absence of pain") is the only thing that is desirable as an end.[2] The HTV implies that things other than pleasure can only be instrumentally good—such things as knowledge, love, and virtue are valuable only insofar as they tend to promote pleasure or diminish pain. It also implies that when making overall assessments about the non-instrumental value of someone's life (e.g., judging whether someone has a good or bad life) the only considerations that are relevant are facts about the pleasures and pains that the person experiences.

My definition of the HTV is neutral between quantitative and qualitative hedonism. The quantitative HTV holds that the value of pleasures and pains is solely a function of their quantity (intensity and duration). Quantitative hedonism implies that the non-instrumental value of a person's life is determined solely by the amount of pleasure and pain that she experiences. The qualitative HTV denies that questions about the non-instrumental value of someone's life are reducible to questions about the quantity of pleasure and pain he experiences. According to Mill's version of qualitative hedonism, the value of pleasures is a function of both their quantity and quality. Other things equal, the more intense a pleasure or the longer its duration, the more valuable it is; a "higher" pleasure is more valuable than a "lower" pleasure of equal quantity. In order to be plausible, the HTV must construe "pleasure" and "pain" very broadly to include any kind of pleasant and unpleasant experience, e.g., feeling sad, depressed, anxious, feeling contented, and enjoying an activity.[3] The HTV would be *very* implausible if it implied that physical pleasures and pains are the only things that are non-instrumentally good or bad. It would be possible to have a very pleasant life, even if one experiences more physical pain than physical pleasure. Similarly, it would be possible to have a very miserable life even if one experiences more physical pleasure than physical pain.

3. The Concepts of Pleasure and Pain; Considerations That Support the Motivational Theory of Pleasure/Pain

The content of the HTV depends on what sorts of experiences we count as pleasures and pains. One of my main conclusions in chapters 1 and 2 is that a number of standard arguments for and against the HTV depend on controversial assumptions about the proper analysis of pleasure. Among other things, I argue that Mill's qualitative HTV is incoherent, given a "motivational" theory of pleasure/pain. These are significant results because it is likely that the motivational theory is true. The motivational theory of pleasure/pain is more plausible than its main rivals, the "felt-quality" theory and the adverbial theory.

The motivational theory of pleasure/pain is the view that the pleasantness or unpleasantness of an experience is a function of one's desires with respect to it qua feeling. A pleasant experience is an experience that one prefers to have rather than not have (abstracting from all considerations about its consequences and preconditions); an unpleasant experience is an experience that one prefers not to have (abstracting from all considerations about its consequences and preconditions). William Alston defines the motivational theory of pleasure as the view that

> To get pleasure is to have an experience which, as of the moment, one would rather have than not have, on the basis of its felt quality, apart from any further considerations involving consequences.[4]

The motivational theory provides a plausible account of what all of the many different kinds of experiences we call pleasures have in common. (For all of the disagreement about the meaning of "pleasure," there seems to be considerable agreement about the extension of the term, i.e., which experiences are pleasant and which are not.) The felt-quality theory and the adverbial theory cannot give a satisfactory account of what all pleasures have in common.

The felt-quality theory holds that the pleasantness or unpleasantness of an experience is determined solely by its felt introspectable or phenomenological qualities. Pleasure is not a simple kind of sensation like the sensation of being burned. Nor are pleasantness and unpleasantness manifest isolable qualities of experience in the way that the perceived or phenomenological property of redness is. Pleasant experiences are extremely varied in their felt qualities; it's not obvious that they share any common phenomenological properties. The heterogeneity of pleasures is a serious problem for the felt-quality theory.[5] Consider the pleasures of orgasm, the pleasure of being rubbed or massaged during sexual activity, the pleasure of warming oneself by a fire, the pleasure of eating delicious food, the pleasure of quenching one's thirst, the pleasure involved in being pleased or elated about good news, the pleasure of enjoying a game of tennis, the pleasure of reading a good story, and the pleasure of laughter and humor. It's not obvious that there is any common felt quality they all share. The same is true of unpleasant experiences. By contrast, my visual experiences of a red flag, a red firetruck, and red paint clearly share a common property. The motivational theory gives a plausible explanation of what all pleasant experiences have in common—they are all desired for their felt qualities.

In response to this objection, some defenders of the felt-quality theory claim that pleasantness and unpleasantness are "feeling tones" of conscious experience. The classic statement of this view is Karl Duncker's paper "Pleasure, Emotion, and Striving."[6] Duncker never defines or explains what this feeling tone is—he apparently takes it to be an unanalyzable notion. But he presents many examples to help us focus our introspection. My own introspection and that of many others fails to discern a feeling tone of pleasantness that is shared by all pleasant experiences. The feeling tone of pleasantness, if it exists at all, is a subtle and elusive quality of our experience that is difficult to isolate. Duncker's theory cannot adequately account for the ready and easy knowledge we ordinarily have of our own pleasures and pains. It also fails to account adequately for the normative significance that hedonists and most of the rest of us want to ascribe to pleasant and unpleasant experiences. Such a subtle, elusive quality of our experiences can't have the same value and importance that we ordinarily attach to pleasure. Pleasant experiences are valued for their felt qualities and at least some pleasures are taken to be important goods. Qualities that are so difficult to discern can't account for the value we attach to pleasant experiences on account of their felt quality.

The adverbial theory is a behavioristic analysis of pleasure. Gilbert Ryle gives the classic statement of this theory. He presents the adverbial theory as a theory about what it is to enjoy an activity. Ryle holds that one's enjoyment of an activity is not a function of the sorts of experiences one has while engaging in it but rather a function of how one goes about doing it. To enjoy an activity is to go about doing it in a certain way, to be taken up by it, to be absorbed by it, and to give one's heart to it.

To say that a person has been enjoying digging is not to say that he has been both digging and doing or experiencing something else as a concomitant or effect of the digging; it is to say that he dug with his whole heart in his task, i.e., that he dug, wanting to dig and not wanting to do anything else (or nothing instead).[7]

According to Ryle, attending to an activity or giving our heart to it is not separable from the activity itself; it is not a feeling or experience that accompanies the activity.[8]

The adverbial theory is not applicable to many important types of pleasures. Certain kinds of pleasant experiences do not involve being engaged in or taken up by any activities. The pleasure I derive from a warm bath or having my back rubbed does not consist in my attending to some activity. Similarly, feeling pleased about good news is not a case of doing something with one's heart in it. The adverbial theory is a non-starter as a general theory of pleasure that is supposed to explain what *all pleasures* have in common. It is also doubtful that the theory affords a plausible account of what all pains or unpleasant experiences have in common.

The foregoing considerations favor the motivational theory. It seems clearly preferable to its main rivals. This adds to the significance of some of my conclusions in chapters 1 and 2, especially the significance of my claim that Mill's "qualitative hedonism" is incoherent, given the motivational theory. But the argument I have offered here for the motivational theory is not decisive. There are alternative theories of pleasure and objections to the motivational theory that I have not considered. My larger claims in this book do not presuppose the truth of the motivational theory. In particular, my arguments against the HTV do not depend on the assumption that the motivational theory is true.

II. Mill's Proof of Hedonism

1. Introduction

Mill's "proof" of the principle of utility in chapter 4 of *Utilitarianism* is probably the best known argument for the HTV. It is one of the most closely scrutinized passages in the entire history of Western philosophy. There are two standard objections to Mill's argument: (1) Mill's defense of the claim that the only way to show that something is good is to show that it is desired rests on a faulty analogy between "visible" and "desirable." "Visible" means "capable of being seen," but "desirable" does not mean "capable of being desired," rather it means "worthy of being desired"; (2) Mill commits the fallacy of composition in arguing that "each person's happiness is a good to that person, and the general happiness, therefore, [is] a good to the aggregate of all persons." A number of recent commentators have tried to defend Mill against these two criticisms. Some contend that the first criticism misconstrues Mill's intentions and ignores his explicit denial of the possibility of proving first principles.[9] Others have noted a letter in which Mill explains and defends his inference from "each person's happiness is a good to that person" to "the general happiness is a good to the aggregate of all persons." I will argue that Mill's letter provides a plausible defense of this inference. I will not discuss the first objection in any detail. I don't think that Mill adequately defends his claim that the only way to show that something is good is to show that it is desired. I believe, however, that this claim (or something very much like it) is defensible on other grounds, which I will defend at length in chapter 6 and Interlude 2.

The greatest weakness of the proof is Mill's defense of psychological hedonism (PH). PH is the view that happiness (which Mill defines as pleasure and the absence of pain) is the only thing that people desire for its own sake. Not only does Mill fail to give an adequate defense of PH, PH seems to be false. Some people desire such things as fame, money, power, and knowledge for their own sake. Mill concedes that some people desire things other than pleasure/happiness for their own sake. This seems tantamount to rejecting PH. But Mill argues that, when people desire things other than pleasure for their own sake, those things are "desired as part of happiness." This move does not save PH, because in claiming that we desire things other than pleasure "as part of happiness," Mill is abandoning his earlier hedonistic definition of happiness. Mill's attempt to salvage PH rests on an equivocation on the concept of happiness.

I argue that the earlier parts of Mill's proof need to be reconsidered in light of his later distinction between desire and will. Given Mill's very narrow construal of "desire," what is good can't plausibly be equated with that which is worthy of desire but rather needs to be equated with something like "that which is worthy of being both desired and *willed* as an end." I sketch a modified version of Mill's proof which assumes that "good as an end" means roughly "worthy of being both desired and *willed* as an end" and argue that at least some of the premises that are needed to make this argument valid are false. I conclude my examination of Mill's proof by discussing the connection between PH and the HTV; I argue that important normative conclusions *follow* from certain versions of PH. Normative theories are constrained by facts about human nature. If human beings are so constituted as to be incapable of pursuing anything other than pleasure as an end, then we have good reasons for rejecting any non-hedonistic theory of value.

2. Happiness Is a Good

The title of chapter 4 of *Utilitarianism* ("Of What Sort of Proof the Principle of Utility is Susceptible") suggests that the chapter is an argument for utilitarianism. This is misleading; chapter 4 is not an argument for utilitarianism per se; rather it is an argument for the HTV. In chapter 4 Mill assumes (but never defends, or even explicitly acknowledges as an assumption) the truth of a consequentialist theory of right and wrong: one should always act so as to produce the best possible balance of good/bad.

Mill takes questions about what things are valuable as ends (non-instrumentally good) to be questions about what things are desirable as ends (worthy of desire). "Questions about ends are, in other words, questions about what things are desirable" (p. 34). Mill goes on to offer the following argument:

> The only proof capable of being given that an object is visible is that people actually see it. The only proof that a sound is audible is that people hear it; and so of the other sources of our experience. In like manner, I apprehend, the sole evidence it is possible to produce that anything is desirable is that people do actually desire it. If the end which the utilitarian doctrine proposes to itself were not, in theory and in practice, acknowledged to be an end, nothing could ever convince any person that it was so. No reason can be given why the general happiness is desirable, except that each person, so far as he believes it to be attainable, desires his own happiness. This, however, being a fact, we have not only all the proof which the case admits of, but all which it is possible to require, that happiness is a good, that each person's happiness is a good to that person . . . (p. 34)

Mill's preliminary conclusion, that "each person's happiness is a good to that person," is ambiguous. It could be taken to mean either of the following:

Each person's happiness is (non-instrumentally) good or good as an end.

Each person's happiness is an element of his or her own welfare.

In this passage it is unclear whether Mill is attempting to defend the hedonistic theory of value or the hedonistic theory of personal welfare. This ambiguity can be resolved by examining a letter in which Mill clarifies a later passage from chapter 4. This letter responds to a question about the passage in which Mill argues that "each person's happiness is a good to that person, and the general happiness, therefore, [is] a good to the aggregate of all persons" (p. 34).

This passage has been very widely discussed. Some commentators take Mill to be claiming that since each person's happiness is a part of her own welfare, each person's happiness is part of the good or welfare of every other person.[10] So interpreted, Mill's argument seems to commit the fallacy of composition. Mill's letter, however, explicitly rejects this interpretation and claims that his arguments are intended to establish conclusions about what things are (non-instrumentally) good.

> As to the sentence you quote from my "Utilitarianism," when I said that the general happiness is a good to the aggregate of all persons I did not mean that every human being's happiness is a good to every other human being; though I think, in a good state of society & education it would be so. I merely meant in this particular sentence to argue that since A's happiness is a good, B's is a good, C's a good, etc., the sum of all these goods must be a good.[11]

When Mill says that someone's happiness is a good, he means that it is good as an end, or non-instrumentally good. In light of Mill's letter, we should take the earlier passage in which Mill reaches the preliminary conclusion that "each person's happiness is good to that person" to mean roughly that each person's happiness is good as an end (non-instrumentally good).

The first part of Mill's argument can be summarized as follows:

1. To be good as an end (non-instrumentally good) is to be desirable (worthy of desire) as an end.

2. Each person desires his/her own happiness for its own sake.

3. Something is non-instrumentally good (desirable) if, and only if, someone desires it for its own sake.

Therefore:

4. Each person's happiness is good as an end (non-instrumentally good).

Assessment of the Foregoing Argument.   The conjunction of premises 2 and 3 entails 4. 1 does not entail 3, but 3 is plausible only if 1 (or something very much like 1) is true. On this reconstruction, the argument is clearly valid, but is it sound? Are all of the premises true? I will be very brief here, since my main criticisms of Mill concern later stages of the argument (his defense of psychological hedonism). For the purposes of my later criticisms, it is not necessary for me to either defend or attack premises 1–3. I will defend 1, or something quite similar to it, at length in chapter 6. I'm not sure whether or not 2 is true. The apparent existence of people who desire their own unhappiness and misery because of guilt (Dostoyevsky's novels abound with characters of this sort) creates problems for 2. Perhaps these cases can also be explained away; perhaps people who seek earthly misery seek it as a means to redemption (and ultimately greater happiness) in the hereafter. I will not speculate further on this matter. Even if cases of this sort (and perhaps also cases of masochism) make premise 2 untenable, Mill might be able to salvage the argument by showing that it is irrational not to desire one's own happiness. Premise 2 could be modified as follows:

2′.   It is rational for every person to desire her own happiness as an end, and it is irrational for any person not to desire her own happiness as an end.[12]

Mill's argument for premise 3 is widely discussed and widely criticized.[13] I will not venture into this familiar territory here. However, I would like to note a reason for thinking that, *as stated*, premise 3 is false. If some states of affairs are such that (i) some people desire that they exist for their own sake and (ii) some other people desire that they not exist for their own sake, then 3 implies that both the occurrence and non-occurrence of those states of affairs is non-instrumentally good. Suppose that I have a non-instrumental desire that I be happy. Suppose also that someone who dislikes me desires that I not be happy (and desires this independently of its consequences). 3 implies that my being happy and my not being happy are both non-instrumentally good. Mill might reply by claiming that cases of this sort could not occur because psychological hedonism is true. But this would be implausible; some people do exhibit the kind of ill will toward others described in this case. I say a good deal more about the possibility of conflicting desires in chapter 3 (3.II.6) and chapter 8 (8.IX).

Returning to the argument, the next step in Mill's argument is his claim that "each person's happiness is a good to that person, and the general happiness, therefore, [is] a good to the aggregate of all persons" (p. 34). Given Mill's letter cited earlier, this passage does not make the dubious claim that each person's happiness contributes to the welfare of every other person but instead makes the rather innocuous inference from 4 to the following:

5.   The general happiness is non-instrumentally good.

3. *Happiness Is the Sole Good*

Up to this point Mill's argument shows at most that happiness is *one of the things* that is non-instrumentally good. It does not show that happiness is the *only* thing that is non-instrumentally good. Mill writes:

> Happiness has made out its title as *one* of the ends of conduct . . . but it has not, by this alone, proved itself to be the sole criterion. To do that, it would seem, by the same rule, necessary to show, not only that people desire happiness, but that they never desire anything else. (pp. 34–35)

Mill's argument requires the following premise:

6.   Happiness is the *only* thing that people desire for its own sake. (Happiness is the only ultimate object of our desires. The other things we desire are desired only as means to happiness.)

The conjunction of 2, 3, and 6 entails Mill's desired conclusion:

7.   Each person's happiness is non-instrumentally good and nothing other than happiness is non-instrumentally good.

Premise 6 is ambiguous. It might be taken to mean either of the following:

6a.   The only thing that anyone desires for its own sake is her *own* happiness.

6b.   The only thing that anyone desires for its own sake is her own happiness or the happiness of others.

Mill accepts 6b and rejects 6a. 6a is a (strong) version of psychological egoism, a view that he explicitly rejects.[14] 6a also seems to be inconsistent with utilitarianism. If psychological egoism is true and I am *incapable* of desiring anything other than my own welfare, then it would seem to follow that I am incapable of desiring the general welfare for its own sake and thus incapable of directly pursuing the utilitarian end.

6b seems to be open to many obvious objections and counterexamples. Such things as virtue, wealth, fame, and power seem to be desired by some people as ultimate ends. Mill concedes that such things are desired for their own sake. Pleasure, whether our own or that of others, is *not* the only ultimate object of our desires.

[P]eople . . . desire, for example, virtue and the absence of vice no less really than pleasure and the absence of pain. (p. 35)

[V]irtue is not the only thing originally a means . . . which . . . comes to be desired for itself, and that too with the utmost intensity. . . . . Money is, in many cases, desired in and for itself; the desire to possess it is often stronger than the desire to use it, and goes on increasing when all the desires which point to ends beyond it, to be compassed by it, are falling off. (p. 36; see also p. 37)

This concession seems to commit Mill to abandoning psychological hedonism (PH). Mill tries to reconcile this concession with PH by arguing that when things other than pleasure are desired as ends, they are "desired as a *part* of happiness." He continues:

It may, then, be said truly that money is desired not for the sake of an end, but as part of the end. From being a means to happiness, it has come to be itself a principal ingredient of the individual's conception of happiness. The same may be said of the majority of the great objects of human life: power, for example, or fame. . . . In these cases, the means have become a part of the end. . . . What was once desired as an instrument for the attainment of happiness has come to be desired for its own sake. In being desired for its own sake it is, however, desired as *part* of happiness. (p. 36)

It results from the preceding considerations that there is in reality nothing desired except happiness. Whatever is desired otherwise than as a means to some end beyond itself, and ultimately to happiness, is desired as itself part of happiness, and is not desired for itself until it has become so. (p. 37)

What does it mean to desire something as a part of one's happiness? Mill talks about the "elements of happiness." The elements of a person's happiness are *constitutive* of her happiness, not just *means* to it. Therefore, Mill cannot hold that to desire something as a part of one's happiness is to desire it as a *means* to being happy (where being happy is defined as "pleasure and the absence of pain"). He can't hold this, because he wants to use the notion of desiring something as a part of one's happiness to reconcile PH with the fact that people desire things such as wealth and power for their own sake, not merely as means to pleasure. According to Mill, the person who desires wealth (or fame, etc.) for its own sake does not desire anything other than happiness, because having wealth (or fame, etc.) is an "element of his happiness"—part of what it is for him to be happy. This commits Mill to the following account of happiness:

Each person's happiness is a collection of "elements." The elements of a particular person's happiness may include things other than pleasure. [For one to be a happy person, on balance, is for one to have (many, some, all?) of the elements of one's happiness.]

In trying to defend the proposition that happiness is the only thing that any-one desires as an end, Mill abandons the hedonistic theory of happiness. (Recall that he defines happiness as "pleasure and the absence of pain" p. 7.) Since Mill has abandoned the hedonistic theory of happiness, his argument no longer supports the HTV. If the argument of chapter 4 is to establish the HTV, then happiness must be defined hedonistically. Mill's defense of PH by appeal to the idea of desiring something as a part of one's happiness rests on an equivocation on the concept of happiness.[15]

4. Desire and Will

At the end of chapter 4 of Utilitarianism, Mill draws a sharp distinction be-tween "desire" and "will." He uses the word "desire" in a very narrow and re-stricted sense. To desire something, according to Mill, is to find the thought of it pleasant.

I believe that these sources of evidence, impartially consulted, will declare that desiring a thing and finding it pleasant, aversion to it and thinking of it as painful, are phenomena entirely inseparable or, rather, two parts of the same phenomena — in strictness of language, two different modes of nam-ing the same psychological fact.[16] (p. 38)

According to Mill, desire is a purely passive faculty, a "state of passive sensibility" (p. 38). Desiring something does not entail acting (or being disposed to act) so as to obtain it or bring it about. On Mill's account, "will" is the "active phe-nomenon." To will something is to be disposed to pursue it or bring it about.

Mill's discussion of "desire and will" raises serious problems for the earlier steps in the proof. Premise 1 (to be good as an end is to be desirable as an end) needs to be reconsidered in light of Mill's distinction between desire and will. Given Mill's eccentric use of the word "desire," the claim that the good is what is worthy of desire is equivalent to the claim that the good is what is wor-thy of being the object of pleasant feelings. This may be plausible as a partial account of the meaning of the word "good," but it cannot be a complete ac-count. Being good also entails being worthy of being willed or being sought after. To deny this is to deny the practical or action-guiding import of norma-tive judgments. It is impossible to explain the practical import of value judgments unless we assume that being worthy of being willed or chosen is at least *part* of what we mean when we say that something is non-instrumentally good (see chapter 6 for an extended defense of this claim).[17] If there is no kind of mistake or error involved in pursuing bad things rather than good things (other things being equal), then there is no reason to care whether things are good or bad. In light of Mill's later distinction between "desire" and "will," premise 1 needs to be modified roughly as follows:

1a.   To be good as an end is to be worthy of being both desired and *willed* as an end.

This, in turn, requires Mill to revise earlier parts of his argument. Premise 3 is plausible only on the assumption that "good" means "desirable." Given that the first premise needs to be modified along the lines of 1a, Mill's claim that the only way to show that something is desirable is to show that it is desired is not sufficient to establish the truth of premise 3. In order to show that something is good, we must also show that it is "worthy of being willed."

Perhaps Mill's proof can be salvaged by additional arguments to show that happiness and only happiness is worthy of being "willed" as an end, but that would go far beyond anything that Mill himself does in his proof. Allow me to speculate briefly. Given that premise 1 needs to be modified along the lines of 1a, Mill needs to show that happiness and only happiness is worthy of being both desired and willed as an end. How can Mill show that happiness is the only thing worthy of being willed for its own sake? In order to show this while maintaining the structure of the original argument presented in chapter 4, Mill would need to defend modified versions of premises 2, 3, and 6. With suitably modified premises, the argument would read approximately as follows:

1a.   To be good as an end is to be worthy of being both desired and *willed* as an end.

2a.   Each person both desires and wills her own happiness as an end.

3b.   Something is non-instrumentally good if, and only if, someone desires and wills it as an end.

Therefore:

4.   Each person's happiness is good as an end (non-instrumentally good).

6c.   Happiness is the only thing that anyone both desires and wills as an end.

Therefore:

Happiness and only happiness is non-instrumentally good.

So construed, the argument is valid, but premise 6c seems false; many people both desire and will things other than pleasure as ends. For example, some people both desire and will money as an end. Mill himself seems to grant that 6c is false. Near the end of chapter 4 (pp. 38–39), Mill concedes that we both will and desire as ends things other than happiness.[18]

5. The Connection Between PH and the HTV

For all of its problems, Mill's "proof" is a very important contribution to moral philosophy. Mill directs our attention to the connection between PH and the HTV. PH can be formulated in many different ways; the following do not exhaust the possibilities:

PH1. Pleasure and the absence of pain are the only things that human beings desire (in Mill's sense of "desire") for their own sake, and every instance of pleasure and the absence of pain is desired as an end by (at least some) human beings.

PH2. Pleasure and the absence of pain are the only things that human beings will (in Mill's sense of "will") as ends, and every instance of pleasure and the absence of pain is willed as an end by (at least some) human beings.[19]

The truth of PH1 does not entail the truth of the HTV. PH1 is consistent with axiological nihilism (the view that nothing is good or bad). More contentiously, even if PH1 were true, things other than pleasure and the absence of pain could still be worthy of being pursued for their own sake and thus non-instrumentally good. Similarly, the truth of PH2 does not entail the truth of the HTV. PH2 is compatible with axiological nihilism (the view that nothing is good or bad). But it is difficult to reconcile PH2 with the truth of any *non-hedonistic* theory of value. Given the truth of PH2, non-hedonistic theories of value cannot be practical or action-guiding in the way that theories of value purport to be. Any non-hedonistic theory of value implies that one or more of the following is true: (a) some pleasures aren't non-instrumentally good; (b) some things other than pleasure are non-instrumentally good; (c) some pains (unpleasant experiences) aren't non-instrumentally bad; or (d) some things other than pain are non-instrumentally bad. Therefore, if PH2 and a non-hedonistic theory of value were both true, then it would follow that our ultimate preferences are mistaken or misdirected in at least one of the following ways:

i)   We have ultimate preferences for the existence of things that are unworthy of being pursued for their own sake. (We have ultimate preferences for the existence of every sort of pleasure, but not all pleasures are non-instrumentally good, and thus not all pleasures are worthy of being sought after for their own sake.)

ii) We have ultimate preferences for the non-existence of things that are not worthy of being shunned or avoided. (We have ultimate preferences for the non-existence of every kind of pain, but not all pains are non-instrumentally bad, and thus not all pains are worthy of being shunned for their own sake.)

iii) We fail to have ultimate preferences for the existence of things that are worthy of being sought after for their own sake. (Things other than pleasure are non-instrumentally good and thus worthy of being pursued as ends, but, since PH2 is true, we have no intrinsic preference that they exist.)

iv) We fail to have ultimate preferences for the non-existence of things that are worthy of being shunned for their own sake. (Things other than pain are non-instrumentally bad and thus worthy of being shunned for their own sake, but, since PH2 is true, we have no intrinsic preference that they not exist.)

If PH2 is true, then it is reasonable to assume that human nature is such that it is impossible (under anything like ordinary circumstances) for us to pursue things other than pleasure and the absence of pain as ends. If it is possible in the ordinary course of things for human beings to pursue things other than pleasure and the absence of pain as ends, then presumably some of us would, at least occasionally, pursue them. There have been billions of human beings. It cannot be a coincidence if *all* of the non-instrumental preferences of these billions of human beings have pleasure and the absence of pain as their objects. If this is the case, it must be a consequence of certain features of human nature. Value judgments are ordinarily intended to be action guiding. The judgment that x is non-instrumentally good is intended to persuade us to pursue x as an end. If I try to persuade you to pursue something as an end, I must assume that it is possible for you to do so. There is no point in my urging you to do something that I know is impossible for you to do. But the proponent of any non-hedonistic theory of value seems to be doing precisely this (urging others to do what he takes to be impossible for them to do) if he accepts PH2. If we grant that value judgments must be action-guiding and if we grant the truth of PH2, then we cannot accept a non-hedonistic theory of value. Human nature places limits on what can count as an acceptable theory of value. A plausible theory of value cannot recommend that we pursue as ends things that we are incapable of pursuing as ends.

6. Concluding Remarks about Mill's Proof

If PH2 were true (or if PH1 and PH2 were both true), then we would have reasons to reject all non-hedonistic theories of value. However, PH2 seems to be false, and the falsity of PH2 as a theory about our ultimate preferences creates some presumption for thinking that the HTV is false. We *do* prefer or seek things other than pleasure and the absence of pain for their own sake. Defenders of the HTV must show that these preferences are mistaken or unreasonable. The burden of proof rests with them. Our informed preferences should be presumed to be correct (non-mistaken) in the absence of reasons for thinking to the contrary. Those who defend the HTV need to claim that people's ultimate informed preferences for things other than pleasure and the absence of pain are mistaken. In chapter 2 (2.II.6 and 2.VI) I shall argue that this claim is plausible only on the assumption that moral/axiological realism is true.

III. Sidgwick's Arguments for Hedonism

Sidgwick presents his arguments for the truth of the HTV in "The Ultimate Good," Book III, Chapter XIV, of *The Methods of Ethics*.

1. Sidgwick's Definition of "Pleasure"

Sidgwick's arguments for the HTV depend on his definition of pleasure. Sidgwick gives a preliminary definition of pleasure in the following passage from Book I:

> Pleasure is the kind of feeling which stimulates the will to actions tending to sustain or produce,—to sustain it, if actually present, and to produce it, if it be only represented in idea—; and similarly pain is a kind of feeling which stimulates to actions tending to remove or avert it.[20]

In this passage Sidgwick seems to endorse a "motivational" theory of pleasure. However, in a footnote at the end of the passage Sidgwick refers the reader to later "qualifications and limitations which this proposition requires, before it can be accepted as strictly true."[21] In the later passage to which he refers us (Book II, Chapter II, Section 2) Sidgwick takes up Spencer's view that pleasure "is a feeling which we seek to bring into consciousness and retain there."[22] Sidgwick grants that "pleasures normally excite desire" (he defines desire as "a felt volitional stimulus")[23] but claims that the intensity of a pleasure is not necessarily proportional to the degree to which it is desired:

> [I]t still does not seem to me that I judge pleasures to be greater and less exactly in proportion as they stimulate the will to actions tending to sustain them.[24]

> [I]t seems clear to me that exciting pleasures are liable to exercise, even when actually felt, a volitional stimulus out of proportion to their intensity as pleasures. . . . I also find that some feelings which stimulate strongly to their own removal are either not painful at all or only slightly painful: — e.g., ordinarily the sensation of being tickled. If this be so, it is obviously inexact to define pleasure, *for purposes of measurement*, as the kind of feeling that we seek to retain in consciousness.[25]

Sidgwick then considers the view that pleasure or pleasantness is an introspectable quality of feeling independent of volition "like the quality of feeling expressed by 'sweet.'"[26] He rejects this and goes on to define pleasure as a feeling that the subject apprehends to be "desirable":

> [W]hen I reflect on the notion of pleasure, — using the term in the comprehensive sense which I have adopted, to include the most refined and subtle intellectual and emotional gratifications, not less than the coarser and more definite sensual enjoyments, — the only common quality that I can find in the feelings so designated seems to be that relation to desire and volition expressed by the general term "desirable," in the sense previously explained. I propose therefore to define Pleasure — when we are considering its "strict value" for purposes of quantitative comparison — as a feeling which, when experienced by intelligent beings, is at least implicitly apprehended as desirable or — in the case of comparison — preferable.[27]

Let, then, pleasure be defined as feeling which the sentient individual at the time of feeling it implicitly or explicitly apprehends to be desirable; —

desirable, that is, when considered merely as feeling, and not in respect of its objective conditions or consequences, or of any facts that come directly within the cognisance and judgment of others besides the sentient individual.[28]

Sidgwick holds that judgments about desirability of one's own feelings are infallible. If I have a feeling that I experience as being desirable I cannot be mistaken about its being desirable.[29] Since Sidgwick claims that "desirable" means the same as "good,"[30] his definition of pleasure amounts to the following: a pleasure is a feeling that is experienced as being good. Standard versions of the HTV explain what is good in terms of pleasure. They hold that what is pleasant is "prior to" what is good; we can identify pleasant feelings independently of knowing what is good. Sidgwick's definition of pleasure reverses this relation. On his view, a feeling's being good is prior to its being pleasant. We can't say that a feeling is pleasant without first knowing that it is good. Given Sidgwick's definition of pleasure, the statement that all pleasures are good is analytic.[31] Sidgwick's definition of pleasure, however, does not make it analytic that pleasure is the only thing that is (non-instrumentally) good.

2. The Argument by Elimination

The most common objection to the HTV is that pleasure is not the only thing that is non-instrumentally good (Sidgwick uses the term "ultimately good"). Few critics of hedonism deny that pleasure is a good. Given that pleasure is a good and, more controversially, given that all pleasures are non-instrumentally good, one could establish the HTV by showing that nothing other than pleasure is non-instrumentally good. Sidgwick considers some of the other sorts of things that are commonly claimed to be non-instrumentally good and tries to show that they are not.

Some hold that the moral virtues are non-instrumentally good. Sidgwick argues that certain virtues such as candor, generosity, self-control, and honesty are only instrumentally good because they can be had to excess and/or serve bad ends.[32] For example, one could act courageously in the service of a bad cause. According to Sidgwick, the only virtues that can't be had to excess and can't promote bad ends are justice, benevolence, and wisdom. But the analysis or description of these virtues presupposes an independent and determinate notion of the good. Benevolence must be characterized in terms of doing good. Justice involves the fair distribution of goods and benefits. "Wisdom is insight into the good and means to the good."[33] Any theory of value that construes justice, benevolence, or wisdom as non-instrumental goods is viciously circular. Any understanding of these virtues presupposes a prior and independent account of the good. Thus, these virtues cannot be among the things that are non-instrumentally good.

Assessment.   Suppose that we grant that some virtues can be had to excess or serve bad ends. This shows that having them or having them to a greater degree is not always a good thing (on balance). It does not follow that these virtues can only be instrumentally good. The phenomena to which Sidgwick appeals can also be accounted for by the view that the virtues are always non-instrumentally good, but are *instrumentally bad* when they are had to excess or directed upon inappropriate objects. For the sake of argument, however, suppose that we grant that someone's possessing certain virtues is not non-instrumentally good when she has them to excess or when they are directed upon inappropriate objects. This still leaves open the possibility that those virtues are non-instrumentally good under more restrictive descriptions. For all that Sidgwick has shown, virtues such as generosity might be non-instrumentally good *when they are directed upon appropriate objects and not had to excess.* Aristotle holds that the virtues are constituted by qualities that are vices when had to excess. (This is part of his doctrine of the mean.) Given Aristotle's theory of the virtues, it is incoherent to describe someone as having a virtue to excess. If a quality that constitutes a virtue when not had to excess *is* had to excess, it does not constitute a virtue.

The circularity argument is also inconclusive. Sidgwick is correct in claiming that the concepts of justice and injustice presuppose concepts of goodness and badness which are distinct from the notions of justice and injustice; they presuppose that things other than justice and injustice are good or bad. However, he does not show that we need a complete theory of value in order to understand the notions of justice and injustice. Even if we grant Sidgwick's claim that, in order to define a particular virtue, we need to be able to claim that things other than that virtue are good, it does not follow that the virtue in question cannot be among the things that are non-instrumentally good.

Sidgwick continues the argument by elimination by considering other purported ultimate goods such as goodness of will (being disposed to try to act rightly) and talents. I will not rehearse these other arguments here. The argument by elimination requires Sidgwick to show that nothing other than pleasure is non-instrumentally good. Sidgwick assumes a very strong burden of proof. The failure of any of his arguments (to show of some particular thing that it is not non-instrumentally good) insures the failure of the argument as a whole. Given the indefinite number of possible goods, it seems that the argument by elimination cannot, in principle, be complete.

3. The Ultimate Good Is Desirable Consciousness

Sidgwick's most well-known argument for hedonism is presented in the middle of an argument that purports to show that talents are not non-instrumentally good. He claims that any part of the ultimate good must be a state of consciousness. Physical states, qua physical states, are not non-instrumentally good.

> Let us examine this first in the case of the physical processes. It is in their purely physical aspect, as complex processes of corporeal change, that they are means to the maintenance of life: but so long as we confine our attention to their corporeal aspect, — regarding them merely as complex movements of certain particles of organized matter — it seems impossible to attribute to these movements, considered in themselves, either goodness or badness. . . . [I]f a certain quality of human Life is that which is ultimately desirable, it must belong to human Life regarded on its psychical side, or, briefly, consciousness. . . . [I]t is therefore this Desirable Consciousness which we must regard as ultimate Good.[34]

Even if we grant that the only things that are ultimately good are desirable states of consciousness and that pleasures are feelings that are experienced as desirable, Sidgwick is not yet in a position to claim that pleasure is the only thing that is ultimately good. Two problems remain. First, feelings are not the only states of consciousness; cognition and volition are other kinds of conscious states. (Sidgwick distinguishes between three types of conscious states: feeling, cognition, and volition.)[35] Even if all desirable *feelings* were pleasures, it would not follow that all desirable *states of consciousness* are pleasures. Second, Sidgwick needs to show that those feelings that are desirable are coextensive with those that are *experienced as desirable*. For all that Sidgwick has shown, we might experience as desirable feelings that are unworthy of desire and we might fail to experience as desirable feelings that are worthy of desire.

> At this juncture in the argument Sidgwick states his two needed assumptions. He writes:
>
> (1) Nothing is desirable except desirable feelings, and (2) that the desirability of each feeling is only directly cognisable by the sentient individual at the time of feeling, and that therefore this particular judgment of the sentient individual must be taken as final on the question how far each element of feeling has the quality of Ultimate Good.[36]

The entire argument can be summarized as follows:

1. To be (non-instrumentally) good is to be worthy of being desired for its own sake.

2. Pleasure is any feeling that is experienced as desirable.

3. No state of the universe is non-instrumentally good unless it includes consciousness.

4. Feelings are the only desirable (non-instrumentally good) states of consciousness.

5. Feelings are desirable (non-instrumentally good) to the extent that they are experienced as desirable. Each person is the final authority about the desirability of her own experiences. No one can be mistaken in apprehending an experience as desirable or undesirable.

Therefore:

Pleasure is the only thing that is non-instrumentally good.

Assessment. The argument, as I have reconstructed it, is valid. If all of the premises are true, then the HTV must be true. I accept something very similar to premise 1 and will defend it at considerable length in chapter 6. The following case is an apparent counterexample to 2: someone takes pleasure in another person's misfortune but regards her own pleasure in this as inappropriate and shameful. She does not believe that her feeling is desirable and does not experience it as desirable. Such cases are common; many people have pleasant experiences which they do not take to be desirable (good) qua feelings. I am inclined to accept premise 3. Conceived of simply as physical states (the movements of bodies), such things as the exercise of talents or virtues do not possess non-instrumental value. They possess no value apart from their connection with conscious states. Consider the following thought experiment: imagine a world exactly like ours except that there is no consciousness. In this world there are automatons who look just like us, move in just the same ways that we do, and create the same kinds of physical structures that we do. Such a universe possesses no value; the existence of such a universe is not preferable to a universe in which nothing exists.[37] Granting this, Sidgwick's argument shows that consciousness is a part of any good state of affairs; states of affairs that don't involve consciousness in some way can't have any value. But we cannot infer that the value of a state of affairs is simply a function of the conscious states that comprise it. Physical states that have no value in themselves might still contribute to the value of more encompassing states of affairs. (Moore makes this criticism in a well-known passage in *Principia Ethica* which I quote below.)

Sidgwick defends premise 4 by arguing that other kinds of conscious states (cognition and volition) possess no value apart from the feelings with which they are usually associated:

> I think, however, that when we reflect on a cognition as a transient fact of an individual's psychical experience, —distinguishing it on the one hand from the feeling that normally accompanies it, and on the other hand from that relation of the knowing mind to the object known which is implied in the term "true" or "valid cognition"—which is seen to be an element of consciousness quite neutral in respect of desirability: and the same may be said for Volitions, when we abstract from their concomitant feelings, and their relation to an objective norm or ideal, as well as from all their consequences. It is no doubt true that in ordinary thought certain states of consciousness—such as Cognition of Truth, Contemplation of Beauty, Volition to Realize Freedom or Virtue—are sometimes judged to be preferable on other grounds than their pleasantness: but the general explanation of this seems to be (as was suggested in Book ii chap ii #2) that what in such cases we really prefer is not the present consciousness itself, but either effects on future consciousness more or less distinctly foreseen, or else something in the objective relations of the conscious being, not strictly included in his present consciousness.[38]

This argument commits the same fallacy as the argument for premise 3. Suppose that we grant that no cognitions or volitions possess value apart from their connection with feelings. We cannot conclude that the value of a state of consciousness is simply a function of the value of the feelings which it includes. Pleasure together with the cognition of beauty might be more valuable than pleasure alone. Moore makes this point very forcefully in the following passage from *Principia Ethica*:

> [F]rom the fact that no value resides in one part of a whole, considered by itself, we cannot infer that all the value belonging to the whole does reside in the other part, considered by itself. Even if we admit that there is much value in the enjoyment of Beauty, and none in the mere contemplation of it, which is one of the constituents of that complex fact, it does not follow that all the value belongs to the other constituent, namely the pleasure which we take in contemplating it. It is quite possible that this constituent also has no value in itself; that the value belongs to the whole state, and to that only: so that both the pleasure *and* the contemplation are mere parts

of the good, and both of them equally necessary parts. In short, Prof. Sidgwick's argument here depends upon the neglect of that principle, which I tried to explain in my first chapter and which I said I should call the principle of 'organic relations'. The argument is calculated to mislead, because it supposes that, if we see a whole state to be valuable, and also see that one element of that state has no value *by itself*, then the other element, *by itself*, must have all the value which belongs to the whole state. The fact is, on the contrary, that, since the whole may be organic, the other element need have no value whatever, and that even if it have some, the value of the whole may be very much greater.[39]

Sidgwick does not give us adequate reasons to accept premise 5. As Sidgwick notes, feelings are directly cognizable by those who have them. This means that each person is in a better position than anyone else to judge the desirability of his own feelings. However, it does not follow that such judgments are infallible. For all that Sidgwick has shown, there might be states of consciousness that are good or bad independently of whether they are apprehended as desirable (or would be apprehended as desirable under appropriate circumstances). For example, it might be the case that pleasure in the misfortune of others is bad, independently of anyone's beliefs or attitudes about taking pleasure in the misfortune of others. (This view presupposes the truth of moral/axiological realism.) There are serious questions about the value of malicious pleasure; like so many of the other issues discussed in the first five chapters of this book, these questions turn on what we say about the issue of moral/axiological realism and cannot be settled simply by appeal to the beliefs of those who enjoy malicious pleasures. The fact that Genghis Khan regarded his own malicious pleasures as good doesn't (by itself) show that they were (non-instrumentally) good.[40] I address the value of malicious pleasures in chapter 2.III (also see 2.VII).

4. The Systemization Argument or Argument from Theoretical Simplicity

Sidgwick concedes that common sense holds that things other than pleasure are non-instrumentally good. But he claims that the things other than pleasure that are said to be part of the ultimate good are all productive of pleasure and esteemed by common sense roughly in proportion to this.

> The second argument, that refers to the common sense of mankind, obviously cannot be made completely cogent; since, as above stated, several cultivated persons do habitually judge that knowledge, art, etc.—not to speak of virtue—are ends independently of the pleasure derived from them.[41]

But we may urge not only that all these elements of the "ideal good" are productive of pleasure in various ways; but also that they seem to obtain the commendation of Common Sense, roughly speaking, in proportion to the degree of this productiveness.[42]

Sidgwick goes on to support this claim with several illustrations. He argues that knowledge and virtue are valued roughly in proportion to their conduciveness to happiness.[43] He concludes this argument by claiming that alternative theories do not provide as good a way of systemizing our beliefs about the ultimate good.

> If, however, this view be rejected, it remains to consider whether we can frame any other coherent account of Ultimate Good. If we are not to systematize human activities by taking universal happiness as their common end, on what other principles are we to systematize them? . . . I have failed to find—and am unable to construct—any systematic answer to this question that appears to me deserving of any serious consideration: and hence I am finally lead to the conclusion . . . that the Intuitional method rigorously applied yields as its final result the doctrine of pure Universalistic Hedonism.[44]

Sidgwick assumes that we should endeavor to formulate and accept systematic principles that account for our particular beliefs about normative questions. Sidgwick's argument can be reconstructed roughly as follows:

1. The HTV gives us a systematic explanation of our (defensible) common-sense beliefs about value and prudence, etc.

2. No other theory of value of which we are aware can explain and systemize our (defensible) beliefs about value as well.

3. We are rationally required to try to give systematic explanations of our (defensible) beliefs about important matters. We should accept the best available theory that systemizes our beliefs about a set of important issues.

Therefore:

We must provisionally accept the HTV.

As I have reconstructed it, this argument is valid. But is it sound? Are all the premises true? It would be uncharitable to take premise 1 to say that we need to give a systematic theory that will accommodate *everyone's* beliefs about questions of value. Different people's beliefs about questions of value are often sharply inconsistent. No theory can systemize inconsistent beliefs. To be plausible, the systemization argument presupposes a distinction between defensible and indefensible beliefs about value. Premise 1 assumes that there is a single coherent set of (defensible) common-sense beliefs about questions of value. As the numerous thought experiments of chapters 2 and 3 will make clear, people differ sharply in their intuitive beliefs about many questions of value. There simply is no single coherent body of common-sense beliefs that everyone accepts. Many, perhaps even most, people have common-sense beliefs that conflict sharply with the HTV; thought experiments about pleasure machines make this particularly clear (see chapter 2.II). In order to make premise 1 plausible, Sidgwick would need to give us criteria for distinguishing between defensible and indefensible beliefs about value and reasons for thinking that many common intuitive judgments that conflict with the HTV are indefensible.

Sidgwick does not adequately defend premise 2. His defense is inadequate on two counts: (i) he doesn't acknowledge the extent to which the HTV conflicts with most people's beliefs about a wide range of cases, and (ii) he doesn't spend enough time examining alternative theories of value, e.g., the desire-satisfaction theory of value or Aristotelian theories of value, to show that they are less able to systemize "our" beliefs about value than the HTV. Further, chapters 2 and 3 will give reasons for thinking that premise 2 is false. Chapter 2 examines objections to the HTV. These objections show that the HTV conflicts sharply with most people's beliefs about what kinds of lives are good and bad. In chapter 3, I will argue that the rational desire-satisfaction theory of value avoids almost all of these objections and is not open to nearly as many intuitive objections as the HTV. It seems to square better with most people's intuitive beliefs about value than the HTV. While reading chapters 2 and 3, the reader should ask herself which of these two theories best squares with her intuitive beliefs about what things are good and bad. The reader should also consider Thomas Hurka's argument (briefly described in chapter 5.IV that his version of the Aristotelian theory of value best captures what "we" believe about value. Hurka defends his theory on the grounds that it provides a better systematic account of our intuitive beliefs about value than any alternative theories of value.

I will not attempt to assess premise 3. It raises very general questions about philosophical method which I cannot deal with here. Sidgwick defends his view of philosophy at length in other writings.[45]

CHAPTER 2

Objections to the Hedonistic Theory of Value

There is a long history of objections to the HTV. This chapter examines some of the most important objections: the satisfied-pig objection and its recent incarnation in thought experiments about pleasure machines; objections to the effect that pleasure in the bad and undeserved pleasure are not good; Nietzsche's objection that the HTV is an unduly pessimistic theory, and objections to the HTV's temporal neutrality. All of these objections appeal to allegedly counterintuitive consequences of the HTV. Almost all of them appeal to disputed intuitions—intuitive judgments that at least some people reject. I will argue that these objections cannot be adequately assessed apart from answering foundational or metaethical questions about the status of moral intuitions. An examination of the objections and thought experiments discussed in this chapter makes clear that many people have ultimate desires and preferences for things other than pleasure. Defenders of the HTV must claim that these desires or preferences are mistaken. I shall argue that the claim that all of these preferences are mistaken is plausible only if moral/axiological realism is true.

I. The Satisfied-Subhuman (Satisfied-Pig) Objection

1. Introduction

Few people deny that pleasure is a good or that pleasure/happiness is an element of the good life.[1] The most common and persistent criticism of the HTV is that pleasure is not the only thing that is good as an end or the only thing that makes for a good life. It is frequently argued that the HTV commits one to the absurd view that a very pleasant "subhuman" life would be preferable to an ordinary human life. This argument can be formulated in general terms as follows:

1. If the HTV were true, then it would be better to have a very pleasant subhuman life than an ordinary human life.

2. It would not be better to have a very pleasant subhuman life than an ordinary human life.

Therefore:

The HTV is false.

This sort of argument was first presented in Plato's *Philebus* where Socrates attempts to reduce the HTV to absurdity by showing that the HTV commits one to the view that, provided one's life were sufficiently pleasant, to have a life "without reason, memory, knowledge, and true judgment" (a life comparable to that of a "shellfish") would be to enjoy the highest good and to have "all that one could want."[2] Mill's formulation of the satisfied-subhuman/pig objection is the version most familiar to contemporary philosophers. Many recent formulations of the objection appeal to the allegedly counter-intuitive consequences of the HTV in hypothetical situations in which one is asked to choose between being attached to a "pleasure machine" and living an ordinary human life.

2. Mill's Two Formulations of the Satisfied-Pig Objection

Mill's initial statement of the objection is found in the following passage from *Utilitarianism* where he says with reference to the "Epicurean theory of life" (HTV):

> Now such a theory of life excites in many minds, and among them in some of the most estimable in feeling and purpose, inveterate dislike. To suppose that life has (as they express it) no higher end than pleasure—no better and nobler object of desire and pursuit—they designate as utterly mean and groveling, as a doctrine worthy only of swine. (p. 7)

Mill concedes that the HTV implies that humans and pigs have the same ultimate end: pleasure. He argues, however, that, since human beings have different capacities and different likes and dislikes than pigs, the things that give pleasure to pigs will not provide pleasure to human beings. The HTV does not imply that a contented pig provides a useful model of a good life for humans to pattern their own lives after.

> When thus attacked, the Epicureans have always answered that it is not they, but their accusers, who represent human nature in a degrading light, since the accusation supposes human beings to be capable of no pleasures except those of which swine are capable. If this supposition were true, the charge could not be gainsaid, but would then be no longer an imputation; for if the sources of pleasure were precisely the same to human beings and to swine, the rule of life which is good enough for the one would be good enough for the other. The comparison of the Epicurean life to that of beasts is felt degrading, precisely because a beast's pleasures do not satisfy a human being's conceptions of happiness. Human beings have faculties more elevated than animal appetites and, when once made conscious of them, do not regard anything as happiness which does not include their gratification. (pp. 7–8)

Mill then proposes a very different line of defense for the hedonist. Hedonists, he claims, can consistently attach greater intrinsic (non-instrumental) value to "higher pleasures" than "lower pleasures."

> [U]tilitarian writers in general have placed the superiority of mental over bodily pleasures chiefly in the greater permanency, safety, uncostliness, etc., of the former—that is, in their circumstantial advantages rather than in their intrinsic nature. And on all these points utilitarians have fully proved their case; but they might have taken the other and, as it may be called, higher ground with entire consistency. It is quite compatible with the principle of utility to recognize that some kinds of pleasure are more valuable and more desirable than others. It would be absurd that, while in estimating all other things quality is considered as well as quantity, the estimation of pleasure should be supposed to depend on quantity alone. (p. 8)

Mill goes on to formulate and defend his "qualitative" version of the HTV. The qualitative HTV distinguishes between "higher" and "lower" pleasures and claims that, other things equal, higher pleasures are more valuable than lower pleasures. Mill's qualitative hedonism can be stated roughly as follows:

1. All pleasant experiences are non-instrumentally good and nothing else is non-instrumentally good.

2. All unpleasant experiences are non-instrumentally bad and nothing
    else is non-instrumentally bad.

3. All other things (intensity and duration) being equal, "higher pleasures"
    have greater value than lower pleasures.

According to Mill, a pleasure (x) is "higher" than another pleasure of equal
quantity (y) provided that "all or almost all who have experience of both give a
decided preference" to x over y "irrespective of any feeling of moral obligation
to prefer it."[3] By contrast, the traditional HTV or "quantitative hedonism"
holds that any two pleasures of equal quantity (intensity and duration) must
have exactly the same non-instrumental value. According to the quantitative
HTV, the non-instrumental value of a person's life is determined solely by
how much pleasure and pain he experiences.

Mill defends qualitative hedonism and rejects the quantitative HTV. His
arguments culminate in the following passage:

> It is better to be a human being dissatisfied than a pig satisfied; better to be
> Socrates dissatisfied than a fool satisfied. And if the fool, or the pig, are of a
> different opinion, it is because they know only their own side to the ques-
> tion. The other party to the comparison knows both sides. (p. 10)

Quantitative hedonism implies that it is better to be a satisfied pig than a dissatisfied human being (the pig has a positive balance of pleasure to pain—more
pleasure than pain—whereas the dissatisfied human has a negative balance—
more pain than pleasure.) Mill *wants* to say that a dissatisfied human has a better
life than a satisfied pig. In order to maintain this view, Mill believes that he
must reject quantitative hedonism.

Mill's second version of the contented-pig objection can be formulated as
follows:

1. If the (quantitative) HTV were true, then it would be better to be a sat-
    isfied pig than a dissatisfied (unhappy) human being.

2. It would *not* be better to be a satisfied pig than a dissatisfied human
    being.

Therefore:

The (quantitative) HTV is false.

The second version of the contented-pig objection is, on the face of it, a
much stronger objection than the first. Quantitative hedonists such as Epicurus

can give plausible reasons for thinking that, ordinarily, it is undesirable to pursue "lower pleasures" to the exclusion of "higher pleasures." However, given a choice between being a satisfied pig and a dissatisfied human being, quantitative hedonists cannot consistently defend the preference for "higher" over "lower" pleasures.[4] It seems that the quantitative hedonist must say that it would be better to be a satisfied pig than a dissatisfied human being.

The second version of the argument, as I have formulated it, is valid; it has the logical form of a *modus tollens* argument. If we take the expression "satisfied pig" to mean "a pig who experiences considerably more pleasure than pain throughout his life" and "dissatisfied human being" to mean "someone who experiences considerably more pain than pleasure throughout her life," then premise 1 is clearly true. If quantity of pleasure and pain is the only ultimate measure of value, then someone who has more pleasure than pain has a better life than someone who has more pain than pleasure. The only serious question about the argument is the truth of premise 2. Mill defends premise 2 by appealing to our preferences about living the life of a non-human animal:

> Few human creatures would consent to be changed into any of the lower animals for a promise of the fullest allowance of the beast's pleasures. (p. 9)

As Mill formulates the argument, premise 2 seems too indeterminate to have a clear truth value; it is not sufficiently clear what kinds of lives are being compared. We have no right to say that one life is better than another unless we have a clear understanding of the lives being compared. Given the indeterminacy of the lives being compared in 2, the following sort of confusion is possible. When you and I are asked to assess the truth of 2 we each imagine and compare different pairs of lives. You compare a pig in "hog heaven" with an extremely unhappy and unfortunate human being whose life is so bad that he wishes that he had never been born. On the other hand, I compare a moderately unhappy human being with a moderately satisfied pig. On the basis of these comparisons, I claim that premise 2 is true and you claim that it is false. We disagree about the truth of 2. It is possible, however, that our disagreement is based on a confusion. We might both agree that (i) it would be better to be a moderately unhappy human being than a moderately satisfied pig and (ii) it would be better to be a pig in hog heaven than an extremely miserable human being whose life is so bad that he wishes he had never been born.

We can make 2 more determinate by taking it to mean that "it is *always* better to be a dissatisfied human than a satisfied pig" (or perhaps, more simply, "*any* human being has a better life than *any* pig"). When 2 is understood in this way, its truth is open to question. Some human lives are (arguably) so painful and unpleasant as to be not worth living. Imagine a victim of severe burns who is constantly in intense physical pain. His pain is so intense as to render him incapable of thought, deliberation, or the exercise of any other "higher" human capacities. Suppose also that it is impossible to reduce his pain as long as he is alive. Such a life, I would submit, is not worth living; ceasing to exist would be preferable to continuing such a life. Mill, however, need not take 2 to mean anything as strong as this. For the purposes of the argument against the (quantitative) HTV, it would be sufficient to find a single case in which a dissatisfied human being has a better life than a satisfied pig. The following argument would suffice for the purposes of refuting the (quantitative) HTV.

1a.   If the (quantitative) HTV were true, then it would *always* be better to be a satisfied pig who experiences more pleasure than pain than a dissatisfied human being who experiences more pain than pleasure.

2a.   In *some cases* it would be better to be a dissatisfied human being than a satisfied pig. [Some (actual or possible) dissatisfied human beings have better lives than some (actual or possible) satisfied pigs.]

Therefore:

The (quantitative) HTV is false.

This argument is valid, and premise 1a is clearly true. Our ability to assess the truth of 2a is limited by our ability to understand what it would be like to be a pig. Unless we know what it would be like to be a pig, we have no grounds for making judgments about the value of a pig's life. The only competent judge of the value of two pleasures is someone who is familiar with both. Similarly, in order to compare the value of two lives one must have an adequate understanding of what it would be like to live those two lives. Mill recognizes this and asserts that humans are capable of understanding what it would be like to be a pig. Immediately after the passage in which he says that it would be better to be a dissatisfied human than a satisfied pig he writes:

And if the fool, or the pig, are of a different opinion, it is because they know only their own side to the question. The other party to the comparison knows both sides. (p. 10)

This seems plausible at least on the assumption that human beings are capable of having any kind of experience that pigs can have. (I will discuss this matter below.)

There are many hypothetical cases to which one could appeal in support of premise 2a. I will present an example that makes as strong a case for premise 2a (and the argument as a whole) as I think can be made. I will compare the lives of a pig in hog heaven and a moderately unhappy human being.

Hog Heaven. Hog heaven is a place in which pigs are provided with plentiful supplies of tasty food, companions for sex and social interaction, protection from excessive heat and cold, protection from butchers and other predators, leisure, and unlimited opportunities for sunbathing and mudbathing.

The Moderately Unhappy Human Being. Stig is junior faculty member in a university. He is lonely on account of being a single person in a small town with few opportunities to meet eligible members of the opposite sex. He is badly overworked, with a heavy teaching load and unreasonable demands for publication. He suffers a considerable amount of physical pain on account of a chronic lower-back problem. He is disposed to worrying about his problems and often broods about his loneliness and the possibility of becoming unemployed. Much of the time he is in a moderately unpleasant state of emotional pain and experiences considerably more pain than pleasure.

Ideally, we would want to know more about both lives before comparing their value. However, my descriptions are an adequate basis for a rough comparison of their value. It is possible for us to have sufficient understanding of the pig's life to make an informed comparison of the value of a pig's life and the value of a human life. The main sorts of pleasures that pigs enjoy are familiar to most human beings. Sexual pleasures and the pleasures of eating and drinking don't require any special comment, but certain other pleasures warrant a brief comment. Pigs have a great capacity to enjoy the bodily pleasures of warmth and cooling. They love to warm themselves in the sun and cool themselves by wallowing in the mud and then lying around so that the water in the mud evaporates. I have experienced the pleasures of a warm bath when cold and the pleasures of a cool shower on a hot day. My experiences while idly lingering in a warm bathtub, thinking of nothing in particular, are comparable to those of pigs sunning themselves or wallowing in the mud. I am also familiar with the other kinds of pleasures of which pigs are capable. From the standpoint of the HTV, the three most important differences between pigs and humans are the following: (1) pigs are not capable of any of the mental pleasures human beings enjoy, e.g., studying philosophy or laughing at a joke; (2) pigs are not nearly as prone to boredom as humans; (3) pigs are not nearly as prone to emotional suffering (anxiety, guilt, fear, envy, *ressentiment*, hatred, etc.) as human beings. Healthy pigs in hog heaven would experience pleasure most of the time and seldom experience pain.

3. Premise 2a Assessed in Light of the Foregoing Example

I am inclined to think that it is better to be the moderately unhappy human being than the pig in hog heaven. I strongly prefer that I be the moderately dissatisfied human being rather than the pig in hog heaven; I share the preferences that Mill appeals to in his argument. Are my preferences and intuitive reactions decisive evidence for the truth of 2a? Most of the people with whom I have discussed this issue report that they would also prefer to be the dissatisfied human being. Some, however, report that they would prefer to be the satisfied pig. Quantitative hedonists and others who would like to reject premise 2a need to show that my preference that I be the dissatisfied human being is mistaken. (In 2.II.6 I shall argue that this is plausible only on the assumption that axiological realism is true.) Not all non-hedonists bear the same burden of proof in this case. Proponents of the desire-satisfaction theory of value do not need to show that people who would prefer to be a satisfied pig are mistaken in their preferences. Assuming that those people's preferences are rational, the desire-satisfaction theory implies that *their good* would be promoted by being the satisfied pig rather than the dissatisfied human being.

4. Mill's Argument Presupposes the Falsity of the Motivational Theory of Pleasure

The contented-pig objection derives its force from the fact that "we" (supposedly) would prefer living the life of a dissatisfied human being to living the life of a contented pig. Few people would be inclined to accept the crucial premise (2a) unless they preferred (or thought it rational to prefer) to be the dissatisfied human being rather than the satisfied pig. Mill himself takes informed preferences to be the ultimate basis for resolving questions of value. He claims that desire is the only proof of desirability, and he holds that informed desire is the ultimate criterion for distinguishing between higher and lower pleasures. In order to refute the quantitative HTV, the proponent of the contented-pig objection must be able to point to cases in which (1) we prefer the life of a dissatisfied human being to the life of a contented pig and (2) the contented pig has a more pleasant life than the dissatisfied human being. Given the motivational theory of pleasure and pain, however, it is not obvious that such cases are possible.

According to the motivational theory, to say that an experience is pleasant is to say that the person who has it would prefer to undergo it or continue it rather than not, if he were choosing solely on the basis of its felt quality (this rules out choosing because of "any feeling of moral obligation to prefer it" or not prefer it); to say that an experience is unpleasant is to say that the person would prefer not to have it or not continue it if he were considering only its felt quality. The motivational theory can be extended to provide an account of what it is for one experience or set of experiences to be more pleasant than another. An experience or set of experiences (*e1*) is more pleasant (for me) than another experience or set of experiences (*e2*) provided that I would prefer *e1* to *e2*, choosing simply on the basis of their felt characteristics, ignoring all considerations about the causes or consequences of those experiences. This means that if I prefer the experiences of a lifetime devoted to the pursuit of higher pleasures to the experiences of a life in which I only pursue lower pleasures (choosing solely on the basis of the felt character of the experiences) then the life of the higher pleasures is *ipso facto* the more pleasant life (for me). Given the motivational theory of pleasure, it is impossible that there be cases of the sort that Mill appeals to in the second version of the contented-pig objection, i.e., cases in which (i) we compare a non-human life that contains more pleasure than pain with a human life that contains more pain than pleasure (the quantitative HTV implies that the non-human has the better life), but (ii) we prefer the human life to the non-human life, and (iii) the qualitative HTV implies that the human life is better. In order to hold (iii), Mill needs to accept the following: (iv) we would prefer the human life to the non-human life if we judged them only in terms of the felt quality of the experiences that they involve.[5] However, given the truth of the motivational theory of pleasure, (iv) implies that the human life is (on balance) more pleasant than the non-human life and this is inconsistent with (i). Mill's second version of the contented-pig objection which he uses both to attack quantitative hedonism and to defend qualitative hedonism presupposes the falsity of the motivational theory of pleasure/pain. Those who would simply like to use the contented-pig objection to attack quantitative hedonism (but not defend qualitative hedonism) need not reject the motivational theory. If I claim that we would prefer life 1 to life 2 (but do not claim that we would prefer 1 to 2, choosing simply on the basis of the felt quality of the experiences they involve) the motivational theory of pleasure does not require me to say that life 1 contains a greater net quantity of pleasure over pain than life 2.

5. Mill's Qualitative Hedonism

Mill's theory is asymmetrical in that he distinguishes between higher and lower pleasures but does not distinguish between higher and lower pains. This is dubious in light of his criteria for distinguishing between higher and lower pleasures. Pleasure X is a higher pleasure (and thus a more valuable pleasure) than a pleasure of equal quantity Y, provided that all, or almost all, who are acquainted with both pleasures prefer X to Y, "irrespective of any feeling of moral obligation to prefer it." Consider two unpleasant experiences of equal quantity (intensity and duration), X and Y. It is possible that all, or almost all, who have experienced both X and Y have a greater aversion to X than to Y. The logic of Mill's criteria for distinguishing between "higher" and "lower" pleasures commits him to saying that X is worse than Y. Mill's criteria for distinguishing between higher and lower pleasures also commit him to the view that there are many *degrees of quality*, not just the two categories of higher and lower pleasures. Suppose that pleasures X, Y, and Z are all of equal intensity and duration. It is possible that all (or almost all) who are familiar with each prefer Y to Z and prefer X to either Y or Z. Mill's theory implies that X is a higher pleasure than Y and that Y is a higher pleasure than Z.

According to quantitative hedonism, the non-instrumental value of pleasure is solely a function of its intensity and duration.[6] Mill holds that being a higher pleasure confers extra value on a pleasure. For the purposes of the examples below, I will take Mill to mean that quality is a multiplier of the value of pleasure. On this reading, the value of pleasure is the product of its intensity, duration, and quality (the quality number assigned to higher pleasures is greater than the quality number assigned to lower pleasures). Nothing depends on this way of construing qualitative hedonism; my examples could be modified to fit alternative understandings of the way in which being higher rather than lower makes pleasures more valuable.

Let us briefly consider how the qualitative HTV avoids (or claims to avoid) the second version of the contented-pig objection. Suppose that a pig averages 50 units of pleasure (units measured in terms of both intensity and duration) and 3 units of pain each day. Compare the pig's life with that of a dissatisfied philosophy professor who averages 10 units of pleasure and 40 units of pain each day. Suppose that 8 of the professor's units of pleasure are higher pleasures. Mill *wants* to say that the professor has a better life on account of the extra value of his higher pleasures. In order to make this work, he needs to say that higher pleasures are *much* more valuable than lower pleasures. The "multiplier" for the value of higher pleasures would have to be very large. Let's say that higher pleasures are ten times more valuable than lower pleasures of equal quantity. In that case, the total value of the professor's average daily pleasures is 82. We subtract an amount equal to the pain he suffers and get a total net value of 42 per day. The pig is still ahead. In order to get things to work out in this example, Mill must say that higher pleasures are at least 12 times as valuable as lower pleasures of equal quantity. The view that, other things equal, higher pleasures are *much* more valuable than lower pleasures of equal quantity is probably consistent with Mill's intentions (see *Utilitarianism*, pp. 8–9), but I wonder if this is plausible.

Mill's qualitative hedonism presupposes the falsity of the motivational theory of pleasure and pain. Suppose that two pleasures are of equal quantity. Mill's definition of higher pleasures presupposes that it is possible for someone to have a strong preference for one over the other (choosing solely on the basis of their felt quality). He defines higher pleasures as those that are preferred to other pleasures of equal quantity. Given the motivational theory, however, it is not possible that two pleasures are of equal quantity and one is preferred (solely on the basis of its felt quality) to the other. If I prefer one pleasure to another (solely on the basis of their felt quality) the one that I prefer is *ipso facto* of greater quantity. Mill's qualitative hedonism is coherent only if a non-motivational theory of pleasure and pain is correct.[7] It's worth repeating again that I am assuming that Mill's definition of higher pleasures should be construed to mean that the informed judges who choose between two pleasures of equal quantity choose between them solely on the basis of their felt quality. Donner disagrees with my interpretation of Mill on precisely this point; I discuss and criticize her views in 2.II.5.

6. Does Qualitative Hedonism Really Imply
the Things Mill Claims It Implies?

There is apparently a serious discrepancy between what actually count as higher pleasures according to Mill's criterion for distinguishing between higher and lower pleasures and the kinds of pleasures he *wants* to count as higher pleasures. Mill *wants* to say that higher pleasures are coextensive with mental pleasures or pleasures involving the exercise of our "higher capacities."[8] However, it is not true that all, or almost all, people who know both bodily pleasures and pleasures of the intellect always prefer the latter to the former, other things being equal.

People who have a wide knowledge of different kinds of pleasures disagree so much in their preferences about pleasure that Mill's criterion for being a higher pleasure is seldom, if ever, satisfied. It is very difficult to find two pleasures of equal quantity such that "all or almost all who have experience of both" have "a decided preference" for one over the other, "irrespective of any feeling of moral obligation to prefer it."[9] Consider something that Mill *wants* to call a higher pleasure, the pleasure derived from solving a math problem, and something that he *wants* to call a lower pleasure, the pleasure derived from sex or eating. Given the extent to which people's preferences differ, it is unlikely that *all* or *almost all* who have experience of each kind of pleasure have a decided preference for the former, "irrespective of any feeling of moral obligation to prefer it."

Mill attempts to deal with this problem in the following passage:

> It may be objected that many who are capable of higher pleasures occasionally, under the influence of temptation, postpone them to the lower. But this is quite compatible with a full appreciation of the intrinsic superiority of the higher. Men often, from infirmity of character, make their election for the nearer good, though they know it to be the less valuable; and this no less when the choice is between two bodily pleasures than when it is between the bodily and the mental. They pursue sensual indulgences to the injury of health, though perfectly aware that health is a greater good.[10]

Mill claims that those who know both mental pleasures and bodily pleasures choose bodily pleasures over mental pleasures (of equal quantity) only against their better judgment or as a result of weakness of will. This seems false; many people who are acquainted with both intellectual pleasures and sexual pleasures pursue the latter almost to the exclusion of the former. Some do this without any sense that this is against their better judgment or considered preferences. Many would describe this as a case in which people prefer a lesser good (sexual pleasure) to a greater good (intellectual pleasure). But Mill cannot describe the case in this way. Given his account of the difference between higher and lower pleasures, pleasure x can't be more valuable than another pleasure of equal quantity (y) independently of its being the case that people who are familiar with each prefer x to y. On Mill's view, something can't be a higher pleasure independently of what informed human beings prefer.

Another objection to Mill's claim that all or nearly all who are acquainted with both physical and intellectual pleasures prefer the latter is the fact that some people have a preference to experience a wide variety of different kinds of pleasures. Many people lack an invariant preference for physical pleasures over mental pleasures or vice versa. Rather, they desire to experience a wide variety of pleasures. Given that different people's informed preferences between different kinds of pleasures might differ significantly, it is possible that hardly any pleasures count as higher pleasures according to Mill's criteria. There might be few, if any, pleasures that are such that all, or nearly all, who are familiar with them prefer them to other pleasures of the same intensity and duration.

II. Pleasure Machines

1. Introduction

A current staple of objections to the HTV are thought experiments about "pleasure machines." We are asked to imagine the possibility of attaching oneself to a pleasure machine for the rest of one's life. This would result in a considerably more pleasant life than most people enjoy. But, it is argued, an ordinary human life is preferable to living a life attached to a pleasure machine. This argument can be stated more formally as follows:

1. If the (quantitative, qualitative) HTV were true, then it would be better to live a life attached to a particular sort of pleasure machine (a particular sort of pleasure machine must be described) than to live an ordinary human life (a particular sort of life must be described).

2. The ordinary human life in question is better than the life of someone attached to the pleasure machine in question.

Therefore:

The (quantitative, qualitative) HTV is false.

2. Physical Pleasure Machines

An "orgasmatron" would be a machine that gives one continuous, intense sexual pleasure.[11] We can also imagine machines that simulate the experience of eating chocolate ice cream, eating in an expensive restaurant, or taking a warm bath. For my own part, I would strongly prefer a machine that would give me a wide variety of physical pleasures (I will call this a "physical-pleasure smorgasbord machine")[12] to any machine that would give me only physical pleasures of one particular sort. I suspect that most people share this preference (the majority of the students with whom I have discussed this report the same preferences). Consider the following argument:

1. The quantitative HTV implies that spending one's entire life attached to a physical-pleasure smorgasbord machine that gives one continuous, intense pleasure would be preferable to living almost any ordinary human life.

2. Some ordinary human lives are preferable to a life spent attached to a physical-pleasure machine of the sort described in 1.

Therefore:

The quantitative HTV is false.

Assessment of the foregoing argument.   Given a motivational theory of pleasure, the truth of premise 1 is open to question. Many (most) people report that they prefer many ordinary kinds of human lives to living a life attached to a physical pleasure smorgasbord machine. It is possible that some of these people would persist in these preferences if they were judging the various lives solely on the basis of their felt quality. In that case, the motivational theory of pleasure implies that those real lives would (on balance) be more pleasant (for those people) than a life on the physical-pleasure machine, and the quantitative HTV can allow that those lives are better (for the people in question) than a life spent on a physical-pleasure machine. Apart from this, the argument seems quite strong. I have discussed physical-pleasure smorgasbord machines with numerous groups of students. Almost all of them endorse premise 2) and say that they prefer to live a normal human life rather than be irrevocably attached to a physical-pleasure smorgasbord machine. Proponents of the quantitative HTV need to claim that these preferences are mistaken. This claim, I will argue, is plausible only if axiological realism is true (see 2.II.6 and 2.VI).

3. Real-Life-Simulation Machines

A real-life-simulation machine would give one experiences identical to those of someone living a "real life." We could imagine programming the machine to give one the life experiences of a great lover, a great athlete, a great statesman, a great scientist, a great philosopher, a great parent, or some combination of the above. A real-life-experience machine could be programmed to simulate one's most extravagant fantasies. Such a machine could give one "higher pleasures." Both the quantitative HTV and the qualitative HTV imply that life in a real-life-experience machine would be (or could be) noninstrumentally better than an ordinary human life.

Robert Nozick describes a similar experience machine and uses it as part of a thought experiment to determine "*What else can matter to us, other than how our lives feel from the inside?*"[13] Nozick argues that, upon reflection, we will discover that a number of other things do matter to us. "First, we want to *do* certain things and not just have the experience of doing them."[14] Second, we want to be persons of a certain sort. A brain passively undergoing experiences as a result of electrode stimulation cannot be characterized as a courageous, kind, or loving person. We not only care about what kinds of experiences we have but about what kinds of people we are. Third, in an experience machine we are not in "*actual* contact with any deeper reality." I find, on examination, that I strongly prefer lives in which I can act to those in which I cannot. This preference is not consistent with the HTV. According to the HTV, lives in which I act and do things are not preferable to equally pleasant lives in which I do not act.

I will now present further variations on Nozick's example that shed light on the issue of wanting to be in contact with reality. Imagine an "interactive-experience machine" on the model of an interactive video game, except that while on the machine one is not aware of the fact that one's experiences are being caused by the machine (one believes that one is living a "real life"). While connected to such a machine, one can make choices that affect the (apparent) external world one inhabits. Allow me to digress briefly to illustrate how one might be said to *act* while attached to an interactive-experience machine. Suppose that I am attached to such a machine and undergo the experience of being mugged by a large, but unarmed, assailant. I am forced to choose between handing over my money or fighting the mugger. If I choose to hand over my money, I will undergo the life experiences of someone who loses his money. If I choose to fight, I will experience the pain and other consequences of fighting someone much larger and stronger than I. A person attached to this kind of interactive-experience machine could *act* and thereby exhibit moral virtues and vices. Such a person could be said to be kind, or generous, or miserly, or cowardly, etc.[15]

4. The Desire to Interact with Other People

The main difference between being attached to an interactive real-life-experience machine and living a real life is that while attached to the machine the objects of one's experience (both physical objects and other persons) would not be real. For my own part, I have no great concern about the metaphysical status of inanimate physical objects; I would not be distressed to learn that the objects of my experiences are not independently existing physical objects (substances). I would, however, be extremely disconcerted to learn that I am mistaken about the reality of the other conscious beings with whom I seem to interact. In this respect, and in this respect alone, I find the interactive real-life-experience machine less desirable than a "real life." Proponents of the HTV can agree that a universe in which I am the only conscious being is less valuable than one in which their are billions of other conscious beings who enjoy pleasure. (According to the HTV, billions of conscious beings enjoying pleasure is better than one conscious being enjoying pleasure.) The non-existence of other minds would not only detract from the value of the universe, it would also detract from the value of *my own life*. (The HTV cannot account for this.) Most significantly, the non-existence of other people would render most of my activities pointless and futile. I spend the greater portion of my life trying to do things that affect the experiences of others, e.g., talking to my wife and children, lecturing to my students, and writing things for other people to read. All of these activities are pointless and futile unless other minds exist. If other people are not real, then my work as a teacher is as pointless as the actions of an insane person lecturing to an empty room. If my children are mere figments of my imagination, then staying up at night to comfort them when they are ill makes as much sense as staying up at night to comfort a doll. The value of my activities and the value of love and affection are largely contingent on the reality of other people.

Consider the four possible universes described below:

1. The actual universe as common sense supposes it to be. There are other minds with whom we interact and an independently existing physical world.

2. A universe in which I am irrevocably attached to an interactive real-life-experience machine and have *exactly* the same experiences I have in 1. Other minds do not exist; I am the only conscious being in this universe.

3. A universe with billions of brains or minds irrevocably attached to interactive-experience machines. For every sentient being in 1, there is a sentient being in 3 who has exactly the same experiences as the being in 1. These sentient beings act and display virtues and vices but they do not interact with each other. In universe 3 there is a sentient being who corresponds to my wife in the actual universe and who has the same experiences that my wife has in the actual universe. But, in 3, I am not the cause of any of her experiences, and her actions and volitions do not affect me. In universe 3, people do not enter into causal relations with each other. Their actions are related by a kind of "preestablished harmony" like Leibnizian monads.

4. A universe with billions of minds or brains who are interconnected by an interactive real-life-experience machine. Universe 4 differs from 3 in the following respect: in 4 different minds can interact and affect each other's experiences. One interacts with the objects of one's affections.

In this universe, the people whom I seem to know and care about do exist. My actions affect their experiences and their volitions affect my experiences. For example, if I say something unkind to my wife, I cause the pain or distress that she suffers. (Universe 4 is very much like the universe conceived of by Berkeley.)

Hedonists (whether quantitative or qualitative) would regard universe 2 as less valuable than 1, 3, and 4. The HTV implies that a universe in which billions of people experience pleasure is better than a universe in which only one sentient being experiences pleasure. The HTV (whether quantitative or qualitative) implies that universes 1, 3, and 4 have *exactly* the same value. 1, 3, and 4 contain the same number of people and the experiences of the people in the three universes are identical. If the felt character of our experiences is all that matters, then these three universes cannot differ in value. I strongly prefer either 1 or 4 to 3. (I am relatively indifferent between 1 and 4, although I know that many people prefer 1 to 4.) I find, on reflection, that I value or care about some things other than the felt character of my experience (or the felt character of the experiences of other people). I want to act and interact with other minds.

5. Donner's Reply to Nozick

Wendy Donner discusses Nozick's example at length and offers three different lines of defense for the hedonist. First, she argues that Nozick's example is too bizarre and too remote from any actual possibilities to take seriously.

> Although the tank floater example [brain in a vat example] is a logical possibility, it is not a practical possibility and thus need not concern a moral theory that is constructed for the actual world.[16]

There are several problems with this argument. First, a theory of non-instrumental value is more than just a guide to action "in the real world"; it is a theory about what *makes* things good and bad. As such, the HTV has implications for many hypothetical cases. Some of these implications strike many people as mistaken or objectionable. Another problem is that because of advances in neurophysiology and the development of "virtual reality" examples of the sort that Nozick describes may soon become "practical possibilities."

Donner's second reply is that qualitative hedonists can maintain that veridical, authentic pleasures are preferable to illusory or hallucinatory pleasures. The pleasure of winning the Nobel Prize is a higher pleasure than the pleasure of having one's brain stimulated to simulate the pleasure of winning a Nobel Prize.[17] Here, Donner departs from standard versions of hedonism, which hold that the felt or experienced character of one's experiences is all that matters. (Indeed, for this reason, I do not regard her theory as a purely hedonistic theory of value.) Donner takes causal and intentional features of experiences to be relevant to their value. According to her, the experiences I have when I really win the Nobel Prize are better than those that I have when I have the illusion of winning the Nobel Prize, because of their causal and relational properties. No doubt she would claim that the pleasures that I derive from actually interacting with other people are better than those I obtain from falsely believing that I am interacting with other people. Donner never formulates her criteria for determining the quality of pleasures. In this respect, her theory is incomplete; however, her remarks about the pleasure machine suggest the following principle:

> Pleasures whose intentional objects are real (winning the Nobel Prize, being loved by another person) are better than phenomenologically indistinguishable pleasures whose objects are not real, e.g., pleasures created by electrical stimulation of the brain.

This principle has objectionable consequences in the case of malicious or morally objectionable pleasures. The pleasure that a sadist derives from actually torturing someone is not better than the pleasure that he gets from falsely believing that he is torturing someone.

Donner's third argument is an extension of the second. She notes that in the philosophy of mind there is a lively debate between "internalist" and "externalist" accounts of mental states or experiences. Internalist theories about the content and individuation of mental states hold that the identity of mental states is completely independent of any relations they bear to the external world. Externalists hold that the content of mental states cannot be identified independently of a person's social or physical environment. On this view,

> Such mental events as beliefs, desires, and intentions are partly identified and determined by external facts and relations, including social facts and relations.[18]

> The contents of these experiences cannot be individuated by internal properties alone.[19]

Given an externalist account of the content and individuation of mental states, Nozick's example is conceptually incoherent. It is impossible for experiences induced by a pleasure machine to be the same as real or veridical experiences.[20]

If externalism is true, then it is impossible for a person attached to an experience machine to have the same experiences as someone who lives a real life. Even if externalism is true, it is nonetheless possible for us to carry out Nozick's thought experiments if we describe them slightly differently. We can still consider the choice between living a real life and being attached to an experience machine that will give one experiences that are phenomenologically indistinguishable from those one would have in a real life (but which have very different causal and intentional properties). Thus, Donner must fall back on her second line of argument against Nozick, i.e., her claim that the qualitative HTV can allow that the causal or intentional features of experiences are relevant to determining their non-instrumental value.

Donner presents her view as an interpretation of Mill. However, given Mill's phenomenalism (he defines matter as "a permanent possibility of sensation"),[21] it is very unlikely that he would endorse the kind of externalist view of experiences that Donner's view presupposes. According to the sort of phenomenalism Mill endorses, statements about our experiences are logically prior to statements about physical objects; from this it follows that experiences must be capable of being adequately described independently of any reference to physical objects. Donner's reading of Mill obscures the originality of her own view. She proposes her view in the context of defending the HTV against objections. Donner does not offer any positive reasons for thinking that the theory of value that she endorses is true. Her theory of value implies that external states of the world cannot possess any non-instrumental value or contribute to the value of any wider states of affairs apart from their place in pleasant or unpleasant experiences. This assumes the falsity of realist objectivist theories of value such as Moore's according to which states of the physical world can be non-instrumentally good apart from their relations to any sentient creatures.[22] Her theory also presupposes the falsity of desire-satisfaction theories of value according to which states of affairs that are not the causes of, or intentional objects of, pleasure are non-instrumentally good if they are desired (or would be desired by rational people). Thus, like the other theories considered in chapters 1–5, her theory cannot be assessed apart from a detailed examination of metaethical questions.

6. Conclusions

Where do the thought experiments about pleasure machines leave us? Many of the thought experiments and examples proposed in the objections considered here can be questioned on conceptual or metaphysical grounds. Donner and Putnam claim that the hypothetical cases described in standard pleasure machine objections are not possible. Further, at least some of the cases described in these objections may be impossible, given the truth of the motivational theory of pleasure. Apart from these considerations, the thought experiments considered here constitute serious objections to the HTV (both qualitative and quantitative). Many people have apparently rational preferences that are strongly opposed to those that the HTV (both quantitative and qualitative) would endorse. Still, it is open to the hedonist to claim that our informed and apparently rational preferences and intuitions about these cases are mistaken. In order to say this, the hedonist would need to endorse a version of axiological realism according to which facts about the goodness or badness of things are independent of people's actual or informed/rational preferences about them. Axiological realism implies that rational and informed ultimate preferences can be mistaken. (For example, my rational and informed preference for x might be mistaken in virtue of the fact that x is non-instrumentally bad.) Non-realism denies that there are any moral/axiological facts independent of our actual or ideal beliefs, preferences, or attitudes. Given non-realism, there can't be any independent moral/axiological facts in virtue of which our ideal preferences could be mistaken. If axiological realism is false, then we have good reasons for thinking that the HTV is also false. Many people seem to have rational, informed preferences that are contrary to those that the HTV would endorse. Given that realism is false, the hedonist cannot plausibly claim that all of these people's preferences are mistaken.[23]

III. Bad Pleasures, the Pleasures of Bad People, and Moral Goodness

The HTV implies that *all* pleasures (including malicious or sadistic pleasures) are non-instrumentally good. Some philosophers take this to be an unacceptable consequence of the theory. This objection finds its most forceful expression in Brentano. According to Brentano, emotions can be correct or incorrect in just the same way that beliefs and judgments can be correct or incorrect. It is correct to take pleasure in what is good. Brentano takes this claim to be analytic; he defines good as "that which is worthy of love, that which can be loved with a love which is correct."[24] It is incorrect to take pleasure in things that are bad. Pleasure in the bad is itself bad.[25]

A standard hedonist reply is that this objection confuses the instrumental and non-instrumental value of pleasure in the bad. The HTV can give a clear explanation of why the traits of character that give rise to malicious pleasure are instrumentally (very) bad and why malicious pleasure itself is instrumentally bad. Because of the possibility of confusing instrumental and non-instrumental value, we should try to find examples of malicious pleasure that do not have bad consequences and do not originate in traits of character that have bad consequences. Smart attempts to construct such an example. He asks us to compare the following: (1) a universe containing one sentient being who falsely believes that others are suffering and derives great pleasure from that belief; (2) a universe with no sentient creatures; and (3) a universe in which there is one sentient creature who suffers because he falsely believes that others are suffering. Smart argues that "the universe containing the deluded sadist is the preferable one. After all he is happy, and since there is no other sentient being, what harm can he do?"[26] Smart admits that many of us are likely to find sadistic pleasure repugnant, but he argues that the HTV can give a perfectly good explanation of why we feel this repugnance and why our repugnance is reasonable.

> Our repugnance to the sadist arises, naturally enough, because in our universe sadists invariably do harm. If he lived in a universe in which by some extraordinary laws of psychology a sadist was always confounded by his own knavish tricks and invariably did a great deal of good, then we should feel better disposed towards the sadistic mentality. . . . When a state of mind is sometimes extrinsically good and sometimes extrinsically bad, we find it easy to distinguish between our intrinsic and extrinsic preferences for instances of it, but when a state of mind is always, or almost always, extrinsically bad, it is easy for us to confuse an extrinsic distaste for it with an intrinsic one.[27]

Having considered the matter as carefully as I can, I find that I dislike sadism, apart from any of its harmful effects. I am inclined to think that malicious pleasure is non-instrumentally bad (or at least not non-instrumentally good).

There are similar questions about the value of the pleasure or happiness of morally bad people. Some philosophers contend that the pleasure or welfare of bad people is non-instrumentally bad on account of its being undeserved or constituting a kind of cosmic injustice.[28] Consider the following example:

> You are a soldier in the German army in 1942. Hitler is visiting your unit and orders a large cake. A chef makes the cake and gives it to a subordinate, who sets out to drive the cake to Hitler by truck. The truck is hit by an artillery shell and the driver is temporarily knocked out, but the cake is unharmed. You come upon the truck and have the following choice: (a) do nothing—the driver will regain consciousness and deliver the cake to Hitler—(this will give Hitler great pleasure for one evening) or (b) throw the cake in the mud (no one will see you, and, since the truck was destroyed, everyone will assume that the cake was thrown from the truck by the explosion, and no one will get into any trouble as a result).

I think that it would not be a good thing if Hitler were to get the cake, but Smart would presumably disagree.

Is moral goodness non-instrumentally good? Or, as hedonists claim, does it possess only instrumental value? As a thought experiment, let us imagine the following two universes:

1. A universe in which the only conscious beings are human beings. They are selfish and do not possess any moral virtues. Nonetheless, they have relatively pleasant lives on account of their favorable physical circumstances: they live in a "tropical paradise," they have inherited a great deal of wealth, and they have developed cures for most painful physical ailments, such as arthritis.

2. A universe in which the only conscious beings are human beings. (This universe contains the same number of human beings as 1.) They are extremely altruistic and virtuous and manage to live relatively pleasant lives (their lives are roughly as pleasant as the lives of the people in 1) in spite of their harsh and unpleasant environment. They eke out a meager living in an area much like the Aleutian Islands and suffer from many painful physical ailments. In spite of all this they are happy on account of their warm and pleasant personal relationships.[29]

According to the hedonist, these two universes have the same value. For my own part, I think that the second universe is better than the first (at least I prefer it).

The objections considered in this section rest on disputed intuitions. Therefore, I am not yet in a position to assess their cogency as objections to the HTV. However, in 8.IX I will argue that the desire-satisfaction theory of value gives us reasons to think that moral goodness is non-instrumentally good.

IV. Hedonism and Pessimism: Nietzsche's Objection to Hedonism

Nietzsche raises a serious objection to the HTV in the following passage from *The Will to Power*:

The sum of displeasure outweighs the sum of pleasure; consequently it would be better if the world did not exist" — "The world is something that rationally should not exist because it causes the feeling subject more displeasure than pleasure" — Chatter of this sort calls itself pessimism today! . . . I despise this *pessimism of sensibility*. It is itself a sign of deeply impoverished life.[30]

This can be formulated explicitly as an argument against the HTV as follows:

1. The universe contains more pain than pleasure.

2. The (quantitative) HTV implies that if (the history of) the universe contains more pain than pleasure, then it would be better if the universe had never existed.

3. It is false and absurd to say that it would be better if the universe had never existed.

Therefore:

The (quantitative) HTV is false.

I do not know whether or not premise 1 is true. I am only acquainted with a tiny spatiotemporal portion of the universe and have no evidence for or against the claim that pain outweighs pleasure in other parts of the universe. This argument can be modified to avoid committing ourselves to any sweeping generalizations of this sort. Whether or not the universe as a whole contains more pain than pleasure, it seems clear that the lives of many *individuals* contain more pain than pleasure. The quantitative HTV implies that such lives are, on balance, non-instrumentally bad. We can restate the argument as follows:

1a. The quantitative HTV implies that the lives of people who experience more pain than pleasure are non-instrumentally bad and not worth living, apart from their effect on others.

2a. (At least) *some* human lives are non-instrumentally good and worth living, apart from their effect on others, even though they contain more pain than pleasure.

Therefore:

The quantitative HTV is false.

This argument is valid and premise 1a is clearly true. If 2a is true, then the HTV is false. I believe that 2a is true. My reason for thinking that 2a is true is that there seem to be people who have the following characteristics: (a) they experience more pain than pleasure throughout their lives; (b) they have a rational and informed preference to live rather than cease to exist (or to have never existed), a preference that is based on accurate beliefs about their lives: past, present, and future; and (c) their preference to continue to live would persist even if they didn't have any other-regarding desires (their preference to continue to live is not dependent on other-regarding desires). Given the falsity of realism, the fact that someone has a rational desire to live (and would want to live independently of his other-regarding concerns) is *prima facie* evidence for thinking that his life is non-instrumentally good.

As I have reformulated it, the Nietzschean argument assumes that the benchmark for measuring the value of life is non-existence. A particular life is (on balance) good or worth living provided that it is preferable to not existing at all.[31] Here, it might be objected that we cannot compare the value of any particular sort of life with the value of not existing. The value of my actual life can only be compared with the value of other lives (or other lives that I might have). We can compare the value of a life that contains more pain than pleasure with the value of a life that contains no pleasure and no pain, but we cannot compare the value of a particular sort of life with the value the person's life would have if he did not exist. I cannot say that I am better or worse off now than I would be if I did not exist. For, if I did not exist, there would be no "I" to make any comparisons with; if I do not exist, I cannot be assigned any particular level of welfare or well-being. We cannot say that a person who dies is worse off than she was before she died, because she no longer exists. This is the gist of Epicurus' argument to show that death cannot harm anyone.[32]

Epicurus is correct to say that we cannot compare one's level of well-being while alive with one's level of welfare when one does not exist. It is unclear, however, that this saves the HTV from Nietzsche's objection. The HTV allows us to make judgments about the total value of the universe. According to the quantitative HTV, other things equal, the total value of the universe is increased if an unhappy person (someone who experiences more pain than pleasure) ceases to exist. However, I will not insist on this point here. For, in any case, we can use non-existence as the benchmark for making judgments about people's welfare and the value of people's lives without opening ourselves to the Epicurean objection. Instead of making the inadmissible comparison between one's level of welfare while one exists and one's level of welfare when one does not exist, we can rely on perfectly admissible comparisons between the total (non-instrumental) value of the life one will have if one continues to exist and the total value of the life one will have if one ceases to exist now. My life is worth continuing now if the total value of the life I will have if I continue to exist is greater than the total value of the life I will have if

I cease to exist (now). More intuitively, my ceasing to exist now would be an evil because my continued existence will add to the total value of my life as a whole. To say that my life as a whole is worth living is to say that the total net value of my entire life is greater than the total value my life would have had if I had ceased to exist immediately after I began to exist.[33]

The hedonist can at least partly defuse the Nietzschean objection by appealing to the motivational theory of pleasure. Given the motivational theory of pleasure, we measure the quantity of pleasures and pains in terms of our preferences between different experiences and different groups of experiences. According to the motivational theory, a person's life contains more pain than pleasure if, and only if, he would prefer non-existence to his actual life, choosing simply on the basis of the felt character of his experiences. If someone prefers to undergo the experiences he will have if he continues to exist rather not have any experiences at all (choosing solely on the basis of the felt quality of the experiences), then the motivational theory implies that the remainder of his life contains more pleasure than pain. However, the motivational theory still allows for the possibility of cases of the following sort: (a) person S experiences more pain than pleasure throughout his life; (b) S has a rational and informed preference to live rather than cease to exist (or have never existed), a preference that is based on accurate beliefs about his life: past, present, and future; (c) S's preference to continue to live would persist even if he didn't have any other-regarding desires (his preference to exist is not dependent on other-regarding desires); and (d) S would not prefer to continue to live if he were choosing solely on the basis of the *felt character* of his experiences. If true, a through c provide *prima facie* evidence for the claim that the person's life is worth living, and, given d, the motivational theory of pleasure does not require us to say that the person's life contains more pleasure than pain.

V. Time Preference

According to standard versions of the HTV, the non-instrumental value of pleasures is independent of their temporal order and position in one's life as a whole. Other things being equal, the pleasures one has at one time are no more or less valuable than the pleasures one has at other times.[34] In his essay "Goodness and Lives," Michael Slote attacks hedonism and other theories of value that imply that temporal place and order are irrelevant to the value of the goods within a person's life.

The fact that goods occur at one time (of life) rather than another is generally held to make no difference to the overall goodness of lives or to the existence of reasons for actions, and this rejection of 'time preference' can be found across a wide spectrum of moral theorists. But . . . I shall argue that time preference is not the atypical or irrational phenomenon that so many otherwise divergent theorists assume and that our ordinary thinking quite naturally ascribes unequal importance to different periods of life.[35]

Slote claims that successes or failures in the "prime of life" are more important than successes or failures at other times. Success or good fortune in the prime of life can "make up for" failure or bad luck in one's youth but not vice versa.

> I believe that such a division into 'times of life' tends to be accompanied, in most of us, by a sense of the greater importance or significance of certain times of life in comparison with others, and what I first want particularly to stress is the lesser seriousness with which we regard the successes and misfortunes of childhood (including adolescence) when considering, in the rough and ready way we sometimes do, how fortunate someone has been in life. I think we have a definite tendency to discount youthful misfortune or success in the way that can be seen, for example, in what we think and say about someone who won all the prizes and captained all the teams in school, but whose later life seems dull or unfortunate by comparison. . . . Schoolboy (or schoolgirl) glories cannot compensate for (cannot make up for) what happens later in life.[36]

Slote also claims that a life that slowly progresses to some great achievement or good fortune is preferable to one in which the same sort of achievement or good fortune comes early in life and is then followed by decline.

> A given man may achieve great political power and, once in power, do things of great value, after having been in the political wilderness throughout his career. He may later die while still 'in the harness' and fully possessed of his powers, at a decent old age. By contrast, another man may have a meteoric success in youth, attaining the same office as the first man and also achieving as much good; but then lose power, while still young, never to regain it. Without hearing anything more, I think our natural, immediate reaction to these examples would be that the first man was more fortunate, and this seems to suggest a time preference for goods that come late in life.[37]

Brentano and Chisholm defend much the same view as Slote. Note the following passages from Brentano:

It is not merely the summation of the elements in an order that is to be considered as a good; the order itself must be taken into consideration.[38]

Let us think of a process which goes from good to bad or from a great good to a lesser good; then compare it with one which goes in the opposite direction. The latter shows itself as the one to be preferred. This holds even if the sum of the goods in the one process is equal to that in the other.[39]

Chisholm writes the following:

> If A is a situation in which a certain amount of value x is increased to a larger amount y, and if B is like A except that in B there is a decrease from the larger amount of value y to the smaller amount x, then A is preferable to B.[40]

We need to know more about the details of these cases in order for our judgments about the desirability of the lives in question to carry much weight. When we flesh out such cases, it is evident that the HTV can account for the fact that it is *often* better to achieve success later rather than very early in life. Those who enjoy very early success are less likely to appreciate it and more likely to take it for granted than those who wait longer. People who enjoy early success followed by later failures are likely to feel disappointment and bitterness about the decline of their fortunes.

Slote responds to this objection in the following passage:

> [T]he person who achieves and loses high office when he is still relatively young may well hope and have reason to expect to gain power again, whereas the politician who is in the political wilderness throughout his early and middle years may easily stop expecting to gain power. And in that case, the man who succeeds late may have *fewer* of the pleasures of anticipation or hope than one who achieves early success. . . . It seems, rather, to be a matter of sheer preference for goods that come later, of our assumption, even, that a good may itself be greater for coming late rather than early in life.[41]

We still need to know much more about the two lives being compared in order to be justified in having any strong views about which is better. Among other things, we need to know how much pain and dissatisfaction the loss of power causes the first politician. We also need to know how dissatisfied the second is while in the political wilderness and how long he is able to savor his eventual success (success can come too late in life to be adequately appreciated and relished). My intuitions about which life is better depend very much on the attitudes of the two individuals about their lives. How satisfied or dissatisfied are they with their lives? Given the strong correlation between contentment and pleasure and discontentment and pain, it is not possible to describe the case in such a way that later success clearly seems better without also describing it in such a way that later success is preferable on hedonistic grounds.

Slote's view that the phenomena he describes are explained by "sheer preference for goods that come later" is unsatisfactory. If goods that come later in life (generally) are more valuable than those that come earlier, then there must presumably be some reason for this.

J. David Velleman offers an interesting extension of Slote's arguments.[42] He accepts Slote's arguments to show that the value of a person's life cannot be determined by simply adding up the values of the various goods that comprise it, but he rejects Slote's explanation of why this is so.

> The reason why later benefits are thought to have a greater impact on the value of one's life is not that greater weight is attached to what comes later. Rather, events are thought to alter the meaning of earlier events, thereby altering their contribution to the value of one's life. . . . The preference elicited by Slote's example must depend on something more than the mere effects of timing. . . . The event's meaning is what determines its contribution to the value of one's life.[43]

> [A]n event's contribution to the value of one's life depends on its narrative relation to other events. . . . How the value of one's life is affected by a period of failure combined with a period of success, for example, cannot be computed merely from the timing of these periods and amounts of well-being they contain. Their impact on the value of one's life depends as well on the narrative relations among the successes and failures involved.[44]

Velleman does not propose any kind of systematic theory of narrative value; however, he offers several intuitively plausible examples of how the narrative history of one's life is relevant to its value. According to Velleman, the "meaning" of a misfortune within one's life is altered if it later has positive instrumental value. For example, "An edifying misfortune is not just offset but redeemed, by being given a meaningful place in one's progress through life."[45]

Velleman's description of these matters strikes me as extremely insightful. The "meaning" events acquire in the narrative history of one's life (and one's informed view of one's life as a whole) can have an important effect on one's overall welfare. The redemption or non-redemption of past misfortunes is a very real phenomenon that can dramatically affect the value of one's life. But Velleman's arguments do not conclusively refute the HTV and other summative theories of the good. The problem is that it is difficult to hold other things equal in our comparison cases when we bring in the idea of "redeeming" past misfortunes and other good or bad narrative features of our lives. These narrative features themselves characteristically produce pleasure and pain, and contentment and discontentment. Suppose that we imagine three lives of the sort that Velleman wants us to contrast. Life 1 involves an early failure F_1 that is redeemed by later success S_1. Life 2 involves an early success S_2 (S_2 is equal to S_1) followed by a later failure F_2 that is never redeemed (F_2 is equal to F_1). Life 3 involves an early failure F_3 followed (but not redeemed) by a later success S_3 (F_3 is equal to F_1 and F_2, and S_3 is equal to S_1 and S_2). Velleman and Slote would say that, other things being equal, life 1 is better than life 2, even though the sum of the goods in the two lives is the same. (Velleman would claim that 1 is better than either 2 or 3.) It seems to me, however, that an important reason why we prefer successes that redeem past misfortunes to those that do not is that they give us pleasure and contentment. A past misfortune that embitters one may be a constant source of pain and discontentment unless it is redeemed. When I imagine these three lives, I am not imagining three lives with equally good parts or elements. As I imagine it, life 1 involves more pleasure and less pain (and more contentment) than lives 2 and 3. I would raise the following dilemma for Slote and Velleman: either (i) the three lives are as I imagine them and the value of their parts differs significantly, in which case summative theories of value can account for the fact that 1 is better than 2 and 3; or (ii) the person who has life 1 takes no pleasure or satisfaction in the thought that his past misfortunes have been redeemed, in which case it is not clear that their having been redeemed is of any benefit to him.

Slote and Velleman claim that in a wide range of cases "we" will agree that certain lives are clearly better than others, even though the ones we think are better are not preferable on hedonistic grounds alone. It is unclear, however, whether the lives that they ask us to compare are equally good from a hedonistic point of view. Given this, and given the likelihood of conflicting intuitions about those cases in which hedonistic reasons do not make good fortune later in life preferable to earlier good fortune, their arguments cannot be considered conclusive. The thought experiments the authors describe, however, are very helpful in revealing our own preferences. On examination, I find that I care deeply about the narrative structure and temporal ordering of various goods within my own life. It also seems to me that my concern is at least partly independent of hedonistic considerations. In chapter 3 I will argue that the considerations advanced by Slote and Velleman strongly support global over summative versions of the desire-satisfaction theory of value. Slote and Velleman say much that is true and insightful. I believe that their insights can plausibly be incorporated into global versions of the desire-satisfaction theory of value. Our rational ultimate preferences for our lives may include the preference for successes that redeem past failures over successes that do not.

VI. Preliminary Conclusions

Some of the thought experiments and examples considered in this chapter can be questioned on conceptual or metaphysical grounds. Putnam and Donner claim that the hypothetical cases described in standard pleasure machine objections to the HTV are impossible. Further, some of the cases described in standard objections to the HTV may be impossible, given the truth of the motivational theory of pleasure.

Some defenders of the HTV (Mill and Brandt) take preferences or informed preferences to be the ultimate criterion of value. They try to defend the HTV by appealing to facts about what we prefer (or would prefer if we were fully rational). This view must be rejected in light of our results here and in chapter 1; many people's informed preferences are contrary to those that the HTV would endorse.

Most of the objections discussed in this chapter appeal to the allegedly counter-intuitive consequences of the HTV. Most of these objections appeal to disputed intuitions and, therefore, must be regarded as inconclusive in the absence of a defense of the intuitive judgments being appealed to. Those who attack hedonism by appealing to intuitive judgments about controversial cases need to show why their intuitions are correct and the hedonist's mistaken. However, these same objections suggest a much stronger objection to the HTV. The thought experiments that these objections employ reveal that many apparently rational and well-informed people have preferences contrary to those that the HTV would endorse. For example, many ostensibly rational people would prefer to live a "normal" human life to being attached to an electronic pleasure machine, even though the life they would have while attached to the pleasure machine would afford them much more pleasure and much less pain. Proponents of the HTV need to claim that the preferences of these people are incorrect or mistaken. This claim is plausible only if axiological realism is true; proponents of the HTV are committed to endorsing axiological realism. Axiological realism holds that there are facts about what things are good or bad that are independent of our actual or ideal desires/preferences. Axiological realism implies that informed ultimate preferences can be mistaken. (For example, my informed preference for x might be mistaken in virtue of the fact that x is non-instrumentally bad.) Non-realism denies that there are any moral/axiological facts independent of our actual or ideal preferences. Given non-realism, there can't be any independent moral/axiological facts in virtue of which ideally rational preferences could be mistaken.

The Desire/ Preference-Satisfaction Theory of Value

Introduction

Some of the standard arguments for and against the HTV take people's desires or rational desires/preferences (I use the terms "desire" and "preference" inter-changeably) to be the ultimate standard for settling debates about questions of value. Mill argues that pleasure is the only thing that is non-instrumentally good because pleasure is the only thing that is desired for its own sake. Others hold that the HTV is false because we desire things other than pleasure for their own sake. Given the widespread appeal to what we desire in arguments about standards of value and the widely accepted view that "good" means the same as "desirable" or "worthy of choice" (a view I will defend at length in chapter 6), the preference-satisfaction theory of value seems to be a plausible alternative to the HTV.

The desire-satisfaction theory of value has been adopted by many utilitarians, most notably R. M. Hare, James Griffin, and John Harsanyi.[1] The desire-satisfaction theory of value (or welfare) is widely endorsed by economists, in part, because it is thought to provide a better basis for measuring utility and making interpersonal comparisons of utility than alternative theories. Three notable non-utilitarian philosophers, Rawls, Gauthier, and von Wright also defend desire-satisfaction theories of value (or welfare).

[O]ur good is determined by the plan of life we would adopt with full de-liberative rationality if the future were realized in the imagination.[2]

Value, then, we take to be a measure of individual preference—subjective because it is a measure of preference and relative because it is a measure of individual preference. What is good is good ultimately because it is preferred, and it is good from the standpoint of those and only those who prefer it.[3]

Among major historical philosophers, Spinoza is the clearest proponent of the desire-satisfaction theory of value.

From what has been said it is plain, therefore, that we neither strive for, wish, seek, nor desire anything because we think it to be good, but, on the contrary, we adjudge a thing to be good because we strive for, wish, seek or desire it.[4]

I will present several different versions of the desire-satisfaction theory and formulate what I believe to be the most plausible version(s) of the theory. I then consider a number of objections to the desire-satisfaction theory. Some of these objections presuppose the truth of moral/axiological realism. I will argue that, in the absence of adequate reasons for thinking that moral/axiological realism is true, my preferred version of the desire-satisfaction theory of value can be defended against these objections. This chapter does not offer any positive arguments in favor of the desire-satisfaction theory. I give a qualified argument for the rational desire-satisfaction theory of value in Interlude 2. This argument rests on assumptions that will be defended in chapters 6 and 7.

I. Some Versions of the Desire-Satisfaction Theory

There are many possible versions of the desire-satisfaction theory; it is important to indicate the range of possibilities before proceeding further.

1. Theory of Value versus Theory of Personal Welfare

In the literature the desire-satisfaction theory is usually presented and discussed as a theory of personal welfare rather than a theory of value. The truth of the desire-satisfaction theory of personal welfare does not entail (and is not entailed by) the truth of the desire-satisfaction theory of (non-instrumental) value. It would be consistent to accept the desire-satisfaction theory of welfare and still hold that certain states of affairs that are not constitutive of the welfare of any sentient being, e.g., the existence of unperceived beautiful objects or unperceived ugly objects, are non-instrumentally good or bad. It is also possible that certain states of affairs that are constitutive of people's welfare, e.g., the happiness of evil people, are not non-instrumentally good. Kant and Ross, for example, hold that the happiness of bad people is not a good thing,[5] but, presumably, they would not deny that the happiness of bad people is beneficial *to them* or contributes to their welfare. Nonetheless, there are important connections between theories of value and theories of personal welfare. Most objections to the desire-satisfaction theory of welfare are also objections to the desire-satisfaction theory of value. With one exception (see 3.II.5), all of the objections that I consider in this chapter are objections to both the desire-satisfaction theory of value and the desire-satisfaction theory of welfare. Any plausible theory of value must allow that human welfare (or at least some instances of human welfare) is non-instrumentally good.

2. A Theory about What Things Are Non-instrumentally Good or a Criterion of Value

The desire-satisfaction *theory of value* can be construed as either a theory about what things are non-instrumentally good and bad or as a criterion of non-instrumental value. On the first interpretation, the desire-satisfaction theory is the view that the satisfaction of someone's desires is the only thing (or state of affairs) that is non-instrumentally good. On the second interpretation, the desire-satisfaction theory is not a theory about what things are good and bad, but rather a *criterion of value*, i.e., a theory about what *makes* things good or bad. The desire-satisfaction criterion of value says that what *makes* something (non-instrumentally) good/bad is that it is desired (or would be desired by someone who was rational). The desire-satisfaction criterion of value commits one to axiological non-realism. Roughly, axiological realism says that certain things are good or bad independently of peoples' (actual or possible) beliefs, desires, or attitudes about them. The desire-satisfaction criterion of value denies that things are good or bad independently of our actual or ideal desires about them. The desire-satisfaction theory of value (as a theory about what things or states of affairs are non-instrumentally good) differs from the desire-satisfaction criterion of value in that it is consistent with moral/axiological realism. It would be consistent for an axiological realist to hold that the state of affairs someone having an actual (ideal) desire that is satisfied is the only state of affairs that is non-instrumentally good and that this is true independently of people's beliefs or attitudes. To my knowledge, no important philosophers have defended the desire-satisfaction theory as a theory about what things are non-instrumentally good. The major versions of the desire-satisfaction theory defend the theory either as a theory of welfare or as criterion of non-instrumental value (or both).[6] I defend the desire-satisfaction *criterion of value*. Unless I indicate otherwise, I shall take the desire-satisfaction theory of value to mean the desire-satisfaction criterion of value.

Some philosophers defend hedonism as a theory about what things are good and bad by appealing to the desire-satisfaction criterion of value. For example, in his paper "Fairness to Happiness," Brandt attempts to defend the HTV by arguing that it is likely that our desires for pleasant experiences are our only rational non-instrumental desires (he argues that it is likely that they are the only non-instrumental desires that would survive full information and maximal criticism).[7] Mill's proof of hedonism is also an attempt to defend hedonism as a theory about what things are good by appealing to a desire-satisfaction criterion of value. Mill defends hedonism as a theory about what is non-instrumentally good or bad on the grounds that "happiness" (pleasure and the absence of pain) is the only thing that anyone desires for its own sake. Nietzsche also defends a monistic theory of value by appealing to a monistic theory of desire or motivation. He claims that power is the only thing that is good as an end because power is the only thing that we desire or pursue as an end (see 4.I.1 and 4.IV.4 for a discussion of this argument). I don't think that the desire-satisfaction criterion of value supports the HTV or any other monistic theory about what things are non-instrumentally good or bad. Many people have non-instrumental preferences for things other than pleasure, and there is no reason to think that all such preferences are irrational. The numerous thought experiments presented in chapter 2 illustrate this. If we accept the desire-satisfaction criterion of value, we must hold that many different kinds of things are non-instrumentally good (see 8.IX).

3. Actual versus Ideal Desires

The actual-desire theory of value says that what makes something non-instrumentally good is that someone desires it for its own sake. The ideal- or rational-desire theory of value says that what makes something good is that rational people *would desire* it for its own sake.[8]

When our actual desires are ill informed or the result of false beliefs, satisfying them can be bad or harmful for us. Suppose that I am thirsty and desire to drink water from a stream, not knowing that it was poisoned by a chemical leak at a nearby factory. I will die if I drink from the stream. Satisfying my desire to drink from the stream would clearly be bad for me. The actual-desire theory can account for this; it says that the satisfaction of any one of my actual desires is good for me, *other things equal*, but it does not imply that satisfying a desire is always good for me, on balance. Drinking poisoned water from the stream would not promote the overall satisfaction of my actual desires. Indeed, it would make it impossible for me to satisfy any of my other desires. Acting on irrational or ill-informed desires often frustrates *other desires* that are of greater importance to the agent. The actual-desire theory does not imply that one promotes one's personal welfare by satisfying such desires; it is a more defensible theory than is often supposed. However, in 3.II.1 and 3.II.5 I discuss objections that favor the ideal-desire theory over the actual-desire theory. My arguments for the desire-satisfaction theory in Interlude 2 also provide reasons for preferring the ideal-desire-satisfaction theory of value to the actual-desire-satisfaction theory of value.

4. Summative versus Global Desire-Satisfaction Theories[9]

According to summative desire-satisfaction theories, the non-instrumental value of one's life (or, alternatively, one's personal welfare) is a function of the satisfaction or non-satisfaction of one's individual desires. The value of one's life (or one's level of welfare) is determined by "summing" the satisfaction and non-satisfaction of all one's individual desires. Global theories say that the non-instrumental value of one's life (or one's overall level of welfare) is a function of the satisfaction of one's global desires, i.e., one's desires for one's life as a whole.

The global view is preferable to the summative view. Most people's global preferences exhibit what Moore calls "organic unity." My overall preferences about my life as a whole are not the sum of my individual preferences. I not only care about the various parts of my life and about obtaining the objects of my individual desires, I also care about how my life hangs together—I care about the global and narrative features of my life. My concern with these global or narrative features is rational. The burden of proof lies with proponents of the desire-satisfaction theory who claim that our global desires are mistaken when they are not identical to the sum of our individual desires. The arguments of Slote and Velleman discussed in chapter 2.V also provide strong reasons for preferring the global version of the desire-satisfaction theory to the summative version. It is perfectly rational for people to care about the global or narrative features of their lives. Here one might object that the foregoing argument only shows that global desires are rational, not that they take precedence over non-global desires when the two kinds of desires conflict. To the extent that (informed) global desires might conflict with other desires, global desires should take precedence over the other desires in determining what is good or good for one. Everything I do affects my life as a whole and the narrative history of my life. If I prefer something without considering how having it would affect my life as a whole and the narrative history of my life, my preference is not fully informed. Fully informed desires would necessarily be global desires; they would consider the object of the desire in the context of one's life as a whole and the narrative history of one's life. So, to the extent that we have reasons to prefer the *rational-*, or informed-, desire-satisfaction theory of value (welfare) to the *actual*-desire-satisfaction theory, we also have reason to prefer global versions of the theory to summative theories.

5. Restricted versus Unrestricted Desire-Satisfaction Theories of Welfare

The unrestricted version of the desire-satisfaction theory of *welfare* says that *any* state of affairs can be the object of a desire whose satisfaction is relevant to one's welfare. Restricted versions say that there are restrictions on the kinds of desires whose satisfaction is logically relevant to one's welfare. Parfit offers the following objection to the unrestricted version. Suppose that I feel sorry for a sick man and come to desire that he be cured (this could be a rational desire). Later he is cured, but I have no knowledge of this, and his being cured does not affect me in any way. The unrestricted version implies that his being cured promotes my own welfare. But this seems objectionable; it's hard to see how his being cured can benefit me. Parfit holds that our welfare is determined by the satisfaction (or non-satisfaction) of "our preferences about our own lives."[10] This seems plausible as far as it goes, but he provides no explanation or elaboration of this restriction. Parfit needs to explain what he means by preferences that are and are not "about our own lives."

Mark Overvold noted the same problem several years before Parfit's book appeared. To date, Overvold has proposed the most detailed and plausible formulation of the restricted version of the desire-satisfaction theory of welfare. Overvold takes Brandt's definition of self-interest in "Rationality, Egoism, and Morality"[11] as his point of departure. In this paper, Brandt claims that the actions that are in a person's self-interest are the same as those that the person would perform if (1) "his desires and aversions at the time were what they would be if he had been fully exposed to available information," and if (2) he were fully informed and vividly aware of all the relevant facts.[12] Overvold objects to Brandt's theory on the grounds that it makes self-sacrifice logically impossible, unless the agent acts on the basis of incomplete information or irrational desires. In order to be a genuine case of self-sacrifice, an act must be (a) voluntary, (b) informed (the agent must be aware of the loss to her own welfare and must be aware of alternatives more favorable to her own interests), and (c) contrary to the agent's self-interest. According to Brandt's theory, however, any act that fully satisfies conditions (a) and (b) *ipso facto* maximizes one's self-interest and thus cannot be an act of self-sacrifice. On Brandt's theory, it is logically impossible for a rational and fully informed person to perform an act of self-sacrifice.[13] Brandt's theory makes the thesis of psychological egoism trivially true.[14] Brandt now concedes this objection and has abandoned the desire-satisfaction theory of welfare for other reasons I discuss in 3.II.3.[15] With appropriate modifications, Overvold's objection can be generalized to apply to other versions of the desire-satisfaction theory.[16]

Overvold does not claim that his objection refutes the desire-satisfaction theory of welfare; rather, he formulates a restricted version of the theory. Overvold's general strategy is to restrict the kinds of desires that can count as logically relevant to the determination of a person's welfare or self-interest. A person's welfare is determined only by his desires for states of affairs of which he is an essential constituent, i.e., those states of affairs such that the person's existing at time t is a logically necessary condition of the state of affairs occurring at t. Overvold formulates his restricted version of the desire-satisfaction theory as follows:

> An act maximizes S's self-interest if it is the act (or one of them) that S would most want performed if he were fully informed of all the relevant facts, but choosing only on the basis of his rational desires and aversions for features and outcomes of the act that are such that S's existence at t is a logically necessary condition of the proposition asserting that the outcome or feature obtains at t.[17]

Overvold claims that one's other-regarding desires and one's desires for things that happen when one does not exist are not logically relevant to one's self-interest. With the addition of this restriction, the desire-satisfaction theory allows for the logical possibility of fully informed acts of self-sacrifice. Suppose that, acting on the basis of full information and rational desires, a woman willingly gives up her life or most of her money to save another person's life. Earlier formulations of the desire-satisfaction theory make it a conceptual truth that this act promotes her own self-interest (welfare). Overvold's theory avoids this absurd consequence. On the basis of the totality of her desires, the woman preferred to give up her life. If, on the other hand, she had chosen solely on the basis of those desires that meet Overvold's restriction (which excludes her desires for the welfare of others), she might have preferred not to give up her life. In that case, we could say that giving up her life was not in her self-interest and that it *might* have been an act of self-sacrifice.

Overvold and Parfit raise serious objections to the unrestricted desire-satisfaction theory of welfare. The desire-satisfaction theory of welfare needs to be restricted to allow for the logical possibility that a fully informed person could perform acts of self-sacrifice. Whether Overvold's theory is fully satisfactory is open to question (I have raised difficulties with the details of his theory elsewhere).[18] Nonetheless, to date, it is the best and most fully developed attempt to restrict the desire-satisfaction theory, and it is a theory that lends itself to further refinement and improvement.

Overvold's arguments concern the desire-satisfaction theory of *welfare*. We need to ask whether the desire-satisfaction theory of *value* should be restricted along the same lines as Overvold's theory. In 3.II.7 I distinguish between what I call the "welfarist" and "non-welfarist" versions of the preference-satisfaction theory of value. The welfarist theory can readily incorporate Overvold's restriction; the non-welfarist theory cannot so easily accommodate it. I do not have decisive reasons for preferring either the welfarist or non-welfarist version of the theory. Thus, I take to it be an open question whether the desire-satisfaction theory of value should be restricted along the lines of Overvold's theory.

6. The Relevance of Things That Happen after One Dies to One's Personal Welfare (or the Value of One's Life)

Overvold holds that the only states of affairs that are logically relevant to a person's welfare or self-interest are those such that the person's existing at t is a logically necessary condition of the state of affairs existing at t. He takes this to imply that things that happen after one dies (and does not exist) are irrelevant to one's welfare. He writes "it is hard to see how anything which happens after one no longer exists can contribute to one's self-interest."[19] I believe that Overvold is mistaken about implications of his theory for this issue. Clearly things that happen when one does not exist cannot affect one. Events that happen after I have ceased to exist cannot, through a process of backwards causation, affect me while I exist. Overvold's theory, however, allows that facts about what *will happen* when one no longer exists can be logically relevant to assessing one's level of welfare while one is alive. While they are alive, many people rationally desire to be *doing* work that will make a lasting contribution to human knowledge and human welfare. There is no reason to think that such desires cannot be rational. Such desires satisfy Overvold's criteria for being logically relevant to one's welfare; the state of affairs—S's doing work that makes a lasting contribution to human welfare—cannot obtain at t unless S exists at t. But whether or not S is actually satisfying this desire in the present depends upon what will happen after he is dead and no longer exists. If his work will benefit humanity long after his death, then, *while he is alive*, he is satisfying his desire to do work of lasting benefit to humanity. If his work will not benefit anyone after his death, then, *while he is alive*, he is failing to satisfy this desire. Overvold's theory makes facts about what will happen after one's death relevant to determining how well one is faring while one is alive.

Whatever Overvold's intentions may have been, I think that we should welcome this consequence of his theory. Let me present an example that I hope will persuade the reader. Suppose that a scientist (S) devotes his entire adult life to carrying out an unorthodox program of scientific research. S subordinates all of his other aims and pursuits to his work. He does this in the hope that his work will help advance scientific knowledge and contribute to the development of new technologies. He also hopes that he will eventually be recognized for his work. S dies before his work is completed or recognized. Either of the following might hold true after S dies (for the purposes of this example, I shall assume that there is no afterlife and that people cease to exist when they die):

1.   One hundred years after S's death someone else will find his old records and carry out an experiment that S had planned. This experiment will have startling results and lead to major advances in scientific theory and to the development of new and innovative technologies. S will receive credit for his work and become an important figure in all subsequent histories of science and technology.

2.   S and his work will be completely forgotten soon after his death. No good will ever come of his life's work.

Inasmuch as S had a rational preference for 1 over 2 while he was alive, proponents of the desire-satisfaction theory should hold that, *while S is alive*, facts about what will become of his work after he dies are logically relevant to his present welfare. It's not that in the future, when he no longer exists, events will affect him. Rather, while he is alive, facts about the future (which we cannot know until the future) are logically relevant to determining how well he is faring. Given 1, while he was alive, S was engaging in important and highly beneficial work that would eventually alter the history of science. Given 2, S's work and sacrifice are for naught; while he is alive it can truly be said of him that his work is in vain—he is doing work from which no good will ever come.

There is much more to be said about the bearing of posthumous events on personal welfare. I refer the reader to several recent discussions of Overvold's treatment of this issue.[20] I suspect that Overvold would want to add further restrictions to ensure that desires to do things that will have consequences after one dies do not count as logically relevant to one's welfare. The desire-satisfaction theory can be modified to account for a wide spectrum of views on this issue.

I believe that whatever we say about the bearing of posthumous events on a person's *welfare* while she is alive should also apply to the desire-satisfaction theory of *value*. If we accept the desire-satisfaction theory of value, we should say that events that happen after one dies and no longer exists can be logically relevant to the value of one's life. The scientist in the example presented above has a better life, other things being equal, if he is doing work that will benefit humanity after he dies.

7. A Further Restriction for the Desire-Satisfaction Theory of Value

According to the desire-satisfaction theory of *welfare*, one's own welfare is determined by the satisfaction or non-satisfaction of one's *own* desires. My welfare is determined by the satisfaction or non-satisfaction of my desires; your welfare is determined by the satisfaction or non-satisfaction of your desires. The satisfaction or non-satisfaction of *other people's desires* is not logically relevant to one's own welfare. According to the desire-satisfaction theory of *welfare*, a particular occurrence or event might contribute to one person's welfare and detract from another's. Should the desire-satisfaction theory of *value* be restricted in the same way? Should we say that only the satisfaction or non-satisfaction of one's own desires is logically relevant to the non-instrumental value of one's own life, or should we not place any restrictions on whose desires are relevant to the value of one's life (or anything else)? Note the difference between the following two formulations of the desire-satisfaction theory of value:

1. The non-instrumental value of someone's life is determined by the satisfaction or non-satisfaction of her desires (or her rational desires, i.e., the desires she would have if she were rational). The satisfaction or non-satisfaction of other people's desires is not logically relevant to the non-instrumental value of one's own life. The lives of individual people are the locus of value (nothing can be non-instrumentally good unless it contributes to the value of someone's life).

2. The non-instrumental value of anything is determined by the satisfaction or non-satisfaction of everyone's (rational) preferences. Anyone's preferences are logically relevant to determining the non-instrumental value of anything. Anything can be non-instrumentally good or bad if it is the object of someone's (rational) preferences or aversions.[21]

(1 and 2 do not exhaust the possibilities, but it's not essential to list all possible versions of the desire-satisfaction criterion of value.) We could restrict 1 further along the lines of Overvold's theory and say that the non-instrumental

value of someone's life is determined by the satisfaction or non-satisfaction of her (rational) desires about her *own life*. So modified, 1 implies that one's "external preferences" (one's preferences about things other than one's own life) are not logically relevant to the value of one's life.[22] The lives of different people often "overlap" so that an event that is part of one person's life is also part of another person's life. (The happiness of my daughter is also the happiness of my wife's daughter.) If the desires (or rational desires) of different people conflict, then 1 implies that one and the same event could enhance the (non-instrumental) value of one person's life and detract from the value of the other's life. Together, the desire-satisfaction theory of welfare and the view that welfare and only welfare is non-instrumentally good entail 1. Because of this, and because of its similarity to the preference-satisfaction theory of welfare, I shall refer to 1 as the "welfarist" version of the preference-satisfaction theory of value. (However, 1, itself, does not commit us to endorsing a preference-satisfaction theory of welfare.) Formulation 2 raises questions about relativism. It seems possible that some people rationally desire X and others rationally desire not-X. How should we interpret 2 in such cases? Should we say that X is both good and bad? I discuss this in 3.II.6 and 8.IX.2.

Many people find the desire-satisfaction theory of value attractive because they endorse the idea of "the individual sovereignty of the good"—each person's good is determined by what she desires for *herself* (or would desire for herself were she rational). This idea presupposes the falsity of moral realism, but, given the falsity of realism (which is assumed by all standard versions of the preference-satisfaction theory of value), this idea seems plausible. The welfarist version of the desire-satisfaction theory of value (1) is consistent with the individual sovereignty of good, but the non-welfarist version (2) is not. I'm inclined to favor 1 over 2 for that reason. But I'm not sure that this consideration is decisive, and nothing in the later parts of this book presupposes that 1 rather than 2 is the preferred version of the desire-satisfaction theory of value. I will try to note whenever anything important turns on the difference between the welfarist and non-welfarist versions of the desire-satisfaction theory of value.

8. Summary

There are many possible versions of the desire-satisfaction theory. For the record, I plan to defend the global version of the rational desire-satisfaction theory as a criterion of non-instrumental value. I am not certain whether the welfarist version of the theory should be preferred to the non-welfarist version or vice versa. Nor am I sure whether or not the theory should be restricted along the lines that Overvold proposes.

II. Objections to the Desire-Satisfaction Theory

Many philosophers reject the desire-satisfaction theory on the grounds that it clashes with our intuitions about what kinds of lives are better than others and our intuitions about what sorts of things are most beneficial to individuals. The objection is that, even if they were fully rational and fully informed, some people might prefer "the wrong things." It is possible that a rational person (as defined by the desire-satisfaction theory) could prefer x to y, when y is better than x (or when y promotes his welfare better than x). Intuitive objections to the desire-satisfaction theory assume many forms. I will consider some of those that seem most serious.

1. Preferences for "Lower" or "Subhuman" Lives

Some people might prefer "subhuman" lives to lives in which they more fully develop their "higher" capacities. Rawls asks us to consider the case of a person who possesses the capacity to do important work in applied math, but instead prefers to devote himself to counting blades of grass.[23] Some contend that this person would be better off (or have a better life) if he became a mathematician, even though he prefers to count blades of grass. This objection is reminiscent of the contented-pig objection to the HTV. Rawls presents this case as a possible objection to the desire-satisfaction theory of welfare, but it could also be construed as an objection to the desire-satisfaction theory of value. (For the sake of simplicity, I'll only consider this objection in connection with the welfarist version of the theory. Nothing important hangs on this.)

The preferred formulation of the desire-satisfaction theory holds that our welfare (or the value of our lives) is determined by the satisfaction or non-satisfaction of our rational desires—the desires or preferences that we would have if we were rational and fully informed. This requirement is very demanding. In order to be fully informed, a person's preference for being a grass counter rather than a mathematician would have to involve a vivid understanding of what it would be like to live (and enjoy the satisfactions characteristic of) these two kinds of lives. A fully informed person would also be aware of the many plausible arguments hedonists have given for the instrumental value of developing one's "higher capacities." It is unlikely that anyone who possessed this knowledge would prefer counting grass to other vocations that more fully utilize her "higher" potentials. However, it is possible that some people would rationally choose not to develop their "higher" capacities. The rational-desire-satisfaction theory of value implies that *their* good (or the best life for *them*) does not require the development of their higher capacities. (This only holds for the "welfarist" version of the rational-desire-satisfaction theory.) Below I shall argue that this consequence is acceptable (at least given the falsity of moral realism). But before doing this, let us consider an even stronger version of the objection—what I call the "lobotomy objection."

A person's desire to exercise his higher capacities and his ability to conceive of what it would be to exercise those capacities could be altered through mental impairment. A person who was severely impaired might lack any kind of desire to engage in "higher" activities. The desires of a retarded or mentally impaired person might be much more easily satisfied than those of a "normal person." In light of this, it might be objected that the preference-satisfaction theory of welfare/value recommends that some people cause themselves to become mentally impaired. If I caused myself to become impaired I would be better able to satisfy the desires I would then have than I am now able to satisfy my present desires. Consider the following case:

> I can choose to undergo a special kind of frontal lobotomy that will render me far less intelligent than I now am. It will make me incapable of thinking about science or philosophy, reading "good books," or engaging in serious political discussions. After the lobotomy my desires will change; they will be dominated by an intense desire to collect complete editions of Topps Baseball Cards. My financial circumstances will be such that it will be easy for me to satisfy this desire. Not only will I satisfy a much higher percentage of my desires, but I will be much more satisfied with my life as a whole.

If I have the lobotomy, my global preferences for my life as a whole will be better satisfied than they are now. This is a very serious problem for the actual-desire-satisfaction theory (both as a theory of welfare and a theory of value). It is not, however, a problem for the ideal-desire-satisfaction theory. If I have the lobotomy, I will be able to satisfy fully the global desires that I will then have, but those global desires will not be the desires of a rational person. I will cease to be a rational or competent judge of my own life. According to the ideal-desire-satisfaction theory, the preferences that determine what is best for me are not the preferences that I will have after the lobotomy but the preferences that my ideally rational self (with all of its capacities intact) would have. If I were to undergo a lobotomy, what is best for me would be determined, not by the preferences I would then have, but rather by the preferences that my ideally rational self would have for my self in the lobotomized state. What is best for me in my actual circumstances is determined by what my ideally rational self would want for my actual self. My ideally rational self would not want me to be lobotomized. My ideal global desires are not fully satisfied in my present life, but they are much better satisfied than they would be if I were to undergo a lobotomy. My ideally rational self would strongly prefer my present life (in which my capacities have not been diminished) to my life as a mentally impaired but contented baseball card collector.

The rational-desire-satisfaction theory of value largely avoids the kinds of contented-pig objections that have long been raised against the (quantitative) HTV. The very force of the contented-pig objection as an objection to the HTV consists largely in the fact that, in a wide range of cases, the quantitative HTV seems to imply that subhuman life X is better than "normal" human life Y, even though most of us have a clear and apparently rational preference for life Y over life X. The fact that we rationally prefer life Y over life X entitles us to say that Y is better than X (at least for us). The contented-pig objection can only arise for the rational-desire-satisfaction theory of value in cases in which it is rational for someone to prefer a "subhuman" life to a more ordinary human life. In such cases, however, it is not obvious that the ordinary human life is better for that person. If they were fully informed and fully rational, most people (perhaps the great majority of people) would prefer to develop and exercise their higher capacities and not have those capacities surgically diminished. But it is conceivable that some people would rationally prefer to fail to use (or even prefer to diminish) their "higher" capacities. The rational-desire-satisfaction theory of value implies that the best lives for such people do not involve the full use of their "higher" capacities. But this result is acceptable, barring compelling reasons to accept moral realism. If moral realism is false, then there simply is no fact that it is bad not to develop one's "higher" capacities that is independent of what rational people want or desire. Given that moral realism is false, it is not absurd to endorse the idea of "the individual sovereignty of the good": each person's good is determined by what she desires for herself (or would desire for herself were she rational).[24]

A *final caveat.*   In the preceding discussion, I have assumed the truth of something like the standard full-information theory of rationality. However, in chapter 8 I argue that the divine-preference theory of rationality is preferable to the standard full-information theory. If God prefers that all human beings develop and not diminish their "higher" capacities, then versions of the rational-desire-satisfaction theory of value that employ the divine-preference theory of rationality imply that each person's good is promoted by her preserving and developing her higher capacities. Such versions of the rational-desire-satisfaction theory may be completely consistent with the intuitions of perfectionists and Aristotelians.

2. An Appeal to Our Experience of Value

Some philosophers claim that it is an obvious feature of our moral/axiological experience that we desire things because they are good. This is inconsistent with the desire-satisfaction theory (of value), which says that things are good because we desire them.[25] E. J. Bond writes:

> One reflectively desires the things one does, because one has *discovered* their value. One desires *because* of the value; the value does not exist because of the desire.[26]

If Bond is claiming that all desires (or all desires that we are willing to endorse on reflection) are desires that we have because we believe that the objects of the desires are good, then he is mistaken. At least some people experience "simple wants" and endorse those wants (they take themselves to have reasons to satisfy them) regardless of whether those things are good independently of being desired. Perhaps we should take Bond to be claiming something like the following instead:

> *Sometimes* we desire things because they are good. *Sometimes* we cease to desire things because they are bad. We *sometimes* adjust our preferences in light of normative considerations.

Many people describe their experience in this way; they claim that they desire certain things because those things are good. How should we interpret these reports? Should we take them to be evidence for either or both of the following?

1. Some people desire certain things because they *believe* that those things are good. People adjust their preferences in light of their beliefs about value.

2. Some people desire certain things because those things are good (and good independently of our actual or ideal desires).

The kinds of experiences that Bond and many others report are clear evidence for 1; it would be unreasonable to deny the truth of 1. People *do* adjust their preferences in light of their normative beliefs. Sometimes, as the result of reflection, we come to regard our present preferences as mistaken and adjust them accordingly. But 1 is perfectly consistent with the ideal-desire-satisfaction theory of value.

Proposition 2 presupposes the truth of axiological realism. Do the reports of people like Bond give us compelling reasons for accepting 2? Some people claim that they have direct experience of value. However, we needn't assume the truth of realism in order to account for the sincerity of these reports. "Projectivist" and other non-realist theories hold that these reports are mistaken in that they claim that normative properties are objective in a way that they aren't (see 7.IV).[27] The simple appeal to experience cannot refute projectivism; nor can it establish the truth of realism. Bond's argument must be regarded as question-begging (or at least inconclusive) apart from independent reasons for accepting realism.

3. The Problem of Changing Desires

Brandt raises the problem of changing desires as an objection to the desire-satisfaction theory of welfare. His worries about this problem caused him to abandon the theory.[28] This objection applies equally to the desire-satisfaction theory of value. (Again, I'll only discuss the welfarist version of the desire-satisfaction theory of value.) Let me present a very simple example in order to illustrate the seriousness of the problem. At age forty, my employer asks me to choose between the following two options: (1) maintaining my present salary and retirement benefits and (2) opting for a lower salary with greater retirement benefits. Opting for 1 will give me a higher standard of living for the next twenty-five years. Choosing 2 will enable me to retire comfortably at age sixty. If I choose 1, I will not be able to retire until I am sixty-eight. I know all the facts and my preference is rational. Let us also stipulate that (i) only self-regarding considerations enter into the decision and (ii) I know that I will live to be eighty years old. I now prefer 1 to 2. This is a global preference; I now prefer the life I will have if I choose 1 to the life I will have if I choose 2. But I know that when I turn sixty my preferences will change. If I choose 1, then when I become sixty I will regret having chosen 1 when I was forty. If I choose 2, then for the next twenty years I will regret having chosen 2. On balance, am I better off choosing 1 or 2? How should I weigh the different preferences that I have at different times?

Overvold's theory deals with this kind of case by giving absolute weight to the preferences that a person has *at the time that he acts*. According to Overvold, what promotes my welfare depends on what my ideal preferences are at the time of choice—in this case it depends on my present ideal preferences. Overvold's theory gives undue weight to preferences that I have at the time that I act. My preferences at other times should also count. The perspective of my present preferences should not necessarily take precedence over other perspectives. Granted, I always act in the present, but I will have to live with the consequences of those choices at later times in my life.

Consider another case. Suppose that when I am twenty-five years old my fairy godmother gives me a choice between receiving a hundred thousand dollars when I am thirty years old or receiving a million dollars when I am forty. Assume also that I know that I will live for approximately sixty years. (After I make the choice, she causes me to forget that I ever made it.) Suppose that my ideal preferences about this choice change so that from the ages of ten until twenty-three my ideally rational self will prefer to get a hundred thousand dollars at age thirty. From age twenty-three on, my ideally rational self will prefer to get a million dollars at age forty. According to Overvold, if offered the choice at twenty, it would be in my self-interest (it would maximize my welfare) for me to choose to get a hundred thousand dollars at the age of thirty. If offered the choice at twenty-five, it would be in my self-interest to choose to get a million dollars at the age of forty. Overvold's theory implies that whether or not it maximizes my welfare to get the money at thirty or at forty depends on when I am asked to make the choice. This doesn't seem right. The result of the choice is the same in either case. The time at which I make the choice cannot be so all-important.

There is another problem. The following seems to be at least a conceptual possibility on Overvold's theory. Every act that I perform maximizes my own welfare (according to the lights of his theory). But because my desires are constantly changing, I have an utterly wretched life on account of regret over the past. At every moment in my life I am doing what I most want to do in light of my present desires, but I bitterly regret my entire past life and am profoundly dissatisfied with my life as a whole.[29]

The phenomenon of changing desires is a very serious problem for the desire-satisfaction theory (both as a theory of welfare and a theory of value), but it is not a fatal objection. Concerning the possibility of constant regret on account of changing desires, we should note that a rational and fully informed person would know that changing desires are likely to cause regret and unhappiness in the future. Inasmuch as most of us rationally prefer not to experience unhappiness and regret in the future, we should try to minimize regret by giving weight now to our future preferences. Our actual preferences often change. They often change as a result of changes in what we know or believe. For example, a person may choose a certain career and then later discover that he finds it boring, or that he isn't very good at it, or that there is another career that he prefers. Our rational preferences involve full information. They might not change very much through time; they might not change at all. If our ideally rational preferences don't change at all, then changing preferences cannot be a problem for rational-desire versions of the desire-satisfaction theory. Presumably, God's preferences about our lives don't change over time. (For example, it is not the case that at one time God wants me to retire at age sixty and at some other time God wants me not to retire at age sixty.) Given the divine-preference theory of rationality I defend in chapter 8, my *rational* desires for my own life don't change over time, and Brandt's objection about changing desires evaporates.

Brandt's objection about changing desires only applies if we assume a more conventional theory of rationality such as the full-information theory that Brandt himself defends. For the sake of argument, let us assume something like Brandt's full-information theory of rationality and also assume that ideally rational desires can change through time. This means that what my idealized self desires at one time can conflict with what it desires at some other time. At time t_1 my ideally rational self might prefer X to Y, and at t_2 it might prefer Y to X. (X and Y refer to events that occur at specific times. For example, X might be my receiving a hundred thousand dollars at age twenty, and Y might be my having a son at age thirty-five.) What should we say about such cases? Let me sketch an answer that I will not try to defend fully. We should regard the perspective of each period of time in a person's life as equally important. How my idealized self would view things from one temporal point in my life is no more or less important than how it would view things from some other temporal point in my life.[30] In determining one's welfare or the value of one's life, the rational preferences that one has at one time are no more or less important than those that one has at any other time. Assuming that the preferred version of the desire-satisfaction theory is a global rather than summative theory, we should view my choice between X and Y as a choice between the life I will have if I choose X and the life I will have if I choose Y. Suppose that my ideal global preferences with respect to X and Y change; at some times my ideally rational self prefers the life in which I choose X, at other times, my ideally rational self prefers the life in which I choose Y. On balance, do I have a better life if I choose X over Y? Other things equal, if my ideal preference for the life I will have if I choose X over Y (at times when I have that preference) is stronger than my ideal preference for the life I will have if I choose Y over X (at times when I have it), then I'm better off choosing X. Other things equal, if there are more times when my ideal self would prefer X to Y than Y to X, then I am better off choosing X. In proposing this, I am not abandoning the global theory for the summative theory. The summing that my proposal describes is a summing of rational *global* preferences that I have for my life as a whole at different times, i.e., the rational preferences that I have for my life as a whole at one time and the rational preferences that I have for my life as a whole at some other time.

Other things equal, the rational preferences that I have for my life as a whole at one time are no more or less important than those that I have at other times. At the very least, those who argue that a person's ideal preferences at one time count for more than her ideal preferences at some other time assume a burden of proof to show that a person's assessment of her life from some temporal perspectives is more important than her assessment from other temporal perspectives. The arguments of Slote and Velleman might be taken as evidence for this view. But, as we saw in chapter 2.V, their arguments are not conclusive.

Hare proposes an interesting alternative to my position. He distinguishes between

the preferences that a person has at a particular time regarding *things that happen at that time* (he calls these "now for now" and "then for then preferences")

and

the preferences that a person has at a particular time regarding *things that happen at other times* (he calls these "now for then" preferences).

According to Hare, when such desires conflict, the former always override the latter for determining one's own welfare.[31] When assessing the bearing of some event that occurs at t on one's welfare, the only preferences that matter are the rational preferences that one has at t. Hare's view is open to the same objection I raised earlier against Overvold. Giving absolute weight to my present ideal desires about what happens now leaves open the possibility that at later times my ideal self will regret my present choices. Things that happen in the present are not only important to me at the present time; they are part of the narrative history of my life and are relevant to global assessments of my life that I make at other times.

The foregoing solution to the problem of changing preferences is very sketchy. To the extent that the arguments of this book support, or at least make plausible, the preference-satisfaction theory of value, we have reasons to refine and develop the theory further to deal with problems such as this. Let me note again that whether our rational desires can change over time depends on the theory of rationality we presuppose. Given the divine-preference theory of rationality defended in chapter 8, it is unlikely that our rational preferences change over time. On this view, the objection about changing desires cannot get off the ground.

4. "Irreducibly Social Goods"

Charles Taylor contends that there are "irreducibly social goods."[32] Enjoying a joke or a musical concert together, for instance, is not reducible to individual enjoyments. Such joint activities are, according to Taylor, more valuable than individual activities. Two people enjoying a joke together is more valuable (and more pleasurable) than each enjoying it separately.[33] Certain goods that people value presuppose the existence of complex social or cultural backgrounds and cannot exist in isolation apart from those backgrounds. For example, the existence of a particular language and participatory government presuppose the existence of a certain social and cultural background.[34] Such goods are not "decomposable into states of individuals."[35] Taylor's arguments are part of a more general critique of utilitarianism. He claims that both hedonistic and preference versions of utilitarianism are subjectivist theories that commit one to an untenable atomism about value.

Even if Taylor's arguments refute "atomistic" conceptions of value, they do not give us reasons to reject the desire-satisfaction theory. The desire-satisfaction theory of value is not necessarily an atomistic theory of value. (This statement applies to both the welfarist and non-welfarist versions of the desire-satisfaction theory of value.) The rational-desire-satisfaction theory of value says that what makes something non-instrumentally good is that it would be desired by someone who was fully rational. This doesn't place any constraints on *what things are valuable*. The states that rational people would desire for their own sake might be irreducible to the states of individual people. Rational people might desire "irreducibly social states of affairs." (Indeed, Taylor's arguments show that many rational people do have such desires.) The view that (rational) desires are the ultimate criterion of value doesn't commit us to saying that satisfied desires are the only things that are ultimately valuable.[36] Even Overvold's restricted desire-satisfaction theory of welfare allows that one's own good or welfare may consist in states of affairs of which other people are constituents. According to Overvold's theory, a state of affairs cannot be (logically) relevant to my own welfare unless I am a *part* of it, but it doesn't imply that I am the only person who is a constituent of those states of affairs that are logically relevant to my welfare. Since I am an essential constituent of many "irreducibly social states of affairs," Overvold's theory implies that those states of affairs can be constitutive of my welfare.

5. Desires to Harm or Punish Oneself

In his recent presidential address to the American Philosophical Association, Richard Kraut raises a very serious objection to the desire-satisfaction theory.[37]

He presents this as an objection to the desire-satisfaction theory of personal welfare, but his argument could also be taken to be an objection to the desire-satisfaction theory of value. His objection can be summarized as follows. A person might desire to harm or punish himself. Such desires could be rational in any of the various senses of "rational" proposed by standard versions of the desire-satisfaction theory. But it would be absurd to think that the satisfaction of such desires contributes to the good (welfare) of people who have them. In such cases, people desire to do what is detrimental to their own good (welfare).

> It is conceptually and psychologically possible for people to decide, voluntarily and with due deliberation, to renounce their good in favor of an alternative goal. . . . In fact, they can carry out certain plans precisely *because* they think that it is bad for them to do so. For example, suppose a man has committed a serious crime at an earlier point in his life, and although he now regrets doing so, he realizes that no one will believe him if he confesses. So, he decides to inflict a punishment upon himself for a period of several years. He abandons his current line of work, which he loves, and takes a job he considers boring, arduous and insignificant. . . . His aim is simply to balance the evil he has done to others with a comparable evil for himself. He punishes himself because he regards this as a moral necessity. . . . It would be dogmatic and counter-intuitive to insist that he must benefit from his punishment simply because he desires it. The more reasonable response is to concede that sometimes carrying out one's plans and getting what one above all wants conflicts with one's good.[38]

Proponents of the rational-desire-satisfaction theory must either: (1) deny that it could be rational to desire to punish oneself or (2) deny Kraut's claim that it would be absurd to say that the self-punishment promotes one's own good or welfare (even if one rationally desires to punish oneself).

On the basis of Kraut's description of this case, I'm not sure that we should say that self-punishment is contrary to the person's long-term interests. Certain religious views make it plausible to say that self-punishment can promote one's own good (welfare). Suppose that we add the following details to Kraut's example. The person in question punishes himself in order to atone for his sins and make himself worthy of God's forgiveness. Given the truth of his belief that atonement for a finite period of time is necessary to avoid eternal punishment in the hereafter, it is perfectly plausible to suppose that this kind of self-punishment is in his own self-interest.

Take a slightly different example. Suppose that an atheist who does not believe in an afterlife still believes that he needs to atone for immoral actions that he has performed and submits to a temporary punishment as a penance.

He views his soul as stained or soiled and wants to be punished in order to cleanse his soul. (For the purposes of this example, let us suppose that all of his beliefs about the afterlife are true.) Here, again, it is unclear that the person is harming himself or acting contrary to his long-term self-interest. The person in this example has an interest in his own moral purity.

Sometimes people submit to judicial punishment because they view it as a way to benefit those they have harmed or wronged—the knowledge that one is being punished will please or gratify those they have harmed (or the survivors of those they have harmed). At the end of the movie *Dead Man Walking* a murderer about to be executed expresses the hope that his execution will bring relief to the parents of his victims, who are present at his execution. It is conceivable that someone might punish himself for the same kinds of reasons. Provided that self-punishment is desired for the benefit of others, a modified desire-satisfaction theory of welfare such as Overvold's does not imply that such acts benefit the agent.

In order to make this argument work, Kraut needs to describe the kind of case he has in mind very carefully. The following kind of case seems best for the purposes of Kraut's argument. Someone chooses to ruin his own life by irrevocably consenting to be placed in miserable and frustrating circumstances, e.g., being permanently enslaved or imprisoned, without hope of reward or gain in another life, and (1) this choice is made out of concern for cosmic justice (the belief that one deserves to suffer) and not out of concern for the purity of one's soul or the desire to be rewarded by God; (2) the person does not choose to harm himself for the benefit of others; and (3) the person does not rationally regret the choice for most of the rest of his life. Kraut's example must satisfy condition 3 if he wants to refute the kind of desire-satisfaction theory that I endorse. If the view that I developed in 3.II.3 is incorporated into the desire-satisfaction theory of welfare, then the theory does not imply that a person who rationally chooses to punish himself necessarily promotes his long-term welfare. On my view, whether or not this decision promotes his long-term welfare depends on his rational preferences *at other times in his life*—not just the time at which he makes the choice. If, for most of the rest of his life, the person rationally regrets having chosen to punish himself, then my preferred version of the desire-satisfaction theory of welfare does not imply that he promoted his long-term welfare by punishing himself.

Could it ever be rational to desire to punish oneself on the grounds that one "deserves" to suffer and have one's desires thwarted? The answer depends largely on what kind of theory of rationality we assume. In chapter 8.VIII I defend what I call the divine-preference theory of rationality/value. This view says roughly the following: if there exists a God who created the universe, cares about human beings, and is omniscient, kind, and sympathetic, then God's preferences are the ultimate standard for determining the correctness of our own preferences; my preference that X is correct provided that such a God exists and prefers that I prefer X. It is possible that a God who is kind and sympathetic does not want people to punish themselves in ways that are ultimately harmful to them (as opposed to a punishment that promotes their later redemption). When combined with the divine-preference theory of rationality, the preference-satisfaction theory of welfare (or value) may not have the kind of counterintuitive consequences that Kraut claims. Suppose, on the other hand, that there is a God of the sort that the theory describes who sometimes prefers that morally bad people suffer punishments that do not ultimately benefit them. If this is the case, then the desire-satisfaction theory of *welfare* seems to be untenable. (These would seem to be cases in which it is rational for someone to desire something that is harmful to him.) This, however, would not be evidence against the desire-satisfaction theory of *value*. Rather, it would be strong evidence for claiming that someone's suffering (just punishment) can be non-instrumentally good. Given that the unhappiness of morally bad people is non-instrumentally good, it is not absurd to say that a bad person who punishes herself acts so as to increase the non-instrumental *value* of her own life.

Suppose that a God of the sort that my theory describes does not exist. In that case, we cannot use God's preferences as a standard of rationality. It's not completely clear what sort of standard we should use in that case. (We still might hold that the preferences that such a God *would* have, if he existed, should be the ultimate standard for determining the rationality of our preferences; see 8.VIII.8.) But for the sake of argument suppose that we grant that a more conventional theory of rationality is correct—something like Brandt's full-information theory. Given such a theory, could it ever be rational to desire to punish oneself on the grounds that one "deserves" to suffer and have one's desires thwarted? The answer depends on the status of the view that bad people deserve to suffer. Ross defends this view: he denies that the happiness of morally bad people is non-instrumentally good. His view presupposes the truth of moral/axiological realism; it assumes that the unhappiness of bad people is good regardless of whether they desire to be unhappy (or would desire to be unhappy if they were fully rational). If it is true that bad people deserve to suffer in the sense explained above, then it could be reasonable for someone to desire to punish himself. Suppose that some people deserve to suffer, i.e., other things equal, it is better that they suffer and have their desires frustrated. In that case, it follows that a person who chose to punish herself in the way that Kraut describes would have a *better life* than she would otherwise have. It follows that, other things equal, the world will be a better place if she punishes herself, provided that she really was bad and deserved to suffer. Given that the unhappiness of morally bad people is non-instrumentally good, it is not absurd to say that a bad person who punishes herself acts so as to increase the non-instrumental *value* of her life. (It does seem absurd to say that this person is promoting her own *welfare*.) Suppose that realism is true and it is false that the happiness of bad people is bad. In that case, those who act on the view that the happiness of bad people is bad by punishing themselves cannot be described as fully informed or ideally rational (they are acting on false beliefs).

But let's suppose that non-realism is true. In that case, an ideally rational person could not desire to punish himself because he believes that there is some kind of independent moral fact that his suffering would be good or fitting. (The belief in such facts would, by hypothesis, be a false belief.) Suppose that a non-realist desires that he and other morally bad people be punished and concludes that the welfare of bad people is non-instrumentally bad. If such desires are not rational, then the rational-preference-satisfaction theory of value does not imply that it would be good if this person were to punish himself. On the other hand, if such desires could be rational, then the desire-satisfaction theory of value seems to imply that, other things being equal, it would be a good thing if he punished himself. But this consequence is acceptable; it is not a *reductio ad absurdum* of the theory. Given non-realism, the fact that some bad people rationally desire to punish themselves would be evidence for the view that their unhappiness and illfare are non-instrumentally good.

In the foregoing discussion I have presupposed the welfarist version of the desire-satisfaction theory of value. There are reasons to think that the non-welfarist version of the theory can more readily deal with Kraut's objection. The kind of case that makes Kraut's objection most plausible is one in which someone has an *inappropriate* desire to punish himself even though he satisfies the conditions for being rational. In such cases we suspect that personal idiosyncracies may cause someone to have excessive guilt, even if there is no obvious sense in which he can be said to be irrational. If personal idiosyncracies cause me to have excessive guilt and desire to punish myself, then others who don't share those idiosyncracies may not desire that I punish myself. According to the non-welfarist version of the preference-satisfaction theory, the goodness or badness of my punishing myself is determined by *everyone's* rational preferences, not just my own.

Kraut's arguments are directed at the desire-satisfaction theory of *welfare*. I have tried to show that his arguments do not refute the desire-satisfaction theory of *value*. My argument may not fully succeed in answering his objections to the desire-satisfaction theory of *welfare*.

6. Relativism

Some might object that the preference-satisfaction theory commits us to relativism since people's (rational) preferences could conflict. If one person rationally prefers that X and another person rationally prefers that not-X, then the preference-satisfaction theory of value implies that X is both good and bad. This objection does not apply to the preference-satisfaction theory of *welfare*. Even if the rational preferences of different people conflict, the theory implies that judgments about someone's welfare are perfectly objective. A person's welfare is determined by the satisfaction or non-satisfaction of *his own preferences* (or his preferences about his own life). Whether or not other people have preferences that conflict or do not conflict with one's own is irrelevant to one's own welfare. The preference-satisfaction theory of welfare allows that one and the same event could detract from one person's welfare and enhance the welfare of another person, but this is not relativism. The theory allows that judgments about each person's welfare are objectively true. Similar remarks apply to the welfarist version of the preference-satisfaction theory of value (but see the second-to-last paragraph of 8.IX.2 for a needed qualification). Suppose I desire that X and you desire that not-X. Suppose also that X is something that can plausibly be regarded as a part of both of our lives. The welfarist theory implies that, other things being equal, the occurrence of X enhances the value of my life and detracts from the value of yours.

Consider the view that the only state of affairs that is non-instrumentally good (bad) is someone's having a preference that is satisfied (not satisfied). Earlier I contrasted this version of the desire-satisfaction theory of value with those versions that construe the theory as a *criterion of value* (3.I.2). This view clearly does not commit us to relativism. Suppose that I rationally prefer X and you rationally prefer not-X. Suppose also that X occurs. According to the view in question, something good has happened (my desire has been satisfied) and something bad has happened (your desire has been thwarted). On the present view, this judgment is perfectly clear and objectively true. To make overall or on balance judgments of value, we simply sum individual instances of satisfied or thwarted preferences.

The non-welfarist version of the desire-satisfaction theory of value, which holds that being rationally desired by someone (anyone) makes something good and that being the object of a rational aversion makes something bad, likely does commit us to relativism (this is version 2 of the desire-satisfaction theory of value from 3.I.7). Given this view and the fact that people's rational desires sometimes conflict, it seems to follow that some things are both good and bad. X might be non-instrumentally good in virtue of S's rationally desiring it and non-instrumentally bad in virtue of S1's rationally desiring not-X. Proponents of the non-welfarist version of the desire-satisfaction theory of value can avoid committing themselves to formal contradictions by denying that normative judgments are objectively true or false. Instead they might say something like the following: "It's true for one person that X is non-instrumentally good and true for others that X is non-instrumentally bad." (I develop this idea at greater length in chapter 8.IX.) People's *actual* desires often conflict. Therefore, the non-welfarist version of the actual-desire-satisfaction theory of value clearly commits us to some sort of relativism. However, it's not so clear that people's *rational desires* can conflict. We need to examine the concept of rationality before we can speak to the issue of whether the rational preferences of different people can conflict. Any answer we give to this question presupposes a particular theory of rationality. In chapter 8 I will formulate several different theories of rationality that I take to be plausible. The theory of rationality that I take to be most plausible (the divine-preference theory of rationality) may not commit us to relativism. An alternative theory of rationality (which I call "informed-preference theory") probably commits us to relativism (see chapter 8.IX).

For the sake of argument, let us grant that people's rational desires sometimes conflict and that the non-welfarist version of the desire-satisfaction theory of value commits us to some kind of normative relativism. It is not clear that this is a decisive objection to the theory; we need independent reasons for thinking that relativism is false. Given independent reasons for accepting a theory that commits us to relativism, we may have to live with relativism, however disconcerting we may find it.

Conclusion

I defend the global version of the rational-desire-satisfaction theory as a criterion of non-instrumental value. This theory avoids the kinds of contented-pig objections that are so problematic for the HTV. At the intuitive level, it seems much more plausible than the HTV. The theory can be defended against recent objections by Brandt, Taylor, and Kraut. The desire-satisfaction theory of value (as I construe it) entails the falsity of realism. Therefore, the case for or against the desire-satisfaction theory depends on the case for or against realism. Objections of the sort proposed by Bond presuppose the truth of axiological realism. These objections are question-begging in the absence of reasons for thinking that axiological realism is true.

Because I haven't yet discussed realism, I am not yet in a position to offer any positive arguments in favor of the desire-satisfaction theory. I discuss realism in chapter 7 and offer qualified (positive) arguments in favor of the rational-

desire-satisfaction theory of value in Interlude 2. This argument rests on premises defended in chapters 6 and 7.

The plausibility of the rational-desire-satisfaction theory of value depends,
to a very large degree, on the kind of theory of rationality we employ. I discuss
the concept of rationality at great length in chapter 8. A number of recent papers present objections to full-information versions of the desire-satisfaction
theories of welfare. The objections presented in these papers are objections to
normative theories that rely on full-information theories of rationality. I discuss
these objections in chapter 8 and argue that standard full-information theories
of rationality are untenable. I defend a divine-preference theory of rationality.
Many of the objections to the desire-satisfaction theory considered in this
chapter evaporate if we accept the divine-preference theory of rationality.

CHAPTER 4

Nietzsche's Theory of Value and the Good Life: The *Übermensch* Ideal

Introduction

Nietzsche's ideal of the *Übermensch* is an important vision of the good life; it is also the key to understanding Nietzsche's own positive theory of value. Nietzsche takes "strength," or "power," to be the ultimate standard of value. On his view, strong people have good lives and weak people have bad lives. Nietzsche defends the view that strength, or power, is the standard of value in a number of passages. It is unclear exactly what Nietzsche means by "strength" or "power." He never defines these terms, nor does he ever give necessary and sufficient conditions for being a strong person. However, we can reconstruct Nietzsche's concept of strength or power, and thus his theory of value, on the basis of his detailed description of the (very) strong person (the *Übermensch*).

This chapter consists of four parts. In part I, I will argue that Nietzsche has a theory of value and that he takes strength or power to be the ultimate standard of value. Part II lists and describes some of the major characteristics Nietzsche ascribes to the strong person (the *Übermensch*). In part III, I propose an interpretation of Nietzsche's theory of value. Part IV is an assessment of the *Übermensch* ideal and Nietzsche's theory of value. Nietzsche defends his theory of value by appealing to his theory of the "will to power." This argument is unsuccessful because Nietzsche fails to provide an adequate explanation and defense of his theory of the will to power. However, if his theory of the will to power were true (if it were true that all human behavior aims at power and power alone), then we would have reasons to accept power as the standard of value (or at least to reject all other alternative theories of value). I will argue that Nietzsche's theory of value is separable from his moral theory; one can accept Nietzsche's theory of value without accepting his "immoralism." Objections to Nietzsche's immoralism are not necessarily objections to his theory of value. I will also argue that ideals of value such as the *Übermensch* have considerable importance from the standpoint of the rational-desire-satisfaction theory of value. An ideally rational person must be able to vividly imagine the kinds of lives envisaged in such ideals and the process of imagining such lives is likely to alter the kinds of preferences that she would have for her own life. Some people find, on due consideration, that they desire to possess some of the characteristics that Nietzsche ascribes to the *Übermensch*.

I. Does Nietzsche Have a Theory of Value?

1. *Some Textual Evidence*

In a number of passages Nietzsche claims that strength or power is the ultimate standard of value: strong people have good lives, and weak people have bad lives. He goes so far as to say that power is the "objective measure of value."

> What is the objective measure of value? Solely the quantum of enhanced and organized power. (WP 674)

> What determines rank, sets off rank, is only quanta of power, and nothing else. (WP 855)

> What determines your rank is the quantum of power you are; the rest is cowardice. (WP 858)

> I teach No to all that makes weak—that exhausts. I teach Yes to all that strengthens, that stores up strength, that justifies the feeling of strength. (WP 54)

> What is good?—All that heightens the feeling of power, the will to power, power itself in man. What is bad?—All that proceeds from weakness. What is happiness? The feeling that power *increases*—that resistance is overcome. *Not* contentment, but more power; *not* peace at all, but war; *not* virtue, but proficiency. . . . The weak and ill-constituted shall perish: first principle of *our* philanthropy. (AC 2; see also WP 55, 382, 660, 710, 713, 856; and GM II.12)

One of Nietzsche's basic criticisms of conventional moralities is that they weaken and thus harm the "higher types" of people who adopt them.[1] These criticisms presuppose that strength or power is also the standard for measuring personal welfare. In *The Will to Power* Nietzsche claims that the value of particular moral codes should to be measured by the standard of "life."

> What are our evaluations and moral tables really worth? What is the outcome of their rule? For whom? In relation to what? — Answer: for life. (WP 254; see also WP 298, 354; and GM Pref. 3)

Moralities that "enhance" life are good; those that harm it or detract from it are bad. This does not constitute a departure from the view that strength or power is the ultimate standard of value, for strength or power is the standard by which Nietzsche measures the "enhancement" of life. Immediately after the passage quoted above, Nietzsche goes on to add:

> But *what is life?* Here we need a new, more definite formulation of the concept "life." My formula for it is: Life is will to power. (WP 254; see also WP 706)

Nietzsche makes value judgments throughout his writings. He uses strength as the standard of value in making these judgments. The question is: what sort of status does he assign to these judgments? Does he consider them to be true or correct? Does he take them to be justified in a way that conflicting judgments are not? There is considerable evidence for the view that Nietzsche takes his own value judgments and standards of value to be correct and justified in a way that alternative value judgments and theories of value are not.

In *The Will to Power* Nietzsche writes:

> There is nothing to life that has value except the degree of power — assuming that life itself is the will to power. (WP 55)

This appears to be a rough analogue of Mill's argument for hedonism: power is the only thing that is pursued for its own sake, therefore it is the only thing that is good for its own sake. Both Mill and Nietzsche defend monistic theories of value by appealing to monistic theories of human motivation. Both claim that pleasure/power is the only thing that is good as an end, because pleasure/power is the only thing that is desired or pursued for its own sake.[2] According to Nietzsche, all human behavior can be explained in terms of the "will to power," or the drive to increase and expend one's power.[3] Nietzsche understands the will to power as a drive or tendency to behave in certain ways rather than a conscious desire or a motive of intentional actions. He tries to explain the behavior of plants and other non-sentient things in terms of the will to power.[4] Further, he holds that states of consciousness and mental events have no causal efficacy with respect to behavior.[5]

WP 710 also provides evidence for my interpretation. In this passage Nietzsche suggests that we should attempt to see whether "a scientific order of values" can be constructed on a numerical scale measuring force (power):

> Our knowledge has become scientific to the extent that it is able to employ number and measure. The attempt should be made to see whether a scientific order of values could be constructed simply on a numerical and measurable scale of force—all other "values" are prejudices, naiveties, misunderstandings. They are everywhere *reducible* to this numerical scale of force. The ascent on this scale represents every rise in value; the descent on this scale represents diminution in value. Here one has appearance and prejudice against one. (For moral values are only apparent values compared with physiological values.)

Nietzsche doesn't explicitly claim that it is possible to construct a "scientific order of values" on a numerical scale. But he clearly considers this to be a serious possibility and strongly suggests that his own "physiological" standard of value has much more claim to being considered correct than moral values (standards).

2. Danto's Objection

Arthur Danto claims that Nietzsche is an axiological nihilist[6] on the basis of the following passage:

> The feeling of valuelessness is attained when one apprehends that the general character of existence must not be interpreted with the concept of "purpose," of "oneness," or of "truth. . . ." The world fails to have in the plenitude of happenings any overarching unity; the character of existence is not "true," it is *false*. . . . One has no longer any ground to persuade himself of a *true* world. . . . In brief, the categories "purpose," "oneness," and "being," with which we give a value to the world, are now withdrawn by us—and the world now looks valueless. . . .[7]

According to Nietzsche, the categories of "purpose," "unity," and "truth" ("true being") do not apply to the universe. The universe has no goal or purpose; there is no unifying principle that explains all events; and there is no "true world," i.e., there are no "things in themselves" as opposed to "mere appearances." If we judge the world in terms of these categories, it seems to be valueless. But, Danto to the contrary, Nietzsche does not conclude that the concepts of value and disvalue have no application to the world or things in the world. Rather, he concludes that we ought to question our reliance on these three categories. We need to create new standards for judging things.

> Once we have devalued these three categories, the demonstration that they cannot be applied to the universe is no longer any reason for devaluing the universe. (WP 12) [This passage is from the very next paragraph after the passage cited by Danto above.]

> *Our* pessimism: the world does not have the value we thought it had. . . . it seems worthless. . . . That is precisely how we find the pathos that impels us to seek *new values*. In sum: the world might be far more valuable than we used to believe; we must see through the naiveté of our ideals, and while we thought that we accorded it the highest interpretation, we may not even have given our human existence a moderately fair value. (WP 32)

3. Nietzsche's Rejection of "Unconditional" Standards of Value

There are passages in which Nietzsche denies the existence of any "absolute" or "unconditional" standards of morality or value.[8] Nietzsche's rejection of "unconditional" standards of value is perfectly consistent with my interpretation, because it is possible that he takes his own standard of value to be only conditionally true. This seems to be precisely his view: Nietzsche thinks that the truth of his standard of value is conditional on the truth of his doctrine of the will to power (see the passage from WP 55, cited in 4.I.1).

4. Nietzsche's Denial of the Existence of Moral Facts

The most serious challenge to my interpretation is the fact that there are places in which Nietzsche says that there are "no moral facts."

> My demand upon the philosopher is known, that he take his stand *beyond* good and evil and leave the illusion of moral judgment *beneath* himself. This demand follows from an insight which I was the first to formulate: that *there are altogether no moral facts*. Moral judgments agree with religious ones in believing in realities which are no realities. Morality is merely an interpretation of certain phenomena — more precisely a misinterpretation. (TI VII.1)

> *My chief proposition: there are no moral phenomena, there is only a moral interpretation of these phenomena. This interpretation itself is of extra-moral origin.* (WP 258; see also WP 786)[9]

These passages seem to show that Nietzsche holds that moral judgments cannot be true or justifiable. They do not show, however, that he thinks that value judgments cannot be true or justifiable. Nietzsche uses the term "morality" in a very narrow sense. In his sense of the term "moral" *(moralisch)*, not all value judgments are moral judgments. Nietzsche's assertion that *moral judgments* can't be true or rationally justified does not commit him to the view that *value judgments* cannot be true or rationally justified.

Earlier, I quoted a passage in which Nietzsche assesses the "value of moral evaluations." He claims to have a higher (non-moral) standard by which to evaluate moral standards. This presupposes that at least some *value* judgments are not *moral* judgments. There are many other places in which he distinguishes between moral and non-moral values.[10] The fact that Nietzsche denies that *moral judgments* can be true or justifiable is perfectly consistent with the view that he takes certain kinds of *value judgments* to be both true and justifiable. Nietzsche is a "moral nihilist" in his own narrow sense of the word "moral," but he is not an axiological nihilist or irrationalist.[11]

Nietzsche denies the objective truth or reasonableness of all judgments that make use of the concepts of guilt, retribution, and moral praiseworthiness and blameworthiness.[12] This, he says, follows from the fact that people do not have "free will."

> *The error of free will* . . . the doctrine of the will has been invented essentially for the purpose of punishment, that is, because one wanted to impute guilt. . . . Men were considered "free" so that they might be judged and punished—so that they might become *guilty*. . . . Christianity is the metaphysics of the hangman. (TI VII.1–2; see GS 110, 345; and HA I.39, in which Nietzsche also rejects the idea of free will)

Nietzsche rejects the notion of moral (as opposed to legal) justice and injustice.[13] It also seems likely that he would deny the objective truth of judgments that make use of the concepts of right and wrong or moral duty (obligation). He almost never makes use of these concepts in his own value judgments.

Nietzsche rejects the morality of "good and evil" and all of the distinctive kinds of judgments and concepts that are a part of it. However, his rejection of morality (good and evil) does not constitute a rejection of all value judgments that make use of the concepts of good and bad. Nietzsche makes this explicit in the following passage from the *Genealogy of Morals*:

> [I]t has long since been abundantly clear what my *aim* is, what the aim of that dangerous slogan is that is inscribed at the head of my last book *Beyond Good and Evil*. At least this does *not* mean "Beyond Good and Bad." (I.17)[14]

5. A Final Caveat

In trying to show that Nietzsche accepts the theory of value that I attribute to him, I have relied heavily on passages from *The Will to Power*. Nietzsche never submitted these writings for publication. Many readers will regard my evidence as inconclusive because of my reliance on passages from *The Will to Power*. However, the evidence that I have marshaled at least shows that Nietzsche seriously considered the idea of endorsing a theory of value based on the notion of strength, or power. Even if I am mistaken in thinking that Nietzsche endorses a theory of value, it is still worth asking whether the *Übermensch* ideal points to any specific theory of value or whether any specific theory can be extracted from this ideal. Nietzsche's pronouncements about value are of great interest to philosophers. It is important to ask whether there is any systematic unity underlying Nietzsche's value judgments and whether they are roughly consistent with any particular theory of value. No one should object to attempting to extract systematic accounts of value from episodes in a novel or play. Similarly, no one should object to attempting to extract a systematic theory of value from Nietzsche's many pronouncements about good and bad. My aim in this chapter is to reconstruct the theory of value that is suggested by Nietzsche's description of the *Übermensch* and numerous pronouncements about good and bad and ask whether that theory is plausible. This project is worth pursuing regardless of whether Nietzsche accepts or endorses a theory of value in the ordinary sense of the term.

II. Nietzsche's Description of the Strong Person (*Übermensch*)

Before turning to Nietzsche's description of the strong person, we should first note that some of the characteristics we ordinarily associate with strength, or power, play no role in Nietzsche's account. Often when we describe someone as a "powerful person," we mean that she has great "social power" or the ability to control or affect the lives of others by means of force or persuasion. A strong person in Nietzsche's sense does not necessarily have social/economic power. Members of the lower classes have little social/economic power. But, according to Nietzsche, many of the strongest individuals belong to the lower classes.

> Where one must seek the stronger natures . . . they prosper most often in the lowest and socially most abandoned elements. (WP 887)

Nietzsche would also reject the view that social power is *sufficient* for being a strong person, since he says that weaker, degenerate types of people often occupy positions of great social power.[15] I think it unlikely that Nietzsche takes social/economic power to be constitutive of strength, or power. In any case, it seems clear that he does not regard it as an important constituent of personal strength. Note the attitude about worldly power or social/economic power evident in the following passage:

> One pays heavily for coming to power: power *makes stupid*. The Germans—once they were called the people of thinkers: do they think at all today? The Germans are now bored with the spirit, the Germans now mistrust the spirit; politics swallows up all serious concern for really spiritual matters. *Deutschland, Deutschland über alles*—I fear that was the end of German philosophy. (TI VIII.1)

"Strong" sometimes means "tough," "durable," or "fit for survival." However, according to Nietzsche, having this kind of strength is neither necessary nor sufficient for being a strong person. It also seems doubtful that he would regard the ability to survive as an important constituent of strength, because he says that the lower (weaker) types of human beings generally have a greater capacity for survival than the higher types.

> Among men, too, the higher types, the lucky strokes of evolution, perish most easily as fortunes change. . . . The higher type represents an incomparably greater complexity—a greater sum of coordinated elements: so its disintegration is also incomparably more likely. (WP 684; also see GM I.17)

Natural selection and the struggle for survival do not favor the survival of the best individuals of a given species. "Strange though it may sound, one always has to defend the strong against the weak" (WP 685).

We can now turn to the characteristics that Nietzsche ascribes to the strong person (*Übermensch*).

1. Self-Control, Strong Passions, and "Good Instincts"

Nietzsche takes self-control to be an essential feature of the strong person.

> The essential feature is precisely *not* to "will"—to *be able* to suspend decision. All unspirituality, all vulgar commonness, depend on the inability to resist a stimulus: one *must* react, one follows every impulse. (TI VII.6)

Or, to speak more definitely, the inability *not* to respond to a stimulus—is itself merely another form of degeneration. (TI V.2; see also WP 45, 47)

One way of controlling one's passions is to eliminate or "extirpate" them.

> The most famous formula for this is to be found in the New Testament, in that Sermon on the Mount, where incidentally, things are by no means looked at from a height. There it is said, for example, with particular reference to sexuality: "If thy eye offend thee, pluck it out." (TI V.1)

A strong person is capable of controlling his passions without extirpating them; it is only the degenerate who cannot do without such radical expedients.[16] But it's not just that a strong person doesn't *need* to extirpate his passions; he can't do this without ceasing to be a strong person. A strong person must have strong passions. The passions are "great sources of strength" (WP 383), "the mightiest natural powers" (WP 386).

> The highest man would have the greatest multiplicity of drives in the relatively greatest strength that can be endured. Indeed, where the plant "man" shows himself strongest, one finds instincts that conflict powerfully (e.g., in Shakespeare), but are controlled . . . the greatest perhaps also possess great virtues, but in that case also their opposites. I believe that it is precisely through the presence of opposites and the feelings they occasion that the great man, the *bow with great tension*, develops. (WP 966; also WP 98, 928, and Z Prol. 3)

Here, as in other places, Nietzsche emphasizes that a strong person must have the full spectrum of typical human passions.

> For every strong and natural species of man, love and hate, gratitude and revenge, good nature and anger, affirmative acts and negative acts, belong together. (WP 351)

"Emotional deadness" is the most distinctive characteristic of the "last man," who represents an antithesis to the *Übermensch* (Z Prol. 5).

A strong person must have "good instincts." Her passions are such that she almost always promotes her own welfare by acting on them. She no longer needs to control or resist harmful impulses; she doesn't have any (bad) impulses that need to be resisted. Nietzsche writes:

To *have* to fight the instincts—that is the formula of decadence: as long as life is ascending, happiness equals instinct. (TI II.11)

What is it fundamentally that allows us to recognize *who has turned out well?* . . . He has a taste only for what is good for him. (EH I.2; see also AC 6; and WP 384, 906, 1003)[17]

Nietzsche emphasizes the importance of being able to act spontaneously (on instinct) without deliberating about what to do.[18] In order to be able to act in this manner without harming oneself, one must have "good instincts." According to Nietzsche, psychic harmony and good instincts are attained through a process of self-discipline[19] and sublimation.[20]

The foregoing provides us with some clues as to what Nietzsche means by "strength." Strong passions are important because they provide one with energy.[21] A person's strength is at least partly a function of his energies; a strong person must have a great amount of energy.[22] She must also be able to use this energy wisely and efficiently.

That which constitutes growth in life is an ever more thrifty and more far-seeing economy, which achieves more and more with less and less force— as an ideal, the principle of the smallest expenditure. (WP 639; see also WP 800, and TI IX.37)

Nietzsche seems to be committed to the view that one's strength is to be measured or determined at least partly in terms of one's ability to do or achieve various things. Increasing the efficiency with which one uses one's energies contributes to one's strength only to the extent that it enables one to accomplish more with one's limited energy (force).

2. Independence of Mind, Self-Esteem, and the Independence of Self-Esteem

Nietzsche attaches considerable importance to independence of mind and takes it to be an essential feature of the strong person.

Greatness of soul is inseparable from greatness of spirit. For it involves *independence*. (WP 984)

Independence of the soul—that is at stake here! No sacrifice can then be too great: even one's dearest friend, one must be willing to sacrifice for it. (GS 98; see also GS 7; and Z I.22.iii)

The strong person is not a member of the "herd" of which Nietzsche speaks so contemptuously; she is self-directed and is not a conformist. The high valuation Nietzsche places on non-conformity can be explained in terms of some of his other views. He says that the basic values of European societies of his time are "unnatural" and "life denying."[23] The "higher types" of people who adopt these values become weak and sick as a result. At most, this only shows that being a conformist is incompatible with being a strong person if one lives in a society that has the wrong sorts of values. Conformity per se doesn't necessarily lead to the adoption of harmful values. However, conformity is incompatible with the kind of creativity ("being a creator of new values") that Nietzsche takes to be essential for being an *Übermensch* (see chapter 4.II.7).[24]

According to Nietzsche, the need for the approval and admiration of others is a mark of deficient self-esteem or self-love.

> You cannot endure yourselves and do not love yourselves enough: now you want to seduce your neighbor to love, and then gild yourselves with his error. . . . You invite a witness when you want to speak well of yourselves; and when you have seduced him to think well of you, then you think well of yourselves. (Z I.16)

> [W]ho could fathom the full depth of the modesty of the vain man? . . . It is from you that he wants to acquire his faith in himself. . . . He even believes your lies if you lie well about him; for, at bottom, his heart sighs: what am I? . . . The vain man is unaware of his modesty. (Z II.21; see also BG&E 261; GS 330; and HA I.583)

The vain man is weak because he is dependent on the approval of other people. His self-respect is extremely vulnerable to changes in public opinion. A strong person doesn't need the approval of others; his power no longer needs proving, he disdains to please.[25]

3. Lightheartedness (Übermütigkeit)

Nietzsche says that a strong person would be "joyful,"[26] "gay," "cheerful," and "lighthearted" *(übermütig)*.[27] Nietzsche defines *Lust* (joy, pleasure) as the "feeling of power" that a person derives from accomplishing things and overcoming obstacles.[28] Given this and given that "strength" is to be defined largely in terms of the ability to accomplish things, it would seem to follow that the strongest people experience the most joy (pleasure). A strong person has "good instincts" in the sense described in 4.II.1. Because of this, she can "let go" and act in a spontaneous (uninhibited) manner without harming herself. She doesn't need to worry about every single decision she makes. Inasmuch as excessive worry and lack of spontaneity rob life of much of its joy and pleasure, lightheartedness can also contribute to the pleasantness of one's life. The strong person's courage enables her to be lighthearted in the face of adversity.[29] Her tremendous self-esteem allows her to be indifferent to public opinion and the disapproval of others. She rejects conventional morality and with it the notions of free will, guilt, and responsibility. Because of this, she doesn't dwell on her own shortcomings and misdeeds.

> To be incapable of taking one's enemies, one's accidents, even one's misdeeds seriously for very long—that is a sign of strong, full natures in whom there is an excess of power to form, to mold, to recuperate and to forget. (GM I.10)

Lightheartedness is incompatible with *ressentiment*, which Nietzsche takes to be paradigmatic of weakness and degeneration.[30] According to Nietzsche, *ressentiment* is a kind of impotent hostility. It is "the submerged hatred, the vengefulness of the impotent" (GM I.10). Max Scheler proposes an interesting analysis of *ressentiment* on the basis of Nietzsche's many scattered remarks. He defines *ressentiment* as a reliving or reexperiencing (as opposed to a mere recollection) of certain hostile emotions, feelings of hatred, envy, revenge, and the like.[31] *Ressentiment* characteristically involves a feeling of weakness or impotence since it results from an inability to "act out" one's hostile feelings, e.g., the inability to avenge past wrongs and the inability to acquire the things for which one envies others.[32] Nietzsche and Scheler are especially concerned with the role *ressentiment* plays in the genesis of values and moral codes. However, what is important for our purposes here is Nietzsche's claim that a strong person would be relatively free from *ressentiment*. Many of the factors that often give rise to hostile feelings, for instance, dissatisfaction with one's own life and lack of self-respect,[33] would not be operative in the case of the strong person.

4. Amor Fati

"*Amor fati*" (love of fate) or an affirmative attitude about one's own life and the universe as a whole is another characteristic of the strong person. Nietzsche uses the doctrine of "eternal recurrence" as a test of strength. A strong person must be able to take pleasure in the thought that the entire course of history (including his own life and everything that happens to him in his life) will occur over and over again an infinite number of times in the future.[34] People who are dissatisfied with their own lives and/or the state of the universe would presumably not be pleased at the thought of eternal recurrence. People who hope for a better life in the hereafter would also be distressed with the idea of eternal recurrence. Nietzsche overemphasizes the importance of eternal recurrence as a test of strength or *amor fati*, because passing this test doesn't guarantee that one has the sort of love of one's own fate that Nietzsche requires for being an *Übermensch*. Consider the case of an atheist who does not believe in an afterlife and who expects the universe to reach a state of static entropy at some time in the future. For her to be pleased at the prospect of eternal recurrence amounts to little more than her thinking that her present life and the universe, as they are, are "better than nothing" (it is better that they continue as they are rather than cease to exist). However, *amor fati* requires much more than this:

> My formula for greatness in a human being is *amor fati*: that one wants nothing to be different, not forward, not backward, not in all eternity. Not merely bear what is necessary, still less conceal it . . . but love it. (EH II.10)

> Such an experimental philosophy as I live . . . wants rather to cross over to the opposite of this—to a Dionysian affirmation of the world as it is, without subtraction, exception, or selection—it wants the eternal circulation: the same things, the same logic and illogic of entanglements. The highest state a philosopher can attain: to stand in a Dionysian relationship to existence—my formula for this is *amor fati*. (WP 1041; see also Z IV.19.ix and IV.19.xi)

According to Nietzsche, an *Übermensch* would be perfectly pleased with the way the world is. However, it's difficult to see how anyone who accepts Nietzsche's theory of value could be perfectly pleased with the state of the universe. According to Nietzsche, the universe is not as good as it might have been. People aren't nearly as strong as they might have been. The universe would be better if the *Übermensch* would finally appear; or better still, if all people were *Übermenschen*. I don't see how these views can be reconciled with the attitude that "one wants nothing to be different." Nietzsche is aware of this difficulty (see note 34). Here one might try to defend the consistency of Nietzsche's view by claiming that an *Übermensch* would not necessarily have to accept or live by Nietzsche's theory of value. On this reading, Nietzsche distinguishes sharply between the correct standard or criterion of value (power) and the values or set of values whose adoption would best foster one's self-development. Nietzsche, however, never provides us with an example of a set of values that would enable one to take a thoroughly optimistic view of the universe. His own theory of value falls far short of this objective. This failure is evident in nearly all of his writings; his contempt and scorn for the great majority of human beings is hardly the attitude of a man who "wants nothing to be different."

5. Kindness

Nietzsche says that an *Übermensch* would be kind—at least to the weak.

> [Y]ou who are good and just . . . What is great is so alien to your souls that the *Übermensch* would be awesome to you in his kindness. (Z II.21; see also Z I.3)

There are a great many passages in Nietzsche's writings that appear to contradict this. Nietzsche's admiration for certain types of cruel people, barbarians and "blond beasts of prey," is consistent with his ascribing positive value to kindness. Nietzsche does not admire warriors and barbarians for their cruelty, but rather for their joyfulness, lightheartedness, and strong natural passions. Further, the warrior or barbarian is *not* Nietzsche's ideal. His discussion of the "Three Metamorphoses of the Spirit" (Z I.1) makes this clear (see also BG&E 257). The camel (the ordinary civilized person, a "tamed beast of burden") represents the lowest stage of human development. The lion (the warrior, barbarian) represents a higher stage. But the child (the creative person) occupies the highest level. According to Nietzsche, a strong person would not be kind to others out of a sense of pity or moral duty. However, a strong person would be free from many of the typical motivations for being cruel or unkind, e.g., *ressentiment* (touchiness, vindictiveness, and envy) and dissatisfaction with his own life.

> [M]an has felt too little joy: that alone, my brothers, is our original sin. And learning better to feel joy, we learn best not to hurt others or to plan hurts for them. (Z II.3; see also TI VI.2; and HA I.588)

Having tried to make a case for the consistency of Nietzsche's view that an *Übermensch* would have to be kind, I must conclude by noting that there are numerous passages in which Nietzsche recommends that ordinary people be treated ruthlessly and their interests sacrificed to promote the interests of exceptional people (some of these passages are quoted in 4.IV.2.B). Presumably, Nietzsche would recommend that an *Übermensch* sacrifice the welfare of ordinary people provided that this benefits her. This seems inconsistent with kindness as it is ordinarily understood.

6. Generosity

An *Übermensch* would be very generous.[35] She is not only generous, she is also magnanimous in her giving. She does not expect thanks, and she does not give in order to have others beholden to her.[36] She is extremely wary of arousing feelings of shame in those to whom she gives.[37] Whenever necessary, she will allow others to steal from her rather than cause them to feel ashamed for being dependent on her.[38] In these respects the *Übermensch* is considerably more magnanimous than Aristotle's "high-minded man." Note Aristotle's description of the high-minded man in the following passage:

> He is the kind of man who will do good, but who is ashamed to accept a good turn, because the former marks a man as superior, the latter as inferior. Moreover, he will requite good with a greater good, for in this way he will not only repay the original benefactor but put him in debt at the same time by making him the recipient of an added benefit. The highminded also seem to remember the good turns they have done, but not those they have received. For the recipient is inferior to the benefactor, whereas a highminded man wishes to be superior." (*Nicomachean Ethics* 1124b)[39]

Nietzsche does not take this kind of generosity to be inconsistent with psychological egoism. The strong person is completely selfish, even when he acts generously.[40] The generosity of the *Übermensch* is a natural "overflowing" of an "overrich" and "overfull" life.[41]

7. Creativity, Creative Genius

Another characteristic Nietzsche takes to be essential for being an *Übermensch* is creativity, or creative genius. He says that "the highest individuals are creative men."[42] All of the historical individuals for whom Nietzsche expresses great admiration are creative geniuses of one sort or another. It is significant that Nietzsche lavishes more praise on Goethe than on any other historical personage. In "The Three Metamorphoses of the Spirit" the child, or the creative person, represents the highest stage of the spirit. Nietzsche's admiration for Napoleon does not constitute a counterexample to my claim that being a creative genius is necessary for being an *Übermensch*, since Nietzsche admired Napoleon for his vision of a united Europe with a cosmopolitan culture free of petty national rivalries (see GS 362 and WP 104).

Nietzsche attaches great value to the ability to do creative work in art, music, philosophy, and other artistic and intellectual fields. For him, however, the most important kind of creative ability is the ability to "create new values."

Order of Rank: He who *determines* values and directs the will of millennia by giving direction to the highest natures is the *highest* man. (WP 999)

The most powerful man, the creator, would have to be the most evil, inasmuch as he carries his ideal against the ideals of other men and remakes them in his own image. Evil here means: hard, painful, enforced. Such men as Napoleon must come again and again and confirm the belief in the autocracy of the individual. (WP 1026)

Around the inventors of new values the world revolves: invisibly it revolves. (Z I.12)

Companions the creator seeks . . . fellow creators, the creator seeks—those who write new values on new tablets. (Z Prol. 9; see also Z I.9, II.18, III.12.xi, III.12.xvi, and WP 23, 32)

Formulating and articulating new *standards of value*, e.g., moral, axiological, and aesthetic standards, counts as "creating new values." Sometimes people use or suggest new standards without ever articulating them. The first "impressionist" may have never formulated the new standards he used in his art. We still might want to say that he created new aesthetic standards (values). Sometimes we speak of people creating new standards in a particular field simply because they do work of exceptional quality. It's not clear what Nietzsche would say about this or the case of the first impressionist. It might be suggested that Nietzsche takes "creating new values" to include "creating objects of value" or "things which have value." This is possible. However, this interpretation is not supported by any of the passages cited above. Nietzsche does not use either the word *Wertsachen* or *Wertgegenstände* (objects of value) in any of these passages.

In other passages, Nietzsche construes "creating values" very differently to include any acts of valuing (esteeming) things. Nietzsche denies that things have value independently of being valued or esteemed. All value is *created* by individual acts of valuing and esteeming things. On Nietzsche's view, things are good because they are valued; they are not good independently of being valued.

Verily, men gave themselves all their good and evil. Verily, they did not take it, they did not find it, nor did it come to them as a voice from heaven. Only man placed values in things to preserve himself—he alone created a meaning for things, human meaning. Therefore he calls himself "man," which means: the esteemer. To esteem is to create: hear this, you creators! Esteeming itself is of all esteemed things the most estimable treasure.

Through esteeming alone is there value: and without esteeming the nut of existence would be hollow. Hear this, you creators! (Z I.15)

We who think and feel at the same time are those who really continually *fashion* something that had not been there before: the whole eternally grown world of valuations, colors, accents, perspectives, scales, affirmations, and negations. The poem that we have invented is continually studied by the so-called practical human beings (our actors) who learn their roles and translate everything into flesh and actuality, into the everyday. Whatever has *value* in our world now does not have value in itself, according to its nature—nature is always valueless, has been *given* value at some time, as a present—and it was *we* who gave and bestowed it. (GS 301)[43]

On one reading, only very rare and exceptional individuals can "create values" (only exceptional people are capable of creating new standards of value). On another reading, almost all human beings can "create values" (almost all human beings are capable of esteeming things). If esteeming or valuing something entails desiring it, then Nietzsche's theory seems to be a kind of desire-satisfaction theory of value.

III. A Reconstruction and Interpretation of Nietzsche's Theory of Value

It is very difficult to reconstruct Nietzsche's theory of value from his picture of the *Übermensch*. Even if we were confident that we had a complete list of all of the essential features of an *Übermensch* (I do not claim to have provided one here), we would still need to determine which of those features Nietzsche takes to be desirable for their own sake. There might be features of the *Übermensch* that Nietzsche does not value for their own sake but simply regards as necessary conditions for (or invariable consequences of) other valuable characteristics. Since he never explicitly addresses this issue, we can't be certain which of the characteristics of the *Übermensch* Nietzsche takes to be constitutive of power (value).

Three interpretations of Nietzsche's theory of value seem at least initially plausible.

1. First Interpretation

The ultimate standard of value is creative artistic and intellectual "power." On this view, the psychological traits of the *Übermensch* are just means to enhancing his creative powers. Such characteristics as self-esteem and strong passions are valuable only insofar as they promote creativity.

This interpretation cannot be reconciled with Nietzsche's intense dislike and scorn for certain creative geniuses, e.g., St. Paul and Martin Luther. Nietzsche regards them as sick and profoundly unhealthy. He seems to regard their "sickness" as something undesirable in itself; it is not just something that is bad when it hampers people's creative powers. Nietzsche's criticisms of "art for art's sake" also weigh heavily against this interpretation.[44]

Not only is the first interpretation dubious as a reading of Nietzsche, the theory it attributes to him is implausible in its own right. Psychological health is not necessary for creativity. The tormented genius is all too common a phenomenon. It would be implausible to hold that the life of the miserable, deranged creative genius is just as desirable as the life of a creative genius who is also a joyful, lighthearted Übermensch.

2. Second Interpretation

Strength or power means health; psychological health is the sole standard of value. The primary basis for this interpretation is the fact that Nietzsche often uses the words "weak" and "strong" interchangeably with "sick" and "healthy." According to this interpretation, Nietzsche values creative activity only as a means to psychological health. In order to achieve psychological health, one must sublimate or spiritualize one's desires. Nietzsche says that sublimation is the only way to control one's passions without thereby weakening and destroying them (D 109). Sublimation is a redirection of one's energies. All other methods for attaining self-control, e.g., extirpation of the passions, diminish one's energies. They involve a weakening of certain desires without a corresponding strengthening of other desires. Roughly speaking, sublimation, as Nietzsche and Freud conceive it, is a redirection of one's energies. The goal of sublimation is to control certain unwanted desires by redirecting the energies one uses to satisfy them into other pursuits (D 109). To spiritualize one's desires is to sublimate them by means of spiritual or mental activities, e.g., art, music, poetry, and philosophy. Spiritualization is a special kind of sublimation.[45] Nietzsche prefers that we spiritualize our passions rather than merely sublimate them. In at least one place he seems to say that one can't successfully sublimate one's desires unless one spiritualizes them (TI V.1).

The second interpretation is implausible. It cannot do justice to the great value Nietzsche attaches to creative genius and achievement. There is no reason to think that the great artist sublimates his desires any better than the lesser artist, but clearly Nietzsche values great artists much more than lesser artists. According to the second interpretation, Nietzsche holds that engaging in spiritual activities is necessary for psychological health, and he values spiritual activities only as means to psychological health. The view that spiritual activities are necessary for psychological health seems to assume that spiritualization is the only form of sublimation that can be successful. Whether or not Nietzsche endorses it, the view that creative spiritual activities are the only reliable means for sublimating one's desires is implausible. So long as one finds two activities equally satisfying and equally absorbing, they will be equally effective as ways of sublimating one's desires. Many people find the kinds of spiritual activities Nietzsche recommends more engrossing and more satisfying than more common pursuits. Other people, however, find other sorts of activities, such as gardening, athletics, and child-rearing, equally satisfying. Many people succeed in sublimating their desires without spiritualizing them.

Nietzsche would have us engage in creative spiritual activities rather than more humble pursuits. If the preceding argument is correct, then this cannot be recommended to us simply because of its consequences for our health. Nietzsche is committed to the view that creative activities have greater non-instrumental value than other sorts of activities.

3. Third Interpretation

Nietzsche attaches non-instrumental value to both artistic and intellectual creativity and to characteristics constitutive of psychological health, e.g., strong, harmonious passions and self-esteem. This interpretation avoids the problems of the first two interpretations. According to this third interpretation, Nietzsche does not have a simple or unified theory of value; the things he values all fall under the following two headings:

1.   Creative artistic and intellectual powers

2.   Psychological health

IV. An Assessment of Nietzsche's Theory of Value

1. Should Nietzsche's Theory of Value Be Rejected on Moral Grounds?

It might be objected that the *Übermensch* ideal is morally deficient in that an *Übermensch* is (or could be) a morally bad person, completely lacking moral virtues such as justice, benevolence to others, and the willingness to sacrifice himself for the sake of the less fortunate.[46] This objection assumes the stand-point of conventional morality, or at least a standpoint not greatly at odds with conventional morality. I will attempt to defend Nietzsche's theory of value against this objection. I accept the moral views presupposed by this objection and will attempt to show that accepting Nietzsche's theory of value is consistent with rejecting his immoralism. Nietzsche's theory of value and his "immoralism" are *separable*.

I take the following principles to be at least part of conventional moral views about right and wrong in contemporary Western societies:

1. All mentally competent people have moral obligations; their actions can be right or wrong.

2. All mentally competent people have moral obligations to *all other human beings*. Other things equal, it is wrong to harm any other human being (including the many people Nietzsche regards as inferior).

3. Other things equal, people have a duty to help other human beings when they are able to do so (at least provided that helping others does not require one to sacrifice one's own interests).

The objection at issue raises two key questions:

1) *Must* an *Übermensch* be immoral by reference to conventional morality, i.e., must an *Übermensch* be the sort of person who often performs acts that are wrong (or seriously wrong) according to the standards of conventional morality?

2) *Could* an *Übermensch* be immoral by reference to the standards of conventional morality?

The answer to the first question is no. An *Übermensch* need not be immoral. One can find many shocking passages in which Nietzsche seems to endorse immoral actions. However, there is nothing in Nietzsche's theory of value or description of the *Übermensch* that commits him to the view that an *Übermensch* must be immoral. Some of the worst forms of immorality are incompatible with one's being an *Übermensch*. An *Übermensch* couldn't perform wrong actions out of rancor or viciousness. An *Übermensch* might be someone whose actions are nearly always consistent with the demands of conventional morality. Here I appeal to underdetermination; the essential features of the *Übermensch* underdetermine the morality or immorality of her actions. Nothing in the description of an *Übermensch* requires that she act contrary to conventional morality. A person blessed with exceptional good fortune would not need to harm others (or violate other rules of conventional morality) in order to promote her self-development. To make this a bit more concrete, let me give a brief description of an *Übermensch* who is not immoral. Imagine a creative artist who devotes most of her time to her work. She has achieved great critical success at an early age and has inherited large sums of money and, thus, does not need to step on others or violate the prohibitions of conventional morality in order to promote her own "growth and development." She is generous and has a kindly disposition. This inclines her to help others in the ways required by conventional morality. These characteristics are compatible with the other characteristics Nietzsche takes to be essential for being an *Übermensch* — there is no reason why such a person couldn't be an *Übermensch*. The answer to our first question, then, is no. There is no reason why an *Übermensch* would have to be immoral by standards of conventional morality.

Consider a slightly different version of question 1. Would it be possible for an *Übermensch* to *accept* and *follow* the demands of conventional morality (as opposed to merely acting in ways that do not violate the demands of conventional morality)? For instance, could an *Übermensch* feed the hungry out of a sense of duty as opposed to a feeling of generosity that "overflows" from a good life?[47] Nietzsche seems to say no. A central tenet of his critique of Christian morality is that it has disastrous consequences for those who accept it (or at least for most of the "naturally superior" people who accept it). Others (most notably Scheler) have speculated on the question of whether a strong person or *Übermensch* could be a Christian or accept Christian morality.[48] I can't do justice to this question here. I would simply observe the following. We need not accept Nietzsche's contention that being an *Übermensch* is incompatible with accepting and following Christian morality or any other form of conventional morality. To reject this contention is not to reject his theory of value. We must distinguish between his theory of value and his theory about the harmfulness of conventional morality or Christian morality. Nietzsche appeals to his own theory of value in arguing that conventional morality is harmful. In this sense, his critique of conventional morality presupposes his theory of value. However, his theory of value does not presuppose the correctness of his contentions about the harmfulness of conventional morality; it would be consistent to accept the former, but reject the latter.

Now let us turn to the second question: *could* an *Übermensch* be immoral by reference to conventional standards of right and wrong? An *Übermensch* couldn't be immoral in the way that cruel and hateful people such as Hitler are immoral. But an *Übermensch* could treat "inferior" people ruthlessly in pursuing her own self-fulfillment and other goals. An *Übermensch* could be immoral in the way that Napoleon was immoral. Nietzsche shocks and appalls us again and again by endorsing precisely this. I appeal again to the underdetermination of the essential characteristics of the *Übermensch*. There is no reason why someone possessing the essential features of an *Übermensch* could not be indifferent to the welfare of ordinary people and ruthless in the pursuit of her goals. So the answer to question 2 is yes—an *Übermensch* could be immoral.

This, however, is not a decisive objection to Nietzsche's theory of value. We must distinguish sharply between a theory of the good life or personal welfare and a theory of right and wrong or a theory about what constitutes an ideal moral agent. The fact that the *Übermensch* ideal is not plausible as a theory of right and wrong or a theory of moral goodness is not an objection to it as a theory of the good life. Nietzsche's theory of value implies that one could flourish or have a good life and yet be morally bad. Is this so shocking? The hedonistic theory of value and actual-desire versions of the desire-satisfaction theory of value have precisely the same consequence. But they are seldom attacked for this reason. For my own part, I think that moral goodness is non-instrumentally good because it is rational to desire it for its own sake (see 2.III and 8.IX). But, from the perspective of common sense or conventional morality, it is not absurd or obviously false to hold that moral goodness has only instrumental value.

Nietzsche claims that all moral judgments are mistaken. He does not make moral judgments (in his narrow sense of the word "moral"; see 4.I.4) and he seems indifferent to moral considerations. Moral judgments are judgments about the rightness or wrongness of actions, the justice or injustice of laws or institutions, or judgments about the praiseworthiness or blameworthiness of people. Nietzsche is a moral nihilist (in his narrow sense of the word "moral"), but he is not an axiological nihilist. Nietzsche makes value judgments, and he thinks that they make sense. Recall the following passage from *The Genealogy of Morals* quoted earlier:

> [I]t has long since been abundantly clear what my *aim* is, what the aim of that dangerous slogan is that is inscribed at the head of my last book, *Beyond Good and Evil*. At least this does *not* mean "Beyond Good and Bad." (I.17)

Nietzsche wants us to reject or "go beyond" judgments of good and evil (what he calls "moral judgments"). But he does not want us to reject or "go beyond" value judgments of good and bad.

Most of us think that both moral judgments and value judgments make sense. Making moral judgments and holding that they can be true or justified is inconsistent with accepting Nietzsche's moral theory, but it is perfectly consistent with accepting his theory of value. One could accept a consequentialist or a Rossian theory about right and wrong and still accept Nietzsche's theory of value.

2. Other Objections to Nietzsche's Theory of Value

A. Very few people are capable of being an *Übermensch*. Throughout *Zarathustra* Nietzsche says that there has not yet been a single *Übermensch*. It might be objected that such an unattainable ideal cannot serve as a standard for judging the value of the lives of ordinary people. Given that I have no realistic hope of becoming an *Übermensch*, how can it make sense to judge the value of my life by reference to the *Übermensch* ideal? Nietzsche might reply that the great majority of human beings have bad lives that are not worth living. This reply evinces the kind of pessimism he disavows, but often succumbs to. Alternatively, Nietzsche could claim that the *Übermensch* is an ideal of the *best life* and that ordinary people should judge the value of their lives by how closely they approximate the *Übermensch* ideal, i.e., one has a good life to the extent that one's life resembles or approximates that of an *Übermensch*. It is unclear whether or not Nietzsche holds this view. However, whether or not he does, it is a view he *could endorse* without greatly modifying his theory of value.

B. Nietzsche says that the higher types of people are so much more valuable than the lower types that we are justified in sacrificing the majority for the sake of a few exceptional people. Note the following passages (I could supply many others):

[M]ankind in the mass sacrificed to the prosperity of a single *stronger* species of man—that would be an advance. (GM II.12)

What is the ape to man? A laughingstock or a painful embarrassment. And man shall be just that for the overman: a laughingstock or a painful embarrassment. (Z Prol. 3)

The weak and ill-constituted shall perish: first principle of *our* philanthropy. And one shall help them to do so. (AC 2)

[C]oncerning the evolution of mankind: perfecting consists in the production of the most powerful individuals, who will use the great mass of people as their tools. . . . (WP 660; see also WP 859, 866, 997; BG&E 258)

Many people (myself included) think that Nietzsche radically undervalues the lives of ordinary people. For the sake of argument, let us grant this. Is this an objection to his theory of value? Is someone who embraces the *Übermensch* ideal committed to accepting Nietzsche's exceedingly low valuation of ordinary human beings? In the dreadful passages cited above, is Nietzsche correctly following the implications of his theory of value or is he simply revealing his own pathology (or both)? Nothing else Nietzsche says in his discussion of the notion of strength or power commits him to saying that people differ so greatly in their strength or power that the value of an exceptional person exceeds the value of the lives of thousands or millions of others. He never proposes any standards for measuring or quantifying power. I conclude much as I did in 4.IV.2.A; even if Nietzsche's theory of value commits him to saying that the value of the life of an exceptional person exceeds the value of the lives of thousands or millions of others, his theory would not have to be greatly modified in order to avoid this consequence.

It is commonly claimed that "perfectionist" moral theories such as Nietzsche's commit one to antiegalitarian political views. Thomas Hurka disputes this claim in his book *Perfectionism*.[49] His arguments (which I take to be largely successful) are worth sketching here. Hurka combines a perfectionist theory of the good with a standard agent-neutral consequentialist theory of right and wrong. According to Hurka, the state should maximize the (total/average?—Hurka is unclear on this point) perfection of all human beings, counting everyone equally. He claims that, given certain plausible empirical assumptions, e.g., that most humans have talents that can be perfected and that wealth has diminishing marginal utility in promoting the perfection of any given person, his version of perfectionism requires an egalitarian distribution of resources in moderately affluent societies. When combined with ordinary forms of consequentialism, perfectionist theories of the good do not imply that societies should devote most of their resources to fostering the perfection of the few. Hurka concedes, however, that if a society is very poor and cannot afford to educate all of its members, the long-term development of human perfection may require that the society devote a disproportionate share of its resources to educating the few.[50]

Hurka formulates a view that he calls "maximax perfectionism":

> "According to maximax, each agent's overriding goal should be not a sum or average of lifetime value, but the greatest lifetime value of the single most perfect individual or, if perfections are not fully comparable, of the few most perfect individuals."[51]

Maximax perfectionism is sharply antiegalitarian. There may be no limit to the resources that could be devoted to furthering the perfection of the most talented. Hurka conjectures that Nietzsche held something like maximax perfectionism. This interpretation is plausible in light of some of the passages quoted in this section (4.IV.2.B). However, it would be perfectly consistent for someone to accept Nietzsche's theory of the good life without accepting maxi-max perfectionism.

Here, and earlier, I have spent a good deal of time trying to answer some of the intuitive objections to Nietzsche's theory. My reasons for this are twofold. First, the views and moral intuitions to which they appeal are widely and firmly held—I hold them myself. Second, I want to show that Nietzsche's theory of value is largely independent of his immoralism. One needn't accept his immoralism in order to accept his theory of value. Like many readers, I find that I have very mixed reactions to Nietzsche. I find his views both attractive and repellent to a very high degree. My distinction between Nietzsche's moral theory and his theory of value helps to explain this reaction. Many of us are repelled by his moral theory (or non-theory) but find his theory of value plausible and suggestive.

3. The Will to Power and Power as the Standard of Value

Does Nietzsche's theory of the will to power as an explanatory principle give us reasons for accepting power as the standard of value? This question is very similar to the question I addressed at the end of my discussion of Mill's proof in chapter 1.II.5. (The question I addressed there is whether the truth of psychological hedonism provides reasons for accepting the hedonistic theory of value.) Most of what I said in chapter 1 applies here. The truth of Nietzsche's view that the will to power explains all human behavior does not entail the truth of Nietzsche's theory of value—accepting the will to power as an explanatory principle is consistent with not accepting any theory of value. But the truth of the will to power (as an explanatory principle) would provide reasons for rejecting any alternative theory of value. If human beings are so constituted that they can only seek power as an end, then there is no point in accepting any theory of value which attaches non-instrumental value to anything other than power. John Wilcox puts this very well. According to Wilcox, if the doctrine of the will to power is correct, then Nietzsche's standard of value does not *need* to be justified.

> If he is right, we all seek power, first and most fundamentally; and we all *must*—this is the nature of a living being. But if that is true, then, in a sense, the norm of power does not have to be justified; we are confronted with a *fait accompli*—in ourselves. It is as if we had all accepted the norm and cannot now reject it. It is our standard and it *must be*—there is no alternative to it.[52]

The most serious problem with Nietzsche's argument is his failure to give an adequate explanation or defense of his theory of the will to power. He never explains this doctrine clearly nor does he ever make clear what kind of empirical evidence would count for or against its truth. In the absence of further clarification and defense of the theory of the will to power as an explanatory principle, Nietzsche's attempt to establish power as the standard of value by appealing to the truth of the will to power must be regarded as inconclusive. The prudent reader will, of course, want to make her own assessment of Nietzsche's theory of the will to power. I can only report that I do not understand it and that I have searched in vain for empirical content, content that would allow us to regard actual or possible empirical data as evidence for or against the theory.

4. An Assessment of Nietzsche's Theory from the Standpoint of the Rational-Desire-Satisfaction Theory

In order to assess the *Übermensch* ideal as a theory of value we need to ask the following questions:

a) Are all of the characteristics that Nietzsche takes to be constitutive of strength or power non-instrumentally good?

b) Is there anything else that is non-instrumentally good?

According to the rational desire-satisfaction theory of value, something is non-instrumentally good provided that one would desire it if one were rational. If someone would have a non-instrumental desire to possess certain features of the *Übermensch* if he were fully rational, then his possessing those features would be non-instrumentally good (this holds, given what I called the "welfarist" version of the rational-desire-satisfaction theory of value). On the other hand, if someone would not desire to possess certain features of the *Übermensch* if he were fully rational, then those characteristics are not constitutive of his own good and his possessing them would not be non-instrumentally good. On reflection, many of us have ultimate desires for the existence of moral goodness, both in ourselves and others. (See 2.III for a thought experiment that bears on this question.) These seem to be desires that would persist, even if we were fully rational. Thus the rational-desire-satisfaction theory seems to imply that moral goodness (or at least certain instances of it) is non-instrumentally good (also see 8.IX). Nietzsche does not ascribe any intrinsic value to moral goodness; the rational-desire-satisfaction theory of value seems inconsistent with his theory on this score. There may also be people who are such that if they were fully rational they would not desire to possess certain characteristics Nietzsche ascribes to the *Übermensch*. Unlike Nietzsche's theory, the rational-desire-satisfaction theory of value denies that it would be non-instrumentally good if these people possessed the characteristics in question.

The foregoing points notwithstanding, ideals of value such as the *Übermensch* play an important role in the rational-desire-satisfaction theory of value. In order to be fully informed, our desires must be informed by a vivid knowledge and understanding of ideals of the good life. Among other things, we must know what it would be like to be an *Übermensch*. At least some of us will alter our preferences in light of this knowledge. Some people who have no intrinsic desire to develop their "higher" artistic and intellectual capacities would acquire this desire if they had a vivid understanding of what it would be like to do so. My intrinsic preferences concerning my own psychological traits have changed in light of consideration of the *Übermensch* ideal. Among other things, I desire to be lighthearted and free from *ressentiment* in the way that an *Übermensch* is. I would also like to have the generosity, self-esteem, and "good instincts" of an *Übermensch*. These are not preferences that would be likely to be altered if I gained further information—they are desires that I would have if I were fully informed and fully rational.

Human Purpose and Human Nature: Aristotelian Theories of Value

Introduction

Aristotle and others in the Aristotelian tradition use the notion of human purpose or human nature as the foundation for theories of value. They hold that
to have a good life is to fulfill one's purpose or essential nature as a human
being.

In the first section of this chapter, I examine Geach's attempt to defend an
Aristotelian theory of value by appealing to the meaning of the word "good."
Geach claims that, in senses that are central to morality and value theory, the
word "good" involves implicit reference to the purpose or function of human
beings. But he does not propose or defend any particular theory of human
purpose or function. I will argue that, in the absence of a fully developed theory of human purpose or function that yields a plausible theory of value, we
should not accept Geach's theory.

The other sections of this chapter examine three different conceptions of
human function (essence) and theories of value based on them. Section II
considers the view that having a good life consists in fulfilling the purpose(s)
for which one was created. I formulate several versions of the theory. On some
formulations, this theory is open to decisive objections (these objections are
analogues of standard objections to the divine-command theory of moral
rightness). However, one version of the theory (a divine-purpose theory of
value that is an analogue of Adams's latest formulation of the divine command
theory of right and wrong) is not open to any obvious objections. This theory
assumes the falsity of axiological realism; thus, any positive argument for
thinking that it is true presupposes reasons for thinking that realism is false. In

chapter 8, I return to this topic and offer a qualified defense of two versions of the desire-satisfaction theory of value. One of these theories (and the one I favor) is a divine-preference/purpose theory of rationality/value.

In section III, I consider several standard interpretations of Aristotle's theory of value. I argue that, on certain interpretations, Aristotle's theory is open to serious objections. I consider alternative interpretations that do not open Aristotle's theory to these objections. On those readings that avoid the objections, however, Aristotle does not have a purely functionalist theory of the good; his functionalist principles are supplemented by other, independent normative principles. None of the standard interpretations of Aristotle attributes to him a theory of human purpose or human nature that by itself can form the foundation of an adequate theory of value.

Section IV examines Thomas Hurka's attempt to base a theory of value on the concept of human nature. Hurka's view is roughly that to have a good life is to develop to a high degree those characteristics or abilities that are essential for being human. Hurka's theory is arguably the most plausible version of the Aristotelian theory of value to date. However, I shall argue that Hurka fails to give adequate reasons for accepting his theory.

I conclude that, to date, proponents of theories of value based on the idea of human purpose or human essence have not given us adequate reasons for accepting those theories. However, the examination of ideals of the good life defended by Aristotle and others in the Aristotelian tradition is important, given the rational-preference-satisfaction theory of value. In order to be fully informed, our preferences must be based on a vivid awareness of what it would be like to live the kinds of lives they take to be ideal. It is very likely that our rational desires would be altered by such knowledge; if we were fully informed and fully rational, many of us would want our lives to possess some of the features of the lives described in these ideals.

There are many different things one might mean by "the purpose or function of human beings." In some of these senses, the purpose or function of human beings clearly cannot provide a plausible foundation for normative theories. (a) Sometimes "function" refers to socially determined roles, as in the statement "one of the functions of KGB agents is to suppress all criticism of the state." We can talk about the function of fathers, teachers, and police officers. This particular notion of function cannot serve as the basis for a plausible theory of value, since there is no reason to think that it is always a good thing for someone to fulfill the function of a socially or conventionally defined role. Throughout human history, social conventions have created many bad or morally objectionable roles. (b) We might say that human beings have a purpose in the same sense that biological organs do: the purpose/function of the heart is to circulate blood, the purpose of the liver is to remove toxins from the body. However, since human beings are not parts of a larger biological organism, this theory rests on a faulty analogy. (c) We might take the purpose of someone's life to mean "the various purposes or goals that he has that give him reasons to want to continue living." The view that to have a good (or "meaningful") life is to fulfill (or largely fulfill) one's own goals and purposes is frequently associated with existentialism.[1] I will not consider this view in the present chapter since it seems to be a version of the desire-satisfaction theory.

I. Geach's Argument for Functionalism

1. Attributive and Predicative Adjectives

Geach distinguishes between attributive and predicative adjectives. Consider the statement "x is an AB" where "x" is an expression that names (or refers to) a particular thing, e.g., "Bob" or "this"; "A" is an adjective; and "B" is a noun. The adjective "A" is predicative in the statement "x is an AB," provided that "x is an AB" is equivalent to "x is A *and* x is B." Any adjective that is not predicative is attributive. If "x is an AB" is not equivalent to "x is A *and* x is B," then A is an attributive adjective.[2] For example: "red" is a predicative adjective. The statement "this is a red pen" is equivalent to "this is red and this is a pen." "Large" and "fast," respectively, are attributive adjectives in the following two sentences:

> "Mickey is a large mouse." (This is not equivalent to "Mickey is large and Mickey is a mouse.")

> "Gertrude is a fast snail." (This is not equivalent to "Gertrude is fast and Gertrude is a snail.")

When an adjective is used attributively, its meaning depends on the kind of noun to which it applies. The meaning of "small" depends on the kind of thing to which it applies. A small galaxy is much larger than a large mouse. The largeness or smallness of something is relative to the kind of thing it is. We can say that something is a large or small house (dog, galaxy, etc.), but it makes no sense to say that something is a large or small thing without saying what kind of thing it is.

2. Geach's Thesis

Certain central uses of the word "good" are clearly functionalist. To say that something is a good watch or a good knife is to say that it serves well the function for which it was created (it keeps time well, or it cuts well). In these cases, the word "good" is used attributively. Geach contends that all legitimate uses of the words "good" and "bad" (including those central to morality and the theory of value) are attributive:

'[G]ood' and 'bad' are always attributive, not predicative, adjectives.[3]

[T]here is no such thing as being just good or bad, there is only being a good or bad so and so.[4]

3. An Objection

Some normative judgments have the grammatical form of predicative statements. Consider the following:

Lincoln is good.

Courage is good.

Pleasure is (non-instrumentally) good.

Geach concedes that such uses of the word "good" appear to be predicative. But he claims that, in these contexts, "good" implicitly refers to the goodness of a certain sort of thing.[5] This account is a plausible reading of the first two sentences. It is plausible to take "Lincoln is good" to mean "Lincoln is a good man" or "Lincoln is a good human being." It is plausible to take "courage is good" to mean "courage is a good trait of character." It is unclear, however, that "pleasure is (non-instrumentally) good" can be construed as an attributive use of the word "good." "Pleasure is a good human feeling" and "Pleasure is a good experience" are very strained readings of "Pleasure is (non-instrumentally) good." Geach needs to give us an account of the purpose or function of human feelings (or an account of the purpose of human beings that explains the role of pleasure in human life).

4. Does Geach's Attributivism Commit Us to the View That There Are Many Different Concepts of Goodness?

Geach considers the objection that his attributivism commits him to the view that the word "good" has different meanings when ascribed to different kinds of things, e.g., watches and knives. A good knife is a knife that cuts well and holds an edge well. A good watch is a watch that keeps time well. Geach's answer to this objection is that to say that something is a good X means that it serves or fulfills the function of Xs well.[6]

For Geach the key notions are those of a "good/bad man [human being]" and a "good/bad human action."[7] Geach, however, does not give criteria for distinguishing between good and bad human actions, nor does he give an account of the function or purpose of human beings and human actions. Given the incompleteness of his theory, it is at best an open question whether the notion of purpose or function can serve as a plausible basis for a theory of good/bad human beings and good/bad human actions. (I will have more to say about this in 5.I.5 and 5.I.6.)

5. Can Attributivism Account for the
Commendatory Meaning of "Good"?

According to Geach, "good" (in senses relevant to morality and value theory) is a commendatory term; it commends or expresses a favorable attitude about the things to which it is ascribed. To say that pleasure is good is to commend pleasure or recommend that people pursue it. To say that courage is good is to commend it. But "good" in the attributive sense does not always commend the things to which it applies. In ordinary contexts, to call someone a good bank robber or a good liar is not to commend her. Geach attempts to answer this objection by arguing that calling something a "good X" involves a conditional or hypothetical commendation of it. To say that something is a good X implies that if you want Xs, it is the sort of X you should want.

> It belongs to the *ratio* of 'want', 'choose', 'good', and 'bad', that, normally, and other things being equal, a man who wants an A will choose a good A and will not choose a bad A—or rather will choose an A that he thinks good and will not choose an A that he thinks bad. This holds good whether the A's we are choosing between are knives, horses, or thieves.[8]

"He is a good torturer" implies "If you want a torturer, he is the kind of torturer you should want." Geach's view does not do justice to the unconditional condemnation that certain kinds of moral/value judgments express. "Torture is a bad action" implies something much stronger than "If you want human actions, this is not the kind you will want." An even more serious problem for Geach is that the statement "If you want human actions, you will want good ones" has no clear meaning. By contrast, the statement "If you want a knife, then you will want a good one" is perfectly clear and seems to be true. We know what knives are *for*. It is not clear or non-controversial what human actions are *for*. Geach makes no attempt to explain what human actions (or human beings) are *for*, much less to defend such a view (see 5.II for more on this subject).

6. Good and Bad Purposes

We can make (and need to make) value judgments about purposes and functions themselves. We can ask if it is good that something serves its function well. Some things, e.g., instruments of torture and malicious lies, are such that it is not a good thing if they function well or achieve their intended purpose(s). Does Geach's theory permit us to say that certain purposes or functions are bad? Can he say that it is bad that an instrument of torture fulfills its function? For Geach, something that serves its function well can be bad only to the extent that it involves *something else* not serving *its* function well. Geach might say that it is bad that an instrument of torture functions well because torturing someone is a bad human action. Being a good torturer is incompatible with being a good human being. Not only do we want to say that being a good torturer is incompatible with being a good human being, but that, on balance, it is better or more important to be a good human being than to be a good torturer. If Geach's theory is to serve as the basis for a plausible ethical theory, he needs to provide a basis for saying that certain functions (the function of human beings or the function of human actions) are better or more important than others. It is very difficult to see how the criteria for ranking functions could, themselves, be functionalist, and thus it is difficult to see how any purely functionalist theory of value could be plausible.

On Geach's view, we cannot make sense of the question of whether it is good to fulfill one's function or purpose as a human being.[9] However, it is perfectly proper to ask whether or not it is good to fulfill one's function as a human being, and, *prima facie,* it is a serious failing of Geach's view that he closes this question. For all that I have shown here, there may be some concept of human purpose such that it makes no sense to ask whether it is a good thing to fulfill one's purpose as a human being. We have no reason to think that there is such a concept, however, until Geach or someone else proposes and explains it.

Geach's theory is incomplete. He needs to explain what he means by the purpose or function of human beings and human actions. We need to examine fully developed accounts of human purpose or function. The next three sections of this chapter examine theories of value based on specific notions of human purpose or function. On all of these particular accounts of human purpose or function, it is an open question whether it is good to fulfill one's purpose or function as a human being. All are open to the same last objection I raised against Geach's theory—they don't give us a cogent answer to the question "Why is it good to fulfill one's purpose or essential nature as a human being?"

II. Good as the Fulfillment of the Purpose for Which One Was Created

The view that I want to consider here is the following:

> P.   For one to have a (non-instrumentally) good life is for one to fulfill the purpose for which one was designed and/or created.

Geach's arguments might be taken to support P. The rationale for this can be stated as follows: "Good" is used in the same sense whether it is applied to persons or to artifacts. Just as a good knife is one that serves well the purpose for which it was designed and/or created, so a good human being (or human being who has a good life) is one who serves well the purpose or function for which she was designed and/or created.

P is ambiguous because the expression "purpose for which one was designed and/or created" can be understood in a number of different ways (the following list does not purport to be exhaustive):

1.   The purpose(s) (if any) for which one's parents created (conceived) one

2.   The purpose(s) (if any) for which God designed and created one as an individual

3.   The purpose(s) (if any) for which God designed and created human beings

Using these three notions of purpose, we can distinguish between the following three versions of P:

> P1.   To have a good life is to fulfill the purposes for which one's parents created one. To have a bad life is to fail to fulfill the purposes for which one's parents created one. If there is no purpose for which one's parents created one, then one cannot have a good or bad life.[10]

> P2.   To have a good life is to fulfill the purposes for which God designed and created one as an individual. To have a bad life is to fail to fulfill the purposes for which God designed and created one. If there is no purpose for which God designed and created one, then one cannot have a good or bad life.

> P3.   To have a good life is to fulfill the purposes for which God designed and created human beings. To have a bad life is to fail to fulfill the purposes for which God designed and created human beings. If there

is no purpose for which God designed and created human beings, then one cannot have a good or bad life.

P1 is an extremely implausible position. It implies that a child conceived by her parents so that they can sell her into slavery or prostitution has a good life provided she fetches a high price. To my knowledge, no philosopher has ever defended P1.

P2 and P3 hold that the purposes or designs of God are the ultimate standard for judging the value of human life. Both P2 and P3 imply that if there is no God, or if God did not design and create us for a purpose, then no one can be said to have a good or bad life.[11] Surely, though, we can judge some lives to be good and others bad, even if there is no God. P2 and P3 imply that any kind of life (however wretched and miserable) would be a good life provided that it helped to fulfill God's purpose in creating us. For example, if God created human beings as a source of malicious pleasure for himself, then P3 implies that the more pain and suffering one experiences, the better life one has.[12] Here, it might be objected that, since God is good, he could not have designed and created human beings to be the source of malicious pleasure or for any other bad purpose. But this reply assumes that there are standards of goodness and badness independent of God's purposes, in which case P2 and P3 cannot be the only ultimate standards of value. Proponents of P2 and P3 thus face the following dilemma: either (a) for God to be morally good is for God to fulfill his own purposes, in which case God's being morally good places no constraints on what sorts of purposes he can have and the objection about God's being cruel cannot be answered or (b) moral goodness is determined by standards independent of God's aims and purposes, in which case God's aims and purposes are not (the only) ultimate standards of value.

We can avoid the objection about God being malicious if we modify P2 and P3 by requiring that God be kind or loving. So modified, P2 would read as follows:

P2a.   To have a good life is to fulfill (most of) the purposes for which *a loving God* designed and created one as an individual. To have a bad life is to fail to fulfill the purposes for which a loving God designed and created one. If there is no purpose for which a loving God designed and created one, then one cannot have a good or bad life.[13]

P2a avoids the objection that we might have been created as a source of malicious pleasure for our creator. But it is still open to the objection that it implies that lives can't be good or bad unless there is a loving God who designed and created us for certain purposes.

This last objection can be avoided if we further refine P2. Consider the following:

> P2b.   If there is a loving God who designed and created human beings for a purpose, then (i) to have a good life is to fulfill (most of) the purposes for which *a loving God* designed and created one as an individual; (ii) to have a bad life is to fail to fulfill the purposes for which a loving God designed and created one. If a loving God who designed and created human beings for a purpose does not exist, then the goodness or badness of human lives is determined by the most plausible alternative theory of value.[14]

According to P2b, if there is a loving God who designed and created human beings for a purpose, then the goodness or badness of human life is determined by reference to God's purposes. But P2b also allows that there can be valid standards of good and bad, even if a loving God who designed and created human beings for certain purposes does not exist. I have considerable sympathy for P2b; indeed, the view I defend in chapter 8 closely resembles P2b. P2b avoids the serious intuitive objections which beset the other analogues of the divine-command theory that we have considered here. However, we haven't yet given any positive reasons for accepting it. P2b presupposes the falsity of strong forms of axiological realism according to which some things are good or bad independently of the beliefs, aims, and attitudes of God or any other rational being. (P1, P2, P3, and P2a also presuppose the falsity of this strong form of realism.) Since P2b is inconsistent with realism, we need to examine the case for and against axiological realism before we will be in a position to endorse P2b.

III. Aristotle

1. Aristotle's Functionalist Theory of the Good

Aristotle seeks to discover what is the highest good or highest good for human beings. According to Aristotle, *eudaimonia* is the highest good.

> Let us discuss what is in our view the aim of politics, i.e., the highest good attainable by action. As far as its name is concerned, most people would probably agree: for both the common run of people and cultivated men call it *eudaimonia* and understand by being *eudaimon* the same as "living well" and "doing well." (*Nicomachean Ethics* 1095a14–20)

Aristotle notes that there is considerable disagreement about what *eudaimonia* is. Some say that it is pleasure; others say that it is wealth or honor (1095a22; cf. 1095b14–1096a5). I follow most commentators in taking Aristotle to hold that it is a conceptual truth that anyone who is *eudaimon* has a good life; *eudaimonia* means roughly "good life."[15] I also take it that, for Aristotle, there is no distinction between the concepts of personal welfare and a good life. This reading is strongly supported by 1098b, where Aristotle writes, "we have all but defined *eudaimonia* as a kind of good life and well-being."

According to Aristotle, whatever constitutes the highest good, or *eudaimonia*, must have the following formal features:

1. It must be something for the sake of which everything else is done (1097a).

2. It must be desired for its own sake and never as a means to something else (1097b).

3. It must be "self-sufficient," i.e., it must be "that which taken by itself makes life desirable and deficient in nothing."[16]

Aristotle appeals to 2 to show that the highest good cannot be pleasure, honor, intelligence, virtue, or wealth. Pleasure, honor, intelligence, virtue, and wealth can all be desired partly for their own sake, but they are also desired as means to *eudaimonia* (1097a33–1097b5).

Aristotle then proposes a functionalist account of the human good. He claims that just as the goodness of a flute player or sculptor resides in his proper function *(ergon)*, so "the good of man" resides in "whatever is his proper function" (1097b):

> [J]ust as the goodness and performance of a flute player, a sculptor, or any kind of expert, and generally of anyone who fulfills some function or performs some action, are thought to reside in his proper function, so the goodness and performance of man would seem to reside in whatever is his proper function. (1197b22–27)

Aristotle then considers the objection that human beings have no proper function and replies as follows:

> Is it then possible that while a carpenter and a shoemaker have their own proper functions and sphere of action, man as man has none, but was left by nature a good-for-nothing without a function? (1097b)

The proper function of human beings must be something that distinguishes them from other living things, Aristotle continues:

> What can this function possibly be? Simply living? He shares that even with plants, but we are now looking for something peculiar to man. Accordingly, the life of nutrition and growth must be excluded. Next in line there is a life of sense perception. But this, too, man has in common with the horse, the ox, and every animal. There remains then an active life of the rational element. The rational element has two parts: one is rational in that it obeys the rule of reason, the other in that it possesses and conceives rational rules. Since the expression "life of the rational element" also can be used in two senses, we must make it clear that we mean a life determined by the activity, as opposed to the mere possession, of the rational element. For the activity, it seems, has a greater claim to be the function of man. The proper function of man, then, consists in an activity of the soul in conformity with a rational principle. (1097b–1098a)

Merely fulfilling one's function is not sufficient for having a good life. The human good requires excellent functioning.

> In speaking of the proper function of a given individual we mean that it is the same in kind as the function of an individual who sets high standards for himself: the proper function of a harpist, for example, is the same as the function of a harpist who has set high standards for himself . . . the full attainment of excellence must be added to the mere function. . . . We reach the conclusion that the good of man is an activity of the soul in conformity with excellence or virtue, and if there are several virtues, in conformity with the best and most complete. (1098a)

To have a good life (to be *eudaimon*) is to live a life in which one engages in excellent activities that utilize abilities unique to human beings. A good life is a life of excellent activity.

> [E]udaimonia is a certain activity of the soul in conformity with perfect excellence. (1102a)

Aristotle devotes most of the *Nicomachean Ethics* to a description of distinctive human excellences (or virtues) such as courage, self-control, generosity, justice, practical wisdom, and theoretical wisdom. In order to have a good life, one must possess these excellent traits of character. But possessing these virtues is not sufficient for *eudaimonia*. One must also possess certain external goods and good fortune so that one can fully engage in excellent activities.

> Is there anything to prevent us, then, from defining the *eudaimon* man as one whose activities are an expression of complete excellence, and who is equipped with external goods, not simply at a given moment but to the end of his life? (1101a)

In order to understand Aristotle's account of *eudaimonia*, we need to understand what he means by virtue or excellence *(aretē)*. Aristotle holds that there are two kinds of human virtues: moral virtues and intellectual virtues (1103a). Aristotle defines "virtue" in the following passage:

> [E]very virtue or excellence (1) renders good the thing of which it is an excellence, and (2) causes it to perform its function well. For example, the excellence of the eye makes both the eye and its function good, for good sight is due to the excellence of the eye. Likewise, the excellence of a horse makes it both good as a horse and good at running, at carrying its rider and facing the enemy. Now, if this is true of all things, the virtue or excellence of man, too, will be a characteristic which makes him a good man, and which causes him to perform his own function well. (1106a)

Aristotle takes pleasure to be a necessary condition of virtuous activity. For example, a truly generous person must take pleasure in generous actions. A person who gives to others but does not take pleasure in doing so is not generous (1099a; see also 1104b). The connection between virtue and pleasure is explained by Aristotle's theory of pleasure. He characterizes pleasure as "unobstructed activity" (1153b) or "the completion of action" (1175a).[17] If *eudaimonia* consists in excellent activity, and if excellent action must be complete and unobstructed, then it follows that excellent action must be pleasant. Thus, on Aristotle's view, there is a necessary connection between *eudaimonia* and pleasure.[18] A *eudaimon* life (a life characterized by excellent activity) must contain a considerable amount of pleasure. In places, Aristotle seems to say something stronger than this, namely, that those people who have *eudaimonia* have the most pleasant lives (1099a). He also says that the highest form of *eudaimonia* is the most pleasant (1178a). We might be tempted to conclude that Aristotle's theory is extentionally equivalent to the hedonistic theory of value, but this is not the case. Aristotle holds that things other than pleasure are noninstrumentally good (1172b). Further, he denies that all pleasures are good in themselves; the pleasures proper to morally bad activities are bad (1175b).

2. Intellectualism

Book X of the *Nicomachean Ethics* raises extraordinary difficulties for interpretations of Aristotle's theory of *eudaimonia*. In Book I.7, Aristotle defines the good life as one of excellent or virtuous activity. He distinguishes between practical or moral virtues and theoretical/intellectual virtues in Book I.13. It seems reasonable to suppose that he takes both to be included in *eudaimonia*. Near the beginning of the *Nicomachean Ethics* (Book I.2 and I.4) Aristotle seems to say that the entire work is concerned with *eudaimonia*. Much of Books II–IX is given to detailed analyses of both the moral virtues, such as courage, justice, and temperance, and the intellectual virtues (practical and theoretical wisdom). Further, at 1097b he seems to say that *eudaimonia* is an inclusive good that includes all other goods.[19] In Book X, however, Aristotle says (or seems to say) that *eudaimonia* is simply contemplation or excellent theoretical activity. A life of practical virtue is *eudaimon* only in a secondary sense.

> *Eudaimonia* is coextensive with study, and the greater the opportunity for studying, the greater the *eudaimonia*, not as an incidental effect but as inherent in study; for study is in itself worthy of honor. Consequently, *eudaimonia* is some kind of study or contemplation. (1178b)

> A life guided by the other kind of virtue [the practical, translator's note] is *eudaimon* in a secondary sense. (1178a)

There is considerable debate among scholars about how we should construe Aristotle's discussion of contemplation in Book X and whether it is consistent with what he says elsewhere in the *Nicomachean Ethics*. Aristotle clearly regards contemplation as the greatest single good and the best or most important constituent of *eudaimonia*. The question is whether, on Aristotle's view, there is anything else that is constitutive of the best life. Some commentators hold that, Book X.6–8 notwithstanding, Aristotle takes *eudaimonia* to be an "inclusive good" consisting of the exercise of both excellent contemplation and excellent practical activity.[20] Other commentators claim that Aristotle holds that *eudaimonia* in the primary sense consists only of contemplation.[21] Aristotle clearly holds that more than one kind of thing is non-instrumentally good (he holds that all virtuous activities and at least some pleasures are good in themselves). This seems inconsistent with the view that the highest good consists of contemplation and contemplation alone, because it would seem that a life of contemplation could be improved by adding other goods. Kraut argues that these views are consistent in light of the fact that Aristotle takes contemplation to be a "dominant good" such that the value of the smallest amount of contemplation exceeds the value of any quantity of other goods.[22] If contemplation is a dominant good in this sense, one always promotes one's own welfare or enhances the value of one's life by maximizing one's opportunities for contemplation; it never makes sense to sacrifice contemplation for the sake of other goods.

It is unclear what exactly Aristotle means by contemplation (*theoria*). Does the discovery of truth or intellectual activity in the pursuit of truth, e.g., working to solve or understand a math problem or trying to formulate an argument clearly, count as contemplation? Or is it restricted to the contemplation of things we already know and have made clear to ourselves? (The argument from divinity discussed below seems to favor the latter interpretation. The gods know everything; their activities do not include the pursuit or discovery of truth.) In the *Metaphysics* Aristotle claims that the value of contemplation is determined in part by the value of the objects being contemplated. The more valuable the object being contemplated, the more valuable the activity of contemplation itself. Since God is the very best thing, the best activity is the contemplation of God (*Metaphysics* 983a5–10, 1026a15–20). (Note the shift from talking about "the gods" to "God.") It follows that the activity of God is self-contemplation (*Metaphysics* 1074a30–35, 1075a5–10). In *Metaphysics* 1026a15–30, Aristotle seems to say that *theoretical* activity is restricted to mathematics, theology, and natural sciences. All other kinds of study, such as politics, have lesser value.

Aristotle's general argument in the *Nicomachean Ethics* to show that *eudaimonia* is contemplation (or that contemplation is the highest form of *eudaimonia*) is roughly that (a) if *eudaimonia* is activity in conformity with virtue and if some particular virtue is the best or highest, then *eudaimonia* must be activity in accordance with the highest virtue or the best features of human nature;[23] (b) theoretical excellence is the highest virtue of human beings and the best feature of human nature.[24] Therefore, *eudaimonia* is contemplation (*theoria*).

> Now, if happiness is activity in conformity with virtue, it is to be expected that it should conform with the highest virtue, and that is the virtue of the best part of us. . . . [I]t is the activity of this part [when operating; translator's note] in conformity with the excellence or virtue proper to it that will be complete happiness. That it is an activity concerned with theoretical knowledge or contemplation has already been stated. (1177a)

In Book X.7–8, Aristotle gives a number of different arguments to show that *theoria* or contemplation is the highest kind of activity: (i) *Theoria* is concerned with the highest objects of knowledge and is the most continuous of any human activity (1177a22–23). (ii) Contemplation is the most pleasant activity (or at least the activity that provides the purest, most certain pleasures) (1177a25). (iii) *Theoria* is more self-sufficient than acts exhibiting practical virtue:

> Like a just man and any other virtuous man, a wise man requires the necessities of life; once these have been adequately provided, a just man still needs people toward whom and in company with whom to act justly. . . . But a wise man is able to study even by himself (1177a28–33).

(iv) Unlike other virtuous activities, *theoria* is always pursued as an end, never as a means (1177b1–15). (v) In 1177b15–25, Aristotle presents the following argument:

1.   Military and political actions are the best and most noble of any actions that exhibit practical virtues.

2.   *Theoria* is better than virtuous military and political actions.

Therefore:

Theoria is the best form of virtuous activity.

Aristotle defends premise 2 on the grounds that (a) political and military actions are pursued for the sake of other ends but *theoria* is pursued only as an end;[25] (b) *theoria* is more leisurely and free from fatigue than military and political actions; and (c) *theoria* is more self-sufficient.
    (vi) In 1178a5–8, Aristotle presents the following argument:

> [W]hat is by nature proper to each thing will be at once the best and most pleasant for it. In other words, a life guided by intelligence is the best and most pleasant for man, inasmuch as intelligence, above all else, is man. Consequently, this kind of life is the most *eudaimon*.

In 1178a he also repeats the self-sufficiency argument.
    (vii) Aristotle's final argument to show that *theoria* is the highest good is often called "the argument from divinity."

> We assume that the gods are in the highest degree blessed and *eudaimon*. But what kinds of actions do we attribute to them? Acts of justice? Will they not look ridiculous making contracts with one another, returning deposits, and so forth? . . . Nevertheless we all assume that the gods exist and,

consequently, that they are active. . . . Now, if we take away action from a living being, to say nothing of production, what is left except contemplation? Therefore, the activity of the divinity which surpasses all others in bliss must be a contemplative activity, and the human activity which is most akin to it is, therefore, most conducive to *eudaimonia*. . . . The gods enjoy a life blessed in its entirety; men enjoy it to the extent that they attain something resembling the divine activity; but none of the other living beings can be *eudaimon*, because they have no share in contemplation or study. So *eudaimonia* is coextensive with study. (1178b8–31)

This argument can be summarized as follows:

1. The gods are the most *eudaimon* beings.

2. The *eudaimonia* of the gods consists in contemplation.

3. Human *eudaimonia* is closely analogous to that of the gods. Whatever is constitutive of the *eudaimonia* of the gods is also constitutive of human *eudaimonia*.

Therefore:

Human *eudaimonia* consists in contemplation.

Aristotle does not explicitly state premise 3, but clearly 3 is necessary in order for the argument to be valid. Aristotle defends premise 2 in 1178b8 (cited above), but in Book X he gives no reasons for accepting either 1 or 3.

3. Two Readings of Aristotle's Functionalism

Aristotle holds that to have a good life is to fulfill one's function (*ergon*) as a human being. The proper function of human beings consists in the exercise of abilities or characteristics unique to human beings. So, for Aristotle, *eudaimonia* consists in excellent activities that utilize uniquely human characteristics. However, Aristotle's view about the exact relation between *eudaimonia* and uniquely human characteristics and abilities is unclear. Are excellent actions that involve the exercise of any uniquely human characteristics/abilities constitutive of *eudaimonia* or is *eudaimonia* restricted to the excellent exercise of some subset of uniquely human characteristics? This question makes clear the difference between the following two interpretations of Aristotle's functionalist theory of value:

A1. For a human being to have a good life is for her to perform her function well. The proper function of human beings consists in excellent actions that utilize abilities or capacities unique to human beings. (Actions that exhibit the excellence of *any* uniquely human capacities are constitutive of *eudaimonia*.)

A2. For a human being to have a good life is for her to perform her function well. The proper function of human beings consists in excellent actions that utilize abilities or capacities unique to human beings, but not *every* uniquely human characteristic is part of the proper function of human beings. (*Eudaimonia* is constituted by actions that exhibit the excellence of *certain* uniquely human capacities, but not all uniquely human capacities are such that actions that exhibit their excellence are constitutive of *eudaimonia*.)

4. Criticisms of A1 and A2

Both A1 and A2 are open to serious criticisms. (Here I am concerned with the merits of A1 and A2 as theories of value rather than their merits as interpretations of Aristotle. For criticisms of A1 and A2 as interpretations of Aristotle see 5.III.5.) The fact that an ability is unique to human beings is not a reason for thinking that it is either good or bad for humans to develop that ability. A1 claims that all uniquely human abilities are good (or at least that activities that display their excellent use are good). For all that we know, however, certain ostensibly bad characteristics of human beings are unique to humans. It is possible that the ability to lie and the ability to plan and wage wars are uniquely human.[26]

Interpretation A2 avoids this objection, and, in light of Aristotle's discussion of intellectualism in NE X.6–8, it seems closer to Aristotle's intentions than A1. However, A2 has some unacceptable consequences. It is possible that there are *no* abilities unique to human beings. For all that we know, there are extraterrestrial species who have all of the abilities humans have. If there are such beings, then A2 implies that, since there are *no abilities* unique to human beings, there is *no* proper function of human beings. Aristotle clearly holds that activities exhibiting excellences of rationality are constitutive of *eudaimonia*. If we take him to hold A2, we must also take him to be saying that rationality is at least one of the uniquely human abilities whose excellent exercise is constitutive of *eudaimonia*. If he holds A2, Aristotle is committed to the view that the value of rationality and its exercise is *contingent* on its being unique to us. However, the value of rationality is *independent* of these considerations.

Whether or not there are other rational species should not affect our estimation of the value of our own rationality. Thomas Hurka makes this point nicely in the following passage:

> To say that a property is distinctive of humans is not just to say something about humans. It is to say that the property is possessed by humans *and not by other species*. It is to say as much about non-humans as humans, and how can facts about non-humans affect *our* nature and *our* good?[27]

If we take Aristotle to hold A2, then we need to give an account of how he distinguishes between uniquely human characteristics that are a part of our proper function and those uniquely human characteristics that are not. In certain passages (1098a17–20, 1177a11–13), Aristotle seems to say that rationality is the best or highest capacity of human beings. Other capacities such as the ability to lie or wash one's hands compulsively (which, for all we know, are uniquely human) are not good. Perhaps Aristotle holds that, in order to be a part of the proper function of human beings, an ability or capacity must be both uniquely human and non-instrumentally good. On this reading, Aristotle has standards of good and bad that are independent of the notion of human function or purpose. However, Aristotle never gives a clear statement of these other standards, and it is difficult to see how these other standards themselves could be purely functionalist. On this reading, the ultimate basis or foundation of Aristotle's theory is unclear.

5. Some Alternative Readings of Aristotle's Functionalism

Thomas Hurka attributes the following view to Aristotle:

A3.   To have a good life is to develop to a high degree those characteristics that are both unique to humans and essential for being human. (The development of any such characteristic is constitutive of a good life.)[28]

Inasmuch as such characteristics as lying and killing others for fun are not essential for being human, A3 may avoid the objection that certain uniquely human abilities are bad. However, since it holds that the good life is constituted by activities unique to humans, A3 is open to the main objections raised earlier against A2. A3 implies that if there are no abilities unique to human beings, then there is no special function of human beings.

Further, A1, A2, and A3 are all flatly inconsistent with Aristotle's argument from divinity. Aristotle claims that the highest and best human activity is one that we have in common with the gods. This cannot be reconciled with the idea that our good consists in the development and use of uniquely human abilities.[29] One should hesitate to attribute such an egregious contradiction to Aristotle. In Book I.7, where he sets out the *ergon* argument, Aristotle asks what distinguishes human beings from other living things (plants and animals). It might be suggested that the comparison class for judging what is uniquely human is not all living or conscious beings in the universe, but rather all living things *on earth*. In light of this, we can revise A2 as follows (I will not bother to make the analogous revisions in A1 or A3):

A2a.   For a human being to have a good life is for her to perform her function well. The proper function of human beings consists in excellent actions that utilize abilities or capacities unique to human beings among all the things that live on earth. But not every characteristic unique to humans among earthly creatures is part of the proper function of human beings. (*Eudaimonia* is constituted by actions that exhibit the excellence of *certain* capacities unique to humans among earthly creatures, but not all such capacities are constitutive of *eudaimonia*.)

Why hold A2a? On the assumption that life on earth is the product of conscious design, we might take the fact that this ability is unique to humans to be a good indication that fulfilling God's (the gods') purpose in creating humans requires that we exercise that ability. On this reading, Aristotle takes the purposes of God (or the gods) to be the ultimate standard of value.[30] This view is open to all the same objections as P3 (see 5.II). The restriction to capacities unique to humans "among earthly creatures" is ad hoc. Any attempt to draw inferences about God's reasons for creating human beings must be based on an interpretation of the place of human beings within all of creation, not just their place on earth.

Richard Kraut proposes a very different interpretation of the function argument of Book I. According to Kraut, the function argument does not state any kind of fundamental normative principle like A1, A2, or A2a. Kraut claims that the function argument of Book I can only be understood if we remember that Aristotle makes the following two assumptions:

1.   Human beings have better lives than plants and other animals that live on earth.

2.   The gods have better lives than human beings.[31]

Given that humans have better lives than plants and other animals, it follows that the human good or highest good would have to involve characteristics that humans possess and other living things do not possess. On Kraut's reading, the uniqueness principle is applied only to creatures whose lives are assumed, *independently of any "functionalist" considerations*, to be less valuable than the lives of humans. Since this principle does not apply to the gods, the purpose of human beings need not consist in abilities that the gods lack. On Kraut's reading, it seems as if the notion of function or purpose is *not* the foundation of Aristotle's theory, and it is not clear what that foundation is. We need to ask *why* the lives of human beings are better than the lives of plants and other animals. Kraut does not pursue this question. Many different theories of value are consistent with the claim that humans have better lives than plants and other animals. To the best of my knowledge, Aristotle does not give any explicit defense of this claim, but note the following passage in which he argues that pleasure cannot be the only thing that is good:

> No one would *choose* [emphasis added] to live his entire life with the mentality of a child, even if he were to enjoy the fullest possible extent of what children enjoy; nor would he *choose* [emphasis added] to find his joy in something very base, even though he were to escape any painful consequences. (1174a)

Presumably, Aristotle would also endorse the same kind of argument for thinking that it would be better to be a fully rational adult human being than a non-human animal, no matter how much pleasure the animal enjoys. If Aristotle's answer to the question "Why is it better to be a human being than a plant or some other sort of animal?" is that no human being (or no rational human being) would *choose* to be a "lower animal" rather than a human being, then the foundation of Aristotle's theory seems to be a version of the preference-satisfaction theory. Taking Aristotle's claim that *eudaimonia* must be something that is always desired as an end and never as a means to be the ultimate foundation of his theory of value also involves attributing to him a kind of preference-satisfaction theory of value.

Yet another reading of the function argument is that Aristotle identifies the proper function (*ergon*) of human beings with the essential nature of human beings.[32] On this interpretation, Aristotle holds that *eudaimonia* consists in excellent activities that utilize those abilities and characteristics that are *necessary for being human*. I believe that this is a much more plausible theory of value than A1, A2, A2a, or A3, but I venture no opinion of its merits as an interpretation of Aristotle. Thomas Hurka has recently defended such a view (although he does not attribute this theory to Aristotle). I examine his theory in 5.IV.

IV. The Good Life as the Development of One's Essential Nature as a Human Being

The view that a good life consists in the development of those characteristics that are essential for being human merits special consideration. This view is more plausible in its own right than many of the other views commonly attributed to Aristotle (whether or not this is Aristotle's view is another matter). This position finds its clearest and best statement in Thomas Hurka's *Perfectionism*. Hurka claims this theory avoids the sorts of objections that were raised against A1–A3. While such characteristics as lying and killing for fun might be unique to humans, they are not essential for being human. Hurka is not committed to saying that the development of such characteristics is constitutive of a good life. Hurka's theory also avoids the objection that such characteristics as rationality may not be unique to human beings. Claims to the effect that a certain characteristic is essential for being human cannot be overturned by discoveries that reveal that other species also possess that characteristic. Hurka also claims it as a virtue of his theory that it avoids the "narrow intellectualism" sometimes associated with perfectionism. Certain physical abilities we share with animals are necessary for being human. The good life for human beings consists partly in the perfection of these physical abilities.

Hurka holds that a good life is one that develops to a high degree those properties that are essential for being human.[33] One of the most crucial claims Hurka makes in his book is that, inasmuch as rationality (or the potential to be rational) is essential for being human, the perfection of our rational powers is a very important element of the good human life. It is unclear, however, that being rational is essential for being human. Consider a normal human being who has suffered severe brain damage or a profoundly retarded child of normal human parents. My intuitions strongly support the view that both are human beings (homo sapiens), even though they are neither rational nor potentially rational. Hurka grants that it is possible that some *individual* human beings are not rational,[34] but he claims it is inconceivable that all human beings could lack the *capacity* to be rational.

> We do not think that there were humans in the world until primates developed with sufficient intelligence. . . . If we imagine a species with no capacity for mental life, or with none more sophisticated than that of other animals, we do not take ourselves to be imagining humans. Whatever their physical form they are not of our species.[35]

My own intuitions about this case are not clear, and I will not press this point.

Even if we grant Hurka's claims about the human essence, why should we accept his theory of the good? Why is it good to develop to a high degree those abilities that are essential for being human? The question "Why is it good to develop those features of ourselves that are essential for being human?" or "Why should I develop those features of myself that are essential for being human?" creates a serious dilemma for Hurka. He must choose between the following:

A.   It is good to develop one's rationality *because* rationality is part of the human essence.

B.   It is good to develop one's rationality, but not simply because rationality is part of the human essence. Rationality is good independently of its being essential for being human.

It might be possible to formulate further principles that strike a compromise between A) and B), but I will not attempt to do so here. Given his purposes, Hurka cannot adopt B). To do so would be to abandon any attempt to base a systematic theory of value on the notion of human nature. Proposition B assumes the existence of an *independent* basis for making value judgments. Hurka seems to endorse A; note the following passage:

A generalized perfectionism does imply that, if essentially cruel beings existed, the development of cruelty in them would be intrinsically good.[36]

This commits Hurka to the following more generalized version of A:

A1.   For any species X, and for any ability Y such that Y is essential for being a member of X, it is intrinsically (non-instrumentally) good if a member of X develops Y to a high degree.

A1 has consequences many would regard as counterintuitive. Among other things, it implies that if cruelty were an essential feature of a species, then it would be intrinsically (non-instrumentally) good if a member of that species developed his capacity for cruelty. Cruelty would be an intrinsically (non-instrumentally) good trait in members of that species. Hurka attempts to minimize the counterintuitiveness of this by noting that the value of the perfection of cruelty would likely be outweighed by the evils that cruelty causes.[37] I don't find Hurka's solution to this problem satisfactory, but, given my own reservations about the cogency of appeals to intuitions, I won't press the point.

A more serious problem for Hurka, given that he accepts A and A1, is that he does not explain why we should develop those capacities that are essential for being human. Why should we be concerned to develop our *humanity* rather than any of the many other natures in which we partake? Being a human being is one of the many different descriptions that apply to me; it is only one of many essential natures I possess. In addition to being a human being, I am also a person, an omnivorous mammal, a male human being, a Caucasian human being, a midwesterner, and a blue-eyed mammal. Why should I develop my essential nature as a human being as opposed to my essence as a male animal or a Caucasian (European) human being? Even more problematically for Hurka, why shouldn't a child molester fulfill his essence as a child molester? We could also ask why one should develop *any* of the essential natures in which one partakes?

It will not do to say that the essential features of humans are extremely valuable, but those of male animals or blue-eyed animals are not. For this assumes a standard of value independent of Hurka's perfectionist notion of fulfilling one's essence as a human being. Alternatively, Hurka might appeal to the notion of broader and wider essences. He might say that I should fulfill my essence as a human being rather than my essence as a Caucasian,[38] because the class of human beings is broader than the class of Caucasians. However, the principle to "fulfill one's essence as a member of the broadest category of things to which one belongs" has consequences quite contrary to Hurka's intentions. It does not imply that we ought to fulfill our nature as human beings, but rather that we should fulfill our essences as living things, or spatiotemporal things. Yet another rationale for distinguishing between the property of being human and that of being a child molester or a midwesterner is that only the former is essential to one's being numerically the same individual one is. My being human is essential to my being my actual self but my being a midwesterner is not—I might not have been a midwesterner. This reply is unconvincing on two grounds. First, it's not clear that being human is essential to our personal identity. I think it makes perfect sense to imagine that I could have been a non-human animal. At the very least, Hurka needs to defend a view of personal identity and explain why this is impossible. Second, this argument answers the question "Why is it good for us to develop those properties essential to our being human?" only by raising other equally difficult questions to which there is no obvious answer: Why is it good to develop those properties that are essential for one's personal identity as a numerically distinct individual? Why are those features we possess that are essential for our personal identity more valuable than those that are not?

There may be an answer to the question "Why should I fulfill my essence as a human being, rather than my essence as a male animal?" that does not presuppose the existence of an independent standard of value (independent of human essence). At least, my foregoing argument does not show that there cannot be. However, in the absence of a cogent answer to the question "Why should I fulfill my essential nature as a human being?" we have no reason to accept Hurka's theory.

Hurka would no doubt protest my claim that he hasn't given any reasons for thinking that it is good for humans to develop those of their features that are essential for being human. This claim is justified by appealing to his theory, which, in turn, is justified by the method of "reflective equilibrium." Hurka endorses the method of reflective equilibrium as the basis for justifying ethical theories:

> A substantive defense of perfectionism must follow the same lines as a defense of any morality. It must show that the theory coheres with our intuitive moral judgments at all levels of generality or in Rawls's phrase, is in "reflective equilibrium" with all of these judgments.[39]

According to Hurka, a plausible moral theory or theory of value must satisfy the following conditions: (1) its basic idea must have "intrinsic appeal"; (2) it must have intuitively acceptable consequences for particular cases; and (3) it must give a satisfying rationale for our intuitions.[40] Hurka gives no defense of these methodological strictures, nor does he give any satisfactory account of the problem of conflicting intuitions. Some people have intuitions about particular cases that conflict with Hurka's theory. If condition 2 is taken to mean that moral theories must be consistent with *everyone's* intuitions, then Hurka's theory does not satisfy condition 2, and it seems unlikely that any coherent theory could satisfy it. Hurka might modify his position and defend a modified coherentism, according to which theories of the good must be consistent with *reliable* or *correct* intuitive judgments about the good. But this would require him to propose and defend criteria for distinguishing between correct and incorrect intuitive judgments of value. It is not clear that plausible criteria can be formulated and defended. Nor is it clear that such criteria, taken together with a modified coherentism, support Hurka's version of perfectionism. Nothing I have said here shows that this cannot be done, but Hurka himself hasn't done it.

Concluding Remarks

Many of the theories examined in this chapter are clearly implausible, however, my arguments in this chapter do not show that all theories of value based on the notion of human function or human essence are mistaken. I have not examined all of the possible versions of this theory. Further, two of the theories I have examined, P2b and Hurka's theory, aren't open to any obvious refutations. However, Hurka doesn't offer adequate positive reasons for thinking that his theory is true, nor have we yet seen positive reasons for endorsing P2b (among other things we need to examine the case for and against realism). In chapter 8, I will defend a version of the desire-satisfaction theory that closely resembles P2b.

Standard versions of the ideal-desire-satisfaction theory of value make the desires human beings would have if they were fully rational the ultimate criterion of value. It is likely that, in the great majority of cases, standard versions of the ideal-desire-satisfaction theory agree with Aristotle and Hurka about the goodness or badness of particular lives. For it is likely that, on reflection, most of us will find that we want to develop many of the "higher human capacities" that Aristotle and Hurka take to be constitutive of a good life. The desire-satisfaction theory and Aristotelian theories will sometimes yield conflicting judgments about particular cases. It is conceivable that some individuals are such that their ideal desires would not require them to develop their "higher capacities." Alternatively (and more probably), the ideal desires of some people might include intrinsic desires for things other than the development or perfection of their higher capacities. For example, someone's ideal desires might include desires for physical ("lower") pleasures. Suppose that S is such a person and that he is forced to choose between two lives, L1 and L2. L1 involves a slightly higher level of "perfection" than L2, but L2 involves a much higher level of physical pleasure than L1. S would prefer L2 to L1 if he were fully informed and fully rational. Aristotelian/perfectionist theories imply that L1 is better than L2. But the ideal-desire-satisfaction theory implies that L2 is better than L1.

The ideals of the good life proposed by Aristotle and Hurka have an important place in standard versions of the rational/ideal-desire-satisfaction theory of value. Ideally rational preferences would be informed by a vivid awareness of what it would be like to live the kinds of lives that these philosophers take to be ideal. Many of us are such that our preferences are altered (or would be altered) by such knowledge. I find on examination that I am inclined to prefer the kind of "well-rounded life" that involves the development of many different kinds of abilities. Hurka argues that the ideal life involves the development and use of a wide range of human abilities.[41] When I contrast a life of passive pleasures (in a pleasure machine) with an equally pleasant life resulting from the active use of a wide range of my abilities, I find that I strongly prefer the latter. There is every reason to think that this preference would persist if I were fully informed or fully rational. Here I am presupposing the standard full-information theory of rationality or something similar to it. In practice, the rational-desire-satisfaction theory may also yield results largely consistent with Aristotelian theories, given the divine-preference theory of rationality. However, any speculations we make about God's ultimate preferences are highly fallible (see 8.IX.1).

The Need for Metaethics

Mill's argument for the HTV by appeal to psychological hedonism and Nietzsche's argument for power as the ultimate standard of value by appeal to his theory of the will to power are both unsuccessful. Mill and Nietzsche fail to give an adequate defense of the explanatory principles to which they appeal (psychological hedonism and the will to power). Almost all of the other arguments considered in chapters 1–5 appeal to intuitive normative judgments about particular cases, e.g., the judgment that a dissatisfied human being has a better life than a satisfied pig. These arguments appeal to disputed intuitions. Many people agree with Mill's claim that it is better to be a dissatisfied human being than a satisfied pig. Others, however, reject this claim. Moore defends the claim that unperceived beauty is intrinsically good by appealing to his intuitions about the value of a beautiful universe in which there are no sentient beings who perceive or appreciate its beauty and an ugly universe in which there are no sentient beings who perceive its ugliness.[1] I (and many others) reject Moore's intuitive judgments about this case. Hurka appeals to intuitive judgments about particular cases in support of his Aristotelian theory (he takes these judgments to be evidence against both hedonism and the desire-satisfaction theory). I find that my own intuitions conflict with at least some of Hurka's.

The history of philosophical debate about first-order questions of value reveals a tremendous amount of disagreement between the intuitions of different philosophers. Ostensibly reasonable people often disagree sharply in their normative intuitions. Philosophers cannot, in good conscience, defend or attack particular theories of value simply by appealing to disputed intuitions. When we discover that other people have intuitions that are opposed to our own, we are not entitled to assume that ours are correct and those of the other people mistaken—at least not without being able to give reasons for thinking that this is the case.[2] Most traditional arguments for or against particular theories of value are inconclusive because they are conducted at the intuitive level.

Some philosophers try to use people's informed or rational preferences (between different kinds of lives) as the basis for defending or criticizing first-order theories of value. The fact that rational people prefer life X to life Y is taken to be decisive evidence for thinking that X is better than Y. This strategy presupposes the falsity of axiological realism (moral realists claim that our rational preferences *can* be incorrect or mistaken). In order to assess arguments that appeal to people's rational preferences, we need to look at arguments for and against axiological realism. As we saw in our discussion of pleasure machines in chapter 2, many apparently informed and rational people prefer less pleasant lives to more pleasant lives. Defenders of the HTV need to say that these preferences are mistaken. This claim is plausible only on the assumption that axiological realism is true. Therefore, the HTV is not defensible unless realism is true. Several other arguments discussed in chapters 1–5 assume either the truth or falsity of realism. In its most plausible forms, the rational-desire-satisfaction theory of value is a non-realist theory that presupposes the falsity of axiological realism (see 3.I.2). Several of the most serious objections to this theory discussed in chapter 3 presuppose the truth of realism.

The plausibility of most of the arguments considered in the first five chapters largely depends on the answer to the following question:

i)   In what sense, if any, can normative judgments be true or correct? Can they be true or correct in the way that realists claim, i.e., can they be true or correct independently of what rational people believe or prefer?

Whatever we say about the evidential status of moral intuitions and informed preferences presupposes an answer to question i. Question i, in turn, forces us to ask the following question:

ii)   What does it mean to say that something is good or bad?

Question ii is prior to question i. Answers to question i presuppose an understanding of what we mean when we say that something is good or bad. Our answers to ii constrain whatever we say about i. Certain theories of meaning entail that moral judgments are statements that are true or false; other theories of meaning imply that moral judgments are not statements that are true or false.

A Look Ahead

In chapters 6 and 7 I will defend the following views, which answer (or partly answer) questions i and ii:

1. At the present time there are no decisive arguments for thinking that axiological realism is true. (It is not unreasonable to reject AR.)

2. "X is (non-instrumentally) good" means (at least in part) that X is desirable or worthy of being desired or pursued as an end.

CHAPTER 6

The Concept of Value:
A Pragmatic Approach

I want to stress again that my main concern is the notion of a good life. Everything that I say about the concept of value should be understood in this light. In asking which of the many alternative concepts of goodness (or which of the many possible analyses of "good") we should accept or employ, I am asking what sort(s) of normative notion(s) we should employ in making overall assessments of our lives. I am concerned with norms for making global assessments of people's lives. There may be other normative notions or concepts of goodness, e.g., good in the sense of good knives, for which my analysis is inadequate.

I. Intrinsic Value and Non-Instrumental Value

1. Moore's Concept of Intrinsic Value

Intrinsic value is the value that something has simply in virtue of its own intrinsic nature, apart from its relations to anything else. The intrinsic value of something is the value that it has in virtue of its non-relational properties. Extrinsic value is the value that something has in virtue of its relations to other things. Moore takes "intrinsically good" to mean "good in isolation":

> To assert of any one thing, A, that it *is intrinsically* better than another, B, is to assert that if A existed *quite alone*, without any accompaniments or effects whatever—if, in short, A constituted the whole universe, it would be

better that such a universe should exist, than that a universe which consisted solely of B should exist instead.[1]

[W]e make judgments of what was called in Chapter II 'intrinsic value'; that is to say, where we judge, concerning a particular state of things that it would be worth while—would be 'a good thing'—that that state of things should exist, *even if nothing else were to exist besides,* either at the same time or afterwards. . . . We *can* consider with regard to any particular state of things whether it would be worth while that it should exist, even if there were absolutely nothing else in the Universe besides.[2]

Moore's analysis can be extended to the notion of intrinsic badness as follows:

A thing (or state of affairs) is intrinsically bad if, and only if, a universe in which it is the only thing that ever exists (occurs) would be worse than a universe in which nothing ever exists.

2. Non-Instrumental (Contributory) Value (NIV)

Many philosophers use the term "intrinsically good" rather indiscriminately to mean both "good in itself" and "good as an end" or "non-instrumentally good." This usage ignores an important distinction. The notion of possessing value in itself or in isolation must be distinguished from that of being good as an end or possessing non-causal or non-instrumental value. We need to make two distinctions: the distinction between intrinsic and extrinsic value and the distinction between being valuable as an end and being valuable as a means.[3] There is no reason to think that everything that has non-causal or non-instrumental value possesses value in isolation, and there is no reason to think that things that possess value in isolation always possess non-causal value when they occur as parts of broader states of affairs.[4] Moore uses his concept of the "organic unity of value"—the value of a whole is not simply the sum of the values of its parts taken in isolation—to make this same point. In our universe things do not exist in complete isolation from everything else. Since we never choose between causing one thing or one state of affairs to exist in isolation and causing it to be the case that nothing ever exists, the question of whether something is intrinsically good (in Moore's sense of "intrinsically good") is of very little, if any, practical importance. What *is* important is for us to know whether or not something will contribute to the value of broader circumstances of which it is always a part.

As a first approximation, we can define the concept of non-instrumentally contributing to the value of a larger situation as follows:

NIV1.   A particular occurrence (x) of a state of affairs is non-instrumentally good (bad) if, and only if, its occurrence contributes to (detracts from) the value of a larger state of affairs, everything else being equal (including causal consequences); i.e., everything else being equal, the larger state of affairs is better (worse) than it would have been if it were not for x.

The problem with this is that something can be part of many different larger states of affairs. One and the same state of affairs might contribute to the value of some larger states of affairs and detract from the value of others. In such cases, we will want to make an "all things considered" judgment about the non-instrumental value of the state of affairs in question, taking everything into account. Abstracting from all causal and instrumental considerations, is it a good thing, on balance, that something happens? When something contributes to the value of certain larger wholes, but not others, our overall assessment of its value should focus on its role in the largest whole of which it is a part. The broadest perspective, taking everything into account, is preferable to more parochial views. Every thing or state of affairs is part of the universe or the history of the universe. To take *everything* into account when assessing the non-instrumental value of something is to consider its place in the universe or the entire history of the universe. In light of this, it seems reasonable to revise NIV1 as follows:

NIV2.   A particular occurrence (x) of a state of affairs is non-instrumentally good (bad) if, and only if, its occurrence contributes to (detracts from) the value of the universe, everything else being equal (including causal consequences and requirements).[5]

NIV2 creates considerable epistemological difficulties when applied. Using NIV2 to make judgments about what things are non-instrumentally (non-causally) good or bad requires us to make judgments about the value of the universe as a whole. Chisholm notes this problem in a different context (in his criticisms of Michael Zimmerman's definition of "intrinsic value"):[6]

But how are we to decide which states of affairs are sufficiently encompassing to merit predication of intrinsic value? Every state of affairs, after all, is a part of a more encompassing state of affairs—*except* for those all-encompassing states of affairs that are sometimes called "worlds." But the assumption that intrinsic value can be attributed only to worlds is inconsistent with our presupposition according to which there are some things we know to be good and some things we know to be bad.[7]

By "intrinsic value" Zimmerman means something close to what I mean by "non-instrumental value." If successful, Chisholm's objections to Zimmerman apply equally to my NIV2. However, NIV2 does not commit us to the kind of skepticism Chisholm's objection alleges. NIV2 doesn't require us to make overall judgments about the value of the universe, taking into account every good and bad thing in the universe (it is impossible for us to make judgments of this sort). It only requires that we make *ceteris paribus* judgments — judgments to the effect that a particular universe is better (or worse) than an otherwise identical universe that differs from it in a certain respect. Consider the following example: Jones is a virtuous person; he feels pleased about the happiness of another virtuous person. This particular occurrence of the state of affairs someone being pleased is non-instrumentally good. Apart from its causal consequences and causal prerequisites, it contributes to the value of the universe (to use Chisholm's terminology, its value is not "defeated" in any larger whole).[8] Other things equal, the universe is a slightly better place than it would otherwise have been because of its occurrence. We can be as sure about this as we can about the statement that a universe in which the only thing that exists is a virtuous person taking pleasure in the thought that another virtuous person is pleased is better than a universe in which nothing ever exists. Nothing Chisholm says speaks against the ultimate priority of the widest possible perspective. Something that contributes to the value of certain larger situations but not to the value of the universe itself is not, on balance, a good thing. If we can't be sure that x contributes to the value of the universe as a whole, then we can't be sure that, on balance, it is a good thing that x occurs. Our lives and events that happen in our lives *do occur* in a larger context. In judging the value of things we cannot ignore or abstract away from the context in which they occur.

II. To Be Good Is to Be Desirable

1. My Analysis

My central contention in this chapter is that being non-instrumentally good entails being desirable or worthy of being desired; a good life is a life that is worthy of being chosen. Given the definition of non-instrumental value presented in 6.I.2, my view is best stated as follows:

> A necessary condition of something's being non-instrumentally (non-causally) good is that it would be correct, in a sense that is opposed to incorrect or mistaken, to prefer (desire, choose) that it exist (occur) rather

than not, everything else (including all of its causal requirements and consequences) being equal. (If something is non-instrumentally good, then it would be incorrect not to prefer that it occur rather than not, everything else being equal.)

If X is non-instrumentally better than Y, then it would be correct, in a sense that is opposed to incorrect or mistaken, to prefer that X exist (occur) rather than Y, everything else being equal.

If life X is non-instrumentally better life than Y, then it is correct, in a sense that is opposed to incorrect or mistaken, to prefer living life X to life Y, other things being equal.

Note that the foregoing principles only give *necessary conditions* for something's being non-instrumentally good (or non-instrumentally better than something else); they do not give necessary and sufficient conditions.

2. The Notion of Correctness

There are many different notions of correctness and incorrectness. My proposed analysis of value doesn't specify any particular notion of correctness. The reader might object that my analysis of value concepts is hopelessly vague. At this stage of the discussion, however, such vagueness is a virtue. At least for now, we should leave open the sense of "correct" in which value judgments assert the correctness of preferences. Before attempting to specify this sense, we should first seek to determine in what sense(s), if any, preferences can be said to be correct. In particular, we need to examine moral/axiological realism and ask whether desires/attitudes can be correct or incorrect in the way that realists claim. If we have good reasons to think that AR is true, we will probably want to define our normative concepts in terms of the realist's notion of correctness. However, in the absence of compelling reasons for thinking that axiological realism is true, we should not make the realist's notion of correct and incorrect desires the central notion in our concept of value. If we do, we may find ourselves committed to an error theory, i.e., a theory according to which value judgments *purport* to be true or correct in some determinate sense of "true" or "correct," but aren't.[9] There are pragmatic reasons to want our concept of goodness to employ a notion of correctness that does, in fact, apply to preferences. Norms for the good life are norms by which to assess our most fundamental goals and commitments. It is not reasonable for us to guide our lives by normative standards and concepts the application of which we believe to involve a systematic mistake or error. It is an important virtue of my theory of meaning that it leaves open questions about the truth of realism. In chapter 7

I will argue that the truth or falsity of realism is, at present, an open question. Our normative concepts should leave open questions about the truth or falsity of realism.

My proposed concept of value leaves open the question of whether normative judgments purport to be correct for *everyone*. When someone says "it is correct to prefer x to y" we need to know *for whom* this is being claimed to be correct. If I assert that x is better than y, does this entail that it is correct for every human being (or every rational being) to prefer x to y or does it only entail that it is correct *for the members of my society/group* (or correct for *me*) to prefer x to y? (There are many other possibilities; I will not try to list them all.) Our conceptual commitments should leave these questions open, at least for now. But, at the very least, it seems clear that we want our concept of good to imply that if I say that x is better than y, then I am saying that it is correct *for me* to prefer x to y (and that it would be *incorrect* for me not to prefer x to y).[10] Judgments about the goodness or badness of one's own life could not have the practical importance that most of us attach to them unless "doing x would cause me to have a much worse life than I would otherwise have" entailed "other things being equal, it would be a mistake for me to do x." A theory of the good life can't guide our choices unless, in some way, it rejects certain choices.[11] A normative theory that doesn't constrain our choices cannot guide them. Thus, any theory according to which "it is correct for me to prefer x to y" simply means the same as "I prefer x to y" cannot guide my choices. Such theories imply that my actual preferences are correct, whatever they happen to be.

3. A Historical Note

The view that "good" means (or at least entails) "desirable" or "worthy of desire" has a long pedigree. It has been accepted by such philosophers as Mill, Brentano, Russell,[12] Korsgaard, Brandt, and Lemos.[13] Similar analyses in terms of the correctness of favorable and unfavorable attitudes are defended by Sidgwick,[14] Ross,[15] Kraut,[16] Ewing,[17] Urmson,[18] and Wellman. Note the following passage from Brandt's *Ethical Theory*:

> "x is better than y" may be said to mean "It is fitting or justifiable to prefer x to y."[19]

Korsgaard writes the following:

> [W]hen I say that something is good I am recommending it as worthy of your choice.[20]

'Good' names the problem of what we are to strive for, aim at, and care about in our lives.[21]

According to Brentano, value judgments are statements about the correctness of love and hatred (*Lieben* and *Hassen*); on his view, whether one loves or hates something is a function of both one's preferences and feelings:

> We call a thing *good* when the love relating to it is correct. In the broadest sense of the term, the good is that which is worthy of love, that which can be loved with a love that is correct.[22]

> One loves or hates correctly provided that one's feelings are adequate to their object—adequate in the sense of being appropriate, suitable, or fitting.[23]

> When we call one good "better" than another, we mean that the one is preferable to the other. In other words, it is *correct* to prefer the one good for its own sake, to the other.[24]

> One loves or hates correctly provided that one's feelings are adequate to their object—adequate in the sense of being appropriate, suitable, or fitting.[25]

Brentano holds that being worthy of being loved is both necessary and sufficient for being non-instrumentally good. Mill's "proof" of hedonism/utilitarianism in chapter 4 of *Utilitarianism* assumes that "good" means "desirable." Mill holds that being worthy of being desired is both necessary and sufficient for being non-instrumentally good. Carl Wellman holds that a necessary condition of something's being good is that it is rational to favor it.

> "This is good" and "no, it is bad" are opposed because, while the former claims implicitly that favor is the rational attitude to take towards the object, the latter claims that disfavor is the rational attitude.[26]

Aristotle takes it to be a conceptual truth that the final good is worthy of desire or worthy of choice.[27]

> [T]he final good seems to be self-sufficient. . . . For the present we define as "self-sufficient" that which taken by itself makes life something desirable and deficient in nothing. It is *eudaimonia*, in our opinion, which fits this description. Moreover, *eudaimonia* is of all things the one most desirable, and it is not counted as one good thing among many others. But if it were

counted as one among many others, it is obvious that the addition of even the least of the goods would make it more desirable; for the addition would produce an extra amount of good, and the greater amount of good is always more desirable than the lesser. (1097b) [Irwin gives a slightly different translation of this passage. Where the Ostwald translation, which I am using, reads "desirable," Irwin reads "choiceworthy."[28]]

4. Analyses of Value in Terms of the Correctness of Other Sorts of Attitudes

The proposed concept of value takes value judgments to entail judgments about *the correctness of preferences*. Why should we take value judgments to be statements about the correctness of preferences, as opposed to statements about the correctness of emotions or other sorts of attitudes? Or, following Brentano, we could take value judgments to be judgments about the correctness of both preferences and emotions (see note 24). Any attempt to define concepts of value in terms of the correctness of attitudes falls into one of the following three categories:

1.   "Good" and "bad" are defined in terms of the correctness of preferences.

2.   "Good" and "bad" are defined in terms of the correctness of attitudes other than preferences, e.g., emotions or feelings.

3.   Some combination of 1 and 2; "good" and "bad" are defined in terms of the correctness of preferences *and* other kinds of attitudes.

I believe that analyses of type 1 are preferable to those of type 2 or 3. My larger purposes in this book, however, only require me to claim that analyses of types 1 and 3 are preferable to those of type 2. For my purposes, it is sufficient to maintain that a *necessary* condition of something's being good is that it is correct to prefer it.

5. Reasons to Reject Analyses of Type 2 and Prefer Those of Type 1

Ideal observer theories of the sort defended by Hume and Firth[29] are the clearest and most promising analyses of type 2. Hume and Firth analyze moral concepts in terms of specific moral sentiments, e.g., moral approbation and disapprobation. I will only examine Firth's theory, but my criticisms apply equally to Hume.[30] Firth analyzes the meaning of moral concepts in terms of the notion of an ideal observer. According to Firth, moral judgments of the sort "x is — — —" (where — — — is a moral predicate such as "good" or "bad" or "right" or "wrong") are to be analyzed along the following lines: "all ideal observers would react in such and such ways to x."[31] (For our purposes here it is not necessary to consider Firth's characterization of ideal observers or ideal moral judges.)[32] Very roughly, to make a favorable moral judgment about something, to say that it is good or right, etc., is to say that all ideal observers would feel "moral approval" for it. To make an unfavorable moral judgment about something is to say that all ideal observers would feel moral disapproval for it.[33] According to Firth, moral approval and disapproval are felt qualities of experience. Firth notes that, for the purposes of his theory, he cannot define moral approval and disapproval as certain kinds of feelings that are produced by one's moral beliefs because that would make his analysis of moral judgments circular.[34] For example, it would be circular to say that "x is good" means "all ideal observers would believe that x is good and, as a result, have such and such a kind of favorable emotion concerning it." Firth also rejects the view that moral approval and disapproval can be identified with desires or feelings of desire.[35] Firth never explains what exactly he means by "moral approval/disapproval" or "the ethically significant reactions of an ideal observer." He expresses strong sympathy for Wolfgang Köhler's view that "the typical moral datum is an obligatoriness or 'demand quality'; which appears in the deliberative consciousness of the moral judge as an ostensible property of an envisaged act or goal."[36] However, he stops short of endorsing Köhler's view.

My own introspection fails to reveal the existence of distinctive experiences characterized by a "demand quality" that are specifiable independently of my normative beliefs. Nor do I have any experiences that in virtue of their phenomenological character alone (independently of my normative beliefs) could be called moral approval or disapproval. Most other philosophers with whom I have discussed the matter report the same.[37] Firth gives no reason for thinking that our failure to experience a demand quality (or moral approval or disapproval) specifiable independently of our moral beliefs constitutes a cognitive failing. There is no reason to suppose that all ideal observers would experience this sort of demand quality. Thus it seems unlikely that all Firthian ideal observers would agree in their reactions about any significant issues.[38] This shows that Firth's theory has far different implications for the issue of relativism than he himself supposes, but it does not show that his theory is mistaken as an analysis of the *meaning* of normative terms.

A more serious problem for Firth is that his theory leaves open the question of why one should pay greater heed to those desires that are consistent with one's felt moral approval and disapproval than to those that are not. Suppose that someone is thinking of committing a murder in order to obtain money and is torn between greed and empathy for the victim. On the whole, he may be more strongly inclined to commit the murder rather than not, even though only his desire not to kill the other person is characterized by a demand quality (or some kind of felt moral approval). Why should he act on the desire that is characterized by the demand quality (moral approval)? Why should he choose the course of action for which an ideal observer would feel moral approval? Why is it in any sense mistaken or irrational for him to act on his strongest informed preferences rather than perform the action for which he would feel moral approval (or the action for which an ideal observer would feel moral approval)? Firth doesn't answer these questions, and in the absence of cogent answers we should not accept his analysis of normative concepts in terms of the moral approval and disapproval of ideal observers.

This objection can be generalized to other analyses of type 2. Take any analysis of type 2 according to which x is good provided that it is correct to have attitude A about x (where A is an attitude that is independent of one's actual or ideal preferences about x). This analysis and analyses of type 1 will yield different results for actual cases only if it can be correct to prefer something without having attitude A about it or vice versa. Suppose that there is a case in which it is correct to have attitude A about x but not correct to prefer x. Given an analysis of type 2, the judgment that x is good simply does not have the action-guiding features that we ordinarily take value judgments to possess. If being good meant being such that it is correct to have attitude A about it, then something's being good would not give a person even *prima facie* reasons to choose it or prefer it. Since we want a theory of the good life to help guide our choices, analyses of type 1 are preferable to those of type 2.

Gibbard's analysis of the meaning of *moral judgments* is also an analysis of type 2. He takes moral judgments in the narrow sense (judgments about right and wrong) to be judgments about the aptness or rationality of feelings of guilt and anger:

> What a person does is *morally wrong* if and only if it is rational for him to feel guilty for having done it, and for others to be angry at him for having done it.[39]

This may be plausible as an analysis (or partial analysis) of the concepts of right and wrong. Anger and guilt may be appropriate responses to certain kinds of actions, but they are not appropriate responses to every kind of bad thing. For example, neither guilt nor anger (directed at any individual person) is an appropriate response to suffering caused by natural disasters. Gibbard's analysis of right and wrong is not plausible if it is extended to provide an analysis of value. (I should stress that Gibbard does not endorse this as an analysis of "good" and "bad," indeed, he accepts something very much like my analysis.)[40] There are many different kinds of good things. It is unlikely that there is any particular kind of feeling or emotion that is appropriate for every good thing or every bad thing. To take just one example: the emotions that are appropriate responses to hard-earned success are different from the responses that are appropriate to good fortune that occurs simply as a matter of luck.

III. The Appeal to Meaning

Much of twentieth-century Anglo-American moral philosophy is devoted to an analysis of the meaning of moral concepts. Proposed analyses or definitions of moral concepts are defended by appealing to the (conventional) meaning of moral terms ("good" and "bad" and "right" and "wrong") in the English language. Many contemporary philosophers have expressed serious reservations about this approach to moral philosophy. For example, Allan Gibbard holds that recent work in philosophy of language, in particular Quine's attack on the analytic-synthetic distinction, casts doubt on the existence of meanings that can be *discovered* through philosophical analysis.[41] I offer no view on the question of the existence of meanings. If meanings don't exist, then clearly it is out of order to defend one's own preferred concept of good by appeal to the meaning of "good."

But, for the sake of argument, let us suppose that the English word "good" (in the sense of "non-instrumentally good" and "good life") has a single determinate meaning. It doesn't follow that our ordinary-language concept of goodness is justified, i.e., that we have any strong reasons to accept or use that concept. It would still be in order for someone to say, "Granted that's what *English speakers (or people in our society) mean* by 'good' or 'good life'; I don't care about what is good or what is a good life in that sense. I think that we should adopt an alternative normative system which does not include that concept of good or anything like it."[42] The same argument would apply even if we could show that there was a single concept of good shared by all cultures/languages. For any concept or definition of goodness that is claimed to capture what "we" mean by good (goodness$_1$), we can imagine an alternative concept of goodness (goodness$_2$). For any feature we ascribe to "our" concept of goodness, e.g., universalizability, we can imagine an alternative concept of goodness that does not have that feature. The deep question here is: which concept of goodness should we be interested in? Should we be interested in goodness$_1$ or goodness$_2$ (or, perhaps, neither)? We cannot avoid this question by adopting more than one concept of value. For in that case, we will still need norms or priority rules for resolving conflicts between those concepts. Suppose that a possible course of action leads to consequences that (on balance) are good$_1$ but bad$_2$. We need to ask which concept of goodness should take precedence in our decision making. Appeal to the ordinary meaning of "good" in "our language" or "our philosophical tradition" cannot answer this question. The appeal to meaning has no force whatever in trying to resolve conceptual disagreements between different societies. Suppose that two societies have different concepts of goodness. We can ask whether one concept (or one conceptual scheme) is preferable to the other. Would the members of one society be advised to drop their concept in favor of the other society's concept? We cannot answer such questions by simply appealing to the concepts employed in our own society.

We have a *choice* between alternative normative concepts. There are many different possible concepts of value that compete for our favor. We can choose whether or not to employ the normative concepts of our own society. Even if there is a clear conventional meaning of "good" in our language or our society, we have the option of employing some other concept of goodness. One of the ultimate aims of moral philosophy is to advise us regarding our choice of normative concepts. It is mere dogmatism unworthy of critical philosophy to confine ourselves to explicating conventional notions and concepts.

One could choose to reject all normative concepts and not use any concept of a good or bad life. However, on due consideration of what it would be like to live a life completely unregulated by overall judgments about the goodness or badness of one's life, most of us will not find this a serious option. Consider what it would be like to choose a career or decide whether or not to get married if one had no standards for making overall evaluations of one's life. My pragmatic arguments are addressed to those who want to employ norms for assessing their lives and who are choosing between different basic normative concepts.

In the foregoing arguments I have assumed that if there are meanings of existing normative concepts, they are constituted by contingent facts of ordinary use and convention. Platonists and others who think that meanings are determined by the existence of essences would object. However, appeal to the existence of essences cannot support any particular concept of goodness. Suppose that I assert that the correct account of goodness is goodness1 by claiming knowledge of an abstract essence of goodness1 (which exists independently of particular instances of goodness1). The proponent of goodness2 can defend her preferred analysis of goodness by claiming knowledge of the essence of goodness2. I can either accept or reject her claim that there exists an essence of goodness2. If I concede that there exists an essence of goodness2, then the dispute between us comes to something like this: Which essence, goodness1 or goodness2, most warrants being called the essence of 'goodness'? Appeal to the existence of essences cannot avail us here. The dispute becomes a dispute about which essence is correctly associated with the *word* "goodness." On the other hand, if I deny the existence of goodness2 and claim that the other person has misdescribed or misperceived goodness₁, then I need to show why it is the other person (and not I) who is misapprehending the essences. This, in turn, would require me to provide plausible criteria for distinguishing between veridical and non-veridical apprehension of essences. (To my knowledge no such criteria exist.)

A Qualification. I have argued that appealing to the (conventional) meaning of normative terms in a particular linguistic community cannot provide decisive reasons for accepting or rejecting any particular theory of value. This is perfectly consistent with saying that being consistent with ordinary usage and the concepts employed in the philosophical tradition is an important desideratum of any concept of value, provided that the concepts employed in ordinary language and the philosophical tradition serve the purposes that we want our normative concepts to serve. Indeed, I shall argue that the fact that my theory of meaning is consistent with ordinary language and the (Western) philosophical tradition is a consideration in its favor (see 6.V.2).

IV. A Taxonomy of Theories of Meaning

I defend my analysis of the meaning of value judgments as the best of all the options prominent in contemporary philosophy. It is important that I not overlook any significant alternative views. Therefore, I need to give a taxonomy of possible analyses of meaning. My taxonomy draws heavily on the recent work of R. M. Hare. According to Hare, all theories of meaning can be classified as either descriptivist or non-descriptivist. Descriptivist theories take moral/normative judgments to be identical with "descriptive statements or judgments." Any theory of meaning that does not take normative judgments to be identical with descriptive statements counts as a non-descriptivist theory. Hare defines "descriptive statements/judgments" as follows:

[A] statement or judgment is descriptive if its meaning (including its reference) determines uniquely its truth conditions and vice versa.[43]

According to Hare,

[D]escriptivists think that for any sentence to have meaning is for there to be some condition under which statements expressed by it would be true; and this in turn would depend on the conditions for the correct application of the descriptive expressions in it.[44]

I would like to add the following qualification to Hare's definition: descriptivist theories of meaning imply that moral/normative judgments are statements that ascribe properties to things. I believe that this is implicit in Hare's definition, but nothing hangs on whether I am accurately representing Hare's view on this point. I shall construe descriptivism as the view that moral/normative judgments are descriptive statements. A judgment or statement is descriptive provided that (i) it ascribes a property to something, (ii) its meaning uniquely determines its truth conditions, and (iii) its truth conditions uniquely determine its meaning. Clause iii implies that theories of meaning according to which descriptive statements constitute part (but not all) of the meaning of normative judgments[45] do not count as "descriptivist theories."

The standard cognitivist theories of meaning, naturalism and non-naturalism, are descriptivist theories; the standard non-cognitivist theories, emotivism and prescriptivism, are non-descriptivist theories. However, the distinction between descriptivism and non-descriptivism is not the same as the distinction between cognitivism and non-cognitivism. Roughly, cognitivism is the view that normative judgments are statements that are true or false. Non-cognitivism is the view that normative judgments are not statements that are true or false. Alternatively, we could define cognitivism as the view that normative judgments *purport* to be true and non-cognitivism as the view that normative judgments *do not purport* to be true. On either definition of cognitivism/non-cognitivism, not all cognitivist theories count as descriptivist theories. It is perfectly consistent to hold that normative judgments are true or correct but deny that they are descriptive statements. Normative judgments could be (or could purport to be) true/correct or false/incorrect, even if their truth conditions do not exhaust their meaning.[46]

Any descriptivist theory of meaning holds that either:

1.   Normative judgments do not entail statements to the effect that it is correct or fitting to have certain attitudes or preferences.

2.   Normative judgments entail statements to the effect that it is correct or fitting to have certain attitudes or preferences.

I shall call descriptivist theories that hold 1 "reductivist descriptivist theories" and descriptivist theories that hold 2 "non-reductivist descriptivist theories." This terminology is idiosyncratic, but it's useful for the purpose of comparing my theory and the main alternative theories.

Reductivist descriptivist theories hold that normative judgments do not entail statements to the effect that it is correct or fitting to have certain attitudes or preferences. Judgments that do not entail statements to the effect that it is correct or fitting to have certain attitudes or preferences are (according to my theory) non-normative statements. Assuming the truth of my theory of meaning, all versions of reductivist descriptivism are false. I claim that normative judgments entail statements about the correctness or appropriateness of preferences or attitudes. If my theory is true, then normative judgments cannot be descriptive statements that do not entail statements about the correctness of attitudes. But my terminology or taxonomy itself does not beg the question against reductivist descriptivism; my definition of reductionist descriptivism does not make it a conceptual truth that reductivist descriptivism is false.

Reductivist descriptivism is roughly the same view that Moore attacks in arguing that at least some fundamental normative concepts are indefinable in the sense that they cannot be analyzed into constituent notions (Moore calls the view that he attacks "naturalism"). What I call "non-reductivist descriptivist theories" is about the same as what is called "non-naturalist theories." Moore's use of the terms "naturalism" and "non-naturalism" is misleading, since, if successful, his arguments against "naturalism" work against any attempt to define good in terms of non-normative properties. His arguments are intended to refute definitions of good in terms of "supernatural" properties such as the property of being commanded by God as well as definitions of good in terms of what we would ordinarily call "natural" properties.

The distinction between descriptivist and non-descriptivist theories of meaning is not equivalent to the distinction between realist and non-realist theories. My theory of meaning is consistent with either realism or non-realism. Given my theory of meaning, moral realism is true if there are facts (independent of our actual or possible beliefs and attitudes) in virtue of which our preferences (or attitudes) about things can be correct or mistaken, and realism is false if there aren't any such facts. Realism is consistent with non-descriptivist analyses of meaning. For example, mixed theories of meaning according to which normative judgments have both descriptive and emotive meaning are non-descriptivist theories (they do not hold that the meaning of normative judgments is exhausted by their truth conditions), but such theories are still consistent with realism. (I discuss a "mixed" theory in 6.VIII.) Further, descriptivist analyses of meaning are consistent with non-realist error theories according to which moral judgments purport to be objectively true or correct but aren't.

V. Pragmatic Criteria for the Choice of Normative Concepts

1. Three Criteria

Questions about the choice of fundamental normative concepts, e.g., "which concept(s) of value should we employ?," cannot be settled by simply appealing to the meanings of words or concepts. Ultimately, the choice of a concept of goodness can only be justified by reference to pragmatic considerations. What sorts of pragmatic considerations should govern this choice? I propose the following three criteria.

i. The concept of value (good and bad) must be one that makes sense of the practical action-guiding significance of questions of value. Standards of goodness and badness are intended to guide choices. Norms concerning the goodness or badness of lives govern our most important choices and commitments as human beings. Norms for the good life are norms for assessing our most general attitudes and commitments. Any concept of good and bad must be able to make sense of why it is advisable to have a good life rather than a bad life. We should take having a "good life" to entail having a "choiceworthy life."

ii. Whatever concept of value we choose must allow for the possibility of disagreement over first-order standards of value and must facilitate rational discussion and debate between individuals or cultures who disagree about first-order standards of value. If there is anything we know about the meaning of "good" in English, it is that people can and do disagree in their value judgments. It also seems that such disagreements can persist, even if people do not disagree about the answers to other ("factual") questions. The pervasive phenomenon of disagreement is one of our surest anchors in moral philosophy/axiology. English speakers often claim that others are mistaken in their normative judgments, even if they learn that others have different descriptive criteria for applying normative terms.[47]

Even if the normative concepts of our own language did not permit disagreement about standards of value, we could learn or create concepts that allow for this sort of disagreement.[48] Independently of considerations about the conventional meaning of the word "good" in English, we have compelling pragmatic reasons to adopt a concept of goodness that makes first-order disagreement possible. Different people often have conflicting attitudes and preferences about various things. For example, some people have very favorable attitudes about the knightly virtues of chivalry and honor; others view them with disdain. It is a deep and important question whether the attitudes and preferences of some people can be said to be more correct or more justified than those of other people. We need normative concepts in terms of which such questions can be raised. By raising such questions we subject our own preferences and practical commitments to criticism. It would be foolish to cut ourselves off from the insights and criticism of others about such matters.

iii. It is conceivable that we would want to reject the notions of value that are employed in ordinary language and Western philosophy (see section III).

But, unless there are strong reasons to reject the concept(s) of goodness employed in ordinary language and Western philosophy, we will want to choose a concept similar to the concept(s) employed in ordinary language and philosophy. Such a concept will enable us to communicate better with others and will give us the benefits of the criticisms and insights of other people and the Western philosophical tradition. Adopting a normative system quite foreign to that of other English speakers and the Western philosophical tradition will put us in the position of having to continually reinvent the wheel. This is not something that we should do without very compelling reasons.[49]

The Western philosophical tradition is an evolving tradition that has been and will continue to be enhanced by contact with other traditions. The Western and English-speaking traditions are not the property of any one racial or ethnic group; many non-Europeans are members of both traditions. The western philosophical tradition not only includes Aristotle and Kant, it also includes St. Augustine, Averroes, Jaegwon Kim, and Anthony Appiah. The English-speaking tradition includes not only Mill and Wilberforce, but also Martin Luther King Jr., Ghandi, Nelson Mandela, and Vaclav Havel. We have reasons to work within the conceptual framework of this tradition. Self-criticism of the tradition must continue, and the kinds of normative concepts that emerge in the future may be quite different from those that we have now. However, we need to live and work within our tradition, and we need to use some concept of value or good and bad to make overall judgments about the value of our lives.

2. My Proposed Concept of Value Satisfies the Three Criteria

(i) *Practice*. In asking what makes for a good life or in formulating ideals of the good life, we are addressing deeply practical questions. How should I live? What sort of person should I strive to be? What goals should I pursue? What sorts of desires, interests, and traits of character should I try to cultivate? Judgments about the goodness or badness of lives recommend certain kinds of lives over others. In recommending one sort of life over another we are not simply emoting or expressing our own preferences. My theory explains the practical import of normative judgments. Normative judgments about the value of people's lives recommend certain kinds of lives over others on pain of error.

If no mistake is involved in preferring x to y when y is better than x, then it's not clear that we should be interested in questions of value. Given my concept of value, it is analytic that a good life is preferable to a bad life. Some alternative concepts of value allow for the possibility that a bad life could be preferable to a good life. There are strong pragmatic reasons not to employ such concepts. We should employ a concept of goodness that helps to guide our actions and choices.

(ii) *Disagreement.* It seems to be possible for people to disagree about the goodness or badness of particular things, even if they agree about all of the relevant factual questions. Disagreement about first-order questions of value presupposes a shared concept (or core concept) of goodness. Suppose that you say that X is good and I say that X is not good. In order for this to constitute a disagreement there must be something that our concepts of goodness have in common—something that you are affirming or doing with respect to X that I am denying or rejecting. If you and I mean completely different things by "good," then "X is good" as said by you is consistent with "X is not good" as said by me. My view permits us to say that this is a genuine disagreement. If I say that X is good and you say that X is not good, I am saying that it is correct (appropriate) to prefer that X exist or occur rather than not, and you are denying that it is correct to prefer that X exist or occur rather than not.

(iii) *Ordinary Language and the History of Philosophy.* My theory captures at least part of what "good" means in English and part of what historical philosophers have meant by good. Aristotle takes his theory of the good life to be much more than an articulation of his likes and dislikes; he takes it to be a view that we disregard on pain of serious error. At the very least, when the historical philosophers say that one life is better than another, they are saying that (other things equal) it is a mistake to prefer the one to the other. If we reject this, then it's not clear how their writings on questions of value are relevant to practice (as they clearly intend them to be). If no mistake need be involved in preferring x to y when y is better than x, then it's not clear that we should be interested in what is good. It is not an open question whether it is correct to pursue the good. To say that something is good is to say that it is worthy of pursuit. In Western philosophy there are perennial questions about value and the good life. Contemporary philosophers are asking (much) the same questions as Mill, Sidgwick, Moore, and the ancients. There is a strong presumption for thinking that our analysis of the meaning of good should be consistent with this; it should permit us to say that Aristotle, Mill, Sidgwick, and Moore mean much the same thing by "good" when they make claims about what things are non-instrumentally good or good as ends. Aristotle and Sidgwick disagree about whether pleasure is the only thing that is good as an end. Sidgwick took himself to be disagreeing with Aristotle and thus employing roughly the same concept of good. Those who claim that he didn't really disagree with Aristotle bear a very strong burden of proof.

VI. Descriptivist Theories

1. Reductivist Descriptivist Theories of Meaning Do Not Satisfy the Three Criteria

According to reductivist descriptivism, "good" (in ordinary English) means the same as "possesses d" (where "d" refers to a reductive descriptive property or some combination of reductive descriptive properties). A reductive descriptive property (p) is a property or combination of properties such that statements ascribing p to X do not entail statements to the effect that it is correct to have certain attitudes or preferences about X.[50] The properties of being pleased with something and being in accordance with the will of God are reductive descriptive properties. Reductivist descriptivist accounts of the meaning of the conventional (English) concept of good are unacceptable because they are unable to account for the pervasive phenomena of disagreement about first-order value judgments and disagreement about standards of value—disagreements that persist, even if people agree about all of the relevant factual questions. The reductivist descriptivist says that things are good because they have d. Suppose that someone else (let us call him "the dissenter") says that X is not good, even though he concedes that X has d. The dissenter recognizes that X is d and, therefore, does not take it to be part of the meaning of good that whatever has d is good. In saying that X is good the descriptivist is not saying anything that the dissenter denies when he says that X is not good. The reductivist descriptivist must say that he is not disagreeing with this *or any other dissenter* who concedes that X has d. Pure reductivist descriptivist accounts of good cannot allow for genuine disagreement over first-order judgments of value between people who know the non-normative facts.

2. Non-Reductivist Descriptivism

Some non-naturalist theories define normative concepts in terms of the notion of fitting or correct attitudes. Ewing and Broad take the fittingness of attitudes to things in the world to be the ultimate moral (normative) property. The goodness or badness (or rightness or wrongness) of things consists in the fact that certain attitudes befit them. The good is that for which desire or a favorable attitude is fitting; the bad is that for which aversion or an unfavorable attitude is fitting.[51] As a theory of *meaning* this sort of non-naturalism is very similar to my own theory except that it employs a very particular concept of fittingness or correctness and claims that a normative judgment asserts the existence of a relational property of fittingness that holds between things and certain attitudes about them. Other non-naturalist theories of meaning, such as Moore's, take goodness and badness to be simple, unanalyzable, non-relational properties analogous to basic color properties.

Both types of non-reductivist descriptivism posit properties whose existence is open to question—it is unclear that these properties actually exist. (I give reasons for questioning the existence of these properties in chapter 7.II.) Thus, *given the success of my arguments in 7.II*, these two types of non-reductivist theories of meaning risk committing us to an error theory. For that reason, these theories of meaning should be rejected; we have a plausible alternative theory of meaning that doesn't risk committing us to an error theory.

VII. Non-Descriptivist Theories

1. Emotivism

Emotivism is a non-descriptivist theory in that it denies that value judgments are statements ascribing properties to things that are true or false. What I call "crude emotivism" holds that value judgments are simply expressions of attitudes or emotions. To say that x is good is to express a favorable attitude about x; to say that x is bad is to express an unfavorable attitude about x.[52] Crude emotivism denies the obvious phenomenon of *disagreement* about questions of value. Consider a paradigmatic case of a moral dispute. One person holds that Stalin was a good man and another holds that he was a bad man. If normative judgments were nothing more than expressions of attitudes or statements about one's attitudes, then this could not constitute a disagreement. The fact that I like Stalin and you dislike him does not constitute a disagreement any more than the fact that I like the taste of chocolate chip ice cream and you don't constitutes a disagreement.

The emotivist theories of Ayer and Stevenson attempt to deal with the problem of disagreement. Stevenson and Ayer would say that normative disagreement consists in the fact that people with different attitudes about something are each attempting to alter the attitudes of the other about the thing in question.[53] According to Ayer, it is part of the meaning of moral judgments that they are intended to affect the attitudes and actions of other people.[54] So, on Ayer's view, to make a moral judgment is to express an attitude with the intention of influencing the attitudes or actions of other people. Stevenson holds that moral judgments have what he calls "dynamic meaning," i.e., it is a part of their meaning that they can be used to influence the attitudes of other people. According to him, "x is good" means roughly "I approve of x; do so as well."[55]

Although the formulations of emotivism proposed by Ayer and Stevenson are a great improvement over crude emotivism, they do not afford a satisfactory account of normative disagreement. In cases of disagreement, people not only try to cause others to share their attitudes, they assert that their own attitudes are correct and that the attitudes of those who disagree with them are mistaken. My disagreement with the person who claims that Stalin was a good man consists (at least in part) in the fact that I take his views and attitudes about Stalin to be mistaken and he takes mine to be mistaken. Emotivism does not provide a satisfactory account of our ordinary-language concept of normative disagreement. On this score, emotivism is even less plausible as an analysis of the concepts of value employed by major figures in the history of philosophy. When Mill and Sidgwick reject non-hedonistic theories of value, they are doing more than simply expressing their attitudes about things other than pleasure and trying to influence the attitudes of others; they are claiming that those who hold non-hedonistic theories are mistaken.

Further evidence on this score can be obtained by examining ordinary cases of "normative change"—cases in which people change their minds about questions of value. Suppose that a person enjoys engaging in sadomasochistic sexual activities. He believes that the pleasure he obtains from these activities is non-instrumentally good. At a later time he comes to believe that sadomasochistic pleasure is non-instrumentally bad and, as a result, comes to have an unfavorable attitude about sadomasochism. Emotivists would describe this case by saying that his attitudes have changed. But this person is not just reporting a change of attitude and/or a change in his intentions with respect to influencing the attitudes of others. He would say that his previous attitude was incorrect and that it has been rectified.[56] In this context it is instructive to contrast moral change with change of taste. I used to dislike the taste of cantaloupes and now I like the way they taste, but I have no inclination to say that my taste has been corrected.[57]

Emotivism is unable to account for the causal efficacy of value judgments and their importance in human affairs. Value judgments could not have the power to influence us in the way that they do unless they purported to be correct. They make a claim on us. Few of us are such conformists that we are moved to adopt the attitudes of our associates, simply in order to share their attitudes. Emotivism makes it a mystery why we should care so much about normative considerations and why people who are independent thinkers and nonconformists are often moved by the normative judgments of others. Few of us take the fact that others hold an attitude and want us to adopt it to be a reason for us to adopt that attitude. Value judgments purport to give *reasons* for adopting certain attitudes and rejecting others. If we took value judgments to be mere expressions of attitudes intended to influence other people's attitudes, it is unlikely that they would have any significant ability to influence our attitudes. If emotivism were a correct account of the meaning of standard normative terms, normative judgments couldn't have the causal powers that they plainly possess.

The emotivist might respond by noting that certain forms of advertising simply depict expressions of favorable attitudes about the product being advertised. These advertisements attempt to influence our attitudes in much the same way that emotivists claim that moral judgments attempt to influence our attitudes. The success of such advertisements shows that emotivism is, indeed, able to account for the causal efficacy of moral judgments. But, even granting the claims about the efficacy of advertisements which do nothing more than depict the expression of attitudes about a product, this reply is inadequate. First, it does not account for the fact that independent thinkers and non-conformists are often moved by the normative judgments of others. Second, even though many people may, other things equal, be inclined to adopt the same attitudes as others, few people take the fact that others hold an attitude and want us to adopt it to be a *reason* to adopt that attitude. Stevenson's theory cannot explain the fact that value judgments purport to give us reasons for adopting certain attitudes and rejecting others.

My theory provides a plausible account of the difference between value judgments and expressions of taste. Expressions of taste are expressions of attitudes or preferences. Sometimes their purpose is merely expressive; sometimes they are intended to influence the attitudes of others; sometimes they are intended to convey information about one's preferences to others. A value judgment asserts the *correctness of* such a preference or attitude. The essential difference between saying "ugh" when tasting a certain flavor of ice cream and saying "malicious pleasure is non-instrumentally bad" is that, in the latter case, one implies that it is correct or fitting to prefer that people not enjoy malicious pleasure and that those who do not have this preference are mistaken. When I express my liking for a certain kind of ice cream with the hope of influencing others to try it, I do not presume that it would be incorrect for another person not to like it. I allow for the possibility that it may be perfectly correct for others not to like it. On the other hand, a snobbish wine connoisseur who believes that my enjoyment of cheap wine is mistaken due to my underdeveloped powers of discrimination and unfamiliarity with good wine might be making value judgments about non-instrumental value. He might be denying that the pleasure I derive from drinking wine possesses any positive non-instrumental value.

2. Prescriptivism

R. M. Hare is the most important defender of prescriptivism. In his first book, *The Language of Morals*, he claims that moral judgments are "universalizable prescriptions."[58] (Hare uses the term "moral judgment" very broadly to include both judgments about the rightness or wrongness of actions and judgments about good and bad.) According to Hare, moral judgments are prescriptions or imperatives on the order of "shut the door" or "stop!" They are distinguishable from other sorts of imperatives in that they are "universalizable." This means that a person who makes a moral judgment about something is committed to making exactly the same judgment about anything that is similar to it in the relevant respects.[59] This view fails to provide an adequate basis for distinguishing between moral judgments and other sorts of prescriptions, e.g., "don't bet on a lame horse" and "don't juxtapose scarlet and magenta." (The last two prescriptions could be universalizable in Hare's sense.) In his later work beginning with *Freedom and Reason* Hare avoids this problem by adding the condition that moral judgments must be "overriding."[60] In *Moral Thinking* Hare writes the following:

> We might suggest as a first approximation that a use of 'ought' or 'must' is a moral use in this sense if the judgment containing it is (1) prescriptive, (2) universalizable, and (3) overriding.[61]

Hare qualifies this by saying that it only applies to "critical moral principles." *Prima facie* moral principles are, by definition, overridable.[62] Hare explains the notion of overridingness in terms of someone treating a prescription as overriding.

> To treat a principle as overriding, then, is to let it always override other principles when they conflict with it and, in the same way, let it override all other prescriptions.[63]

Hare gives the example of a man who endorses the principle "don't juxtapose scarlet and magenta" but violates it to avoid hurting his wife's feelings. Since he allows this principle to be overridden by principles that forbid hurting other people's feelings, he does not treat it as a moral principle. On the other hand, a person who treated the principle "don't juxtapose scarlet and magenta" as overriding would be treating it as a moral principle.

Ordinary value judgments are not overriding in the way that Hare claims (we do not take them to override all other prescriptions). It is perfectly consistent for someone who says that X is non-instrumentally good to hold that X is incompatible with certain greater goods and thus prescribe that X not be sought. Here Hare might protest that his view only commits him to saying that *all things considered judgments* about the value of the consequences of alternative courses of action are overriding. To say that the consequences of action 1 are better on balance than those of action 2 commits one to prescribing that 1 be chosen over 2 and treating this prescription as overriding. (Similarly, Hare says that on balance judgments about right or wrong are overriding, but he does not say that judgments to the effect that something is *prima facie* right or wrong are overriding.) However, if Hare makes this reply, his view rules out non-consequentialist theories of right and wrong simply in virtue of the meaning of normative terms. Substantive issues such as the truth of consequentialism should be left open by our concepts and conceptual commitments. Even if overridingness is part of the concept of moral obligation, it is not clear that judgments about good and bad are overriding in this same way.[64]

According to Hare, to say that x is better than y is to: (i) prescribe that x be chosen over y; (ii) prescribe that x be chosen over y for any relevantly similar x and y; and (iii) treat these prescriptions as overriding. On Hare's view, saying that x is better than y does not imply that it is correct to prefer x to y.[65] Because of this, Hare's theory cannot provide an adequate account of the nature of normative disagreement or the causal efficacy of normative judgments. Suppose that two people disagree about whether x is better than y. When we disagree about whether x is better than y, we are not just prescribing different choices for this and relevantly similar cases; we are claiming that our own preferences are correct and the other person's mistaken. Unless normative judgments purported to be correct in this way, conflicting normative judgments wouldn't constitute a challenge to our own judgments and preferences. Normative judgments could not have the power to sway us and alter our preferences unless they purported to be correct.[66]

VIII. Good and Bad as "Thick" Concepts

Terms such as "generous" and "honest" are "thick" concepts—they have both evaluative and descriptive meaning. "Generous" and "honest" commend the things to which they are applied; they express favorable attitudes (or assert that it is correct to have favorable attitudes) about the things to which they are applied. There are clear descriptive criteria for using such terms. It is a misuse of language to apply them to things that do not satisfy those criteria. It would be a misuse of the word "miserly" to apply it to someone who makes no attempt to accumulate wealth or to someone who gives away almost all of his wealth and money to help other people. It would be a misuse of the word "generous" to apply it to someone who never gives anything (including time or effort) to anyone else even though he has many opportunities to do so.

Good and bad and right and wrong are often taken to be "thin" normative concepts that don't have any descriptive criteria for their correct application. Emotivism and prescriptivism hold that good and bad and right and wrong are "thin" concepts. But a number of contemporary philosophers, most notably Foot and Williams, hold that all (legitimate) normative concepts are thick concepts. Williams holds that, to the extent that "good" and "ought" are thin concepts, we should ignore them or dispense with them in favor of thick normative concepts such as courage and honesty.[67] Foot construes good as a thick concept.[68] According to Foot, "good" has both descriptive and evaluative or commendatory meaning. "Good" commends or expresses a "pro-attitude" about the things to which it is applied. The descriptive meaning of "good" consists in the fact that "good" stands in an "internal relationship" to the objects to which it is applied. This means that there are limits to the things to which "good" can be consistently ascribed. For example, Foot holds that something can be called a "good action" only if it satisfies one of the following conditions: (i) it is the fulfillment of a special duty derived from a role or promise; or (ii) it exemplifies a virtue.[69] Among other things, this means that we can't say that twiddling one's thumbs is a morally good action in the absence of special reasons for thinking that it serves some purpose. The evaluative meaning of "good" consists in the fact that it expresses attitudes and can be used to commend or induce actions.[70]

Can good and bad be plausibly construed as thick concepts? There are many different possible theories that construe good and bad as thick concepts, depending on what kinds of descriptive criteria we employ and what kind of evaluative meaning we ascribe to good and bad. Foot's theory combines (reductivist) descriptivism and emotivism. We could also imagine a theory that combines prescriptivism and descriptivism. Given the success of my earlier criticisms of emotivism and prescriptivism and the success of my arguments to show that being worthy of desire is at least a necessary condition of something's being good, the most plausible versions of the view that good and bad are thick concepts will combine (reductivist) descriptivism with the view that being good entails being worthy of desire. We can formulate this theory roughly as follows: "good" means "has (reductive descriptive property) d and is desirable for that reason." For any such theory, it makes sense to ask whether things with d are worthy of desire and whether they are the only things that are worthy of desire. We need to keep these questions open. As a matter of policy, we should always be willing to consider criticisms of our own normative standards. With this in mind, we recognize that it is possible that, in the future, we will come to reject the evaluations implicit in our thick concept of

the good. If this happens, we will want to be able to continue to make normative judgments, without inventing new concepts. We need a thin concept of
the good that we can continue to employ in making normative judgments, regardless of how we modify our views about what things are good or bad.

The preferred concept of value is one that allows us to describe coherently
and reflect on changes in our first-order normative judgments. We need a concept that will enable people to communicate with each other while leaving
open the questions "Are all things with d desirable?" and "Are things with d the
only things that are desirable?" Consider the following examples of thick normative concepts that embody objectionable evaluations. The terms "nigger"
and "honor" have both descriptive and evaluative meaning. The word "nigger"
only applies to people of (largely) African origin; it cannot be correctly applied
to pale, blond people of exclusively European descent. The word "nigger" also
expresses contempt for Africans. Those who don't think that Africans, qua
Africans, are worthy of contempt do not use the word "nigger." Honor is another example of a thick concept that many people have abandoned because
they reject the evaluations implicit in its use. The word "honor," as it is used
in some warrior societies, requires vengeance exacted by physical violence
to the exclusion of anything that we might call mercy or forgiveness. For
any thick concept that we employ, we should be open to criticisms of the
evaluations implicit in the concept and consider the possibility that they are
mistaken and cease employing the concept. Thus, we need a higher-level
thin concept in terms of which to make assessments of the evaluations implicit in thick concepts.

My concept of the good enables us to leave open the questions "Are all
things with d desirable?" and "Are things with d the only things that are desirable?" We can continue to make judgments about good and bad regardless of
how we answer these questions. If all of our moral concepts were of the thick
variety, dissenters who disagreed with the evaluations implicit in those concepts would need to coin new concepts (and somehow get others to understand them) in order to express their views. It would be extremely difficult to
dissent from the norms of a society that lacked a thin notion of the good (or a
thin version of some other basic normative concept, e.g., moral rightness). We
want a concept that not only permits dissent but fosters it. We must reject the
suggestion that we (generally) replace or ignore thin moral concepts (good,
ought, etc.) and instead focus on thick moral concepts (courage, honesty, etc.).

CHAPTER 7

Moral/Axiological Realism

Many of the arguments for and against particular theories of value discussed in chapters 1–5 presuppose either the truth or falsity of moral/axiological realism (AR). These arguments cannot be assessed apart from a thorough examination of realism. This chapter takes up the long deferred issue of realism. I define moral/axiological realism and then examine what I take to be the most important versions of realism, with particular attention to recent formulations of the theory. I shall argue that there are no compelling reasons to accept realism or any particular version of moral/axiological realism; I do not attempt to show that AR is false. I argue that recent versions of AR are not stated or developed in sufficient detail for us to be able to determine whether they are true or false. Proponents of what I call "Cornell realism" claim that the kinds of moral facts they posit enter into the best explanations we can give of certain human beliefs and behaviors. This, however, is, at best, a conjecture. At the present stage of the development of psychology, we are so far from having an adequate theory to explain human beliefs and actions that we cannot be sure what features an adequate theory would have. Since we don't know what the best possible psychological theory would look like, we cannot be sure that the best theory to explain human beliefs and human actions would make reference to moral facts. Several recent versions of British realism claim that moral properties can be directly perceived. Defenders of this kind of perceptual realism have not given an adequate explanation of the difference between veridical and non-veridical perceptions of moral qualities. I argue that, in the absence of such an explanation, there is no reason to accept the claim that ostensible moral perception involves the apprehension of independent moral facts about what is good and bad.

181

I. The Definition of Moral/Axiological Realism

1. Metaphysical Realism

Before trying to define moral/axiological realism, it would be useful to give a rough definition of metaphysical realism. A special case of metaphysical realism is realism about the physical world. Realism about the physical world is the view that the physical world exists independently of human (or other) minds; it exists independently of being the actual or possible object of knowledge or perception.[1] The notion of "mind-independence" distinguishes metaphysical realism from idealism or phenomenalism. Berkeley grants the existence of physical objects. He is a non-realist because he denies that physical objects are mind-independent. To be a realist about a certain kind of entity or fact x is: (i) to believe that x exists or that there are facts of type x, and (ii) to believe that those entities or facts are (in some appropriate sense) mind-independent. Here I follow Michael Dummett and David Brink. Dummett defines realism as follows:

> [T]he belief that statements of the disputed class possess an objective truth value, independently of our means of knowing it: they are true or false in virtue of a reality existing independently of us.[2]

Brink defines generic realism as follows:

> (1) There are facts or truths of kind *x*, (2) these facts or truths are independent of the evidence for them.[3]

Metaphysical non-realists needn't be solipsists, who deny the existence of "things in themselves" or deny that there is a way things are quite independent of our wants and beliefs. They only need to deny that the things referred to in ordinary language by physical-object terms, e.g., "tables," "chairs," and "atoms," are things in themselves that exist independently of us. Typically, metaphysical non-realists concede that there are things that exist completely independently of us but claim that these things are, in principle, unknowable to us. They deny that things about which it is possible for us to have knowledge exist completely independently of us. Hilary Putnam defends such a view in *Reason, Truth, and History* (Putnam attributes this same view to Kant). Putnam writes:

> [E]verything we say about an object is of the form: it is such as to affect *us* in such-and-such a way. *Nothing at all* we say about any object describes

the object as it is 'in itself', independently of its effect on *us*, on beings with our rational natures and our biological constitutions. It also follows that we cannot assume any similarity ('similitude', in Locke's English) between our idea of an object and whatever mind-independent reality may be ultimately responsible for our experience of that object. Our ideas of objects are not *copies* of mind-independent things. This is very much the way Kant describes the situation. He does not doubt that there is *some* mind-independent reality; for him this is a postulate of reason. He refers to the elements of this mind-independent reality in various terms: thing-in-itself *(Ding an sich)*; the noumenal objects or *noumena*; collectively, the *noumenal world.* But we can form no real conception of these noumenal things . . . (there is *somehow* a mind-independent 'ground' for our experience even if attempts to talk about it lead at once to nonsense.) At the same time, talk of ordinary 'empirical' objects is *not* talk of things-in-themselves, but only talk of things-for-us.[4]

2. Some Recent Definitions of Moral Realism

Most versions of moral realism follow the generic realist pattern noted above; they claim that: (1) there are moral facts, and (2) these facts are mind-independent. Robert Arrington takes moral realism to be the view that there are things in the world independent of the beliefs, conventions, and attitudes of human beings that make moral judgments true. Speaking with respect to the realist's notion of moral facts, he writes:

> More likely the person asking whether there are any moral facts wants to know whether, when such statements are true, they are true by virtue of there being something in the world (to which they correspond) which is independent of human conventions, beliefs and attitudes.[5]

Hare proposes a definition very similar to Arrington's:

> What then does 'ethical realism' mean? On the face of it, it means the view that moral qualities such as wrongness, and likewise moral facts such as the fact that an act was wrong, exist *in rerum natura*, so that, if one says that a certain act was wrong, one is saying that there existed, somehow, somewhere, this quality of wrongness, and that it had to exist *there* if *that* act were to be wrong. And one is saying that there also existed, somewhere, somehow, the fact that the act was wrong, which was brought into being by the person who did the wrong act.[6]

David Brink defines moral realism as follows:

(1) There are moral facts, or truths, and (2) these facts or truths are independent of the evidence for them.[7]

Mark Platts offers a definition very similar to Brink's; it contains something
very close to Brink's two conditions; his definition also includes another condition that makes semantic claims about the meaning of moral terms.
Speaking with respect to the "moral realist view" that he defends, Platts writes:

This thesis has two components: the first is that moral discourse is descriptive in character, that moral statements are descriptive in character, that
moral judgments are assertoric in force; the second is an identification of
the correct semantic treatment of descriptive discourses as the now-familiar
truth-theoretic treatment. . . . [A] full-blown moral realist view emerges
with the addition of two claims about the applicability of the notion of
truth to moral discourse: the first is that if a moral judgment is true, if it hits
its target, that is so in virtue of an independently existing moral reality; the
second is that the realistic truth conditions of a moral sentence, the conditions that determine its meaning, can transcend the recognitional capacities of those who can use and understand that sentence.[8]

Richard Boyd follows the definitions cited above in taking moral realism to
imply that there are independent moral facts, but adds a further epistemic
condition to his definition. He defines moral realism as follows:

1. Moral statements are the sorts of statements which are (or which express
propositions which are) true or false (approximately true, largely false,
etc.); 2. The truth or falsity (approximate truth . . .) of moral statements is
largely independent of our moral opinions, theories, etc.; 3. Ordinary
canons of moral reasoning—together with ordinary canons of scientific
and everyday factual reasoning—constitute, under many circumstances at
least, a reliable method for obtaining and improving (approximate) moral
knowledge.[9]

Standard definitions of realism and moral realism differ from Boyd's in that
they leave open epistemological questions about our knowledge of mind-
independent facts and thus are consistent with moral skepticism. Boyd and
Brink are both unclear in their formulation of the "independence condition."
They take moral facts to be independent of our *actual* beliefs or evidence,
but they don't explicitly say that they take realism to imply that moral facts

are independent of the beliefs or evidence we would have under ideal conditions. There are good reasons to think that they would want their definitions to be understood to imply that moral facts are independent of the beliefs or evidence we would have under ideal conditions. A definition of realism that only included the stipulation that moral facts are independent of our actual beliefs and evidence would count ideal-observer theories as versions of moral/axiological realism. This is surely contrary to the intentions of both Boyd and Brink. Standard versions of the ideal-observer theory say that something is good because an ideal observer (or an ideally rational person) would have a favorable attitude about it; they deny that things can be good or bad independently of the attitudes of an ideal observer. Realists such as Boyd and Brink want to say that things are good and bad and right and wrong independently of the attitudes of an ideal observer.

3. A Proposed Definition of Axiological Realism

I define axiological realism as follows:

> Judgments to the effect that something is non-instrumentally good or bad are objectively true or false, i.e., true or false for all rational beings. These judgments are true or false in virtue of the existence of "facts" about what things are non-instrumentally good or bad. These facts are logically independent of (and not constituted by) the beliefs, attitudes, emotions, or preferences of rational beings (and independent of the beliefs, attitudes, emotions, or preferences that rational beings would have in hypothetical situations).

On the above definition, a divine-command theory of morality would not count as a version of AR. If we modify the definition by replacing the expression "independent of (and not constituted by) the beliefs, attitudes, or desires of any rational beings" with "independent of (and not constituted by) the beliefs, attitudes, or desires of any *human beings*," then the divine-command theory would count as a version of AR. Arrington holds that moral realism commits one to the view that moral judgments are true or false in virtue of corresponding or not corresponding to reality. However, Brink rejects a correspondence theory of moral truth and claims that moral realism is compatible with a coherentist view of moral truth.[10]

The other versions of moral realism presented above entail (my) AR. AR captures at least part of what is generally implied by the term "moral realism." I believe that my definition does justice to what most contemporary philosophers mean by "moral realism," but it is not essential for my larger purposes in

186 VALUE AND THE GOOD LIFE

this book to claim this. My qualified defense of the desire-satisfaction theory of value in Interlude 2 depends on the assumption that, at the present stage of philosophical debate, no version of AR, *as I have defined it,* is worthy of our acceptance. I will not quarrel with those who describe themselves as "moral realists" or "axiological realists" but reject AR. For example, suppose that a proponent of the ideal-observer theory calls herself a moral realist. She defines moral realism as the view that there are moral facts that are independent of our *actual* beliefs and attitudes. It is not necessary for my purposes to reject or refute her views. She and I mean different things by the term "moral realism." This only requires that we be careful to avoid confusion over differences in our terminologies. It is not fruitful to debate about *the* correct definition of moral/axiological realism.

The theory of meaning defended in chapter 6 places constraints on what sorts of theories can count as versions of AR. In order to constitute a moral or normative fact, something must be a fact in virtue of which it is correct or incorrect to desire/pursue certain things. Normative facts (if they exist) constitute constraints on what it is correct for us to prefer. Suppose that an axiological realist claims that it is an objective fact that life 1 is better than life 2. In order for this to be true, it must be the case that I would be making some kind of mistake or error if I preferred 2 to 1, other things (such as the effect of my life on others) being equal. Moral/axiological facts are things that can determine the correctness of desires or preferences. Facts in virtue of which preferences cannot be said to be correct or incorrect do not warrant the label "moral/axiological facts."

According to AR, non-instrumental goodness is logically prior to the correctness of preferences. AR implies that it is correct for me to pursue certain ends *because they are good.* If axiological realism is true and it is an objective fact that life 1 is better than life 2, then I am constrained (on pain of error) to choose life 1 over life 2. According to the axiological realist, it is incorrect for me to prefer 2 to 1, *because* 1 is better than 2. By contrast, an ideal-desire or ideal-observer version of non-realism would say that life 1 is better than life 2 *because* I would prefer 1 to 2 if I were ideally rational (or because an ideal observer would prefer 1 to 2).

Given a (metaphysical) realist view about the truth or falsity of "factual statements," we can distinguish sharply between a factual statement's truth value and the reasonableness of accepting it. Given AR, it is at least possible that all or almost all of one's desires could be mistaken, even if they were informed and rational. Given AR, it might be rational for me to have desires that are nevertheless incorrect. On certain non-realist views this is impossible. Many non-realists hold that for a belief to be true/correct is simply for it to be rational (or ideally rational). Putnam claims that "truth is an *idealization* of rational acceptability."[11]

4. A General Strategy

I will examine a number of prominent versions of moral/axiological realism and argue that none is worthy of our acceptance; all are subject to serious doubts and criticisms. But, no matter how many versions of AR I have examined and criticized, it may still be possible for someone to formulate a better version of the theory—one immune to my doubts and criticisms. Thus my arguments do not show that AR is false. I only claim that, at the present stage of philosophical debate, there is no prominent version of AR worthy of our acceptance. There are no compelling reasons for thinking that AR is true. For my purposes in this book, it is sufficient to defend agnosticism about AR.[12] My strategy in this chapter assumes that any successful argument for the truth of AR would also be an argument for thinking that some *particular version* of AR is true. In the absence of reasons for accepting some particular version of AR, we should not assume that AR is true. There is no presumption, in the abstract, for thinking that AR is true. AR cannot be defended simply on the grounds that normative judgments purport to be objectively true. Certain kinds of non-realist theories (e.g., divine-command or divine-preference theories) are also consistent with the view that normative judgments are or purport to be true. Further, such arguments leave it open for non-realists to endorse an error theory or what Blackburn calls "quasi-realism" (rational-preference theories and ideal-observer theories are both quasi-realist theories).

Very generally, there are two ways of attacking AR (or some particular version of AR): (1) by showing that the qualities or entities posited by the theory don't exist or that we don't have reason to suppose that they exist, or (2) by showing that, even if the qualities or entities posited by the theory exist, they cannot plausibly be identified with goodness and badness. I employ both of these arguments in my criticisms of AR in this chapter.

II. Non-Naturalist Realism

The two most important and influential versions of non-naturalist AR are Moore's view that goodness and badness are simple unanalyzable (non-natural) qualities and the view (defended by Broad, Ewing, and Ross) that moral/normative facts are constituted by (non-natural) relational properties of "fittingness" that hold between the subjects of normative judgments and attitudes about them.

1. Moore

Moore holds that goodness and badness are simple, irreducible properties of things. They are not "natural" properties like redness. Goodness and badness cannot be perceived or apprehended through the five senses. Moore claims, however, that we can have direct intuitive knowledge of goodness and badness. Moore's theory is open to two serious objections: (1) there is no good reason to think that the simple non-natural properties he describes exist; (2) even if there are non-natural properties of the sort Moore posits, it is doubtful that they should be identified with goodness and badness.

Moore says that he "intuits" a simple non-natural property of goodness. For example, he reports that, when he considers or imagines unperceived beauty in "complete isolation" from any of its ordinary causes or effects, he "sees" or intuits that it is intrinsically good. I don't intuit any simple, irreducible non-natural property when I contemplate good things. I have no direct evidence for the existence of such a property. I am very puzzled by Moore's description of goodness as a simple property like yellow. If I look at a white piece of paper, a white shirt, and a picture of Frosty the snowman I "see" a simple irreducible property that all of these things share in virtue of which they are white. On the other hand, if I think of three non-instrumentally good things: sensual pleasure, intellectual pleasure, and benevolence, I fail to "see" any simple non-natural property that they share and in virtue of which they are all good. (My list of good things is controversial, but the same thought experiment works even if the reader substitutes an alternative list of diverse kinds of non-instrumentally good things.) I have asked numerous groups of students to perform this same thought experiment. Almost all of them report the same results. I am confident that the same is true of most of my readers.

Moore and I report very different experiences. There is, however, no great difference between the objects of our thoughts and reflections; we have reflected on the goodness or badness of the same things, e.g., unperceived beauty. One of the following must be the case: (i) I fail to perceive a genuine property of many of the things with which I am acquainted, or (ii) Moore projects on to things qualities that they don't really possess, properties that he takes to warrant or justify his attitudes about those things.

Moore is committed to the view that he is able to discern certain features of reality that I (and most other people) are unable to discern. Sometimes certain people are unable to perceive features of reality that other people are capable of perceiving. Normal-sighted people perceive features of the physical world that blind and colorblind people are unable to perceive. To be blind or colorblind is to lack perceptual abilities that others possess. There is no comparable evidence that supports Moore's view. Blindness is an inability to perceive genuine features of the world. A sighted person crossing a busy street knows things that an unassisted blind person cannot know. It is not clear that my failure to "see" the non-natural property of goodness is an inability to see features of reality. It is possible to give a thorough physiological explanation of the causes of blindness and colorblindness, and there are clear tests for determining who is colorblind and who is not. However, there is no similar explanation of the alleged fact that some people are able to perceive goodness and others cannot; nor is there a comparable test for moral blindness. Further, it is possible to tell a plausible story of how and why Moore's purported intuition of goodness involves a projection of his own views onto the world. Moore was convinced that goodness was a property of things, and that it couldn't be a natural property. Having convinced himself that goodness and badness had to be non-natural properties, he proceeded to "see" them. It is more reasonable to think that Moore is projecting his attitudes onto the world than that he possesses powers of perception that most other people lack.

The reported intuitions of Moore and others do not provide us with adequate evidence for the existence of the non-natural property of goodness. Alternatively, someone might claim that goodness is a non-natural property whose existence is not directly experienced or intuited but, rather, inferred. But, in the absence of a clearer characterization of this property and some reason for thinking that its existence is required in order to explain our moral experience, we don't have adequate reasons for thinking that such properties exist.

Even if there are simple, unanalyzable properties of the sort that Moore describes, they cannot plausibly be identified with goodness and badness—they are not properties in virtue of which desires and attitudes are correct. To say that something is non-instrumentally good implies that we have reasons to choose or prefer it.[13] To say that the pleasure I obtain from drinking a glass of wine is intrinsically good is to say that the pleasure is a worthy or appropriate object of desire and that, *other things equal,* it is worth trying to obtain the pleasure. But it is a mystery why all of this should be so, given Moore's theory. Suppose that a certain act will result in the production of the non-natural property Moore calls goodness. I can't even form a clear notion of this mysterious and elusive property. I don't care whether or not my actions produce it. Further, there is nothing unreasonable about my indifference. If Moore is right about what goodness and badness are, then I don't care whether things are good or bad; and I am not guilty of any kind of mistake or irrationality for not caring.[14] If Moore's view were correct, the fact that something is good would give us no reason to promote its existence or occurrence. But the fact that something is good implies that we have reason to pursue it. This argument can be summarized as follows:

1. If something is non-instrumentally good, then (other things equal) one has reasons to promote its existence or occurrence.

2. Something's having the non-natural property Moore calls "goodness" does not give us any reason to promote it. (It is perfectly reasonable to be *indifferent* to the occurrence or non-occurrence of this mysterious non-natural property.)

Therefore:

Moore's non-naturalism is false (goodness is not identical with the kind of non-natural property that Moore claims it is).

2. The Ewing-Broad-Ross Theory: Normative Properties as Relational Properties

Ewing defends a much more plausible version of realism than Moore. He holds that moral/axiological facts consist in relations of "fittingness" or "appropriateness" that hold between objects and particular sorts of attitudes about them. Non-realist theories such as the ideal-observer theory also make claims about the fittingness or correctness of attitudes. According to the ideal-observer theory, an attitude is correct or fitting provided that it would be shared by all who are fully informed and impartial. This is not what non-naturalist realists such as Ewing have in mind. They take fittingness to be a relation holding between the attitude and the object itself. Ewing holds that the relation of fittingness is unanalyzable and self-evident to intuition.

Certain characteristics are such that the fitting response to whatever possesses them is a pro-attitude, and that is all there is to it.[15]

Broad and Ross defend a very similar view about the nature of moral rightness. Broad writes:

The fundamental fact seems to me to be that rightness is a relational characteristic, and not a pure quality. When I say that *x* is right I am saying something about its relations to certain other terms. Rightness is a species of fittingness or appropriateness, and a term which is 'fitting' must be fitting *to* something. The above, I believe, is a true statement about right-ness, but it is not a definition of it. For, so far as I can see, rightness is quite a unique kind of appropriateness, just as red is a quite unique kind of colour.[16]

Ross defines moral rightness as follows:

'[R]ight' means 'suitable', in a unique and indefinable way which we may express by the phrase 'morally suitable', to the situation in which the agent finds himself.[17]

In this passage, Ross is concerned with the meaning of the word "right." Since he also thinks that the word "right" refers to a genuine property of things that exists independently of our actual or possible beliefs and attitudes about those things, he is a realist. Thus, this passage is a description of what he takes to be moral facts. The Ewing-Broad-Ross theory has many virtues. It accounts for the practical, action-guiding character of normative judgments; it also explains the supervenience of moral/normative properties on natural properties.

I agree that particular sorts of attitudes *can* be described as fitting or not fit-ting certain objects. But it is unclear that this fittingness or unfittingness con-sists in a simple, unanalyzable relation that we immediately apprehend. The alternative thesis that we are just projecting relations of fittingness onto the world rather than perceiving something that is really there is supported by the phenomenon of disagreement. People often disagree about whether a certain attitude is appropriate for a certain object. Ewing is committed to the view that many people incorrectly perceive relations of fittingness. He owes us an explanation of how to distinguish between correct and incorrect perceptions of fittingness. If relations of fittingness were features of the world and most hu-mans were able to perceive them, then we should expect there to be far more agreement over normative questions than there is. (At least we should expect there to be more agreement about which attitudes are appropriate in cases in which people agree about the "factual" properties of the things in question.) In the absence of evidence for thinking that many or most people are defi-cient in their ability to perceive normative properties (evidence of the sort that we have to show that deaf people are deficient in their ability to perceive sound), it is more reasonable to deny that unanalyzable relations of fittingness are part of the furniture of the universe than to think that some people have special perceptual powers to perceive moral facts that most other people lack. (For further arguments on this point see 7.IV.)

I haven't shown that the Ewing-Broad-Ross version of non-naturalism is false. I have only argued that its proponents have not given adequate reasons for accepting it. They need to give us a plausible theory of correct and incorrect perception of the relation of fittingness and some explanation of the causal mechanisms involved in that perception.

III. Cornell Realism

1. Cornell Realism and the Open-Question Argument

"Cornell realism" is so named because its main adherents are associated with Cornell University, either as faculty or students. A salient feature of Cornell realism (I am thinking particularly of Boyd, Brink, and Sturgeon) is that, while it claims that moral properties are identical with (or "constituted by") non-normative or natural properties, it does not take statements to the effect that a particular natural property constitutes a particular moral property to be analytic. Cornell realists claim that their view is invulnerable to objections of the sort that Moore raises in *Principia Ethica*.

Before examining Cornell realism, it would be useful to briefly sketch Moore's arguments against ("analytic") naturalism. As I noted earlier in chapter 6.IV, Moore's arguments in chapter 1 of *Principia Ethica* are directed against naturalism and the "naturalistic fallacy." Moore's choice of the terms "naturalism" and "non-naturalism" is unfortunate. If successful, his arguments not only show that good can't be defined in terms of "natural" qualities such as pleasure or the satisfaction of desire, they also show that "good" cannot be defined at all in non-normative terms.[18] Moore claims that "good" is indefinable:

> Or, if I am asked "How is good to be defined?" my answer is that it cannot be defined, and that is all that I have to say about it.[19]

In claiming that "good" cannot be defined, Moore means that the word "good" refers to a property (goodness) that cannot be analyzed or broken down into constituent properties or elements. By contrast, the property of being a horse can be analyzed into constituent properties. To be a horse is to be "a hoofed quadruped of the genus Equus."[20] Like the property of being yellow, goodness is a simple, unanalyzable, property. Moore's "open-question" argument can be summarized roughly as follows. Consider any definition of "good" that claims that goodness is identical with a complex property (P). It will always make sense to ask if P is good.

> [W]hatever definition be offered, it may always be asked, with significance, of the complex so defined, whether it is itself good.[21]

But it makes no sense to ask whether P is P, and it makes no sense to deny that good is good. Therefore, good cannot be identical with P. Moore says that even if there are universally true statements about what things are good, they cannot be used to define "good," since their denial or negation would not be self-contradictory.[22] For example, even if it were true that pleasure, and pleasure alone, is good, we could not define good as pleasure, because it is not self-contradictory to deny that pleasure is good, and it is not self-contradictory to deny that only pleasure is good. According to Moore, no definition of "good" in terms of "X" can be correct unless is it self-contradictory to deny that X is good. This commits Moore to the view that good can't be identical with P, unless statements to the effect that P is good and statements to the effect that what is good is P are analytic.

Moore's argument assumes that if two terms, "a" and "b," refer to properties, they cannot have the same meaning unless the statements "What is a is b" and "What is b is a" are analytic. Many contemporary realists contend that this assumption has been refuted by Putnam's discussion of natural kinds. According to Putnam, there are true identity statements about natural kinds, even though such statements are not analytic. For example, water is H_2O (the property of being water is identical with that of being H_2O), even though the statement that water is H_2O is synthetic.[23] Cornell realists concede that statements identifying moral properties with natural properties are not analytic. Sturgeon holds that moral facts are identical with natural facts, but he does not take statements asserting the identity of moral facts and natural facts to be analytic.[24] Brink says that moral properties are constituted by natural properties in the same way that a table is constituted by atoms, or water is constituted by H_2O.[25] Brink claims that the constitution of moral facts by natural facts is a "synthetic moral necessity."[26] Boyd holds that moral properties are physical properties but claims that moral properties cannot be analytically defined in terms of physical properties.[27]

2. The Explanatory Significance of Moral Facts

The most influential and widely discussed arguments for and against Cornell realism center on the question of whether or not moral facts are necessary for explanatory purposes. Recent discussion of this question begins with Gilbert Harman's book *The Nature of Morality*.[28] Harman argues that it is unnecessary to posit the existence of moral facts in order to explain phenomena.

> Nevertheless, observation plays a role in science that it does not play in ethics. The difference is that you need to make assumptions about certain physical facts to explain the occurrence of the observations that support a

scientific theory, but you do not seem to need to make assumptions about any moral facts to explain the occurrence of the so-called moral observations I have been talking about. In the moral case, it would seem that you need only make assumptions about the psychology or moral sensibility of the person making the moral observation. In the scientific case, theory is tested against the world.[29]

Several prominent American realists (including Boyd, Brink, Railton, and Sturgeon) argue that moral facts are (or are likely to be) part of our best explanation of certain phenomena. Sturgeon claims that moral facts help to explain certain actions performed by individuals (e.g., Hitler killed millions of Jews, because he was morally depraved)[30] and also help to explain why we have certain beliefs (the unusual badness or wrongness of British and French slavery in North America explains the beliefs of those in the antislavery movement that emerged in Britain, France, and the English- and French-speaking parts of North America during the late eighteenth and nineteenth centuries).[31]

The realist philosophers in question have not made an adequate case for the explanatory necessity of moral facts. It is possible to give perfectly good explanations of human actions and moral beliefs without invoking the existence of moral facts. A non-realist explanation of Hitler's actions might go as follows:

Hitler was a very bitter and angry person. Because of various false beliefs about Jews (most importantly his belief that Jews were responsible for Germany's defeat in World War I)[32] he found hatred for the Jews to be a satisfying way of releasing his pent-up hostility and anger. His moral beliefs did not place any bounds or restraints on his expression of that hatred.

We can explain the emergence of the large-scale moral opposition to slavery in nineteenth-century Britain, France, and English- and French-speaking parts of North America roughly as follows:

Certain moral principles that imply that slavery is wrong (e.g., the principle that all human beings have a right to liberty) first became widely accepted in English- and French-speaking countries during the eighteenth and nineteenth centuries. The principles espoused by the leaders of the American and French Revolutions imply that all forms of slavery are wrong, and, despite considerable obfuscation and self-deception on this point, this came to be generally acknowledged. Why didn't moral opposition to slavery among people who were not themselves victims of slavery arise on a comparable scale in other slave-holding societies in Latin America, Africa, the Middle East, and the Orient? Slavery, as practiced in these other times and places, did not conflict (or did not conflict sharply) with publicly acknowledged moral principles in the way that it did in the French- and English-speaking parts of North America in the eighteenth and nineteenth centuries. The other societies did not endorse, nor were they founded on, moral principles asserting the right of all "men" to liberty. The extreme psychological and physical cruelty of Anglo-French slavery, in particular the dehumanization of its African victims, also aroused the sympathies of people and helped to create conscientious opposition to slavery.[33]

Here the reader might object that the details of these historical events are irrelevant to arguments about the truth of moral realism. I disagree. The need for moral facts cannot be posited in the abstract. Realists can't plausibly argue that we need to posit moral facts for explanatory purposes unless they can point to *particular phenomena* whose explanation requires the existence of (particular) moral facts. Thus, it is important to examine the details of the examples Cornell realists take to be the best evidence for their view.

3. Sturgeon's Counterfactual Test

Sturgeon suggests that we can test the claim that moral facts are relevant to explaining certain phenomena (in this case, Hitler's actions) by asking the following counterfactual question: Imagine that the moral facts in question did not exist, would the phenomena they are alleged to explain still have occurred? Sturgeon claims that the answer is no: if the moral facts in question did not exist, the events that they explain would not have occurred. If Hitler hadn't been morally depraved, he wouldn't have started Word War II, and he would not have ordered the Holocaust.

Harman's thesis implies that the supposed moral fact of Hitler's being morally depraved is irrelevant to the explanation of Hitler's doing what he did. (For we may suppose that if it explains his doing what he did, it also helps explain, at greater remove, Harman's belief and mine in his moral depravity.) To assess this claim, we need to conceive a situation in which Hitler was *not* morally depraved and consider the question whether in that situation he would still have done what he did. My answer is that he would not, and this answer relies on a (not very controversial) moral view: that in any world at all like the actual one, only a morally depraved person could have initiated a world war, ordered "the final solution," and done any number of other things Hitler did. That is why I believe that if Hitler hadn't been morally depraved, he wouldn't have done those things, and hence that the fact of his moral depravity is relevant to an explanation of what he did.[34]

Sturgeon claims that if the natural facts that constitute Hitler's moral depravity, e.g., his cruelty, did not exist, he would not have done the things he did. But Harman would not accept this reading of the counterfactual test. Harman wants us to consider the situation in which all of the natural facts constituting a moral fact remain the same but the moral fact does not exist. We must imagine a case in which Hitler has all of the same natural properties he actually has but is not morally depraved. Sturgeon continues:

> But Harman, it is fairly clear, intends for us *not* to rely on any such moral views in evaluating his counterfactual claim. His claim is not that if the action had not been one of deliberate cruelty (or had otherwise differed in whatever way would be required to remove its wrongness), you would still have thought it wrong. It is, instead, that if the action were one of deliberate, pointless cruelty, but this *did not make it wrong*, you would still have thought it was wrong. And to return to the example of Hitler's moral character, the counterfactual claim that Harman will need in order to defend a comparable conclusion about that case is not that if Hitler had been, for example, humane and fair-minded, free of nationalistic pride and racial hatred, he would still have done exactly as he did. It is, rather, that if Hitler's psychology, and anything else about the situation that could strike us as morally relevant, had been exactly as it was, but this had *not constituted moral depravity*, he still would have done exactly what he did.[35]

If we imagine cases in which all the natural facts constituting Hitler's moral depravity are the same but Hitler is not morally depraved, the same phenomena supposedly explained by the fact of his depravity would still occur (he would still begin wars and order the deaths of millions of innocent people). But Sturgeon contends that the antecedent of this counterfactual statement is necessarily false. It is necessarily false that something could have all the same natural properties that it now has but not have the same moral properties. (For example, it is necessarily false that Hitler could have all the same natural properties he actually had and not be morally depraved.)

> Now the antecedents of these two conditionals are puzzling. For one thing, both are, I believe, necessarily false. I am fairly confident, for example, that Hitler really was morally depraved, and since I also accept the view that moral features supervene on more basic natural properties, I take this to imply that there is no possible world in which Hitler has just the personality he in fact did, in just the situation he was in, but is not morally depraved.[36]

4. The Inconclusiveness of Arguments about Explanation

The main point of disagreement between Harman and Sturgeon is their understanding of the antecedents of conditional statements such as the following:

> If Hitler had possessed all of the natural properties he in fact possessed but his having those properties did not constitute his being morally depraved, then he still would have started World War II and ordered the Holocaust.

Sturgeon claims that the antecedent of this statement is necessarily false; Harman denies that the antecedent is necessarily false. Sturgeon claims that it is impossible that Hitler could have possessed the natural properties that he possessed (e.g., being cruel and being a mass murderer) without being morally depraved. (More generally, he assumes that it is impossible that something could possess certain natural properties, x, y, and z, without possessing moral property m.) Sturgeon's argument *assumes* that x, y, and z constitute m. Unless x, y, and z constitute m, there is no reason to suppose that it's impossible that something could possess x, y, and z without possessing m. However, the claim that moral facts are constituted by natural facts in this way is the central tenet of Cornell realism. Sturgeon's discussion of the counterfactual test presupposes the truth of Cornell realism. Harman claims that Hitler could have possessed exactly the same natural properties that he possessed without this constituting the fact that he is depraved. More generally, Harman *assumes* that it is possible that something could have natural qualities x, y, and z (which realists take to be constitutive of a certain moral property m) but not have m. His discussion of the counterfactual test assumes that Cornell realism is false — it assumes that natural properties (x, y, and z) do not constitute moral property (m).

In their discussions of the counterfactual test, Sturgeon assumes the truth of Cornell realism and Harman assumes its falsity. Both arguments *seem* to be question-begging. But Sturgeon is not trying to show that Cornell realism is true (if he were, then his argument *would be* question-begging). Rather, he is trying to answer the objection that moral facts are irrelevant for explanatory purposes. He is trying to show that moral facts can be part of acceptable explanations of human behavior. In order to show this, it is perfectly acceptable to show what follows on the assumption that moral realism is true. (His argument is roughly that if there are moral facts of the sort that his theory postulates, then they can enter into explanations of human behavior.) In discussing counterfactuals of the sort stated above, Harman assumes that Cornell realism is false. This would beg the question if his arguments about explanation were trying to show that Cornell realism is false. But the immediate aim of his argument is only to show that the postulation of moral facts is *unnecessary* for purposes of explanation. For this purpose, it is perfectly legitimate for him to assume that realism is false. He only needs to show that the explanations available to us on the supposition that realism is false are at least as good as the explanations realists propose.

To some extent, Harman and Sturgeon are arguing at cross-purposes. Sturgeon is trying to show that there are no good reasons for thinking that moral facts can't enter into explanations of things. Sturgeon does not try to show that moral facts are part of the best explanatory scheme:

> [M]any moral explanations appear to be good explanations, or compo-
> nents in good explanations, that are not obviously undermined by anything
> else that we know. My suspicion, in fact, is that moral facts are needed in
> the sense explained, that they will turn out to belong in our best overall ex-
> planatory picture of the world, even in the long run, but I shall not attempt
> to establish that here.[37]

He only claims that Harman and others have not adequately made the case against the possibility of moral explanations:

> So, I concede that it *could* turn out, for anything I say here, that moral ex-
> planations are all defective and should be discarded. What I shall try to
> show is merely that many moral explanations look reasonable enough to be
> in the running; and, more specifically, that nothing Harman says provides
> any reason for thinking that they are not.[38]

But Harman doesn't deny that moral facts, if they exist, could help to explain things. He only claims that postulating moral facts is *unnecessary* for explanatory purposes. Sturgeon may have answered the objection that moral facts are "irrelevant" to the explanation of phenomena; he may have succeeded in showing that moral facts (if they exist) can enter into acceptable explanations. He does nothing, however, to counter Harman's claim that moral facts are *un-necessary* from an explanatory point of view.[39] Not only does he fail to answer this objection but an acceptable answer is not available to him, given his version of realism. If moral facts are constituted by natural facts in the way that Cornell realists claim, then moral properties seem to be dispensable for explanatory purposes.[40] Natural properties seem to be doing all of the work in the explanations in question. Nothing is explained by assuming that moral properties are *identical* to natural properties. The best explanations of human behavior available to us at the present time do not make any use of claims to the effect that moral facts are constituted by natural facts. If the realist claims that moral facts are something over and above the natural facts constituting them, then it is questionable whether the other properties that she posits exist, and it is a mystery how those properties cause or explain observable phenomena. Cornell realists don't posit any suspect entities, but their claims about the "constitution" of moral facts by natural facts don't add anything to our existing non-moral explanations.

5. Abductive Arguments for Scientific Realism Contrasted with Abductive Arguments for Moral Realism

It would be instructive to compare abductive arguments for moral realism with abductive arguments for scientific realism. Abductive arguments for (and against) moral realism are weaker than abductive arguments for (and against) scientific realism.

At least some of the arguments for scientific realism that appeal to the truth of realism as the best explanation of the many regularities of our experience are stronger than analogous arguments for moral realism. The entities postulated by scientific realists play a role in sophisticated causal and explanatory theories that have undeniable predictive value. Those who reject scientific realism might contend that they have explanatory and predictive theories that are equally good or better, but that some realist scientific theories have considerable explanatory and predictive powers is beyond any reasonable doubt. By contrast, moral realists have not yet proffered theories developed in sufficient detail to be very useful in explaining or predicting the relevant (moral) phenomena. Consider the debate about the existence of unobservable theoretical entities such as atoms and atomic particles. The alleged causal properties of these entities are very precisely defined. Atomic theory enables us to make predictions and explanations that we could not otherwise make, e.g., predictions about readings on Geiger counters and predictions that it is possible to build enormously powerful bombs with uranium. To date, no moral-realist theory has anything like the explanatory or predictive power of atomic theory. The explanatory and predictive powers of realist atomic theories are much greater than the explanatory and predictive powers of existing moral-realist theories of human cognition and behavior.

I am not claiming that the explanatory and predictive weaknesses of moral-realist theories are evidence for moral non-realism. Psychological theories that make no reference to moral facts also are very sketchy and lack explanatory and predictive power. Given that the explanations and predictions afforded by existing psychological theories are less satisfactory than those afforded by modern physics, the explanatory and predictive powers of those theories afford a weaker basis for arguments for *(or against)* moral realism than the explanatory and predictive powers that the theories of nuclear physics provide for or against scientific realism. We are so very far from having an adequate theory of human behavior that it is impossible to be sure what the best possible theories of human behavior would be like. Therefore, any claims to the effect that the best possible theory for explaining human behavior does or does not countenance moral facts are highly conjectural.

Realists about atomic theory claim that atoms and electrons exist. Non-realists about atomic theory claim at least one of the following: (1) atoms and electrons do not exist, (2) we cannot know that atoms and electrons exist, or (3) statements to the effect that atoms and electrons exist are not meaningful. Realists and non-realists about atomic theory disagree about the existence of (or our knowledge of, or the meaningfulness of statements about) certain entities. Some debates about moral realism concern the existence of disputed entities or properties. Moore asserts the existence of a simple non-natural property of goodness. Moral non-realists (and many realists as well) deny the existence of this property. However, the debate between Cornell realists and non-realists is much different. Cornell realists do not posit any entities or properties whose existence anti-realists deny. Cornell realists and anti-realists disagree about whether natural facts, which they both countenance, are equivalent to or constitutive of moral facts. This debate is more analogous to debates in the philosophy of biology and social sciences between reductivists and non-reductivists than to debates about the existence of unobservable entities such as atoms and electrons. Reductivists deny the existence of such things as species or labor unions on the grounds that they are explanatorily impotent. Reference to species is claimed to be in principle unnecessary for explanatory purposes because any individual of a species is token-identical with its physical composition; reference to labor unions is claimed to be unnecessary for explanatory purposes because a labor union is nothing over and above the individual human beings who constitute it.

There is at least one important difference between debates about reductionism in the biological and social sciences and the debate about Cornell realism. In the case of the entities whose existence is denied by reductivists, there is no serious doubt about *what* constitutes them (or what would constitute them if they existed). We know which physical objects constitute the species tigers. We know which individuals constitute the membership of the United Auto Workers. The reference of such terms as "tigers" and "United Auto Workers" is clear. But the reference of normative terms such as "good" and "bad" and "right" and "wrong" is highly controversial. It is unclear and highly controversial which natural states constitute moral facts. Which natural states constitute something's being good or bad? Which natural facts constitute an action's being right or wrong? The answers to these questions are fiercely debated by philosophers and non-philosophers. The terms of the debate between Cornell realists and their opponents are much less clear than the terms of debates about reductionism in the biological and social sciences.

6. The Need for More Fully Developed Realist Explanatory Theories

For all that I have shown, realist moral facts might be part of the best possible explanations of many phenomena. In order to show that the best explanatory scheme countenances realist moral facts, the realist would need to proffer a sketch of the kind of theory he thinks best explains human cognition and behavior—a theory of human nature that uses moral facts to explain human cognition and human action. (We will not have good reasons to accept the Cornell realist's claim that realist moral facts are part of the best theory for explaining human behavior until he gives us a clearer picture of the kind of theory that he claims will ultimately prove to be the best. Otherwise, we have no clear idea of what we are buying into if we accept his claims about explanation.) The kind of theory Cornell realists need to sketch must include an account of the causal mechanisms by which moral facts influence our beliefs and our behavior. At the present time, we cannot be sure what features an adequate psychological theory would have (nor can we be sure that such a theory is even possible). The claims of both realists and anti-realists will need to be rethought in the light of future work in psychology. Let me give an example to help drive home this point. Consider the following:

1. Very unequal distributions of wealth and property within a society can be just, even if they don't benefit the least advantaged members of the society.

2. Very unequal distributions of wealth and property within a society cannot be just unless they benefit the least advantaged members of the society.

Those who accept realism about questions of distributive justice and injustice must hold that either 1 or 2 is true. But it is unclear that the assumption that 1 is true has any explanatory significance. What things would the fact that 1 is true explain that can't be explained if 2 is true? Should we expect there to be less resentment about economic inequalities that don't benefit the least advantaged if 1 is true? If so, why? In virtue of what is 1 true rather than 2 (or vice versa)? Do true moral beliefs have greater causal efficacy than false moral beliefs? If so, why? In their work to date, Cornell realists have not adequately addressed questions of this sort, much less answered them cogently. Realists need to give an account of the causal efficacy of moral facts. In particular, they need to show why its being *true* (in some realist sense of "true") that something is right or wrong (or just or unjust) explains certain phenomena that are not explained by the fact that some people *believe* that it is right or wrong (or just or unjust). In the absence of such an account, we have no reason to think that moral facts are part of the best explanatory scheme.

There is another important respect in which we lack an adequate basis to assess the truth or falsity of Cornell realism. Any psychological theory that employs moral facts to explain human behavior presupposes (a realist version of) a first-order ethical theory. An explanatory theory that invokes notions of wrongness and justice presupposes a theory about *which* natural properties constitute *which* moral properties (or a theory that makes claims about which moral properties supervene upon which natural properties). The realist needs to justify his own particular first-order views as opposed to alternative views. A solution to the problems of normative ethics is a precondition of any attempt to construct a realist explanatory theory. Among other things, realists who appeal to the concept of justice would have to justify the claim that justice is constituted by (or supervenes upon) actions and policies that maximize expected pleasure or else justify the claim that justice is not constituted by (or does not supervene upon) actions and policies that maximize expected pleasure.

At the present time, the arguments about explanation don't conclusively support either realism or antirealism. The work of Cornell realists justifies a research program to try to construct a (moral realist) theory of human psychology, but we cannot assume in advance that this research program will succeed.

7. Explanation and Justification

In a recent paper David Copp asks whether the explanatory success of moral concepts would (if it could be demonstrated) constitute any kind of answer to moral skepticism.[41] His answer is no. Even if moral facts and moral concepts have considerable explanatory utility and are part of the best explanatory schemes for the world, it would not follow that moral theories or moral standards that posit them are justified. Copp offers several plausible examples to illustrate the difference between justification and explanatory success. We can sometimes explain someone's behavior by saying that he is rude, but the success of such explanations doesn't justify prevailing standards of etiquette. Copp's arguments are addressed to the issue of moral skepticism. But they also bear on AR. If successful, Copp's arguments show that AR, as I define it, cannot be defended by appealing to explanatory considerations. AR posits the existence of moral facts that justify preferences and/or attitudes—only facts that justify attitudes can count as moral/axiological facts. If they exist, moral facts of the sort that realists posit imply that certain moral standards are justified or correct. (Copp uses the term "moral fact" in a looser sense; moral facts in his sense don't necessarily justify standards or attitudes.) For my purposes, it is not necessary to assess the cogency of Copp's arguments about explanation and justification. I have argued that, at present, the appeal to the explanatory significance of moral facts does not give us adequate reasons to accept Cornell realism. The success of Copp's arguments would allow us to say something stronger, but it is perfectly consistent with my view.

8. Other Arguments for Cornell Realism

I now want to consider several other arguments for the truth of Cornell realism proposed by David Brink in *Moral Realism and the Foundations of Ethics*.
    a. *Amoralism and Immoralism.* One of Brink's main arguments for realism is that, unlike internalist non-cognitivist theories, realism is able to allow for the conceptual possibility of amoralism and immoralism. An amoralist is someone who accepts moral judgments but is unmoved by them; an immoralist is someone who accepts moral judgments but is motivated, other things equal, to act contrary to them. Brink takes internalism to be the view that a necessary condition of one's accepting a favorable (unfavorable) moral judgment about something is that one actually have a favorable (unfavorable) attitude about it or be disposed to act so as to bring it about (not bring it about). He rehearses these arguments at three different points in his book (pp. 46–50, 59–60, and 83–86) and sets considerable store by them. Brink's argument about amoralism is summarized in the following passage:

> According to the internalist, then, it must be conceptually impossible for someone to recognize a moral consideration and remain unmoved. The fact raises a problem for internalism; internalism makes *the amoralist* conceptually impossible.[42]

Brink also argues that internalism makes immoralism a conceptual impossibility. The internalist might try to answer Brink by denying that there are any genuine cases of amoralism and immoralism; apparent cases of amoralism and immoralism involve people who make moral judgments in an "inverted-commas sense." Brink considers this reply in the following passage:

> We use terms that have a moral sense (e.g., 'good', 'bad', 'right', 'wrong') in a nonmoral, inverted-commas sense when we use these terms, not to express our own moral views but to convey the moral views of others with whom we do not agree. The internalist relies on the possibility of inverted-commas usage of moral language, and replies that people can be unmoved

by considerations that are only *conventionally regarded* as moral, but insists that a genuine amoralist is inconceivable. Apparent immoralists . . . remain unmoved not by what they regard as moral considerations but only by what *others* regard as moral considerations; their own views about morality are really completely different from conventional views.[43]

No doubt some apparent cases of immoralism involve an inverted-commas use of moral terms. But there is no reason to suppose that all such cases can be accounted for in this way. It is logically possible for someone to be indifferent to moral norms he accepts:

> It is simply unclear why we should assume that the person who professes indifference to what she insists are moral requirements is confusedly using moral language in inverted commas or mistaken about what morality requires. We can imagine someone who regards what we take to be moral demands as moral demands—not simply as conventional moral demands— and yet remains unmoved.[44]

I agree with Brink that internalists cannot make sense of amoralism and immoralism. I also agree that it is a serious objection to internalist theories of morality that they make amoralism and immoralism conceptually impossible.[45] But, even if they are completely successful, Brink's arguments against internalism do not support moral realism. Brink's argument rests on the false supposition that all non-realists are committed to "internalism" in his sense of the term. At least some non-realist theories, for example, ideal-desire or ideal-observer theories, are not internalist theories in Brink's sense and allow for the conceptual possibility of amoralism and immoralism. The ideal-observer theory allows for the possibility that someone could think that something was right or wrong but not care. I might recognize that were I an ideal observer, I would do more to help others but not care that this is the case and not be moved to do more to help others in light of this knowledge.

b. *The Possibility of Error.* Brink argues that non-realists cannot adequately account for the fact that moral judgments can be mistaken.[46] On the face of it, this seems false. Any non-realist theory that requires that moral judgments meet certain standards of rationality, e.g., having all relevant information, permits us to say that moral judgments can be mistaken. Brink concedes this point but claims that non-realism cannot account for the fact that our moral beliefs and the attitudes they express could be mistaken even if they were consistent and fully informed.[47] This argument overlooks the fact that certain non-realist versions of the ideal-observer theory hold that being consistent and fully informed is not sufficient for being an ideal observer.[48] These theories imply that moral judgments and the attitudes they express can be mistaken even if they are consistent and fully informed; they imply that moral judgments can be mistaken if the person who holds them lacks other essential features of an ideal observer. Here I suspect that Brink would want to modify his argument and claim that moral judgments can be mistaken even if the person who holds them is rational in any proposed sense of "rational" that is consistent with non-realism. But this argument simply begs the question against non-realist theories, according to which there are no moral facts in terms of which attitudes can be correct or mistaken independently of their rationality. So modified, Brink's argument assumes precisely what non-realists deny. A bit later on, Brink attacks non-realist accounts of moral truth by arguing that truth cannot be identified with justified or rational belief.[49] But, again, this simply begs the question. One of the central questions at issue between realists and non-realists is whether moral judgments are true in some sense that is independent of canons of rationality. Brink can't defend realism simply by *assuming* that moral judgments are true in the way that realists claim.

IV. Contemporary British Realism

Several distinctive versions of moral realism are prominent in contemporary British philosophy. These theories are very different from Cornell realism and merit examination.

1. Moral Properties as Secondary Properties

John McDowell and Mark Platts hold that moral properties are "secondary properties." Colors are usually taken to be secondary properties. On this view, for something to have a particular color, say, red, is for it to have the property of tending to produce visual experiences of a certain sort in normal perceivers under normal conditions for viewing things.[50]

a. *Platts.* Platts defends the following claims: (1) moral properties are properties things possess in virtue of their "disposition to produce certain perceptions in the mind," and (2) moral properties exist "outside" of our minds.[51] Platts's statement of this view is very sketchy and programmatic. He talks in very general terms about kinds of analyses and doesn't define any particular moral concepts. Nor does he precisely specify any of the experiences or perceptions in terms of which moral properties are analyzed. The closest he comes to giving an analysis of value terms ("good" and "bad") is a passage in which he suggests that the value possessed by an object is its disposition to cause people to "value" it.[52]

The analysis of colors in terms of secondary qualities is plausible on phe-nomenological grounds. There are, indeed, characteristic kinds of experi-ences produced by things that have particular colors. But my own introspec-tion fails to reveal any phenomenologically distinctive kinds of experiences to which good and bad things tend to give rise. Most others with whom I have discussed the matter give similar reports. (See chapter 6.II.5, where I raised this same point as an objection to Firth.)[53] Perhaps we are mistaken about this—perhaps a more careful introspection would reveal certain distinctive kinds of normative experiences. But it falls to Platts to give a more adequate description of the kinds of normative experiences in terms of which he ana-lyzes normative properties. This would help us to focus our introspection. Even if more careful introspection would reveal characteristic kinds of experi-ences associated with valuing things, it is still unclear why the dispositional property of being such as to produce these experiences has any normative au-thority. It is an open question whether we would be mistaken if we ignored these properties or failed to adjust our preferences in light of them. (Again, see 6.II.5, where I raised this same point as an objection to Firth.) Platts's the-ory is not sufficiently complete for us to be confident in judging it to be either true or false.

The pervasive phenomenon of disagreement about normative questions creates serious problems for Platts's claim that moral properties are objective properties of things. If everyone were able to perceive normative properties under normal circumstances, we would not expect there to be nearly as much disagreement about normative questions as we encounter. Platts is committed to the view that many people are deficient in their perception of normative properties—they fail to see things that others who are similarly situated (really) see. In order to make this plausible, Platts needs to give some criteria for dis-tinguishing between veridical and non-veridical perception of normative properties. But he simply doesn't do this. His analogy to color properties is very weak here—indeed, this analogy seems to support the non-realist's position. Physiologists can give a perfectly good account of the causal mechanisms of color perception and the distinction between veridical and non-veridical expe-rience of color. There are good scientific grounds for distinguishing between lighting conditions that are favorable and unfavorable to veridical color ex-perience and clear criteria for saying that some people are deficient in their ability to perceive color (there are clear criteria for saying that someone is blind or colorblind). There is, however, no comparable scientific account of the distinction between veridical and non-veridical moral perception.[54] There is no doubt that blindness and colorblindness constitute perceptual deficien-cies. Normal-sighted people can often identify things in ways that blind and colorblind people cannot. Suppose that we take a green cup and a red cup of the same type and shuffle them around on a table and ask which is the red one and which is the green one. A normal-sighted person will be able to correctly identify the two cups. A person suffering from red-green colorblindness will be unable to do so. There are no comparable tests of "moral blindness." There is no independent way (independent of appeal to the very "moral perceptions" whose status is in dispute) of showing that some people are able to discern moral features of reality in ways that others can't. It is possible that ostensible perceptions of moral properties are simply projections that don't correspond to features of external things. It would be absurd to suppose that colors are "mere projections"—they enable us to make useful discriminations between external objects.

b. *McDowell.* John McDowell holds that value properties are secondary properties independent of any particular experience of them.[55] His papers are focused on replying to Mackie's arguments, which purport to show that realism is false. McDowell is particularly concerned to show that his theory is consistent with the view that value properties are objective properties that exist outside of the mind. He likens value properties to the property of fearfulness and claims that they are properties that "merit" or justify certain sorts of responses. The fearfulness of an object is something in virtue of which it merits fear. Value properties are properties in virtue of which the things merit certain kinds of attitudes.[56] McDowell's theory of meaning is very similar to the theory I defend in chapter 6. But, unfortunately, he never proposes a complete analysis of good and bad or any other normative concepts—he doesn't specify the attitudes that specific normative properties are supposed to merit. Nor does he explain how things can merit certain attitudes, much less defend a realist theory of justified attitudes against the kind of non-realist theory that I defend (my theory holds that something merits a particular attitude in virtue its being rational for people to have that attitude about it). Like Platts, McDowell presents a theory that is simply too vague for us to be able to determine whether it is true or false.

Any full-blown theory according to which normative properties are secondary properties will need to deal with the following problems: (1) it will need to make clear the experiential properties in terms of which value properties are defined; (2) it will need to answer questions about the authority of the experiences in terms of which value properties are defined—why we should pay heed to them and adjust our preferences in light of them; and (3) it will need to give a plausible account of the difference between illusory and veridical experiences of value properties. McDowell has the additional problem of formulating and *defending* a realist theory of how things merit certain sorts of attitudes.

For all that I have shown, there may be some version of the view that normative properties are secondary properties that is plausible or correct, but I

am skeptical that such a theory can adequately resolve the three problems I
noted above. In order to assess this view adequately, we need to consider detailed analyses of specific normative properties, e.g., rightness or badness, in
terms of specific experiences or feelings. Neither Platts nor McDowell provide such analyses. They only sketch the outlines of theories.

2. Normative Properties as Patterns We Perceive

In an earlier formulation of his views, written before *Moral Realities*, Platts
claims that moral properties are objective properties of things constituted by
natural properties in the same way that the dots on a page constitute a pattern
or a picture.[57] Susan Hurley holds a similar view. She likens the ability to see
moral properties to the ability to recognize someone's face.[58] Platts claims that
his theory does not commit him to the view that moral perception involves a
sixth sense or special faculty:

> [I]t is not part of this intuitionism to suggest that we detect the moral as-
> pects of a situation by means of some *special faculty* of the mind, the intui-
> tion. We detect moral aspects in the same way we detect (nearly all) other
> aspects: by looking and seeing. Any further claim, like that positing a dis-
> tinctive faculty of ethical intuition, is a contribution to the unintelligible
> pseudo-psychology of the faculties of the mind.[59]

It is important to note that Platts only defends a realist theory of "thick" moral
concepts, e.g., loyalty, kindness, malice, honesty, and courage.[60]

Disagreement about normative questions creates even more serious problems for the present view. Given the pervasiveness of disagreement about normative issues, Platts and Hurley are committed to the view that many people
are deficient in their ability to perceive moral properties. Hurley is aware that
her theory commits her to this:

> Williams' claim that "the idea that our beliefs can track the truth at this
> level must at least imply that a range of investigators could rationally, rea-
> sonably, and unconstrainedly come to converge on a determinate set of
> ethical conclusions" should not be accepted. What can be supposed . . . to
> be necessary for some person's belief to constitute knowledge . . . is *not* that
> a range of investigators would reasonably and unconstrainedly come to
> converge on it . . . but rather that if the proposition believed weren't true
> the person in question wouldn't believe it (and, perhaps we should add,
> that if it were he would). . . . The failure of these convergence conditions
> does not per se undermine the knowledge of those who possess it. . . . To ig-

nore this is to assume (optimistically? or on political grounds?) too great a uniformity, or potential uniformity among persons and their situations; one person's knowledge does not depend on another's capacity for it.

Some people might simply be better at discovering truths about what should be done, all things considered, than others (who might be better at discovering other kinds of truth). . . . For example, some people have very specific agnosias, or recognitional disabilities. Perhaps the most familiar is prosopagnosia, or inability to recognize faces, on the part of someone whose vision is otherwise unimpaired.[61]

It is possible that many otherwise normal and intelligent people are deficient in their ability to discern normative properties. However, in order to show that this is the case, proponents of this second form of British realism need to give a convincing account of the difference between correct and incorrect perception of normative properties. To date, no one has done so. The ability to recognize faces is a way of finding one's way around in the world. Those with the ability to see faces can make discriminations that others can't. A person who can recognize faces can identify particular people in a crowd without difficulty. There are non-controversial and non-question-begging ways of determining whether or not someone has the ability to recognize faces. If someone's competence in recognizing faces is called into question, we can test her ability without relying on *anyone's* ability to recognize faces. There are independent ways of identifying people, e.g., through fingerprints. There is nothing comparable to this in the case of morality. Suppose that you and I disagree about a thing's normative properties, even though we agree about all of its natural properties. Each of us claims that the other is deficient in his/her ability to perceive normative properties. Given the view in question, there is no non-question-begging way for us to determine whose perceptions are deficient and whose are not. If the present version of realism is true and moral properties are patterns that we perceive, then the only way that I can test someone else's moral perceptions is to appeal to my own moral perceptions. There are no non-question-begging ways to resolve disputes about the veracity of people's moral perceptions. In light of this, the thesis that moral perceptions are merely projections cannot be ruled out.

Platts and McDowell would reject this last argument and claim that our moral sensibility enables us to make discriminations that we could not otherwise make. They center their discussion on thick normative concepts, in particular, the virtues. They claim that when a person wields thick normative concepts there is no clear way to separate her factual beliefs and her attitudes.

According to Platts, people who share different attitudes about something can't be said to "see" the same things[62]:

> [T]o *recognize* the obtaining of, say, some desirable moral feature in a possible state of affairs *is* to desire the obtaining of that state of affairs (though not just that). One cannot see the loyal, the courageous, and so forth *as* the loyal, the courageous, etc., without desiring them. . . . It follows from this thesis that if someone else claims to have seen the same evaluative features of the world as I do while differing from me in the obtaining or the not obtaining of desires directed to those states of affairs, then what he has seen is not the same as what I have seen, that how it looks to him must be different from how it looks to me.[63]

Platts claims that the descriptive meaning of normative terms cannot be specified independently of the value concepts and experiences of those who wield them. A person who does not use a specific term that refers to a virtue (or a person who lacks that virtue) can't adequately pick out those things to which the term applies. It is impossible to give purely descriptive criteria that adequately describe our use of virtue terms. For example, it is impossible to formulate purely descriptive necessary and sufficient conditions for being courageous. The complexity of our use of virtue concepts exceeds any descriptive rules.[64] Only those who wield those concepts and share the evaluations implicit in them can correctly apply them to things.

The claim that people who see the same features of things cannot differ in their attitudes about those things must be construed as an empirical claim—it is logically possible that you and I both see the same features in some situation and yet differ in our attitudes about it. Platts and McDowell make a very sweeping claim that covers a huge number of actual and possible cases. Neither offers anything resembling adequate evidence for this. Often disagreements in attitude are explained by the fact that two people don't "see" the same things. For example, someone's failure to like or appreciate a certain sort of music might be due to his inability to see or discern features that it possesses, e.g., its harmonies or structure. Similarly, my failure to be amused by a joke may be the result of my "not getting it." But this isn't always the case. Some people who possess trained musical ears do not appreciate Bach, and sometimes people "get" jokes without being amused by them. Consider an example more relevant to ethics. Sometimes people fail to be distressed by the suffering of others because they do not fully or adequately perceive it or represent it to themselves. Often people's failure to be moved by other people's suffering is due to their failure to "see" that suffering (or see it with full vividness). It is doubtful, however, that all cases of being unmoved by the suffering of others can be accounted for in this way. Indeed, certain forms of malice seem to involve an acute sensibility to the feelings of others.

Particular kinds of moral training and moral concepts engender characteristic kinds of sensibilities and sensitivities. A person who does not share the moral beliefs of my society may be unable to predict how members of my society use such terms as "brave" and "courageous." But it doesn't follow that people who share the same kind of moral training that I have are able to discern independent features of reality that others cannot discern. The non-realist is equally able to account for the evidence in question. The non-realist would say that the only special knowledge I have in virtue of wielding certain normative concepts is the knowledge of how others who wield the same concepts apply those concepts to things. The question is whether those who wield a particular normative concept are able to see independent features of reality that others cannot see or whether they simply possess the ability to predict how others who wield the same concepts will apply those concepts in ways that others can't. There is no non-question-begging way to show that the former, rather than the latter, is the case.

Even if McDowell and Platts were correct in claiming that those who wield particular normative concepts are able to make discriminations that others cannot make, this does not establish the kind of objectivist (i.e., non-relativist) realism that they want to defend. Here, again, the pervasive phenomenon of disagreement creates serious problems for their views. There are competing moral traditions each of which has its own unique array of thick normative concepts. For the sake of argument, let us grant that wielding certain normative concepts enables people to see things that those who do not wield them cannot see. There is no reason to suppose our own normative concepts are unique in this respect. We must allow that it is possible that certain alternative normative concepts that others use enable them to make discriminations that we cannot make. It is possible that the concept of honor wielded by Mongol warriors (which among other things requires revenge to the exclusion of anything we might call forgiveness or kindness) gave them sensitivities and powers of discrimination that we lack. If different and incompatible moral systems can each claim that their adherents possess powers of discrimination that others lack, then the appeal to such powers can't serve to justify any particular moral system.

It is important to stress that Platts's and McDowell's arguments are confined to thick concepts. Even if they succeed in defending realist accounts of virtue and other thick normative concepts, this leaves open my claim that there is no reason to accept a realist theory of good and bad. (As we saw in 6.VIII, it is not plausible to construe good and bad as thick concepts.) There is nothing in their defense of realist *theories of virtue* that is inconsistent with my claim that, at present, there are no decisive arguments for a realist *theory of good and bad*. It is possible that realism is a plausible theory for some normative notions but not others. Note the following passage from Platts:

> There seems no clear reason for thinking that such a realist view has to be applied either to the whole of moral discourse or to none of it. I wish to consider the realist view primarily as it applies to moral evaluations, to judgments expressible by sentences of forms like 'x is loyal', 'x is kind', 'x is malicious', and so on, where x can be (at least) a person, an action or an attitude. That is, I do not want to consider the particular problems that arise in applying a realist view to sentences like, for example, 'That is what you ought to do', 'That is the right thing (for you) to do', or 'That is what you must do'. In fact, my subject matter is narrower still, since I shall not directly consider general evaluations like 'x is good' and 'x is bad'.[65]

For all of my disagreements with them, I think that McDowell, Platts, and Hurley are correct to stress the importance of moral sensibility and sensitivity. I differ from them in that I do not think that moral sensibility enables us to directly perceive moral facts. Rather, I think that the sensibilities and powers of discrimination whose importance they so rightly stress should be thought of as being requirements for being an ideally rational moral/normative judge. Inasmuch as those with acute sensitivities see things that others fail to see, these requirements can be plausibly imported into full information accounts of rationality (see 8.IV).

Conclusion

Some traditional forms of realism, e.g., "analytic naturalism" and Moore's intuitionism, are open to serious objections, which have been rehearsed and refined in twentieth-century analytic philosophy. Cornell realism avoids the standard objections to earlier versions of moral realism. But Cornell realism has not been formulated in sufficient detail for us to be able to determine its truth or falsity. Proponents of this theory need to give a much more detailed account of the nature of moral facts for us to be able to determine whether the kinds of facts it posits are necessary for explanatory purposes. At the present time, anything we say about the explanatory significance of moral facts is highly conjectural. Psychology, at its present stage of development, does not provide adequate explanations of human beliefs and behavior. It is unclear what sorts of explanations of human behavior would be given by the best possible psychological theories, and it is unclear whether those explanations would involve reference to moral facts. Recent versions of British realism claim that moral qualities can be directly perceived. Since people often disagree in their perceptions of value, such theories are committed to claiming that there are veridical and non-veridical perceptions of moral qualities. Defenders of such theories need to give a precise account of the nature of moral facts and our perception of them and, most importantly, provide means for distinguishing between veridical and non-veridical perceptions of moral qualities. British defenders of perceptual realism have not done any of these things. In the absence of such an account, there is no reason to accept their theories. In other cases in which there clearly are veridical and non-veridical perceptions of reality, e.g., the perception of colors, it is possible to give a perfectly clear and noncontroversial account of the distinction between veridical and non-veridical perception. British realists have not made an adequate case for the claim that ostensible moral perception involves the apprehension of independent moral facts about what is good and bad.

There are many more possible versions of AR than anyone has ever formulated. I don't think that anyone has given adequate reasons for thinking that *all possible* versions of AR are false—the very vagueness and sketchiness of so many recent versions of AR would undermine any such argument. But, for my purposes, nothing crucial hangs on this contention, indeed, I would like to be able to claim that AR is false. That would allow me to give a more straightforward argument in support of the desire-satisfaction theory (a more straightforward argument than the qualified argument that follows in Interlude 2).[66]

A Qualified Argument for the Rational-Desire/ Preference-Satisfaction Theory of Value

Many of the arguments considered in chapters 1–5 are inconclusive because they presuppose answers to certain metaethical questions. We've now examined some of these questions. The conclusions reached in chapters 6 and 7, however, do not give us adequate reasons to endorse any particular first-order theory of value.

In chapter 6 I argued that value judgments entail claims about the correctness of preferences. Saying that something is non-instrumentally good implies that it is correct to prefer it. Chapter 7 did not yield any clear answers to questions about realism. The appeal to considerations of meaning doesn't favor either realism or non-realism. Both realists and non-realists can make sense of the idea that preferences or attitudes can be correct or appropriate. There seem to be no compelling reasons to think that axiological realism (or any particular version of AR) is true. Although my own sympathies and inclinations are strongly antirealist and I think that my arguments weaken the case for realism, I haven't shown that all versions of AR are false. Questions about the truth of AR are extremely difficult and perplexing; the issue may not be rationally decidable at the present stage of philosophical discussion. First-order questions of value cannot be settled as long as questions about the truth of AR remain open. For any first-order theory of value we may propose or defend, it is possible that AR is true and that the true or correct version of AR commits us to a quite different first-order theory of value. There are many possible versions of AR. For almost any first-order theory of value, we can imagine a corresponding version of AR which, if true, would support that (first-order) theory of value.

What can we say about non-realism? Suppose we could show that AR is false. (Or, suppose that Blackburn, or someone else, has shown that AR is false.) Could we draw any conclusions for first-order theories of value? If AR is false, then we have reasons to accept the rational-desire-satisfaction theory of value. Consider the following argument:

1. A necessary condition of something's being non-instrumentally good (bad) is that it is correct (fitting, appropriate) to prefer that it exist/occur (not exist/occur), other things being equal.

2. If AR is false, then preferences can be said to be correct or incorrect in virtue of being rational or irrational.

3. If AR is false, there is no other way in which preferences can (plausibly) be regarded as correct or incorrect. The only plausible theories of correct and incorrect preferences consistent with non-realism are theories of rationality.

Therefore:

If AR is false and some things are non-instrumentally good or bad, then they are good or bad (at least partly) in virtue of the fact that it is rational to prefer them. What things actually are good and bad depends (at least in part) on what it is rational to prefer.

Note that this argument leaves open the possibility that nothing is good or bad; the argument does not attempt to refute axiological nihilism. The argument is valid. Premise 1 is defended at length in chapter 6. I have nothing to add to the arguments I presented there. Premise 2 is surely true. Theories of rationality allow us a way to make sense of the idea that preferences can be correct or incorrect. We can say that rational preferences are correct and irrational preferences are incorrect. The main problem with the argument is premise 3. I haven't given adequate reasons for thinking that 3 is true. At present, theories of rationality are the only theories of correct and incorrect preferences consistent with non-realism that have been seriously developed. However, this doesn't show that premise 3 is true; it leaves open the possibility that alternative theories of correct and incorrect preferences could be developed. However, the fact that alternative non-realist theories of correct and incorrect preferences (attitudes) have not yet been developed shows that theories of rationality are, for better or for worse, the main option for non-realists at present.

An Objection to Premise 3

Here it might be objected that I have overlooked a significant option for non-realists. A non-realist could accept Kant's theory of value or something like it. Korsgaard calls Kant's theory of the good a non-realist theory.[1] There is often a danger involved in trying to fit historical philosophers into later categories that they themselves didn't employ. Nonetheless, I'm inclined to think that Kant is a non-realist in my sense, and I will grant this for the sake of argument. To the extent that it is a non-realist theory, however, Kant's theory of value is also a version of the rational-choice or rational-preference theory of value. Kant bases his theory of the good on a theory of practical reason or rational choice. He distinguishes between two kinds of ends or goods: subjective or conditional ends and objective or unconditional ends.[2] Subjective ends are the objects of our desires and wants. Happiness consists in the satisfaction of these desires.[3] The goodness of subjective ends is conditional in that it is contingent on our desiring and needing them.[4] The goodness of our obtaining these ends (and the happiness that results) is also conditional in a second sense: it depends on our being worthy of happiness, i.e., our being morally good. Kant says that a good will or moral goodness is the only thing that is unconditionally good.[5] It might be more accurate to say that Kant holds that a good will or moral goodness is a *necessary part* of anything that is objectively or unconditionally good. On Kant's view, the highest good (happiness together with moral goodness) is also objectively or unconditionally good. Objective ends come from pure reason—they are ends of pure reason; their goodness does not depend on being the objects of inclinations. Objective goods are *necessary* ends or necessary objects of desire for any rational being.[6] Our nature as rational beings determines us to have moral goodness or a good will as an end. Any rational being has moral goodness as an end. Kant holds that a good will is unconditionally good because rational beings, qua rational beings, are determined to have it as an end. He does not say that rational beings have a good will as an end because it is unconditionally good independently of being an end of pure practical reason.[7] Korsgaard writes the following:

> Kant's answer, as I understand him, is that what makes the object of your rational choice good is that it *is* the object of rational choice. . . . His idea is that rational choice has what I will call value-conferring status.[8]

> Similarly, the argument for the objective goodness of the object of a rational choice is not an ontological one; rather, it is based on Kant's theory of rational action. If we regard our actions as rational, we must regard our ends as good; if so, we accord to ourselves a power of conferring goodness

on the objects of our choice, and we must accord the same power—and so the same intrinsic worth—to others.[9]

Kant's theory of value and the rational-desire/preference-satisfaction theory of value that I favor agree in that they say that what is good and bad is determined by what a rational person would aim at or pursue. It may seem strange to call Kant's theory a *"desire*-satisfaction theory." This strangeness, however, derives from connotations of the word "desire" that are inappropriate, given the role of preferences or desires in my theory. In my theory, desires or preferences are dispositions to act. Like Kant's theory, my theory is based on a theory of rational choice or practical reason.

Almost all contemporary non-realists base their normative theories on theories of rationality or rational-desires/preferences. Theories of value based at least in part on the idea of rational or irrational preferences seem to be the main option for non-realists at the present (those who disagree need to propose an alternative theory of correct and incorrect preferences consistent with non-realism). The content of the rational-desire/preference-satisfaction theory of value depends on what sort of concept of rationality we employ. We need to determine what sort of theory of rationality is most appropriate for use in normative theories. Non-realists haven't paid enough attention to questions about how to justify theories of rationality and choose between alternative theories. In chapter 8 I will try to determine what sort of theory of rationality is most suitable for use in a rational-desire-satisfaction theory of value. Full-information theories of rationality/value/welfare have been very prominent of late. I argue that full-information theories of rationality are untenable. I sketch two alternative non-realist theories of rationality that I believe are tenable: a divine-preference theory and an informed-preference theory. I argue that the divine-preference theory of rationality is preferable to the informed-preference theory, but both theories avoid the objections to standard full-information theories. Rational-preference-satisfaction theories of value that employ one or the other of these two theories are the most plausible theories of value open to non-realists at the present time.

CHAPTER 8

The Concept of Rationality as a Basis for Normative Theories

I. Non-realism and the Concept of Rationality

Some realist moral theories countenance moral facts as preconditions for facts about rationality. According to these theories, moral facts are logically prior to facts about what is rational and irrational. Attitude-independent moral facts, according to certain realist moral theories, determine, at least partly and defeasibly, what is rational and irrational. On these realist moral theories, standards of rationality include such principles as the following: It is *prima facie* irrational to prefer the bad to the good (where what is good or bad is independent of what is rational or irrational); it is *prima facie* irrational to prefer a lesser good to a greater good (where what is good or bad is independent of what is rational or irrational); it is *prima facie* irrational to prefer a greater bad to a lesser bad (where what is good or bad is independent of what is rational and irrational). Gert's theory is a clear example of such a view.[1]

Moral/axiological non-realism, by contrast, denies that things are good or bad or right or wrong independently of facts about the attitudes of moral agents; it also denies that attitude-independent moral facts determine what is rational. Many important non-realist moral theories, including the theories of Rawls, Firth, Gauthier, Brandt, and Hare, are based squarely on theories of rationality.[2] These theories take facts about what is rational or irrational to be logically prior to what is moral; they assume that things are right or good because it is rational to choose them or have a favorable attitude about them.

Theories of rationality such as Gert's, which define what is rational in terms of independent moral facts, are plausible only if AR is true. If there are no moral or axiological facts of the sort that realists claim, then there is no reason

219

why canons of rationality should require that our attitudes or preferences conform to those alleged facts. Non-realist normative theories are inconsistent with theories of rationality such as Gert's. Gert's theory presupposes the existence of independent moral facts of the sort that non-realists deny.[3]

II. The Need to Defend a Particular Theory of Rationality

The sort of non-realist normative theory I defend (the rational-preference-satisfaction theory of value) depends on the notion of rational preferences. In this chapter I will try to formulate a plausible theory of rationality that is consistent with axiological non-realism and yields a plausible version of the rational-desire-satisfaction theory of value. I need to defend one particular theory of rationality as the correct (or most plausible) theory of rationality that is consistent with axiological non-realism. If we base a normative theory on a theory of rationality, small differences in the theory of rationality we employ can make for very large differences in content of the normative theories that emerge. Consider the non-realist moral theories of Rawls, Firth, Gauthier, Brandt, and Hare, which are all based squarely on theories of rationality. Such theories assume three things: (a) that moral realism is false, (b) that there is a conceptual connection between morality and rationality, and (c) that the theory of rationality endorsed by the theory is the correct account of rationality.

Rawls, Firth, Gauthier, Brandt, and Hare are all committed to (c). Because their moral theories have theories of rationality at their foundations, each of these theorists must defend a particular account of rationality. Otherwise, we may reasonably prefer an alternative version of their theory based on a different account of rationality. The arguments these philosophers give for their preferred first-order normative theories are no stronger, in the end, than the arguments they give for their theories of rationality. Rawls's argument, for example, that the parties to the original position would prefer his two principles of justice to the principle of average utility depends on his assumption that it is rational for those in the original position to adopt a maximin strategy, rather than some other strategy, such as the policy of maximizing expected utility.[4] Unless they follow a maximin strategy, people in the original position will have no reason to choose a principle of distribution designed to make the position of the least well-off group as good as possible, instead of an alternative distribution principle that (from the perspective of the original position) might afford them greater expected utility.[5]

Non-realist normative theories based on theories of rationality need to assume (c). Let me briefly illustrate this point in connection with a straightforward non-realist moral theory based on a theory of rationality: Roderick Firth's ideal-observer theory. Firth takes his ideal-observer theory to be both a standard of truth for moral judgments and a theory about what moral judgments mean. Let us grant, if only for the sake of argument, Firth's assumption that a favorable (unfavorable) moral judgment about something is true if, and only if, an ideal observer would have a certain attitude of approval (disapproval) toward the thing in question. (Firth's theory is presented more fully in Chapter 6.II.5.) An ideal observer is an ideally rational moral judge. Any particular characterization of an ideal observer presupposes a certain understanding of what it is to be rational. The characteristics of an ideal observer are essential, at least by Firth's lights, for being a *rational* moral judge. Suppose that Firth were to reject assumption (c) and claim that there is no reason to choose between three contrary theories of rationality, R1, R2, and R3. In that case, he would also have to grant that there is no reason to prefer any one of the following contrary theories of morality over the others: (i) the ideal-observer theory wherein an ideal observer is characterized by R1; (ii) the ideal-observer theory wherein an ideal observer is characterized by R2; and (iii) the ideal-observer theory wherein an ideal observer is characterized by R3.

III. The Appeal to Meaning

No particular theory of rationality can find unqualified support in semantic considerations alone: for example, in *the* meaning of the word "rationality." There is no single specific concept of rationality that accommodates all familiar uses of the term "rational." Even if there were just one widely shared specific notion of rationality in circulation, a troublesome question could still remain open: Why care about being rational in that particular widely shared sense of "rational"? Motivation for this question might run as follows: "Even if the sense in question captures what most English speakers mean when they use the word 'rational,' I do not care to be rational in that particular sense. I simply do not care whether my attitudes and actions satisfy the proposed conditions for being rational. If right and wrong and good and bad are determined by what is rational in that sense of 'rational,' then I care not at all about what is right or wrong or good or bad. Further, there is no reason why I *should care* about what is right or wrong or good or bad; I am not guilty of any kind of mistake or error for not caring."

Given a variety of specific notions of rationality, we evidently cannot use semantic considerations alone to justify, in a non-question-begging manner, the adoption of a particular notion of rationality as a basis for normative theories. Can we give some other sort of justification for adopting a particular non-realist theory of rationality? Let us turn to some pragmatic considerations that seem to favor a full-information theory of rationality.

IV. Rationality and Full Information

Full-information theories of rationality imply that an attitude or action of yours is rational if, and only if, you would endorse that attitude or action were you "fully informed." Richard Brandt is the most influential defender of the full-information theory of rationality. In A *Theory of the Good and the Right*, Brandt writes:

> I shall pre-empt the term "rational" to refer to actions, desires, or moral systems which survive maximal criticism and correction by facts and logic. We could of course use some other term, like "fully informed," but the choice of "rational" seems as good as any.[6]

More recently, Brandt has characterized the prospective use of "would be rational for X to do A" as follows:

> I hereby recommend that X do A, while taking as my objective maximizing satisfaction of the transitive mood-independent ultimate desires of X, as they would be if they had been subjected to repeated vivid reflection on relevant facts, and having as my beliefs about options for actions and consequences those which are justified on X's evidence—a recommendation made because A is that one among the options justifiably believed to be open, choice of which exemplifies a strategy for decision-making which we know will in the long run satisfy the (as above) corrected desires of X as effectively as any other strategy can be known to do.[7]

A constraint on rational action, according to Brandt's account, comes from ultimate desires that are *corrected* in that they have withstood (or can withstand) "cognitive psychotherapy": that is, repeated vivid reflection on all relevant facts, or all relevant information.

Cognitive psychotherapy raises special problems for Brandt's theory.[8] It seems possible that cognitive psychotherapy would fail to extinguish irrational desires in certain cases, but Brandt's view implies that this is logically impossible. Suppose that a desire of yours was caused by obviously false be-

liefs arising just from wishful thinking and that this desire would not be ex-
tinguished in cognitive psychotherapy when those false beliefs are corrected.
Such a desire could nonetheless be irrational, since it is based on obviously
false beliefs. According to Brandt, however, the fact that a desire persists in
the light of cognitive psychotherapy *guarantees* that it is rational. Brandt thus
seems unduly optimistic about the causal efficacy of cognitive psychotherapy.
A full-information account need not, however, incorporate Brandt's theory of
cognitive psychotherapy. A full-information theory can (and, I think, should)
say roughly the following instead:

> Rational or ideally rational desires are those one would have had if one had
> been fully informed (and free of cognitive mistakes) at all times at which
> the desires were being formed.[9]

The effects of past cognitive failings can linger even if their causes are re-
moved. Attitudes that have their origins in one's past cognitive failings aren't
rational, even if those cognitive failings are later corrected.

Certain considerations seem to recommend the full-information theory of
rationality over alternative non-realist theories. First, most psychologically normal adults evidently would be willing, on suitable reflection, to endorse a policy of regulating their attitudes and actions in the light of full information. On
suitable reflection, they would regard the standpoint of full information as
ideal for assessing attitudes and actions. Consider the preferences to purchase
an antebellum mansion, marry the person next door, and pursue a lucrative
career as a surgeon. Most people who have such preferences will be open to
criticizing them in light of new or corrected information, for example, learning that the mansion has termites, knowing vividly what it would be like to be
married to the person next door, or learning that the surgical career is ultimately tedious. Most psychologically normal people would, on suitable reflection, regard full information as an ideal standpoint for deciding these issues.

The second consideration seemingly favoring a full-information account is
that virtually every person has conflicting preferences that cannot all be satisfied. In light of such conflicting preferences, we typically have the meta-
preference that our preferences be satisfied efficiently, with minimal loss —
especially relative to the preferences we deem important. Full information is
arguably the ideal standpoint for satisfying our preferences efficiently. If you
act on incomplete or incorrect information, you may be acting in ignorance
of relevant consequences of your preferences or actions.

In the preceding chapter I discussed several contemporary British realists
(Platts, McDowell, and Hurley) who rightly stress the importance of moral

sensibilities and abilities to make discriminations between things. Full-information theories of rationality are most plausibly construed as holding that the maximal or ideal development of sensibilities and abilities to make discriminations, e.g., seeing the point of a joke, seeing the structures in a poem or piece of music, empathizing with the feelings of others (knowing vividly what it feels like to be in their positions), is part of what is involved in being fully informed.[10] Full information is not exhausted by the kind of knowledge that is easily expressed in lists of propositions, e.g., I will earn more money if I become a stockbroker rather than an artist. It is a much richer and more demanding notion than is generally appreciated.

V. Some Objections to the Full-Information Theory

1. The Objection That We Only Need Reliable Information

Here it might be objected that we are typically only interested in having *adequately reliable* information, not necessarily *all* relevant information. Many people think that they often have adequate information on which to act rationally, even though they lack full information. People rarely take the effort to acquire full information—or even all available information—about a decision. Even so, taking full information as the ideal standpoint for decision making is consistent with rarely desiring full information enough to pay the cost of acquiring it. We seldom, if ever, can acquire all information relevant to assessing our attitudes and actions. You are now incapable, for example, of acquiring all the information relevant to the purchase of a certain used car that interests you. Full information includes not only all facts relevant to the performance of that car, but also all facts about every other similar used car for sale in the nearby area. Given the availability of thousands of similar cars for sale, you could devote an indefinite amount of time, effort, and expense to gathering information about the purchase of a used car. The price, in monetary terms alone, of obtaining all relevant information far exceeds the value of any used car. It would seemingly be irrational, in such a case, for anyone to make the effort to obtain all relevant information. However, this is consistent with the fact that full information is the *ideal* standpoint for making decisions. Saying that full information is the ideal standpoint for making decisions is consistent with the fact that often it is not worth the effort to obtain all relevant information. I shall clarify why this is so.

The claim that full information is the ideal standpoint for decision making entails that, other things equal, we should prefer the second of the following two options:

1. Making the decision in accord with our preferences, given our present incomplete information;

and

2. Making the decision in accord with what we would prefer, given full information.

Regarding a decision between choosing a car in accord with our preferences, given our present incomplete information, and choosing a car in accord with what we would prefer, given full information, most people would probably prefer the latter. The costs and difficulty of obtaining information do not count against the claim that, other things equal, we should prefer 2 to 1.

We typically regard full information as a better standard for decision making than all *available* information. Consider the choice between:

3. Making the decision in accord with what we would prefer, given all information available to us;

and

2. Making the decision in accord with what we would prefer, given full information.

Since it is possible that some important information is now unavailable to us, most of us would prefer 2 to 3. Full-information accounts entail that we should do so.

2. Distress

Some people prefer not to have certain information, even when obtaining it involves no real cost. You may not want to know, for example, the details of torture because having such knowledge would be severely distressing for you. In saying that full information is the ideal standpoint for decision making, one is not committed to having full information or even to preferring that one have full information. One is committed only to preferring that one's decision fit with *what one would prefer, given full information.* Our preferences about the occurrence of torture can fit with what we would prefer, given full information, even if we neither have nor prefer to have full information. This consideration removes the threat from the case involving severe distress. That

case would be troublesome if a full-information account of rationality required that one prefer to have full information; but this is not required.

3. The Objection That Irrational Desires Need to Be Taken into Account

It might be objected that full-information theories of rationality unduly ignore
the importance of taking our irrational desires and aversions into account
when we act. Suppose that I have an irrational fear of dogs. A friend asks me to
take care of his dogs while he is away on vacation. My ideally rational self
would not fear the dogs and would not hesitate to look after them. Given my
intense fear of dogs, however, things are likely to turn out badly if I look after
the dogs. Why should I care that my ideal self wouldn't be afraid of dogs?
Wouldn't it still be foolish for my actual self (with all of its phobias) to take
care of the dogs? I might be incapable of adequately caring for them. Even if I
can take care of them, I am likely to undergo a great deal of distress. In this
case, I should follow my present desires rather than the desires that I would
have if I were ideally rational. This objection can be handled if we invoke the
distinction I made earlier in chapter 3.II.1 between the following:

1.   The choice that my ideally rational self would make for itself.

2.   The choice that my ideally rational self would make for my actual (non-
      ideal) self.

My fear of dogs is unlikely to disappear during my friend's vacation. Thus 2,
and not 1, is the appropriate standpoint for judging my present decision. I
have a strong and perfectly rational aversion to emotional distress. Knowing
that I would likely suffer a great deal of distress if I look after the dogs, my
ideal self would have a strong inclination to prefer that I (with my actual fears
and aversions) not look after the dogs.[11]

VI. More Serious Objections to the Full-Information Theory

1. Do Statements about What We Would Prefer If We Were Fully Informed Have a Determinate Meaning and Truth Value?

Full-information theories of rationality and theories of welfare and value
that employ them rely on counterfactual statements of the following sort: "If I
were fully informed about x, then I would have such and such preferences
about x." However, it is unclear that such statements always have a determinate meaning or truth value.

Full-information theories need to require that information be adequately appreciated. For example, in order for my preferences about whether or not to be a smoker to be fully informed, it is not enough that I know that smoking greatly increases my chances of dying of lung cancer—I must have an adequate appreciation of all the kinds of suffering that having lung cancer would involve. Following Brandt, most defenders of full-information theories of rationality deal with the issue of appreciation by requiring vivid awareness of all information. In the present example, this would require that one be vividly aware of all the kinds of suffering that having lung cancer would involve.

J. David Velleman argues that the idea of someone fully representing certain information to himself does not refer to any determinate state of affairs, because "the same facts can be represented in many different ways with different motivational consequences."[12] He gives the example of a heart patient who is trying to represent facts about heart surgery to himself.

> Surely mental pictures of open-heart surgery would affect me differently from a mental flow chart or narration. Furthermore, each medium of representation affords me considerable latitude in style and perspective. For instance, I can describe the operation in medical jargon, using words like "incision," "suture," "clot," and "hemorrhage": or I can describe it in layman's terms with words like "slice," "sew," "gob," and "gush."[13]

Requiring that the facts be represented in an "ideally vivid" way won't solve this problem since the idea of ideally vivid representation is itself indeterminate—there are different modes of representing facts, e.g, pictures and narratives, and thus there is no obvious sense in which one mode of representation can be more vivid than another (in the way that one picture can be more vivid than another).[14] The full-information theorist might attempt to resolve this difficulty by requiring that one represent the facts to oneself in every possible way—viewing them from every possible angle and in every possible light. However, representing information to oneself in every possible way is not empirically determinate because there is no limit to the number of ways in which we can represent information to ourselves. Velleman writes:

> "[A]ll possible representations" is not empirically determinate, either. The problem is not just that this phrase encompasses more actual languages and graphic conventions than we are capable of testing in practice. The problem is that, in order to yield a satisfactory definition of "good," the phrase would have to encompass every possible language and every possible graphic convention—every mode of representation that we might ever invent in

order to illuminate an issue. And there is no scientific method for generating a catalog of possible future inventions.[15]

The difficulties for the full-information theory are compounded by the fact that human beings are not capable of vividly representing complex sets of facts at a single instant. This raises what Rosati calls the "problem of experiential ordering."[16] In order to represent complex facts adequately they must represent the facts in some kind of order or sequence. No one particular sequence can be said to be *the* correct way to represent those facts. Yet, work in empirical psychology suggests that the order in which we represent the facts may affect our final judgment or attitude about those facts.[17] Suppose that I am comparing different kinds of lives. I must contemplate each kind of life in full detail. There are an extraordinary number of facts that I must represent to myself in order to understand a particular life. Even if we reject Velleman's arguments and grant that there is a single determinate set of facts that I need to represent to myself (and a single determinate way for me to represent each fact) in order to understand a particular life, there are still many different ways I can *order* the representation of these facts to myself. The number of possible orderings of information is greatly increased if I try to compare different lives. If I am comparing different lives, any given life can be represented either first or last. If the way that I order the representations affects my preferences (so that different orderings yield different preferences), then it seems that such statements as "I would have such and such preferences about lives A, B, C . . . Z if I were fully informed about them" may not have any determinate truth value. There are considerations that weaken the force of Rosati's concerns about "experiential ordering." Fully informed persons would be aware of any effects that the way they order information has on their preferences, and this knowledge itself would tend to diminish those effects.[18]

It seems that the full-information theory of rationality implies that sometimes (or often) statements about what someone would desire were she fully informed lack determinate truth value. Those versions of the rational-desire-satisfaction theory of value that employ the full-information theory of rationality imply that some (many) normative judgments lack any determinate truth value. If the statement that I (or we) would prefer X to Y were I (we) fully informed lacks a determinate truth value, then those versions of the rational-desire-satisfaction theory of value in question imply that the statement that X is non-instrumentally better than Y has no determinate truth value. This is not a decisive objection to either theory. Given non-realism, it is not absurd to suppose that many normative judgments have no determinate truth value. It would be a very serious objection to the theory if it implied that *no statements* about what someone would prefer were she fully informed have a determinate truth value. There is, however, no reason to suppose that this is the case. Consider a woman's preference that she never begin to smoke cigarettes. Suppose that if she starts to smoke, she will be unable to quit and will die prematurely of a painful case of emphysema. By taking up smoking, she would cut short and blight what would otherwise be a long and happy old age. There are many different ways in which she can represent the relevant information to herself. But, presumably, all of the different possible ways of representing this information to herself will yield the same overall preference—she will prefer that she not begin to smoke cigarettes.

2. Full Information and the Finite Cognitive Capacities of Human Beings

An even more serious problem for the full-information theory is the following. Full information about those matters relevant to questions about the nature of the good life—knowing vividly and in detail what it's like to live many different kinds of lives—greatly outstrips the cognitive capacities of human beings. In order to be able to represent many different lives to myself in full detail, I would need far greater cognitive capacities than I now have. This creates intractable problems for interpreting the sorts of counterfactual statements the theory relies on, e.g., "If I were fully informed about the nature of lives A–Z, I would prefer life T to all the others." The antecedents of such statements don't pick out determinate states of affairs. My fully informed idealized self is so very different from my actual self that it is impossible to hold other things equal when asking what I would prefer were I fully informed. The person that I would be if I were fully informed is radically different from the person I now am. Rosati questions whether it makes sense to say that this fully informed person is *myself*.[19] I question whether it makes sense to say that someone who is fully informed is a *human being*. The following may help to drive home this last point. Given the laws of human psychology and physiology, the size of my brain limits the amount of information that I can represent to myself. These same laws of human psychology and physiology (in particular, the relatively slow speed of the brain's chemical-electrical impulses) place limits on the size of a brain that can function at all. There is no empirically coherent way of conceiving of a human being who is fully informed.[20]

3. Could Full Information Change Our Motivations for the Worse?

Let's begin by considering the problem of "cognitive overload." Suppose that if you were vividly aware, in excruciating detail, of all the suffering caused by

World War II, you would lose your sanity. In that case, what you would prefer, given full information, is what you would prefer, given a psychological breakdown from cognitive overload. You might, of course, have some bizarre preferences after a psychological breakdown. It is thus doubtful that you would now endorse what you would prefer, given a psychological breakdown.

Don Loeb argues that acquiring complete information might change our motivations for the worse. The motivations we would have if we were fully informed might be worse, for the purposes of determining our good, than our actual desires. Full information might involve knowledge that would make us totally depressed or fearful. Loeb writes:

> What sorts of things would such a person be vividly aware of? He would have to be thoroughly acquainted with every kind of pain imaginable: what it is like to be burned at the stake, what it is like to be burned in an oven, what it is like to be eaten by sharks while drowning. But it is possible that this knowledge would scar him, and leave him no longer caring about anything but avoiding these horrible experiences, or preventing his counterpart from having them. . . . He would also have to know unspeakable loneliness, sadness, and self-doubt. But this knowledge might leave him too depressed to care about his counterpart's welfare.[21]

Loeb speaks with reference to Railton's theory of value according to which what is good for one is determined by what a fully rational and informed version of oneself would want for one's non-ideal self.[22]

The kinds of emotional reactions Loeb describes here (being deeply depressed or being consumed by fear) are incompatible with being fully informed about other things. If I am deeply depressed (or consumed by fear of something), then I am not capable of vividly representing to myself the joys of love and friendship. This kind of depression or fear might also diminish one's means-ends rationality. Suppose that knowledge of both X and Y is relevant to deciding a certain question Z, but vivid knowledge of X would cause one to be so depressed that one couldn't have vivid knowledge of Y. In that case, it follows that it is *impossible* for one to be fully informed about everything that is relevant to Z. (I will have more to say about this objection in 8.VII.3).

VII. An Alternative Informed-Desire Theory

1. A Sketch of the Theory

The knowledge required for being fully informed far exceeds human capacities. There is no empirically coherent way of conceiving of human beings (with human brains) who are fully informed. The informed-desire theory I propose is based on the idea that some cognitive and informational perspectives that human beings are capable of occupying are *better* or *better informed* than others. This theory avoids reliance on counterfactual statements about what humans would prefer if they were omniscient or had superhuman powers. It also deals with some of the problems noted by Velleman and Rosati. In particular, it avoids committing ourselves to the view that there is a single "best" way of representing a large body of information to oneself. My theory implies that sometimes statements about what one would prefer—were one rational—lack determinate truth value, but, as we have seen, this consequence is acceptable.

Even though no single way of representing large amounts of information can be said to be cognitively *ideal*, some perspectives are clearly better than others. For example, my current informational perspective on the morality of Germany's actions during World War II (based on discussions with combatants and civilian victims of Germany's actions and a wide reading of generally reliable historical accounts of the war) is clearly preferable to that of a German soldier who accepted false beliefs about the causes of the war and was ignorant of the Holocaust and the extent to which Germany was harming innocent civilians. The cognitive position of someone who has experienced both physical and mental pleasures is more adequate for assessing the relative value of different kinds of pleasures than the position of someone who has experienced only physical pleasures. The idea of full information can still serve as a regulative ideal for criticizing and correcting our preferences.[23] We can use it to criticize our preferences and to seek ever better cognitive perspectives for assessing them.

The *negative condition* of full information (not having any false beliefs) doesn't raise any of the problems discussed above. My not having any false beliefs (and my not having had false beliefs in the past) is a perfectly determinate state of affairs, and it is compatible with my limited capacities for storing and representing information to myself.

For almost any actual or empirically possible cognitive perspective about a particular normative question, we can imagine how it could be improved or made better by giving the person more information. However, sometimes it seems clear that a person's preferences about certain matters would have been the same even if her cognitive perspective had been better. My standpoint for judging the Holocaust could be improved considerably, but it is extremely unlikely that my overall preferences about the Holocaust (my preference that it not have occurred) would be different if my cognitive perspective had been better. In this case, we have plausible grounds for saying that my preferences are correct. Consider another example. I don't have all information relevant to the question of whether it would be desirable for me to pursue a career as a high-rise construction worker. But, knowing that I am happy with my present career and that I have a fear of heights and a diminished sense of balance because of inner ear problems, my information is *sufficient* for me to be confident in endorsing my current preference for my present career to being a high-rise construction worker. This preference would persist in the light of improved information.

I propose the following as a standard for the correctness of an individual person's preferences:

> COR. It is correct for S to prefer X to not-X (and incorrect for him not to prefer X to not-X) if, and only if, (1) there is at least one empirically possible cognitive/informational perspective (P_1) from which S would prefer X to not-X and (2) there is no other empirically possible perspective (P_2) which is as good as or better than P_1 (for deciding between X and not-X) such that S would not prefer X to not-X from P_2.

COR is an "informed-preference theory of rationality" (as opposed to a full-information theory of rationality). COR is modeled on Crispin Wright's idea of "superassertability." Wright uses the idea of a better or improved cognitive standpoint as the basis for his concept of "superassertability." Superassertability, he claims, is a notion consistent with non-realism that approximates our ordinary concept of truth. A statement is superassertable if, and only if, it is (or can be) warranted and will continue to be warranted no matter how much our evidence (or cognitive positions) are improved. Wright defines "superassertable" as follows:

> A statement is superassertable, then, if and only if it is, or can be, warranted and some warrant for it would survive arbitrarily close scrutiny of its pedigree and arbitrarily extensive increments to or other forms of improvement of our information.[24]

> Once we have the notion of better and worse justification for particular statements, we can understand the notion of a statement's continuing to be justified no matter how much more information we may gather which is germane to its justifiability. Say that a statement is *superassertable* if that is so.[25]

The key idea that COR shares with Wright's concept of superassertability is that, beyond a certain level, improvements to one's cognitive position might not alter one's beliefs or preferences. There are also significant differences.

Wright's concept of superassertability is a concept of objective truth (what it is for a statement to be true for everyone). COR is only a theory of what it is for the preferences of an *individual* to be correct. To say that it is correct for *me* to prefer X to Y does not imply that it is correct for *everyone* to prefer X to Y.

I need to explain what it is for one cognitive perspective to be better than another for making a certain kind of choice or decision. Perspectives are assessed not only by the kind of information they involve but also by the kind of cognitive functioning, e.g., means-ends rationality, that characterizes them. The amount of information that it is empirically possible for us to possess is limited by the constraints of human nature—the size of our brains and memories, limitations on how much information we can represent to ourselves at any one time, and limitations on how long we live. At the limit, the amount of knowledge concerning the choice between X and not-X can't be any greater than the amount that I (with my present abilities) could grasp over the course of a normal human lifetime. For the purposes of interpreting COR, cognitive perspectives should be understood to include not only one's cognitive state at a given point in time but also the history leading up to such a perspective at a given time. For example, even if everything is the same in the present, a cognitive perspective that involves one's having had false beliefs about X and not-X in the past is different than one that doesn't involve one's having had those false beliefs in the past. The latter perspective is, other things equal, a better perspective for assessing the value of X and not-X.

The idea of a better cognitive/informational perspective is admittedly vague and context-dependent. Different kinds of information are relevant to different kinds of choices. A given perspective (P1) might be as good as any other possible perspective that I can have for choosing between X and Y but not be a good perspective for making other choices. The best possible perspective for me to assess the choice between A and B might involve my having so much information about A and B that it would be impossible for me to occupy simultaneously both that perspective and the best possible perspective for me to assess the choice between Y and Z. (It might not be possible for me to have all information included in *both* perspectives.) In judging the merits of different informational perspectives we need to balance considerations of breadth of knowledge (being well acquainted with all the relevant *kinds* of information) and considerations of depth and vividness of knowledge. Consider the following example. I am choosing between alternatives 1 and 2. Alternative 1 will have outcomes A-L, and 2 will have outcomes M-Z. I might spend all my available time trying to acquire very vivid knowledge of A and B. This would presumably not be as good an informational perspective as one in which I have moderately vivid knowledge of A-Z. We can say that, other things equal, the more relevant information one has, the fewer false beliefs one has (about relevant matters), and the better one's means-ends rationality, the better one's cognitive perspective. (If certain information is truly relevant to a certain issue, then, other things equal, one's cognitive perspective is better if one has that information.) Here, it might be objected that additional information could be skewed so as to favor certain preferences or certain views over others. Suppose that there are one thousand facts of which I am ignorant that would (if I knew them) affect my judgment about the morality of x. Five hundred of these facts would incline me to think that x is right (or prefer that x occur), five hundred would incline me to think that x is wrong (or prefer that x not occur). Suppose that I learn a hundred facts that all incline me to think that x is wrong. Has my cognitive situation improved by learning these hundred facts? Does hearing all the truths on one side of a debate, but not the other, make one better informed?

The possibility of skewed information is a problem for COR only if it is possible that there are cases in which the correctness of someone's preferences is determined by the preferences that he would have from skewed informational perspectives. But such cases are not possible, because, for any empirically possible cognitive perspective in which one's information about something is skewed, there is an otherwise similar empirically possible perspective in which one's information is not skewed and that constitutes a better perspective. For any perspective from which one's knowledge is skewed, we can imagine that it could be improved by making it unskewed. In some cases, this will only require giving one additional information. For example, suppose that my cognitive perspective for thinking about the choice of careers is skewed by my having detailed and vivid knowledge of the satisfactions of being a locomotive engineer but having little detailed or vivid knowledge of the frustrations and aggravations that engineers suffer. I can unskew my perspective and thereby improve it by acquiring a vivid and detailed knowledge of those frustrations and aggravations.

2. Relevant Information

Some account of the notion of "relevant information" is in order. One standard view is that relevant information about X is information that makes a difference in one's reactions to X.[26] This view is open to several serious objections: (1) Whether or not a certain piece of information makes a difference to my reaction to X may depend on whether I have certain other information. Ostensibly relevant information might fail to make a difference to my reactions to something if I lack other relevant information. For example, suppose that S's doing X will result in his being unable to do Y and that S has promised to do Y. Whether my knowing that S's doing X will make him unable to do Y affects my reaction to his doing X might depend on whether or not I know that S promised to do Y.[27] (2) Certain information that we think shouldn't affect one's reactions to something might make a difference in one's reactions to it. For example, knowing about someone's ethnicity might cause one to judge her more leniently or harshly than one should.

The following account of relevant information constitutes a significant improvement on the earlier view:

> Information I is relevant to S's assessment of X, provided that (A) having I alters or would alter S's reactions to X (or having I would alter S's reactions to X if S possessed other information that he now lacks), and (B) I's altering S's reactions about X in any of the ways described in (A) is not the result of false beliefs, or desires that result from false beliefs, or any deficiencies of cognitive functioning, e.g., S's making incorrect inferences.

Clause A enables us to avoid problem 1. Even if ostensibly relevant information about X fails to alter our attitudes about X, it might still be the case that it would alter our attitudes about X if we had certain additional information. I doubt that my proposal fully avoids problem 2. I can't assume the existence of any independent moral facts (such as that ethnic discrimination is wrong) that rule out such information as relevant. Very often, partiality toward members of certain ethnic groups is the result of false beliefs about those groups, but we can't assume that this kind of partiality could *never* arise apart from false beliefs. Given non-realism, there is no independent fact of the matter that certain features of things are or are not relevant to their goodness or badness. Given the rational-desire-satisfaction theory of value, whether a certain feature of something makes it good or tends to make it good depends on how we would react to it if we were rational and informed. If we reject realism, then we should also reject the strong intuitions about the relevance or irrelevance of certain information that underlie objection 2.

In light of the difficulties involved in drawing the distinction between relevant and irrelevant information, we might attempt to do without this distinction.[28] I am very tempted by this idea, but it creates problems for COR. COR depends on the idea that certain cognitive perspectives are better than others. If we don't attempt to distinguish between relevant and irrelevant information, then COR can't make use of such principles as the following:

> Other things being equal, cognitive position 1 is a better standpoint for S to assess X than cognitive position 2 if 1 includes relevant information about X that S lacks in 2.

Even if we employ some notion of relevance and count certain information as irrelevant to certain questions, there are many normative questions for which the amount of relevant information far exceeds our capacities for representing information. The information relevant to determining whether or not my present career is the best career for me far exceeds my capacities to represent it to myself. For the purposes of ranking different possible cognitive perspectives in COR, we need some notion of the relative importance or salience of (relevant) information. I despair of giving any general account of this concept; it is far too context-dependent for that. The legitimacy of this concept, however, should not be questioned. At least for most of us, knowing that a certain career would be boring and exhausting (or engrossing and pleasant) is far more significant than knowing whether or not a stranger in a foreign country regards that career as prestigious. (It would be easy to generate many more examples of this sort.)

To the extent that the reader is dissatisfied with the present account of relevant information and questions whether any satisfactory account of this notion is available to defenders of the rational-desire-satisfaction theory of value, she will have additional reasons to prefer the divine-preference theory of rationality to COR. Since God is omniscient and has *all* information, we don't need to ask which information is relevant to God's preferences about X. God's attitudes are based on complete information about everything.

3. How COR Deals with Some of the Earlier Objections

COR talks about empirically possible cognitive positions that do not exceed the intellectual and imaginative powers of human beings. It doesn't require that we try to determine what we would prefer if we had Godlike intellectual powers. COR also addresses some of the problems noted by Velleman and Rosati. It doesn't require that we be able to identify a single best (possible) way of representing information to ourselves. It allows that different ways of representing information might be equally good. COR allows that many statements to the effect that one would or would not prefer something were one fully rational have no determinate truth value, but, as we have seen, this consequence is acceptable.

COR is also able to deal with the problem of cognitive overload. If acquiring further information causes a mental breakdown that disrupts one's cognitive functioning, then it worsens rather than improves one's cognitive perspective. In the case of mental breakdown or collapse there will be independent and relatively non-controversial tests of cognitive functioning, e.g., tests of means-ends rationality and reasoning ability. While suffering from severe depression or wild paranoia, one will be unable to do nearly as well on standard tests of mental ability as one normally does.

COR is able to deal with Loeb's objection about information changing our motivations for the worse. If certain information causes the kind of extreme emotional reaction (extreme fear or deep depression) that Loeb describes, then having that information (even though it is part of *full information*) would, on balance, make one's cognitive perspective worse by making it impossible for one to be vividly aware of *other* relevant information. (Strong emotional reactions might also make one's cognitive position worse by diminishing one's cognitive functioning, e.g., one's means-ends rationality.) If one's having certain information causes this kind of reaction, then at least some cognitive perspectives in which one lacks that information will be better than any perspective in which one possesses it.

Here, it would be helpful to consider a concrete example. Two people (X and Y) are trying to decide which careers they should pursue. Each is choosing between the same options and the options in question include being a firefighter. Since firefighters sometimes suffer severe burns and often help prevent others from being severely burned, knowledge of what it is like to experience the pain of severe burns is clearly relevant to this decision. X's personality is such that were he to experience the pain of severe burns he would become unhinged and be so terrified of being burned that his ability to vividly imagine other kinds of relevant information would be substantially diminished. Person Y could (briefly) experience the pain of severe burns without this diminishing his cognitive functioning in any way. In this case, direct experience of the pain of severe burns is part of the best possible cognitive perspective for Y, but not for X. The best possible perspective(s) for X would still allow him to have a considerable amount of information about the pain of severe burns: he could experience the pain of milder burns and know many facts about the consequences of experiencing the pain of severe burns—including the fact that it would be profoundly disturbing for him.

4. A Further Objection—Hardness of Heart

Velleman and Rosati present a different version of the objection that information might change our motivations for the worse. Rosati says it is possible that full information would render us callous, hard, and indifferent.[29] Velleman observes that "our hearts may grow either hard or tender at the sight of other people's pain."[30] Is this also an objection to COR? For the sake of argument, let us grant that it's possible that exposure to relevant information could make someone cold and hardhearted without, at the same time, diminishing the vividness with which he represents other information. COR and the rational-desire-satisfaction theories of value and welfare that are based on it can still be defended. If there can be cases of this sort, then the welfarist version of the rational-desire-satisfaction theory of welfare/value based on COR implies that one's own welfare or the goodness or badness of one's own life is determined by the preferences that a cold, hardened counterpart of oneself (who is indifferent to the sufferings of others) would have for one's actual self. This is not a decisive objection to such theories. It is not absurd to say that the suffering of others might be irrelevant to *one's own welfare* or the goodness or badness of one's own life. COR allows us to say that the suffering of the hungry is relevant to *their own good* or what is good from their point of view. An informed cold-hearted person would not be indifferent to the starvation of his real counterpart. It should also be noted that COR does not imply that it would be good or rational to decide to become a hardhearted person. Some of my better-informed counterparts might be cold and hardhearted. However, if they had a vivid awareness of all the kinds of pleasures, satisfactions, and ways of life that are unavailable to coldhearted people, they would prefer that I not be a cold-hearted person. Being hardhearted is perfectly consistent with not wanting to be hardhearted. Many coldhearted people are painfully aware of the fact that they would have better lives if they weren't coldhearted.

Here, Rosati and Velleman might say that the problem is not that our better-informed selves might be indifferent to *others*, but rather that they might be apathetic and indifferent about what happens to *themselves*. By way of reply, let me first note that in order for this objection to work the kind of apathy or indifference in question would have to be profound and far beyond any that people ordinarily experience. Consider a person who has decided to commit suicide within a few hours. He will very likely be apathetic and indifferent to what happens to him as long as he remains alive. He might not care if his house burns down, or he loses his job, or he is diagnosed with terminal cancer. But, even in such a state of despair about his actual life, he will still have preferences about other lives that he might have led. He will still wish that his life had gone better and that it had taken a different course long ago. He will not be indifferent to all the *possible* lives he might have led. Thus, if my better-informed counterpart has no greater level of apathy or despair than the typical person who commits suicide, he will be able to have clear and sensible preferences about my actual life. But, if we can, let us imagine a profound apathy that not only involves indifference about the circumstances of one's actual life but indifference about any possible lives that one might have had. Knowledge that caused one to be profoundly apathetic or "numbed" would diminish one's ability to represent other kinds of information to oneself. It's doubtful that this kind of apathy and depression is consistent with having a vivid knowledge of the great goods and bads that life can hold for one. It's unclear that such a person could be *vividly aware* of the great joys that many lovers know.

Full information would include vivid and detailed knowledge of any possible future courses of life that would cause one to become happy and pleased with one's life.

Rosati says that being cognitively ideal is not sufficient for being an ideal advisor for questions about what sort of person to be. Ideal-advisor theories must explicitly incorporate some kind of notion of an ideal person or of being "motivationally ideal."[31] We can't simply let the chips fall where they may and say that our good is determined by the kinds of motivations that would result if our actual motivations were altered by improved information. Rosati does not indicate what kinds of motivations she considers "ideal" for an ideal advisor, nor does she explain how she would justify such claims. She concedes that this proposal involves importing substantive evaluative claims into the notion of an ideal advisor and thus involves abandoning the idea of grounding a theory of the good in an evaluatively neutral conception of an ideal advisor.[32]

In spite of all the problems with full-information theories of rationality, it seems clear that non-realist theories of rationality require some kind of informational component—being rational surely requires being adequately informed. (Rosati herself allows for this.) Even if we accept Rosati's and Velleman's criticisms of purely cognitive and informational theories of rationality, COR seems to be a plausible candidate for the informational component of a theory of rationality.

The argument about information causing people to become hard of heart is a serious objection, and I confess to being unsettled by it. But it is not a decisive objection to COR. That an otherwise attractive theory yields counterintuitive results in a very small number of highly unusual cases cannot be considered a decisive reason for rejecting it. Fortunately, non-realists have a better alternative theory—the divine-preference theory I develop below. But we may still need COR as a "fall-back" theory of rationality in case the sort of God the divine-preference theory describes doesn't exist.

VIII. The Divine-Preference Theory of Rationality

1. Some Virtues of the Divine-Preference Theory of Rationality

In light of the many problems confronting full-information theories of rationality, it is very tempting to adopt a divine-preference theory of rationality. Such a theory can deal with the main problems that beset standard full-information theories: the limitations of human capacities, the indeterminateness of statements about what one would prefer if one were fully informed, and the possibility that full information would bring about some kind of mental breakdown or debilitating emotional reaction. Since God is omniscient, full information doesn't exceed God's capacities. Because of God's unlimited capacities, God can be vividly aware of everything in a single instant. Thus, "the problem of experiential ordering" does not arise for the divine-preference theory. An omniscient God *is* fully informed; the divine-preference theory doesn't need to rely on counterfactual statements about what God's preferences *would be if* God were fully informed. God's actual preferences are completely determinate. Because of God's unlimited abilities, God could be fully informed without this leading to any kind of cognitive breakdown or debilitating emotional reaction.

The cognitive standpoint of an omniscient God seems clearly preferable to any cognitive standpoints that human beings are capable of occupying. To the extent that our actual preferences (or the preferences that it is correct for us to have according to COR) are contrary to God's, we should regard our own preferences as mistaken and less rational than God's.

There are clearly ordinary-language uses of the word "rational" that do not fit with the divine-preference theory. Someone's preferences might be very ill-informed and ill-considered but still be consistent with God's preferences simply as a matter of luck. It seems odd to call such preferences "rational." Similarly, preferences that are as well informed and well considered as humanly possible might be contrary to God's preferences (or the preferences God wants us to have). This, however, is not an objection to using the divine-preference theory as a theory about the *correctness* of attitudes which, in turn, is used as the basis for a normative theory.

2. A Comparison of the Divine-Preference Theory of Rationality and Divine-Command Theories of Right and Wrong

There are obvious parallels between divine-preference theories of rational (or correct) preferences and divine-command theories of right and wrong. The traditional divine-command theory of right and wrong can be stated roughly as follows:

> TDCT. An act is morally obligatory if, and only if, God commands it. An act is morally permissible if, and only if, God permits it. An act is morally wrong if, and only if, God forbids it. What makes an act obligatory is that God commands it; what makes an act permissible is that God permits it; what makes an act morally wrong is that God forbids it. Actions cannot be obligatory, wrong, or permissible independently of God's commands.

The TDCT is open to a number of serious objections and is widely regarded as a hopelessly implausible theory. (i) It implies that nothing anyone does can be morally obligatory or morally wrong unless God exists and commands and forbids us to do certain things. To use the words of Ivan Karamazov, the TDCT implies that "if God is dead, then everything is permitted." (ii) The TDCT implies that *any act* would be right if God commanded us to do it. But certain acts, e.g., acts of cruelty or murder, would be wrong even if God commanded us to perform them. (iii) The TDCT implies that if God is indifferent to human beings and what they do, then nothing can be morally obligatory or morally wrong. It seems that the divine-preference theory of rationality is open to analogous objections: it implies that if God is cruel and prefers that we act cruelly, it would be rational/correct for us to prefer that we act cruelly. It also implies that if God doesn't exist (or if God is indifferent to human beings), then none of our preferences are rational or irrational, correct or incorrect. When taken together with the divine-preference theory of rationality, the rational-preference-satisfaction theory of value commits us to the view that nothing can be good or bad unless God exists.

Robert Adams has proposed a modified divine-command theory that avoids these three objections. Adams's most recent formulation of the divine command theory can be stated briefly as follows:

> If there is a loving God, then (1) an action is obligatory if, and only if, a loving God commands it; (2) an action is morally permissible if, and only if, a loving God permits it; and (3) an action is morally wrong if, and only if, a loving God forbids it. If there does not exist a loving God, then the rightness or wrongness of actions is determined in some other way.[33]

Adams holds that if there is a loving God, then right and wrong are determined by God's commands; if there does not exist a loving God, then right and wrong are determined in some other way. Adams's theory avoids the first objection. Adams's modified DCT also avoids the second objection. It does not imply that we would be morally obligated to obey God's commands if God commanded cruelty. If God commanded cruelty for its own sake, he would thereby show himself to be unloving; a loving God would not command cruelty. Adams's theory does not imply that we would be obligated to follow the commands of an unloving God. Since a loving God would not be indifferent to human beings, Adams's theory avoids the third objection (God's being loving entails that he loves human beings).

Given the seriousness of objections (i), (ii), and (iii) and analogous objections to the divine-preference theory of rationality (value), it is preferable to model the divine-preference theory along the lines of Adams's theory rather than the TDCT.

3. Some Versions of the Divine-Preference Theory and Reasons to Accept One Particular Version

Consider the following:

1. If there exists a loving and omniscient God who created the universe and human beings for certain purposes/reasons, then God's preferences are the ultimate standard for the correctness/rationality of human preferences. If a loving and omniscient God does not exist, then the correctness or rationality of human preferences is determined in some other way. (I take omniscience to include what Firth calls "omnipercipience" or ideal vividness of knowledge; it involves a vivid understanding of the feelings of others. I take it that there can be at most one omniscient creator of the universe.)

1 says that *if* there exists a loving and omniscient God who created the universe and human beings for certain purposes/reasons, *then* God's preferences should be considered ideal; we should regard God's preferences as the ultimate standard for judging the correctness of our own preferences. 1 makes God's *actual* preferences the ultimate standard for the rationality or correctness of human preferences, provided that a loving, omniscient creator of the universe exists. Note that 1 does not require that God be omnipotent.

Alternatively, we could say that the ultimate standards for judging our own preferences are the preferences that a loving and omniscient creator *would have* if such a being existed:

2. The correctness/rationality of human preferences should be judged by the preferences that a loving and omniscient God who created the universe and human beings for certain purposes/reasons would have *if such a God existed.*

Although I am indebted to Adams for my formulations of 1 and 2, I doubt that he would accept either 1 or 2 or want to use them as basis for a theory of good and bad. Adams does not defend the divine-command theory as a theory of value. His theory of *moral rightness* is consistent with saying that some things are good or bad independently of God's commands or preferences. Indeed, Adams claims that certain judgments about what is good and bad are true independently of God's commands.[34]

It would be instructive to contrast 1 and 2 with the ideal-observer theory (IOT). Standard versions of the IOT hold that the reactions of an ideal observer determine the truth or falsity of normative judgments. They hold roughly the following: a favorable (unfavorable) moral judgment about X is true provided that, *if s/he existed,* an ideal observer (or all ideal observers) would have a favorable (unfavorable) attitude about X. These theories do not posit the actual existence of an ideal observer. 2 is similar to the ideal-observer theory in that it takes the preferences that God would have (if God existed) to be the ultimate standard of rationality. There may be truths about what God would prefer (if God existed), even if God doesn't actually exist. According to 2, the rationality of preferences is independent of whether God actually exists. 2 is a kind of ideal-observer theory. It differs from standard versions of the IOT in that it takes God, rather than a super-duper human being, to be the ideal observer. By contrast, 1 makes God's actual preferences the ultimate standard of rationality only if a loving and omniscient creator of the universe actually exists.

I think that we should prefer 1 to 2. Assuming that axiological realism is false, the essential features of a loving and omniscient creator would seem to underdetermine the creator's preferences. These characteristics are compatible with different kinds of psychological characteristics and inclinations. There is no reason to think that all possible omniscient and loving creators would have the same preferences about *everything.*[35] Nor is there reason to think that every possible loving and omniscient being who created the universe would create the universe for exactly the same reasons. The following scenario makes clear what is at stake between 1 and 2. Suppose that there is an omniscient and loving creator of the universe who has clear preferences about how human beings live their lives. Suppose also that certain other possible omniscient loving creators of the universe would have different preferences about how humans live their lives. According to 1, God's actual preferences determine what it is correct to prefer (and thus what is good and bad). But 2 implies that God's actual preferences have no priority over the preferences of other possible Gods. In such a case, I think that we should accept the implications of 1 and say that what is correct for us to prefer is determined by God's *actual preferences.* There are pragmatic reasons (perhaps largely prudential) for us to harmonize our preferences with God's. But aren't God's actual preferences arbitrary since they could have been different without God's losing any of God's perfections? God might have had different preferences than those God actually has. God might have designed the cosmos and our place in it for different purposes than those God has in fact designed them for. God might not have created the earth or human beings at all—God might have chosen to create other forms of intelligent life instead. But the contingency of (at least some of) God's actual preferences and designs does not alter the fact that we have reasons to submit to those plans and preferences. Given the existence of purposes within a particular plan of creation (which has its source in an omniscient and loving being), we have reasons to fulfill those purposes. If there exists a wise, omniscient, and loving creator of the universe who has a plan for the universe in which human beings play a role, then it makes sense for us to fulfill our purpose in that plan. If such a God exists, then it is reasonable for us to try to live in accordance with God's plan and not resist our natural ends and the design of the universe. It would be reasonable for us to defer to the superior knowledge and wisdom of such a God, just as it is reasonable for small children to defer to the wishes of their parents, provided that the parents are loving.

Full information relevant to the preference between x and not-x would include knowledge of God's preferences (if any) concerning x and not-x. For deciding between x and not-x, any cognitive perspective in which I know God's preference between x and not-x (and God's *reasons* for preferring what God prefers) would be better than any otherwise identical perspective in which I lack this information. Many of us would be strongly inclined to defer to God's preferences in case they conflict with the preferences that we would have independently of knowing God's will. (I have argued that it would be reasonable for us to defer to God's preferences in such cases.) God's reasons for preferring some things to others (insofar as human beings could understand them) might seem very compelling to us. 1 and COR might be extentionally equivalent in what they say about the rationality of the preferences of such people. But assuming that there are people who would *not defer* to God's preferences (even if they knew as much as it is possible for humans to know about God's reasons for preferring what God prefers) 1 and COR are not extentionally equivalent.

There is a serious ambiguity in 1 and 2 that needs to be addressed. Is the correctness of my preference for X over Y determined by whether God prefers (or would prefer) X to Y? Or is it determined by whether God prefers (or would prefer) that *I* prefer X to Y? This question makes clear the difference between the following:

a.   If a loving and omniscient creator of the universe has a certain preference (p) (or if a loving omniscient creator of the universe would have p if such a God existed), then it is rational (correct) for *any person* to have p.

b.   If a loving and omniscient creator of the universe prefers that person S have a certain preference (p) (or if a loving omniscient creator of the universe would prefer that S have p if such a God existed), then it is rational (correct) for S to have p.[36]

It is conceivable that in some cases God prefers X to Y, but does not prefer that each person prefer X to Y. Consider the following example. Let X be Richard Nixon's ceasing to be president in 1974 and Y be Nixon's remaining as president until the end of his term. It is conceivable that God prefers X to Y, but also prefers that Nixon's wife and daughters prefer Y to X. If God values loyalty and personal attachments, he might want people to be partial to others in certain cases. The sorts of considerations that favor 1 over 2 are also reasons to favor (b) over (a). If there is a loving, omniscient, and extremely powerful God who created the universe and human beings for certain reasons, it is reasonable for us to submit to God's will. (a) commits one to defying God's will in cases of the sort we are imagining here.

4. The Euthyphro Objection

In the *Euthyphro*, Socrates considers the view that "the pious (just) is what is loved by all the gods." This view implies that things are pious (just) because they are beloved by the gods. He objects to this on the grounds that the gods love the things they love because those things are pious (just); this implies that things are pious (just) independently of being loved by the gods. The analogue of this objection for 1 and 2 is something like the following:

> 1 and 2 imply that what makes a preference rational or irrational (correct or incorrect) is that God has it (or would have it, or would prefer that we have it). But God prefers certain things because it is rational or correct for God to do so; it is rational for God to prefer some things to others because those things are good or bad (independently of God's preferences). Therefore, some preferences must be rational or correct independently of God's preferences.

This objection presupposes the truth of AR, and, therefore, is not an objection to the position that I am considering here, namely, that, *given non-realism*, 1 and 2 are plausible theories of rationality (or correct and incorrect preferences). It is widely assumed that Socrates' argument refutes the kind of divine-love theory of justice/morality that Euthyphro defends. But this is far from clear. Socrates' argument presupposes the truth of a very strong version of moral realism. To the extent that moral realism is problematic, so is Socrates' argument.

There is another slightly different objection to 1 lurking in the *Euthyphro*. The objection is that 1 makes God's preferences "arbitrary." Given 1, God can't have reasons to prefer one thing to another. If God's preferences are arbitrary, we have no reason to conform our preferences to God's. This objection, however, is not persuasive. 1 implies that if there is a loving and omniscient God who created the universe for certain reasons, then things can't be good or bad independently of God's preferences. This means that God can't prefer x to y *because* x is better than y (independently of God's preferences). But it leaves open the possibility that God could have *other reasons* for preferring x to y. 1 is consistent with saying that God prefers some things because of God's loving nature and omniscience.[37]

5. A Serious Objection: What Does It Mean to Say That God Is Loving?

I need to explain what it means to say that God is loving. Given that the divine-preference theory of rationality is to be used as part of a non-realist normative theory, certain plausible accounts of the nature of God's love are not open to us. We cannot say that God's being loving consists in the fact that God desires what is good for earthly creatures. It would be viciously circular to say that what is good and bad is determined by what a loving God desires and then go on to define what it is for God to be loving in terms of what is good and bad for humans (independently of what God prefers). Many philosophers and theologians have proffered analyses of "love." Almost all of these analyses imply that at least a *necessary* condition of someone's loving another person is that she desires (or seeks to promote) the good of the other person.

Aristotle defines *philia* (love, friendship) as a mutual feeling of good will. According to Aristotle, two people love each other provided that each desires the other's welfare for its own sake and each is aware of the other's good will.[38] David Hamlyn says that loving someone entails wishing her well, desiring her welfare.[39] Gabriele Taylor claims that a necessary condition of one's loving another person is that one wants to benefit her.[40] Sidgwick holds that love always involves "a desire to do good to the object beloved."[41] Robert Brown says that loving someone "implies wishing to benefit the person and advance the person's welfare."[42] McTaggart's definition of love is a notable exception. McTaggart defines love as a "liking" for another that is intense and passionate.[43] Although he says that we generally desire to do good to any person we love, he denies that benevolence (or desiring to do good to the other) is a necessary condition of love. He goes so far as to say that it is possible to desire the illfare (bad) of those we love.[44] Given McTaggart's conception of love, it's not clear that the requirement that God be loving can serve the purpose it serves in Adams's theory—restricting the kinds of preferences that God can have so that God's preferences can provide the basis of a plausible normative theory.

Some definitions of love presuppose an independent concept of goodness in a different way. According to these definitions, loving someone entails that one judges that she is good or worthy of love; people are loved for the qualities that those who love them take to be good or desirable.[45]

The definitions of love surveyed above are all definitions of what it is for one person or human being to love another. It's not clear that these definitions are adequate as an explication of divine love. There are a number of notable theological discussions of the concept of divine love (agape). Anders Nygren characterizes God's love (for human beings) as "spontaneous," "unmotivated," and "indifferent to value." God's love is not a response to the value of human beings or their worthiness to be loved.

> Agape is creative love. God does not love that which is already in itself worthy of love, but on the contrary, that which in itself has no worth acquires worth just by becoming the object of God's love. Agape has nothing to do with the kind of love that depends on the recognition of a valuable quality in an object; agape does not recognize value, but creates it. Agape loves, and imparts value by loving. The man who is loved by God has no value in himself; what gives him value is precisely the fact that God loves him. *Agape is a value-creating principle.*[46]

Nygren's claim that God's love creates value suggests that he might hold something like the divine-preference theory of value. But it is unclear whether Nygren's theory is a plausible theory of value without presupposing some *independent* account of the human good. The question is whether God's desiring what is good for us (where what is good for us is independent of what God desires for us) is a necessary condition of God's love. Nygren is unclear about this. Outka, who draws heavily on Nygren, gives an account of agape that presupposes an independent notion of human welfare. Outka characterizes agape as:

> [A]n active concern for the neighbor's well-being which is somehow independent of particular actions of the other.[47]

Given standard analyses of "love," what is good for another person must be independent of what one desires for her. Loving another person places constraints on what kinds of desires one can have. But the divine-preference theory of rationality taken together with the kind of rational-preference-satisfaction theory of value I want to defend implies that nothing is good or bad (or good or bad for someone) independently of God's desires. What is good or bad (or good or bad for someone) is simply what God desires (for someone). On these assumptions (that loving someone entails desiring what is good for her and that the divine-preference theory of value is true), God's being loving can't place any limitations on the kinds of preferences God can have, and the requirement that God be loving can't do the kind of work it does in Adams's theory. Given standard analyses of love, 1 seems likely to yield unacceptable consequences analogous to the second objection (ii) to the TDCT. This is not a problem for Adams. Since Adams holds that some things are good independently of God's will, he can say that "God is loving" means that God desires what is good for earthly creatures (where what is good for us is independent of what God desires or commands).

In this respect, Adams's divine-command theory of right and wrong is less problematic than divine-preference theories of good and bad. But this plausibility is bought at a price. Adams's theory is a hybrid theory according to which facts about what is right and wrong are determined by what a loving God commands and forbids, and facts about what is good and bad are independent of God's will. On Adams's theory, facts about what is good and bad severely constrain what sorts of things a loving God can command. To the extent that God is loving, God can't command us to do things that are bad or harmful for human beings.

It is important to ask whether we can base a theory of value or *a complete normative theory* on the will of God. Is it plausible to hold that God's will is the ultimate standard for *all normative judgments*? (This question is all the more pressing in light of the objections to alternative theories of value noted elsewhere in this book.) My theory is a more robust and unqualified kind of divine-will theory than Adams's. I haven't said anything about right and wrong in the present book, but my theory is consistent with a divine-command or divine-will theory of right and wrong. Indeed, my arguments for the divine-preference theory of rationality (value) seem to commit me to a divine-will theory of right and wrong. (In contrast, Adams's theory of right and wrong is not consistent with a divine-will theory of value.)

6. An Improved Formulation of the Divine-Preference Theory of Rationality/Value

It is likely that any plausible concept of love (whether human or divine) presupposes independent notions of good and bad or welfare. But rather than abandon the divine-preference theory of rationality/value, we should try to determine whether we can suitably restrict or modify the theory by requiring that God possess certain other characteristics that do not presuppose independent notions of value or welfare. What characteristics do we need to ascribe to God in order for God's preferences to constitute a plausible criterion of rationality (value)? I propose the following.

1. First, we need to assume that God is not indifferent to human beings but rather cares very deeply about us. We need to assume that God designed and created human beings for certain reasons and regards us as a very important part of creation. On this understanding, God has an intrinsic, or non-instrumental, concern for us; God is not concerned with us simply for instrumental reasons. God has plans and desires for human beings; we please and disappoint God in the ways we live our lives. If God is coldhearted and indifferent to humans and all other rational beings, then there is no reason for us to make God's preferences the ultimate standard for judging the goodness or badness of our lives.

It is conceivable that God is kindly and sympathetic to many other rational creatures in the universe but indifferent to human beings. Imagine also that God's lack of concern for human beings is not simply the result of limitations in God's knowledge or powers. God knows about us and *would* care about us if we were more virtuous (kinder and less selfish, and so forth). God might regard us as the products of a botched or unsuccessful experiment that was improved on later.[48] This is a very unsettling and distressing possibility. What, if anything, would follow from this? One might conclude that if God is indifferent to us, then we should be indifferent to ourselves and each other; nothing that happens to us can be good or bad. I'm inclined to think that even if God were indifferent to us for the kinds of reasons in question, it would still make sense for us to employ standards of good and bad in order to try to make the best of our lives; it would still make sense for us to say that some lives are better than others. I won't speculate about this further. My contention here is that if there exists a certain kind of God (a God who, among other things, does care about us), then we should take God's preferences to determine the rationality or correctness of our own preferences. For my purposes here, it's not essential to make claims about what follows if a different sort of God exists.

2. God must be kind and sympathetic. There is no reason for us to take God's preferences to be authoritative for us if God is cruel and delights in our suffering and frustration. It might be imprudent for us to resist God's preferences if God is cruel. But, if God is cruel, we do not have reason to prefer that things happen as God desires or to make God's preferences the ultimate standard for the correctness of our own preferences. To say that God is kind and sympathetic means more than that God is not cruel or malicious. God's being kind and sympathetic in the sense I am proposing here means that, other things equal, God is distressed by our suffering and pleased by our pleasure. Other things equal, God is inclined to remove our suffering. This is consistent

with saying that God has other ends (other things that God wants for humans) that require that God not intervene to relieve or eliminate human suffering. The world is very far from being a hedonistic paradise. A God sufficiently powerful to have created the universe could have done many things to make human life more pleasant and less painful than it generally is. If an omnipotent and omniscient God exists (or if a God sufficiently powerful and knowledgeable to have created the universe exists), then God clearly permits a great deal of suffering that God might have prevented.

This characterization of God's kindness and sympathy needs to be supplemented further. We cannot allow that God permits or desires our suffering for *any reason whatever*. Suppose that God permits our suffering in order to satisfy certain whims in the way that the Roman emperor Caligula is said to have ordered that many people be impaled so that he could view their red blood against the green grass. Alternatively, God might permit or ordain human suffering and moral depravity for their literary and dramatic value. The purpose of human suffering might be to allow God a vivid and dramatic form of literary/cinematic entertainment. These and other similar possibilities can be ruled out if we require that God's reasons for allowing human suffering not be selfish or self-interested. God ordains suffering for *our sake*, i.e., for the sake of its effect on us. For example, it might be the case that God permits suffering in order to fully realize the conditions of morality or free moral agency. According to John Hick, God allows suffering in order for human beings to become autonomous moral agents and develop moral virtues such as compassion and generosity as a result of their own free actions. Hick claims that this process of "soul building" continues in the afterlife.[49]

The characteristics (of God) described above are purely "descriptive." Unlike the concept of love, they do not presuppose notions of good and bad or welfare that are independent of God's preferences.

I can now state my "final" version of the divine-preference theory of rationality/value:

> If there is an omniscient God who designed and created the universe and human beings for certain purposes/reasons, cares deeply about human beings, and is kind, sympathetic, and unselfish (in the ways explained above), then God's preferences are the ultimate standard for the correctness/rationality of human preferences and for the goodness or badness of things. (If such a God exists, it is rational (correct) for person S to have a certain preference (p) if, and only if, God prefers that S have p.) If such a God does not exist, then the correctness or rationality of human preferences (and the goodness or badness of things) is determined in some other way.

If a God of the sort that I have described exists, then we should take God's preferences to be authoritative for us. God's preferences determine what it is rational for us to prefer and what is good and bad. (I should reiterate that everything I say in this chapter is said on the assumption that AR is false. If AR is false and there exists a God of the sort I have described, then we should take God's preferences to be authoritative for us.)

Suppose that there exists a God who created the universe but does not fully satisfy these conditions. For example, suppose that there exists a creator of the universe who is not omniscient but still vastly more knowledgeable (and vastly more knowledgeable about human affairs) than any human being. I believe that if such a God possessed all of the other characteristics described above, then God's preferences should be considered authoritative for us. (There are many other possible deities who fail to fully satisfy my conditions.) But I won't press this point or attempt to defend it further. I will content myself with the claim that if there were a God who possessed *all of these characteristics*, then God's preferences should be authoritative for us.

Here one might object that the divine-preference theory is demeaning to humans and human autonomy; it requires us to be servile and surrender our autonomy to God. The attitudes toward God it prescribes are unworthy of rational adults and, at best, befit children. The relations between children and their parents point the way to a plausible reply to this objection. It is reasonable for young children to submit to the authority of their parents (provided that their parents are kind and loving). If there exists a God of the sort I have described here, then our position with respect to God is similar to that of a young child to her parents, and it is reasonable for us to submit to God's authority and accommodate our preferences to God's. God's knowledge and wisdom exceed our own by at least as much as the knowledge and wisdom of parents exceed that of their young children.

One might respond to all of this by claiming that the divine-preference theory of rationality/value is true but uninteresting, since the existence of so much evil and suffering in the universe is clearly incompatible with the existence of the sort of God that the theory describes. If there were a God of the sort that I have described, then it would be reasonable for us to take God's preferences to be the ultimate standard for assessing the correctness of our own preferences, but it's clear that such a God does not exist. For my own part, I believe that the existence and magnitude of suffering and moral badness is compatible with the existence of the kind of God I have described. Such a God might have *reasons* to permit so much suffering and moral badness to exist. I do not claim to know what reasons such a God has (or might have) for permitting so much suffering to exist; I only claim that such a God *might* have reasons to permit so much suffering. But, short of writing at length on the problem of evil, I can't adequately defend this here. So I should simply say that I am assuming that the traditional atheistic arguments from evil are not decisive—they do not establish the non-existence of God. (For more on the problem of evil see 8.VIII.7.C.)

The question I am addressing here is the following: Is the existence of so much evil and suffering in the world compatible with the existence of an omniscient God who designed and created the universe and human beings for certain purposes/reasons, cares deeply about human beings, and is kind, sympathetic, and unselfish? This question is slightly different from the question that is asked in standard discussions of the problem of evil: Is the existence of so much evil and suffering in the world compatible with the existence of a God who is omnipotent, omniscient, and perfectly good? The sort of God that the divine-preference theory describes needn't be omnipotent although, of course, an omnipotent God could fit this description. In this respect, the problem of evil may be less of a difficulty for my position than it is for theists who claim that God is omnipotent. It is conceivable that the extent of evil and suffering in the world is incompatible with the existence of an omniscient, omnipotent, and perfectly good being but, nonetheless, compatible with the existence of the kind of God my theory describes.[50]

Clearly the interest or importance of the divine preference theory of rationality/value depends on the likelihood that a God of the sort that it describes exists. In this connection, it is interesting to note that Mackie seems to concede that if God created humans for certain purposes, then God's purposes could plausibly be construed as the basis for objective values. But he dismisses ethical theories based on the notion of divine purpose because he thinks it very unlikely that God exists.[51] The conception of God that I have sketched here is consistent with Judeo-Christian theism; it pictures God as a kindly, caring parent and creator of the universe.[52] But this conception of God does not presuppose the truth of any particular version of Jewish or Christian theism.

7. Three Final Objections Considered

A. *Does my theory make the statement that God is good trivially true and uninformative?* If what is good/right is good/right because it is consistent with God's will, then the statement that "God's will is good" or "God has a morally good character" becomes the trivial "God's will is consistent with God's will."[53] The statement that "God is good" means that "God's character is consistent with God's will." Given the divine-preference theory of value, a person's character is good to the extent that God prefers that her character be as it is or be other than it is. God is good or God's character is good to the extent that God's character is as God prefers it to be. This is not trivially true. God may not be as God wants to be; God may prefer that God's character be other than it is. God might suffer from weakness of will; God may have desires God prefers not to have and is unable to control. (This, I take it, could not be a problem for an omnipotent God. I also take it that the will of such a God would not be a plausible standard of value.)[54] A more serious objection to my theory is that it seems to commit us to the view that any possible God must be good, provided that God's character is consistent with God's will. This is objectionable. We don't want to hold that any powerful omniscient God or any powerful omniscient creator of the universe is good provided that God's character is as God prefers it to be. This would be consistent with saying that a cruel, unkind, and uncaring God is good. But my theory doesn't commit us to this. The will or preferences of a God who was cruel and uncaring wouldn't constitute a plausible standard of value. My theory holds that God's preferences are the ultimate standard of value only if God is kind and caring. In order for God's preferences to constitute the ultimate standard of good and bad, God must be kind and caring. Given that a kind, caring, and omniscient God exists, God's preferences are the ultimate standard for judging the goodness or badness of everything, including God's own character.

Note: The statement "God is good" may be analytic in the sense that "God" is an honorific title so that we will refuse to grant the title of "God" to any being whom we do not take to be good. But the view that "God" is an honorific title in this sense is perfectly consistent with my view that the statement "God is good" is not trivial or uninformative. The objection that I am considering here is not an objection to the view that "God" is an honorific title in this sense.

B. *Does the divine-preference theory commit us to an infinite regress?* My theory implies that God's having a certain preference is not itself good (or bad) unless God prefers that God have (or not have) that preference. Only those preferences that God reflectively endorses can be good. It might be objected that the divine-preference theory commits us to an infinite regress. If God prefers that X, then God must prefer that he prefer that X; if God prefers that he prefer that X, then God must prefer that he prefer that he prefer that X, and so on. This, however, is not a serious problem for my view. First, my theory does not imply that God must have an infinite number of higher-order preferences for every single preference he has in order for anything to be good or bad. My view only implies that the state of affairs God having a certain preference is not itself good or bad unless God has a higher-order preference that he have or not have it. Second, the possibility of an infinite regress of higher-order preferences cannot be dismissed in the case of an omniscient being. God could have an infinite number of higher-order preferences.

C. *Does the divine-preference theory of value make it impossible to raise the traditional problem of evil?* If God's will is the ultimate standard of good and bad, then nothing God does (including his having created this world, instead of some other world) can possibly count as evidence against his goodness. It seems as if the problem of evil can't even arise on my theory. No conceivable facts about the extent of suffering in this world could count as evidence against God's goodness. If God's preferences are the standard of value, then whatever world God chose to create must be at least as good as any alternative world that he could have created instead. God can't possibly be faulted for having created this world as opposed to some other world that was within God's power to create. The problem of evil seems to disappear, given the divine-preference theory of value. This might be taken to be a *reductio ad absurdum* of the divine-preference theory. The problem of evil is a real problem. It is a serious question whether the existence of so much evil in the world counts as evidence against the existence of a good God. Any theory that denies that this is a serious and open question is *ipso facto* unacceptable.

However, the divine preference theory of value allows us to say that the existence of evil raises questions about the existence of God. The existence of so much suffering (and ostensibly pointless suffering) can be taken as evidence against the view that there exists a God who has the qualities that make God's will a plausible standard of good and bad. The existence of so much suffering in the world could be taken to be *prima facie* evidence against the existence of a kind, caring, and powerful God. We might also take the evils of the world to be evidence that there does not exist a God who is omniscient, omnipotent, kind, and caring. But if there exists a God of the sort that my theory describes, then it makes sense to say that God's will is the ultimate standard of value. If we accept the divine-preference theory of rationality/value and there exists a God of the sort that my theory describes, then God's will is the ultimate standard of value. Whatever God prefers is better than what God prefers it to. Given all of this, this world must be at least as good as any alternative world that God could have created instead, and we can't fault God for having chosen to create this world instead of some other world that was within God's power to create. But the divine-preference theory of value is perfectly consistent with our taking the existence of so much suffering to be evidence for the non-existence of a kind and caring God. We can also take it as evidence for the non-existence of a kind, caring, and omnipotent God. If, as I believe is the case, we have good independent reasons for accepting the divine-preference theory of value (the very qualified version of the theory that I endorse), then we have reasons to accept its implications for the problem of evil.

8. A Fall-Back Theory of Rationality

For all that I have shown (or can show) in this book, it is an open question whether or not there exists an omniscient God who designed and created the universe and human beings for certain purposes/reasons, cares deeply about human beings, and is kind, sympathetic, and unselfish. (In order to avoid repeating this cumbersome expression, I will use the expression "kindly omniscient creator of the universe" to refer to this kind of God.) We need a "fall-back" non-realist theory of rationality in case a kindly omniscient creator of the universe does not exist. I have formulated a plausible alternative non-realist theory of rationality: the informed-preference theory (COR). Another alternative for non-realists would be to say that what is rational (correct) for us to prefer is determined by what a kindly omniscient creator of the universe *would* prefer if such a God existed. According to this view, it is rational (correct) for someone to have a certain preference, provided that all possible kindly omniscient creators of the universe would prefer that she have that preference. This view is a kind of ideal-observer theory. A very similar view (2) was discussed in 8.VIII.3. I shall refer to this view as the "ideal-observer version" of the divine-preference theory of rationality. Given non-realism, the essential features of a kindly omniscient creator of the universe underdetermine the creator's preferences for us. It seems likely that there are cases in which some possible kindly omniscient creators of the universe prefer that I have preference X and other possible kindly omniscient creators of the universe prefer that I not have preference X. The ideal-observer version of the divine-preference theory of rationality implies that my preference (X) is neither correct nor incorrect (neither rational nor irrational).

How shall we decide between COR and the ideal-observer version of the divine-preference theory of rationality? If the preferences of *all* possible kindly omniscient creators of the universe conflict with those that COR deems to be correct, then I am inclined to think that we should take the preferences that those hypothetical Gods would endorse to be ultimately correct. The cognitive perspective of an omniscient God is far superior to any perspective that human beings are capable of occupying. Suppose that *all* possible kindly omniscient creators of the universe prefer that I have a certain preference (p), but COR implies that it is not correct for me to have p. To the extent that the preferences that I would have from the best cognitive perspective that I am capable of occupying differ from those that all possible kindly omniscient creators of the universe would want me to have, the former are the result of limitations of human knowledge and cognitive functioning. In this respect, the ideal-observer version of the divine-preference theory seems preferable to COR. On the other hand, we might want to claim that a person's preferences about X could be correct or incorrect, even if possible kindly omniscient creators of the universe would disagree in their preferences about that person's preferences about X. The following compromise theory accommodates both of the views stated above:

> If a kindly omniscient creator of the universe does not exist but all possible kindly omniscient creators of the universe would prefer that S have preference X, then it is correct (rational) for S to have X. If a kindly omniscient creator of the universe does not exist and it's not the case that all possible kindly omniscient creators of the universe would agree in their preference about S's having X, then the correctness of S's preference X is determined by COR.

There is much more that would need to be done in order to defend a particular theory of rationality as the preferred "back-up" non-realist theory of rationality. For all I have shown here, there may be better alternative back-up theories of rationality available to non-realists. But I won't pursue this issue further. For my purposes, it's sufficient to note that non-realists who endorse the divine-preference theory of rationality have at least one plausible "back-up" theory of rationality, in case a God of the sort described by the divine-preference theory does not exist.

IX. What Things Are Good? — Implications of the Theories of Rationality

What are the implications of the theories of rationality presented above when they are incorporated into the rational-desire-satisfaction theory of value? What things count as good and bad according to the theories that result? Let me offer some brief conjectures.

1) The Implications of the Rational-Desire-Satisfaction Theory of Value When Combined with the Divine-Preference Theory of Rationality (on the Assumption That There Exists a God of the Sort the Theory Describes)

Let us first consider the implications of the present view for questions about the objectivity of value judgments. Are value judgments objectively true or false? We can say that a statement or judgment is true for *someone*, provided that it is correct (in a sense that is opposed to mistaken) for her to accept it (see 6.II.2 for a discussion of the notion of correctness). We can distinguish between two different notions of objective truth. In one sense, a judgment is objectively true, provided that it is true for *all human beings*; a judgment is objectively true, provided that it is correct (in a sense that is opposed to mistaken) for all human beings to accept it. There is also a stronger notion of objective truth. To say that something is objectively true in this stronger sense is to say that it is true for *all possible rational beings*. In this sense, a judgment is objectively true, provided that it is correct (in a sense that is opposed to mistaken) for all possible rational beings to accept it. Kant claims that moral principles are true or valid for all possible rational beings. The view that normative judgments aren't objectively true or false is often called "metaethical relativism."[55]

As I formulate it, the divine-preference theory of rationality says that if there exists a kindly omniscient creator of the universe, then the correctness of our preferences is determined by God's preferences and, if such a God does not exist, then the correctness of our preferences is determined in some other way. This theory implies that if God prefers that I prefer X to Y, then it is correct for me to prefer X to Y. When combined with the divine-preference theory of rationality, the rational-preference-satisfaction theory of value implies that if there exists a kindly omniscient creator of the universe who prefers that all human beings (or all possible rational beings) prefer that X occur, other things being equal, then it is true for all human beings (or all possible rational beings) that X is non-instrumentally good. If, in many cases, God (a God who is kindly and omniscient, and so forth) wants all human beings (or all possible rational beings) to have a certain preference, then the present view implies that many normative judgments are objectively true in the sense of being true for all human beings (or true for all possible rational beings). If God wants everyone to have the same preferences about everything, so that whenever God wants a human being (or a possible rational being) to prefer X to Y, God also prefers that every other human being (or every other possible rational being) prefer X to Y, then the present view seems to commit us to a full-blown objectivism according to which all normative judgments are either objectively true or objectively false.

It is not obvious, however, that whenever God wants one person to have a certain preference, God also wants everyone else to have the same preference. It is conceivable that in some cases God prefers that some human beings have preferences that conflict with the preferences God wants other humans to have. God might prefer that I prefer that X exist and also prefer that you prefer that X not exist (see 8.VIII.3 for a defense of this). The non-welfarist version of the desire-satisfaction-theory (see 3.I.7 for an explanation of this version of the theory) seems to imply that X is both good and bad—X is good insofar as it is correct for me to prefer that it exist, and X is bad insofar as it is correct for you to prefer that X not exist. On pain of embracing contradictions, proponents of the present theory can't say that judgments about the non-instrumental value of X are objectively true or false. Instead, they could say that it's true for me that X is non-instrumentally good and true for you that X is non-instrumentally bad. Alternatively, they could adopt Gauthier's terminology in *Morals by Agreement* and say that X is good from the standpoint of one person and bad from the standpoint of another person.[56] Given that there are cases of this sort, the non-welfarist version of the divine-preference theory of value is inconsistent with a thoroughgoing objectivism but rather seems to commit us to a moderate version of metaethical relativism according to which some normative judgments are objectively true or false and at least some other normative judgments are not. (I am assuming that a kindly omniscient God who created the universe would want all human beings (or all possible rational beings) to share certain preferences, such as an aversion to cruelty.)

As we saw in chapter 3.II.6, the welfarist version of the rational-desire-satisfaction theory of value is compatible with the view that all value judgments are objectively true or false even if it is possible for rational people to have conflicting preferences. According to the welfarist version of the desire-satisfaction theory, the goodness or badness of *my* life is determined by the satisfaction or non-satisfaction of *my* rational desires (or my rational desires for *my own life*), and the goodness or badness of *your* life is determined by the satisfaction or non-satisfaction of *your* rational desires (or your rational desires for *your life*). These judgments can be objectively true even if the rational preferences of different people sometimes conflict. (On the present view, if God prefers that I prefer that my life have a certain feature X rather than Y, then it is objectively true that my life is better if it has X rather than Y. This is true regardless of what preferences God wants other people to have about this matter.)

[*Our knowledge of God's preferences.*]   What are the epistemological consequences of the view under consideration? How can we know what God's preferences are? Possible sources of knowledge include the following: (1) direct personal revelation from God; (2) knowledge of general principles revealed in the texts or doctrines of a religious tradition, e.g., the Bible or the Koran; (3) philosophical theology; and (4) trying to become more like God ourselves—more knowledgeable and kind.

Questions about the epistemological consequences of the divine preference theory of rationality/value raise many substantive religious and epistemological questions I cannot address here. Short of being given direct personal knowledge of God's preferences, we are left by the divine-preference theory with considerable uncertainty about the answers to many normative questions. This uncertainty is appropriate even if we grant that the doctrines of one particular monotheistic religion are true and its scriptures divinely in-spired. The major monotheistic religions (Judaism, Christianity, and Islam) claim that some standards of conduct (right and wrong) have been revealed in their scriptures,[57] but these scriptures do not propose theories of value or the good life. Nor do they purport to explain in any detail God's reasons for creat-ing human beings. Ultimate standards of value are not stated in the sacred texts of these traditions.

The difficulty of discerning God's purposes or ultimate ends for human be-ings is complicated by the possibility or likelihood that there is an afterlife. Most theists, that is, most Christians and Muslims, believe in an afterlife, an afterlife that continues forever. Given the existence of an afterlife, the basic category of value/welfare is not a good or bad earthly life (a life that rarely lasts more than eighty-five years) but a good or bad *existence* (an existence that con-tinues forever). The total value of an afterlife that goes on forever is very much greater (perhaps infinitely greater) than that of a finite earthly life. Given our ignorance about the afterlife, our ignorance about the ways our earthly lives affect our afterlives, and our ignorance about how we will view our earthly lives from the perspective of our afterlives, it is possible that we are seriously mistaken about what sorts of earthly lives make for a good or bad existence.

This view about our ignorance of God's will (insofar as it might constitute the *ultimate standard of value*) is consistent with fairly orthodox versions of theism. Many orthodox theists hold roughly the following:

> We have knowledge of our own moral obligations, but we don't know God's ultimate aims or purposes for us and thus don't know what standards of value God employs (or what standards of value are consistent with God's will). Our lives serve divine purposes and ends. We trust that God's pur-poses are loving and benevolent, but we don't know what they are.

These skeptical comments notwithstanding, the traditional problem of evil suggests some reasonable conjectures about God's will and purposes. Many proposed solutions to the problem of evil make conjectures about God's rea-sons for permitting such extensive suffering to exist. Some of these conjec-tures are more reasonable than others. It is reasonable to suppose that God's preferences are not in accordance with the HTV: that is, it is reasonable to think that God does not aim to maximize the balance of pleasure over pain for sentient creatures (to the exclusion of everything else). A kindly, sympathetic, and omniscient God sufficiently powerful to have created the universe could have done many things to make human life more pleasant and less painful. All of us can easily imagine many things such a God could have done to bring this about. If such a God exists, then there must be other things God values and seeks to promote. The world, as we know it, is very far from being a hedonistic paradise. It is highly implausible to suppose that God designed it as part of a plan to create sentient creatures whose existence is as pleasant as possible. If God permits human suffering for the sake of greater goods humans enjoy in the afterlife, then those goods must include things other than pleasure. For any pleasures we might enjoy in the hereafter, a God sufficiently powerful to have created the universe could have so constituted us that we could enjoy those pleasures without prior suffering. It won't do to claim that reflection on one's past suffering will enhance the pleasures one enjoys in heaven; God could give people in heaven false memories of past suffering. On purely hedonistic grounds, this would be preferable to our experiencing suffering in our earthly lives.[58] Every remotely plausible traditional answer to the problem of evil, e.g., the free-will defense, presupposes that things other than pleasure have non-instrumental value.

Many theists who have attempted to solve the problem of evil (see 8.VII.6 for a brief statement of the problem) say roughly the following:

> God permits human and animal suffering in order that people freely develop and exercise moral virtues. The kind of moral goodness that results from the exercise of free will is a great good that outweighs the badness of all the suffering that occurs.

John Hick endorses this view, but he claims that this solution to the problem of evil is plausible only on the assumption that the process of moral development or "soul making" in human beings continues in the afterlife.[59] He doesn't claim that the moral goodness humans develop *in this world* is a sufficiently great good to outweigh the evil of earthly suffering. Hick's position, like most other discussions of the problem of evil, presupposes that there are axiological facts *independent of God's will.* Hick assumes that there are (independent) facts such as that the goodness of human moral virtues outweighs the badness of human suffering. Clearly, someone who accepts a divine-preference theory of value can't say this. According to the divine-preference theory, there aren't any facts about what things are good and bad that are independent of God's will. Nonetheless, this reply to the problem of evil gives us a reasonable conjecture as to *why* a kindly or loving God would permit so much suffering, and, to the best of my knowledge, it is our only reasonable guess as to why a kindly God would permit so much suffering. Therefore, I conjecture the following: if there exists a kindly omniscient God who created the universe, then God wants us freely to develop moral virtues or moral goodness, and this is at least *part* of the reason God allows so much suffering to exist. God values moral goodness and moral virtues as ends in themselves, not simply as means to promoting other ends such as happiness. Given the divine-preference theory of value, it follows that moral goodness/moral virtue has great value.

In this context, we should note the important distinction between (1) the view that the moral life and the elements constituting it (moral actions and morally good traits of character, and so forth) are non-instrumentally good and (2) the view that they are good simply as a means to improving the value of human life (where the goodness or badness of human life is ultimately determined by things that are not constitutive of moral goodness or the moral life). Hedonists are committed to a purely instrumentalist view of the value of morality. Kant, by contrast, attaches great non-instrumental value to moral goodness (what he calls "a good will").

To my knowledge, every plausible theistic response to the problem of evil that attempts to explain *why* God allows so much suffering to exist attaches great value to moral goodness that develops from the exercise of free will. (The divine-preference theory of value, of course, holds that the value of moral goodness/virtue, and everything else, depends on God's will.) I conjecture that theists who hold that God is omniscient, sufficiently powerful to have created the universe, and kindly or loving must reject an instrumentalist view of the value of morality. It's always possible for the theist to take a skeptical line and say that there *might* be great goods other than moral goodness for which evils and suffering are necessary. (Or, to put this in a way that is consistent with the divine-preference theory, there may be other things a kindly omniscient God wants to bring about that require God to permit so much suffering to exist.) I have done nothing to gainsay the more skeptical view. Perhaps theists should simply say that there *might* be great goods for the sake of which human suffering is necessary and that the atheistic argument from evil cannot rule out this possibility. However, if we attempt to conjecture *why* God allows so much suffering to occur, our best guess (or part of our best guess) is that God seeks to promote moral goodness that results from free will. It's an open question whether we should make such a conjecture, but, if we do, this is our best guess.

Many theists claim that the (or an) ultimate purpose of human life is to enter into some kind of relationship with God and that this was at least part of God's reason for creating human beings. This view, however, does not explain why God permits so much suffering, nor does it answer questions about God's ultimate standards of value or God's reasons for wanting to have close relations with human beings. The view in question is perfectly compatible with the view that God allows so much suffering in part to allow us freely to develop moral goodness. We might say that the purpose of human suffering is to freely develop traits of character that will enhance our relationship to God. God, on this understanding, wants the company of morally good creatures.

God presumably had reasons for creating *this* world, as opposed to other possible worlds. God might have created creatures very different from human beings. God *chose* to create human beings and everything else that makes up this world. These choices were presumably motivated by God's ultimate preferences and concerns. What of God's ultimate will and ends can we discern from this? Aristotelians might be tempted to claim that we can discern God's will by examining human nature and human abilities and capacities; God wants us to develop the abilities and capacities God gave us. The problem with this is that God may not desire the development of all human abilities and characteristics as ends in themselves. God may even be averse to the development of certain abilities (for example the ability to wage wars or inflict harm on others) but allow them for the sake of the development of our moral characters.

Others who have undergone edifying religious experiences may be in a better position to discern God's will, but my own position gives me ample grounds for epistemic modesty and fallibilism about these matters. It is possible that the best way for us to determine what God wants is to try to become more like God ourselves, kinder, more caring, more empathetic, and more knowledgeable, and see how this affects our own preferences. Note that this goes beyond just trying to be better informed and more rational in some conventional sense of "rational." It involves trying better to approximate God's motivations. Thus, in practice, trying better to approximate God's motivations is significantly different from following COR or another more conventional version of the rational-desire-satisfaction theory.

2. The Implications of the Rational-Desire-Satisfaction Theory of Value When Taken Together with the Informed-Preference Theory of Rationality (COR)

The numerous thought experiments of chapters 2 and 3 reveal that many (most?) people have ultimate desires for a number of different kinds of things. In addition to pleasure, many (most?) people desire such things as fame, power, knowledge, and moral goodness for their own sake. In many cases, these desires are not the result of false beliefs, incomplete information, or any other apparent cognitive failings. For any given person, we can imagine ways in which his cognitive position for assessing his preferences could be improved upon. But it is likely that many people would have intrinsic preferences for many different kinds of things even if their cognitive positions were as good as possible. Therefore, it seems likely that, when taken together with COR, the rational-preference-satisfaction theory of value (both the welfarist or non-welfarist versions) supports value pluralism, according to which a number of different kinds of things such as pleasure, pain, moral goodness, and the full development of one's artistic and intellectual abilities are non-instrumentally good and bad.[60]

Given COR, it seems that rational people could have conflicting preferences about certain matters. Suppose that COR implies that it is correct for me to prefer X to Y. (There is at least one cognitive standpoint (s) from which I would prefer X to Y that is better than any other standpoint from which I would not prefer X to Y.) COR doesn't imply that it is correct for everyone else to prefer X to Y. It might also be the case that there is at least one cognitive standpoint (s1) from which you would prefer Y to X that is better than any other standpoint from which you would not prefer Y to X. For example, it might be the case that both (i) it is correct for some people to prefer W1 (a world in which there is a certain amount of happiness and moral goodness) to W2 (a world in which there is substantially less happiness and substantially more moral goodness) and (ii) it is correct for some other people to prefer W2 to W1. There is nothing in COR that rules this out.[61]

As we saw in 3.II.6 and 8.IX.1, even if it is possible for rational people to have conflicting preferences, the *welfarist* version of the rational-desire-satisfaction theory of value does not necessarily commit us to relativism about value judgments (see below for a qualification). According to the welfarist version of the desire-satisfaction theory, the goodness or badness of my life is determined by the satisfaction or non-satisfaction of my rational desires (or my rational desires *for my own life*), and the goodness or badness of your life is determined by the satisfaction or non-satisfaction of your rational desires (or your rational desires *for your life*). These judgments can be objectively true even if the rational preferences of different people sometimes conflict. This notwithstanding, on the present view, what makes a person's life good or bad is "relative to" that person's rational desires for her own life. Suppose that, were I fully rational, I would desire that I have mathematical knowledge as an end in itself and that, were you fully rational, you would not desire that you have mathematical knowledge as an end in itself. Then, on the present view, my having mathematical knowledge would be non-instrumentally good, but your having such knowledge would not be.

Assuming that COR implies that it is correct for some people to have preferences that conflict with the preferences that it is correct for others to have, the *non-welfarist version* of the rational-desire-satisfaction theory of value that employs COR is incompatible with a thoroughgoing objectivism according to which all value judgments are objectively true or false. Rather, it seems to commit us to metaethical relativism. Suppose that it is correct for one person

(S), to prefer that X exist (occur) rather than not, other things being equal, and correct for another person (S1), to prefer that X not exist or not occur, other things being equal. The non-welfarist version of the desire-satisfaction theory implies that it's true for S that X is non-instrumentally good and true for S1 that X is non-instrumentally bad.

[Relativism versus Irrationalism.]   The non-welfarist version of the rational-desire-satisfaction theory of value combined with COR seems to commit us to a version of metaethical relativism. It may even imply that *no* normative judgments are objectively true or false (either in the sense of true or false for all human beings or true or false for all possible rational beings).[62] But, even if this view implies that no normative judgments are objectively true or false, it does not commit us to an "anything goes" kind of irrationalism according to which whatever normative judgments someone accepts are "true for him." Given COR, certain preferences one actually has (and the normative judgments one bases on them) could be incorrect in virtue of being based on false beliefs or incomplete information.

Still, it might be argued that the present view commits us to a kind of relativism that is inconsistent with its being important and desirable to subject our own normative judgments and preferences to rational criticism. There is no point to subjecting our views about a particular normative question to rational criticism unless there is an objectively correct or objectively true answer to that question. If there is no objectively correct answer to a particular question, then any answer is just as good as any other answer, and it's reasonable for us to believe whatever we feel like believing about it.

The foregoing argument is seriously mistaken. Suppose that there is no objectively true answer to a particular normative question. It does *not* follow that any answer to that question is just as good as any other answer. Suppose that I am trying to choose a career and ask which career, on balance, would give me the best life. Suppose that there is no objectively correct answer to this question because there is no single preference about my choice of careers that it is correct for everyone to have. Even if there is no objectively true answer to a given question (no answer that is *true for everyone*), it still might make sense for me to engage in rational criticism and discussion to find the answer that is *true for me*. It might be correct for *me* to prefer that *I* have a certain kind of life, even if it is not correct for everyone else to prefer that I have that same kind of life. Rational criticism can help me find the preferences that it is correct for *me* to have.[63]

Given COR, it is possible that there is no single preference that it is correct for me to have about my choice of careers. It is possible that, for any cognitive perspective from which I would prefer a particular career to all other careers, there is another equally good (or better) cognitive perspective from which I would prefer a different career. In that case, the present view implies that there is no answer to the question "Which career will give me the best life?" that is *true for me* (much less an answer that is objectively true). Even in this case, however, we should resist drawing irrationalist conclusions. The present view still allows us to say that some answers to this question are better than others. Even if there is no single career that it is correct for me to prefer (to the exclusion of all others), COR might still allow that it is correct for me to prefer certain careers to others. It might still be the case that it would be correct for me to prefer any one of careers A, B, C, or D to any careers other than A, B, C, or D. Even in the present case, rational criticism and deliberation can help me find better answers rather than worse ones.

[*Implications of the Present Example for the Welfarist Version of the Desire-Satisfaction Theory That Employs COR.*]   The present example also has important implications for our understanding of the welfarist theory. In the present case, there is no single preference that it is correct for me to have about my choice of careers. Therefore, the welfarist version of the desire-satisfaction theory that employs COR can't say that there is any objectively true answer to the question "Which choice of careers would give me the best life?" If there can be cases of this sort, and I suspect that there can be, then the present view is inconsistent with a thoroughgoing objectivism according to which all normative judgments are objectively true or false. However, this kind of case also shows that the view in question avoids extreme metaethical relativism (the view that no moral judgments are objectively true or false). Given our present assumptions, certain other normative judgments *are* objectively true or false. It is objectively true that choosing career A would give me a better life than choosing career Z and that choosing career B would give me a better life than choosing career Y, and so on.

The kind of (metaethical) relativism that seems to follow from the present theories does not commit us to abandoning criticism of our own preferences and normative beliefs, but it may warrant taking a different view of normative disagreement. Given that normative judgments aren't objectively true or false, we shouldn't assume that one of the parties must be mistaken whenever two people disagree with each other about the answer to a normative question. Nor should we be so concerned to try to persuade others to adopt the views that we hold. Given the kind of relativism in question, I may be leading others into error by persuading them to adopt my beliefs, even if my own normative beliefs are true for me.

3. The Implications of the Rational-Desire-Satisfaction Theory of Value When Combined with the Ideal-Observer Version of the Divine-Preference Theory of Rationality

The characteristics of a kindly omniscient creator of the universe seem to underdetermine the preferences that such a being would have for us. It is possible that some kindly omniscient creators would prefer that all human beings prefer X to not-X and that other possible kindly omniscient creators would prefer that all human beings prefer not-X to X. (There is nothing in the concept of a kindly omniscient creator of the universe that rules this out.) Thus, it is very unlikely that the ideal-observer version of the divine-preference theory of rationality/value permits us to hold that all normative judgments are objectively true or false.[64]

Different possible kindly omniscient creators of the universe might disagree in their preferences about an *individual's* preferences; some might prefer that I prefer X to not-X (other things equal), others might prefer that I prefer not-X to X (other things equal). In such cases, the ideal-observer version of the divine-preference theory of rationality implies that neither my preference for X nor my preference for not-X is rational (correct). Given this, the rational-preference satisfaction theory of value (even the welfarist version of the theory) does not permit us to say that the judgment that X is good or bad is objectively true or false (or even true or false *for me*). This may seem counterintuitive, especially if such cases are common. This kind of case may incline us to prefer the compromise theory (the compromise between the ideal-observer version of the divine-preference theory of rationality and COR that I sketched in 8.VIII.8) to the unmodified ideal-observer version.

The foregoing notwithstanding, all possible kindly omniscient creators will agree about certain matters. They will, other things equal, prefer that pain and suffering not occur and will prefer that human beings not desire the pain and suffering of others for its own sake. When combined with the ideal-observer version of the divine-preference theory of rationality, the rational-preference-satisfaction theory of value seems to commit us to some kind of moderate metaethical relativism according to which some, but not all, normative judgments are objectively true or false. One might try to defend a more narrow and determinate characterization of God for the ideal-observer version of the divine-preference theory of rationality in order to reduce the possibilities for conflicting preferences among different possible Gods. Among other things, we might stipulate that only the preferences of those possible kindly omniscient creators of the universe who would have chosen to create human beings and something like this world are relevant to determining the correctness or rationality of *our* preferences.

X. Conclusion: Prospects for Non-Realist Normative Theories

For better or worse, rational-preference-satisfaction theories of value seem to be the main option for non-realists at present. Those who defend such theories need to defend a particular theory of rationality. Standard full-information theories of rationality that rely on the notion of a fully informed human being are open to decisive objections. The divine-preference theory of rationality is a full-information theory of rationality, albeit one that dispenses with the idea of a fully informed human being. It deals very nicely with the main objections to standard full-information theories and is the basis for a very attractive version of the rational-preference-satisfaction theory of value. If realism is false and there exists a kindly omniscient creator of the universe, then we should take God's preferences to be authoritative for us. The cognitive standpoint of such a God is far superior to any that human beings are capable of occupying, and we have reasons to adjust our preferences in light of such a God's purposes and preferences. If a kindly omniscient creator of the universe does not exist, then we need a "fall-back" theory of rationality. I have proposed two such theories (COR and the hypothetical- or ideal-observer version of the divine-preference theory) that seem plausible and yield acceptable theories of value when combined with the rational-desire-satisfaction theory of value.

Notes

Chapter 1. Arguments for Hedonism

1. G. E. Moore, *Ethics* (Oxford: Oxford University Press, 1965), pp. 24 and 68.

2. J. S. Mill, *Utilitarianism* (Indianapolis: Hackett, 1979), pp. 7 and 34. Unless indicated otherwise, all references to page numbers refer to the Hackett edition of *Utilitarianism*.

3. Cf. Henry Sidgwick, *The Methods of Ethics*, 7th ed. (New York: Dover, 1966), pp. 120–121.

4. William Alston, "Pleasure," *Encyclopedia of Philosophy*, ed. Paul Edwards (New York: MacMillan, 1967), vol. 6, p. 341. Richard Brandt also defends a motivational theory of pleasure. See *A Theory of the Good and the Right* (Oxford: Oxford University Press, 1979), pp. 38–42, and "Fairness to Happiness," *Social Theory and Practice* 15 (1989): 42.

5. Cf. Richard Brandt, *Ethical Theory* (Englewood Cliffs, N.J.: Prentice-Hall, 1959), pp. 303–307, and *A Theory of the Good and the Right*, pp. 35–38.

6. Karl Duncker, "Pleasure, Emotion, and Striving," *Philosophy and Phenomenological Research* 1 (1940): 399–400.

7. Gilbert Ryle, *The Concept of Mind* (New York: Barnes & Noble, 1969), p. 108.

8. Gilbert Ryle, "Pleasure," in *Moral Concepts*, ed. Joel Feinberg (Oxford: Oxford University Press, 1970), p. 25.

9. For places in which Mill denies the possibility of a strict proof of fundamental ethical principles, see *Utilitarianism*, pp. 4–5 and 34.

10. See F. H. Bradley, *Ethical Studies*, 2d ed. (Oxford: Oxford University Press, 1927), p. 114, and Anthony Quinton, *Utilitarian Ethics* (New York: Saint Martin's, 1973), p. 67.

11. J. S. Mill, Letter to Henry Jones, June 13, 1868, in *Collected Works*, vol. 16 (Toronto: University of Toronto Press, 1972), p. 1414. This passage is cited in the following

works: Wendy Donner, *The Liberal Self* (Ithaca, N.Y.: Cornell University Press, 1991), p. 31; Fred Berger, *Happiness, Justice, and Freedom*, (Berkeley: University of California Press, 1984), pp. 57–58; Henry West, "Mill's 'Proof' of Utility," in *The Limits of Utilitarianism*, ed. Harlan Miller and William Williams (Minneapolis: University of Minnesota Press, 1982), p. 30; and Hardy Jones, "Mill's Argument for the Principle of Utility," *Philosophy and Phenomenological Research* 38 (1978): 338–354.

12. In order to make the argument work with 2' instead of 2, we would need to revise 3 as follows:

> 3'. Something (x) is non-instrumentally good (desirable) if, and only if, there is someone who is such that it is rational for her to desire x for its own sake.

13. See G. E. Moore, *Principia Ethica* (Cambridge: Cambridge University Press, 1903), pp. 66–67. Also see Fred Feldman, *Introductory Ethics* (Englewood Cliffs, N.J.: Prentice-Hall, 1978), pp. 44–46, and Rem Edwards, *Pleasures and Pains* (Ithaca, N.Y.: Cornell University Press, 1979), pp. 140–142. Edwards criticizes Mill's analogy between "visible" and "desirable," but he thinks that our being able to desire something is a necessary condition of its being desirable. Some recent commentators defend Mill on this point; see John Marshall, "The Proof of Utility and Equity in Mill's *Utilitarianism*," *Canadian Journal of Philosophy* 3 (September 1973): 17, and Norman Kretzmann, "Desire as Proof of Desirability," in *Mill's Utilitarianism*, ed. Smith and Sosa (Belmont, Calif.: Wadsworth, 1969), p. 115.

14. J. S. Mill, "Remarks on Bentham's Philosophy," *Collected Works*, vol. 10 (Toronto: University of Toronto Press, 1969), p. 14.

15. Moore and Bradley briefly note the same objection, but don't fully develop it. See Moore, *Principia Ethica*, p. 71, and Bradley, *Ethical Studies*, p. 120.

16. D. D. Raphael claims that there are clear counterexamples to Mill's view that desiring something is the same as finding it pleasant.

> Is it true that whenever we have the conative experience of desire, we also have the cognitive experience of thinking that the object of our desire is pleasant? It often happens but not always. I may desire something without raising the question whether it will be pleasant. ("Mill's Proof of the Principle of Utility," *Utilitas* 6 (1994): 58)

I take Mill to be *stipulating* that he is using the word "desire" to name the same thing as "finding something pleasant." If Mill is not giving a stipulative definition, then Raphael's criticisms seem quite in order. Richard Brandt defends a definition of "desire" very similar to Mill's. See "Rational Desires," in Brandt's *Morality, Utilitarianism, and Rights* (Cambridge: Cambridge University Press, 1992), p. 42.

17. Here, it might be objected that, given Mill's associationist psychology, the view that "good" means "worthy of desire" (in Mill's sense of "desire") is sufficient to ensure the action-guidingness of value judgments. Mill claims that "will is the child of desire"; we will things other than pleasure only as a result of habitually associating them with

pleasure (*Utilitarianism*, pp. 36–40). So, if we say that something is worthy of being desired as an end, then (since we know that desire produces will) we are also saying that it is worthy of causing us to pursue it as an end and thus worthy of being pursued as an end. But Mill's associationist principles do not allow him to claim that everything worthy of being desired as an end is worthy of producing the seeking of it and thus worthy of being pursued as an end. Mill does *not* claim that desiring something always causes one to will it. Rather, he claims that if we will something other than pleasure and the absence of pain we must first have desired it. The claim that we come to will *everything* that we ever desire is clearly false.

18. [This is a long, digressive note that probably won't be of much interest to readers who have no special interest in Mill.] Here, it might be objected that Mill's discussion of desire and will and his claim that "will is the child of desire" provides the basis for an improved version of the proof. Before considering this possibility, I first need to explain Mill's claim that "will is the child of desire." Mill concedes that some people will things other than pleasure and the absence of pain as ends. But, according to Mill, we will things other than pleasure only as a result of "habit." All of our ultimate preferences or aversions (willings) for things other than pleasure or pain are formed as a result of habitually associating the objects of those preferences with pleasure or pain.

> [W]ill, like all other parts of our constitution, is amenable to habit, and that we may will from habit what we no longer desire for itself, or desire only because we will it. It is not the less true that will, in the beginning, is entirely produced by desire, including in that term the repelling influence of pain as well as the attractive one of pleasure. . . . How can the will to be virtuous, where it does not exist in sufficient force, be implanted or awakened? Only by making the person *desire* virtue—by making him think of it in a pleasurable light, or of its absence in a painful one. . . . Will is the child of desire, and passes out of the dominion of its parent only to come under that of habit. (*Utilitarianism*, p. 39)

Also note the following passage from Mill's *System of Logic*:

> When the will is said to be determined by motives, a motive does not mean always, or solely, the anticipation of pleasure or a pain. . . . It is at least certain that we gradually, through the influence of association, come to desire the means without thinking of the end: the action itself becomes the object of desire, and is performed without reference to any motive beyond itself. Thus far, it may still be objected, that, the action having through association become pleasurable, we are, as before, moved to act by the anticipation of pleasure, namely, the pleasure of the action itself. But granting this, the matter does not end here. As we proceed in the formation of habits, and become accustomed to will a particular act or a particular course of conduct because it is pleasurable, we at last continue to will it without any reference to its being pleasurable. (*Collected Works*, vol. 8 [Toronto: University of Toronto Press, 1973], p. 842)

Mill thinks that these same "associationist" principles govern the origin of desires. We come to desire things other than pleasure for their own sake as the result of associating them with pleasure.

> [V]irtue is not the only thing originally a means, and if it were not a means to anything else would be and remain indifferent, but which by association with what it is a means to comes to be desired for itself, and that too with the utmost intensity. (*Utilitarianism*, p. 36)

> Life would be a poor thing, very ill-provided with sources of happiness, if there were not this provision of nature by which things originally indifferent, but conducive to, or otherwise associated with, the satisfaction of our primitive desires, become in themselves sources of pleasure . . . Virtue, according to the utilitarian conception, is a good of this description. There was no original desire of it, or motive to it, save its conduciveness to pleasure, and especially to protection from pain. But, through association thus formed it may be felt a good in itself, and desired as such with as great intensity as any other good. (*Utilitarianism*, p. 37)

Mill distinguishes between "original" willing (natural primordial preferences) and non-original willing (acquired preferences). Pleasure and the absence of pain are the only original objects of our will. Our intrinsic preferences for things other than pleasure and the absence of pain are all acquired as a result of associating the objects of those preferences with pleasure (desiring these other things). For example, no one originally (naturally) wills to be virtuous. People will to be virtuous only as a result of desiring to be virtuous (taking pleasure in the thought of being virtuous).

Mill does not use the claim that will is the child of desire as a part of his proof of hedonism. His proof makes no mention of "will." Mill claims that the only way to show that something is desirable is to show that it is *desired*. He never qualifies this by saying that the only way to show that something is desirable is that it is non-habitually desired (willed). However, it might be suggested that Mill's idea that will is the child of desire can be used as the basis for a more plausible version of PH, which, in turn, can be used as the basis of an argument for the HTV. Mill does not succeed in defending conventional versions of PH; he does not show that pleasure and the absence of pain are the only things that human beings desire or will as ends. Indeed, he concedes that some people both will and desire things other than happiness as ends (*Utilitarianism*, pp. 38–39). However, in his discussion of desire and will Mill endorses the following claims:

1. Pleasure and the absence of pain are the only things that human beings non-habitually desire as ends, and every instance of pleasure and the absence of pain is non-habitually desired as an end by at least some human beings.

2. Pleasure and the absence of pain are the only things that human beings non-habitually will as ends, and every instance of pleasure and the absence of pain is non-habitually willed as an end by at least some human beings.

In order to make a valid argument for the truth of the HTV using 1 and 2, we need to assume something like the following:

The only way to show that something is desirable is to show that it is non-habitually desired (willed). Something is non-instrumentally good if, and only if, someone non-habitually desires or wills it.

Mill never defends this assumption and I know of no reasons why we should accept it.

19. I intend PH1 and PH2 to be understood to leave open the question of whether psychological egoism is true. For example, PH1 should be understood to be consistent with either 6a or 6b.

20. Sidgwick, *The Methods of Ethics*, pp. 42–43.
21. Sidgwick, *The Methods of Ethics*, p. 43, n. 1.
22. Sidgwick, *The Methods of Ethics*, p. 125.
23. Sidgwick, *The Methods of Ethics*, p. 43.
24. Sidgwick, *The Methods of Ethics*, p. 126.
25. Sidgwick, *The Methods of Ethics*, p. 127.
26. Ibid.
27. Ibid.
28. Sidgwick, *The Methods of Ethics*, p. 131.
29. Sidgwick, *The Methods of Ethics*, p. 398.
30. Sidgwick, *The Methods of Ethics*, p. 111.
31. Cf. J. B. Schneewind, *Sidgwick's Ethics and Victorian Moral Philosophy* (Oxford: Oxford University Press, 1977), p. 317.
32. Sidgwick, *The Methods of Ethics*, p. 392.
33. Sidgwick, *The Methods of Ethics*, p. 393.
34. Sidgwick, *The Methods of Ethics*, pp. 396–397.
35. Sidgwick, *The Methods of Ethics*, p. 398.
36. Ibid.
37. Moore rejects this. He holds that the existence of unperceived beautiful physical objects is intrinsically good (see *Principia Ethica*, pp. 83–85). In his later book, *Ethics*, Moore retracts this view. He says that "nothing can be an intrinsic good unless it contains *both* some feeling and *also* some other form of consciousness" (p. 107).
38. Sidgwick, *The Methods of Ethics*, pp. 398–399.
39. Moore, *Principia Ethica*, pp. 92–93 (see also pp. 187–197). This criticism has been presented by others. James Seth was apparently the first to formulate the objection. See his paper "Is Pleasure the Summum Bonum?" *International Journal of Ethics* 6 (1896): 422.
40. Genghis Khan is reported to have said the following: "Happiness lies in conquering one's enemies, in driving them in front of oneself, in taking their property, in savoring their despair, in outraging their wives and daughters." See Witold Rodzinski, *A History of China* (Oxford: Pergamon Press, 1979), pp. 164–165.
41. The import of this sentence seems to be that the common sense of mankind cannot be made completely consistent, since some people hold that some things have

value "independently of the pleasure derived from them" and some people (such as Sidgwick himself) deny this.

42. Sidgwick, *The Methods of Ethics*, p. 401.

43. Sidgwick, *The Methods of Ethics*, pp. 401–402.

44. Sidgwick, *The Methods of Ethics*, pp. 406–407.

45. See Henry Sidgwick, *Philosophy, Its Scope and Relations* (London: Macmillan, 1902), and "The Theory of Classical Education," in *Miscellaneous Essays and Addresses* (London: Macmillan, 1904). According to Schneewind, "The belief that philosophy should aim at a complete systemization of knowledge acquired in the special disciplines. . . . underlies all of Sidgwick's writings" (*Sidgwick's Ethics and Victorian Moral Philosophy*, pp. 54–55).

Chapter 2. Objections to the Hedonistic Theory of Value

1. To say that pleasure is an element of the good life is not necessarily to say that *all* pleasures are non-instrumentally good. One could hold that pleasure/happiness is necessary for a good life but still deny that certain kinds of pleasures, e.g., delight in the misfortunes of others, are non-instrumentally good. I consider this issue in 2.III.

2. *Philebus*, 21a–d, trans. Hackforth, in *The Collected Dialogues of Plato*, ed. Edith Hamilton and Huntington Cairns (Princeton: Princeton University Press, 1969).

3. Mill, *Utilitarianism*, p. 8. Also note the following passage:

the test of quality and the rule for measuring it against quantity being the preference felt by those who, in their opportunities of experience, to which must be added their habits of self-consciousness and self-observation, are best furnished with the means of comparison. (*Utilitarianism*, pp. 11–12)

4. Cf. J. J. C. Smart, "Outline of a Utilitarian System of Ethics," in *Utilitarianism For and Against*, ed. J. J. C. Smart and Bernard Williams (Cambridge: Cambridge University Press, 1973):

It is worth while enquiring how much practical ethics is likely to be affected by the possibility of disagreement over the question of Socrates dissatisfied versus the fool satisfied. 'Not very much', one feels like saying at first. We noted that the most complex and intellectual pleasures are also the most fecund. . . . In most circumstances of ordinary life the pure hedonist will agree in his practical recommendations with the quasi-ideal utilitarian. (p. 18)

Smart goes on to observe that disagreements between hedonists and non-hedonists might have important practical consequences in the future if pleasure machines become available.

5. According to Mill, pleasure (x) is of "higher" quality than another pleasure of equal quantity (y) provided that "all or almost all who have experience of both give a decided preference" to x, "irrespective of any feeling of moral obligation to prefer it" (*Utilitarianism*, p. 8). I am assuming that Mill's definition of higher pleasures should be

construed to mean that the informed judges who choose between two pleasures of equal quantity choose between them solely on the basis of their *felt quality*. Wendy Donner disagrees with my interpretation of Mill on precisely this point; I discuss and criticize her views in 2.II.5.

6. Bentham (the archetypal quantitative hedonist) lists seven factors which determine the value of pleasure and pain: (1) intensity, (2) duration, (3) certainty or uncertainty, (4) propinquity or remoteness, (5) fecundity ("the chance it has of being followed by sensations of the *same* kind"), (6) purity ("the chance it has of *not* being followed by sensations of the *opposite* kind"), (7) extent ("the number of persons to which it extends") (*Principles of Morals and Legislation* [New York: Hafner, 1948], p. 30). However, on Bentham's view, only intensity and duration are strictly relevant to determining the non-instrumental value of particular pleasures. Certainty or uncertainty is a relevant consideration when making decisions, but it is not a criterion for assessing the non-instrumental value of actual pleasures. Propinquity is irrelevant to questions about non-instrumental value, since later pleasures do not count for more or less than earlier ones. Fecundity and purity are relevant to the instrumental rather than the non-instrumental value of pleasures. Fecund pleasures tend to produce other pleasures. Impure pleasures tend to produce pain. The category of extent refers to other people having the same pleasure/pain. It is not a category that applies to the individual pleasures (of particular people). Cf. Donner, *The Liberal Self*, p. 25.

7. This criticism has been anticipated by others. Note the following passage from Sidgwick's *The Methods of Ethics*:

> But if we take the definition of pleasure just given—that it is the kind of feeling which we apprehend to be desirable or preferable—it seems to be a contradiction in terms to say that the less pleasant feeling can ever be thought preferable to the more pleasant. (p. 128)

Also see Sidgwick, *The Methods of Ethics*, p. 121, and J. L. Cowan, *Pleasure and Pain* (New York: St. Martin's Press, 1968):

> This distinction in terminology, in short, turns out to be the same. Both boil down simply to preferential choice on the part of the experienced. If those who know both choose, apart from consequences and so on, one mode of existence over another, then, according to Mill, we must say that the chosen mode gives greater pleasure; but whether it is greater in quantity or quality, we are actually given no way of determining. . . . The pleasant, in short, is simply that chosen for itself. Of two objects of choice the more pleasant, call it in quantity or quality as you will, is simply that chosen. (p. 116)

8. Mill, *Utilitarianism*, pp. 8–11. Mill does not explain how to distinguish between "higher" and "lower" capacities.

9. Mill, *Utilitarianism*, p. 8.

10. Mill, *Utilitarianism*, p. 10.

11. Rem Edwards describes such a machine in *Pleasures and Pains*, pp. 60–67.

12. J. J. C. Smart describes such a machine in Smart and Williams, *Utilitarianism For and Against*, p. 19.

13. Robert Nozick, *Anarchy, State, and Utopia* (New York: Basic Books, 1974), pp. 42–45.

14. Nozick *Anarchy, State, and Utopia*, p. 43.

15. Some might argue that an experience machine of the sort that I describe is metaphysically impossible. Putnam gives an elaborate argument to show that the hypothesis that we are brains in a vat (or brains whose experiences are artificially stimulated) is incoherent. See Hilary Putnam, *Reason, Truth, and History* (Cambridge: Cambridge University Press, 1981), chapter 1. Putnam's argument is intended as an argument against metaphysical realism. It is far beyond the scope of the present book to try to assess Putnam's argument.

16. Donner, *The Liberal Self*, p. 71.

17. Donner, *The Liberal Self*, pp. 72–73.

18. Donner, *The Liberal Self*, p. 78.

19. Ibid.

20. For defenses of externalism see Robert Stalnacker, "On What's In the Head," *Philosophical Perspectives* 3 (1989): 287–316, and Tyler Burge, "Individuation and Causation in Psychology," *Pacific Philosophical Quarterly* 70 (1989): 303–322. For a defense of internalism see Jerold Fodor, *Representations* (Cambridge: MIT Press, 1981).

21. J. S. Mill, *Examination of Sir William Hamilton's Philosophy, Collected Works*, vol. 9 (Toronto: University of Toronto Press, 1979), p. 183. See also pp. 180–185; Mill's *System of Logic*, pp. 177 and 179; and John Skorupski, *John Stuart Mill* (London: Routledge, 1989), pp. 229–235.

22. See note 37, chapter 1.

23. I have argued that the HTV is not plausible, given the truth of non-realism. It might be objected that a nonrealist emotivist could accept the HTV. An emotivist might claim that he categorically approves of pleasure and only pleasure and that his approval is independent of whether or not all rational people would desire only pleasure as an end. However, in chapter 6 I argue that emotivism is not a plausible account of the meaning of moral judgments. I also argue that being worthy of being desired is a necessary condition of something's being good. Given the success of my arguments in chapter 6, defenders of the HTV need to say that the desires of people who desire things other than pleasure for their own sake are in some sense mistaken or inappropriate. And *this* claim is implausible, given nonrealism. Given the kinds of theories of rationality consistent with non-realism, many of the desires people have for things other than pleasure seem perfectly rational. (For further arguments on this last point see chapter 8, where I ask the question "What kinds of theories of rationality are consistent with moral non-realism?")

24. Franz Brentano, *The Origin of Our Knowledge of Right and Wrong*, trans. Roderick Chisholm and Elizabeth Schneewind (New York: Humanities Press, 1969), p. 18. Also see the following passage:

Accordingly, everything that can be thought about belongs in one of two classes—either the class of things for which love is appropriate, or the class of things for which hate is appropriate. Whatever falls into the first class we call good, and whatever falls into the second we call bad. (Franz Brentano, *The True and the Evident*, trans. Roderick Chisholm, Ilse Politzer, and Kurt Fischer [New York: Humanities Press, 1966], pp. 21–22)

Brentano uses the terms "love" and "hatred" ("Lieben" and "Hassen") in a very broad sense to designate favorable and unfavorable attitudes. Loving or hating something in Brentano's sense is both a matter of how one is disposed to feel about it and how one is disposed to act. See my book *The Status of Morality* (Dordrecht: Reidel, 1984), pp. 2–3.

25. Brentano, *The Origin of Our Knowledge of Right and Wrong*, pp. 90–91. Cf. Moore, *Principia Ethica*, pp. 209–210; C. D. Broad, *Five Types of Ethical Theory* (London: Routledge & Kegan Paul, 1930), p. 234; and Roderick Chisholm, "The Defeat of Good and Evil," in *The Problem of Evil*, ed. Marilyn Adams and Robert Adams (Oxford: Oxford University Press, 1990), p. 59. Also see Noah Lemos, *Intrinsic Value* (Cambridge: Cambridge University Press, 1994), pp. 74–75, and Thomas Carson, "Happiness, Contentment, and the Good Life," *Pacific Philosophical Quarterly* 62 (1981): 378–392.

26. Smart and Williams, *Utilitarianism For and Against*, p. 25.

27. Smart and Williams, *Utilitarianism For and Against*, pp. 25–26.

28. Immanuel Kant, *Grounding for the Metaphysics of Morals*, 3d ed., trans. James Ellington (Indianapolis: Hackett, 1993), pp. 393–394 (Prussian Academy page numbers). Kant argues that happiness is not good without qualification. A person who lacks a good will is not worthy of happiness. The happiness of such a person is not good. Ross holds that (moral) virtue deserves to be rewarded by happiness and that vice deserves to be rewarded by unhappiness. The happiness of someone who deserves to be happy is good, but the happiness of someone who does not deserve to be happy is bad. The unhappiness of someone who deserves to be unhappy is good. See W. D. Ross, *The Right and the Good* (Oxford: Clarendon Press, 1930), pp. 135–138.

29. Ross offers a similar thought experiment in support of the view that moral virtue is intrinsically good (good as an end):

And if any one is inclined to doubt this and to think that, say, pleasure alone is intrinsically good, it seems to me enough to ask the question whether, of two states of the universe holding equal amounts of pleasure, we should really think no better of one in which the actions and dispositions of all the persons in it were thoroughly virtuous than of one in which they were highly vicious. (*The Right and the Good*, p. 134)

30. Friedrich Nietzsche, *The Will to Power*, trans. Walter Kaufmann and R. J. Hollingdale (New York: Vintage Books, 1968), section 701.

Historical Note. Nietzsche undoubtedly had Schopenhauer in mind when he stated this objection to the HTV. In his essays "On the Suffering of the World" and

"On the Vanity of Existence," Schopenhauer argues that human life is bad, because it involves so much suffering and so much more pain than pleasure (*Essays and Aphorisms*, trans. R. J. Hollingdale [New York: Penguin, 1970]). In these essays *all* of Schopenhauer's arguments to show that life is bad focus on the painfulness and unpleasantness of life and the paucity of pleasure it affords. Although Schopenhauer does not explicitly endorse the HTV, his arguments for pessimism all seem to presuppose the truth of the HTV. In order to make them valid, we must state Schopenhauer's arguments roughly as follows:

1. All (or almost all) human beings experience considerably more pain than pleasure.

2. The quantitative HTV is true.

Therefore:

All (or almost all) human beings have bad lives.

Schopenhauer defends pessimism on the strength of 1. But clearly his arguments are invalid without 2. Hedonistic pessimism is often taken to be a central feature of both Hinduism and Buddhism. Schopenhauer interpreted both Hinduism and Buddhism in this way (see *The World as Will and Representation*, trans. E. F. J. Payne [New York: Dover, 1966], vol. 2, pp. 580, 623, 628, and 643; also see "On the Suffering of the World," in *Essays and Aphorisms*, p. 48).

31. In "The Myth of Sisyphus" (included in Albert Camus, *The Myth of Sisyphus*, trans. J. O'Brien [New York: Albert Knopf, 1955]), Camus claims that the question "Is my life worth living?" is equivalent to the question "Should I commit suicide?" According to Sarah Broadie, Aristotle takes non-existence to be the benchmark for determining whether one has a good life. Broadie says that Aristotle holds that *eudaimonia* is "that in life for the sake of which one is glad to have been born rather than not," in *Ethics with Aristotle* (Oxford: Oxford University Press, 1991), p. 32.

32. Epicurus, "Letter to Menoeceus," in *Letters, Principal Doctrines, and Vatican Sayings*, trans. Russell Geer (Indianapolis: Bobbs-Merrill, 1964).

33. I owe this line of argument to Fred Feldman's book *Confrontations with the Reaper* (Oxford: Oxford University Press, 1992), chapters 8 and 9; see especially pp. 153–154.

34. Cf. Sidgwick, *The Methods of Ethics*, p. 381.

35. Michael Slote, *Goods and Virtues* (Oxford: Oxford University Press, 1983), p. 9.

36. Slote, *Goods and Virtues*, p. 14.

37. Slote, *Goods and Virtues*, pp. 23–24.

38. Chisholm cites this passage from Brentano's *Nachlass* in *Brentano and Intrinsic Value* (Cambridge: Cambridge University Press, 1986), p. 70.

39. Franz Brentano, *The Foundation and Construction of Ethics*, trans. Elizabeth Schneewind (New York: Humanities Press, 1973), pp. 196–197.

40. Chisholm, *Brentano and Intrinsic Value*, p. 71. Noah Lemos also defends this view; see *Intrinsic Value*, pp. 37–40 and 199–200.

41. Slote, *Goods and Virtues*, pp. 24–25.

42. J. David Velleman, "Well-Being and Time," *Pacific Philosophical Quarterly* 72 (1991): 48–77.

43. Velleman, "Well-Being and Time," p. 53.

44. Velleman, "Well-Being and Time," p. 60.

45. Velleman, "Well-Being and Time," p. 55.

Chapter 3. The Desire/Preference-Satisfaction Theory of Value

1. See R. M. Hare, *Moral Thinking* (Oxford: Oxford University Press, 1981); James Griffin, *Well-Being* (Oxford: Oxford University Press, 1986); and John Harsanyi, *Essays on Ethics, Social Behavior, and Scientific Explanation* (Dordrecht: Reidel, 1976), p. 55. Another important utilitarian, Richard Brandt, once accepted the desire-satisfaction theory of welfare but has subsequently abandoned it. I discuss Brandt's reasons for abandoning the desire-satisfaction theory in 3.II.3.

2. John Rawls, *A Theory of Justice* (Cambridge: Harvard University Press, 1971), p. 421.

3. David Gauthier, *Morals by Agreement* (Oxford: Oxford University Press, 1986), p. 59; see also G. H. von Wright, *The Varieties of Goodness* (London: Routledge, 1963), chapter 5.

4. Benedict Spinoza, *Ethics*, trans. William White and Amelia Hutchinson (New York: Hafner, 1949), Part 3, paragraph 9.

5. Kant, *Grounding for the Metaphysics of Morals*, p. 393 (Prussian Academy page numbers). Kant argues that happiness is not good without qualification. A person who lacks a good will is not worthy of happiness. The happiness of such a person is not good. See Ross, *The Right and the Good*, pp. 135–138. Ross holds that (moral) virtue deserves to be rewarded by happiness and that vice deserves to be rewarded by unhappiness. The happiness of someone who deserves to be happy is good, but the happiness of someone who does not deserve to be happy is bad. The unhappiness of someone who deserves to be unhappy is good.

6. Perry construes his theory as a criterion of value. On his view, being valued or desired makes something valuable and anything can be good if it is valued. He is not claiming that the state of affairs someone having an interest or desire that is satisfied is the only thing that is non-instrumentally good (R. B. Perry, *General Theory of Value* [Cambridge: Harvard University Press, 1926], pp. 115–116 and 122).

7. Brandt, "Fairness to Happiness," pp. 33–58.

8. According to the actual desire theory of welfare, a person's welfare consists in the (maximal) satisfaction of her actual desires. The "ideal-desire" theory of welfare says that welfare consists in the satisfaction of people's ideal desires or the desires that they would have if they were fully rational. Von Wright, James Griffin, and John Harsanyi all defend ideal-desire-satisfaction theories of welfare. See von Wright, *The Varieties of Goodness*, chapter 5; James Griffin, *Well-Being*, pp. 11 and 13; and John Harsanyi, *Essays on Ethics, Social Behavior, and Scientific Explanation*, p. 55. Richard Brandt defended the ideal-desire-satisfaction theory of welfare in "Rationality, Egoism, and

Morality," *Journal of Philosophy* 69 (1972): 681–697. The actual-desire-satisfaction theory of value/welfare has few, if any, defenders among contemporary philosophers. Ralph Barton Perry endorses the actual-desire theory of value (or something close to it). He explicitly rejects the view that to be good is to be the object of rational desire or interest (*General Theory of Value*, p. 108). Perry also rejects Brentano's view that to be good is to be the object of "legitimate desire" (p. 81). Perry holds that something is valuable or good if interest is (actually) taken in it (pp. 115–116). Value is a relation between an object and a valuing subject (p. 122). To be good is to be the object of interest. By being an object of interest, Perry means more than just being the object of an actual desire or preference. He says that being the object of interest means the same as being valued if by "valuing" something we mean "liking, desiring or being otherwise favorably disposed to the object" (p. 122).

9. I borrow this terminology from Derek Parfit, "What Makes One's Life Go Best?" in Parfit's *Reasons and Persons* (Oxford: Oxford University Press, 1984), pp. 493–502.

10. Parfit, *Reasons and Persons*, p. 494.

11. Brandt, "Rationality, Egoism, and Morality," pp. 681–697.

12. Brandt, "Rationality, Egoism, and Morality," p. 682.

13. This brief summary oversimplifies the argument. For needed qualifications see Mark Overvold, "Self-Interest and the Concept of Self-Sacrifice," *Canadian Journal of Philosophy* 10 (1980): 105–118. Overvold refines the argument to make the even stronger objection that Brandt's view makes it logically impossible for there to be *any* genuine acts of self-sacrifice. See Brad Hooker, "A Breakthrough in the Desire Theory of Welfare"; Richard Brandt, "Overvold on Self-Interest and Self-Sacrifice"; and Thomas Carson, "The Desire-Satisfaction Theory of Welfare: Overvold's Critique and Reformulation," all included in *Rationality, Morality, and Self-Interest: Essays Honoring Mark Carl Overvold*, ed. John Heil (Lanham, Md.: Rowman Littlefield, 1993).

14. Mark Overvold, "Morality, Self-Interest, and Reasons for Being Moral," *Philosophy and Phenomenological Research* 44 (1984): 499.

15. Richard Brandt, "Two Concepts of Utility," in *The Limits of Utilitarianism*, ed. Harlan Miller and William Williams (Minneapolis: University of Minnesota Press, 1982); see p. 173 in particular. Also see Brandt, "Overvold on Self-Interest and Self-Sacrifice."

16. Von Wright now concedes this criticism; see "A Reply to My Critics," in *The Philosophy of Georg Henrick Von Wright*, ed. P. A. Schilpp and L. E. Hahn (LaSalle, Ill.: Open Court, 1990), p. 776. Von Wright responds to criticisms offered by Thomas Schwartz. Independently of Overvold, Schwartz made essentially the same criticism of the desire-satisfaction theory in his contribution to *The Philosophy of Georg Henrick von Wright*, "Von Wright's Theory of Human Welfare: A Critique," pp. 217–232 (Schwartz's paper was written in the early 1970s, but appeared only in 1990). A slightly different version of the paper, "Human Welfare: What It Is Not," appears in *The Limits of Utilitarianism*, ed. Harlan Miller and William Williams. Schwartz attacks von Wright's theory on the grounds that it makes psychological egoism true by definition. "If whatever I prefer is good for me then I only prefer what is good for me" ("Human Welfare: What It Is Not," p. 199). Schwartz strongly opposes desire-satisfaction theories of welfare. He briefly

considers the possibility of defining welfare in terms of the satisfaction of "strictly self-interested" preferences, but dismisses this possibility in the following passage:

> An analysis of human welfare in terms of strictly *self-interested* preferences would avoid the commitment to psychological egoism. But it would hardly be subjectivist. And it would be circular or nearly so. ("Human Welfare: What It Is Not," p. 200)

Overvold attempts to modify the desire-satisfaction theory by defining human welfare in terms of the satisfaction of "self-regarding" or "self-interested desires." This brief passage by Schwartz (which he does not elaborate on) is not sufficient to show that the desire satisfaction theory cannot be successfully revised in the manner that Overvold proposes.

17. Mark Overvold, "Self-Interest and Getting What You Want," in *The Limits of Utilitarianism*, ed. Harlan Miller and William Williams (Minneapolis: University of Minnesota Press, 1982), p. 188.

18. Carson, "The Desire-Satisfaction Theory of Welfare: Overvold's Critique and Reformulation," pp. 233–246.

19. Overvold, "Self-Interest and the Concept of Self-Sacrifice," p. 108.

20. See Alan Fuchs, "Posthumous Satisfactions and the Concept of Individual Welfare," and Brad Hooker, "A Breakthrough in the Desire Theory of Welfare," both in *Rationality, Morality, and Self-Interest: Essays Honoring Mark Carl Overvold*, ed. John Heil (Lanham, Md.: Roman and Littlefield, 1993). Also see Brandt, *A Theory of the Good and the Right*, p. 330, and Greg Kavka, *Hobbesian Moral and Political Theory* (Princeton: Princeton University Press, 1986), p. 41. Fuchs defends Overvold's view that events that occur after one has ceased to exist are not logically relevant to one's personal welfare. The other philosophers mentioned in this note criticize this view.

21. Perry's theory of value is much more similar to 2 than 1. According to Perry, *anything* can be made valuable by *anyone's* valuing it; there are no restrictions on what sorts of things can be valuable (*General Theory of Value*, pp. 115–116). On his view, being valued or desired by more people makes something more valuable. Other things equal, the more people who value or desire something, the more valuable it is (pp. 604–605, 617–618, and 646–647). Most discussions of the desire-satisfaction theory of value construe the theory along the lines of 1 or 2. But, to my knowledge, no one else explicitly distinguishes between 1 and 2.

22. Ronald Dworkin argues that "external preferences" create serious problems for certain versions of preference-utilitarianism (*Taking Rights Seriously* [Cambridge: Harvard University Press, 1977], pp. 234–238). The problem is roughly that certain versions of preference-utilitarianism imply that a person's preferences for her own life should sometimes be overridden by the ("external") preferences that other people have for her life. Suppose that I rationally prefer that I live a life of kind X to a life of kind Y, but most other people rationally prefer that I live life Y rather than life X. Assume, for the sake of argument, that whether I live life X or Y will not affect anyone else. Lives X and Y are both lives that are lived in isolation from other people. They are both lives that I live while marooned in a remote planet completely cut off from communication

with other people. Preference-utilitarianism implies that it would be better (on balance) if my rational preferences about my own life do not prevail and that, other things equal, it would be right for others to bring it about that I live life Y rather than life X. Preference utilitarians can avoid this objection by opting for a theory of value like 1 (above) and modifying it along the lines of Overvold's theory. Dworkin considers a similar reply, namely revising preference-utilitarianism to say that only one's "personal" preferences count. But he questions whether the distinction between personal and external preferences is sufficiently clear for this reply to succeed.

> Sometimes personal and external preferences are so inextricably tied together, and so mutually dependent, that no practical test for measuring preferences will be able to discriminate the personal and external elements in any individual's overall preference. (*Taking Rights Seriously*, p. 236)

The second formulation of the (rational) desire-satisfaction theory of value (2) cannot incorporate Overvold's restriction or anything like it. It would seem that proponents of 2 need to reject utilitarianism if they want to avoid Dworkin's objection. I would like to comment briefly on Dworkin's argument. First, Overvold's restriction for the desire-satisfaction theory is much more sophisticated and clearly formulated than Dworkin's distinction between "personal" and "external" preferences. Even if Dworkin is correct about the reply he dismisses, this does not show that the reply can't work if it employs something like Overvold's theory. (Dworkin's book was published before Overvold's papers on the desire-satisfaction theory.) Second, Dworkin formulates his objection in terms of the *actual-preference* version of utilitarianism. His examples concern external preferences that are motivated by irrational racial prejudice. It's not clear that his arguments apply to *rational-preference* versions of utilitarianism. Dworkin appeals to cases in which someone's preferences about his own life conflict with other people's preferences about his life. But it is not clear that different people's (ideally) *rational* preferences can conflict. Given the divine preference theory of rationality that I defend in chapter 8, it's doubtful that people's (ideally) rational preferences conflict in this way (see 8.IX.1).

23. Rawls, *A Theory of Justice*, p. 432. I cannot resist the observation that counting things *is* a form of applied mathematics.

24. It's only the welfarist version of the desire-satisfaction theory of value that holds that a person's good is determined by what she (rationally) desires for herself (see 3.I.7).

25. Perry frames the issue nicely in the following passage from *General Theory of Value*:

> the theory of value . . . must locate the seat or *root* of value. . . . Is a thing valuable because it is valued? . . . Or, is a thing valued because it is valuable? (p. 4)

26. E. J. Bond, *Reason and Value* (Cambridge: Cambridge University Press, 1983), p. 45.

27. See also Simon Blackburn's *Essays in Quasi-Realism* (Oxford: Oxford University Press, 1993) for a defense of projectivism; see pp. 55–60 in particular.

28. Brandt, "Two Concepts of Utility," pp. 169–185.

29. Cf. Lynne McFall, *Happiness* (New York: Peter Lang, 1988), p. 72.

30. We should probably restrict this to those times in one's life when one is capable of making rational assessments of one's life as a whole. It's not clear that it makes sense to talk about the global preferences that a newborn infant would have for her life as a whole if she were fully rational and fully informed.

31. Hare, *Moral Thinking*, pp. 105–106.

32. Charles Taylor, "Irreducibly Social Goods," and "Cross-Purposes: The Liberal-Communitarian Debate," both in Taylor's *Philosophical Arguments* (Cambridge: Harvard University Press, 1995), pp. 127–145 and 181–203.

33. Charles Taylor, "Cross-Purposes: The Liberal-Communitarian Debate," p. 190.

34. Charles Taylor, "Irreducibly Social Goods," pp. 136–140.

35. Charles Taylor, "Irreducibly Social Goods," p. 130.

36. Taylor claims that certain collective goods are good whether or not we recognize them or would recognize them as goods if we were rational ("Irreducibly Social Goods," p. 142). Here, Taylor commits himself to moral realism. The desire-satisfaction theory is not consistent with this. But here it is Taylor's realism that is inconsistent with the desire-satisfaction theory. Contrary to what Taylor says, the desire-satisfaction theory can recognize social goods.

37. Richard Kraut, "Desire and the Human Good," *Proceedings and Addresses of the American Philosophical Association* 68 (1994): 39–54.

38. Kraut, "Desire and the Human Good," pp. 40–41.

Chapter 4. Nietzsche's Theory of Value and the Good Life:
The *Übermensch* Ideal

References to Nietzsche's works in this chapter indicate the titles and section numbers of the translations in the bibliography, using the following abbreviations:

AC	*The Anti-Christ*
BG&E	*Beyond Good and Evil*
D	*Daybreak*
EH	*Ecce Homo*
GM	*Genealogy of Morals*
GS	*Gay Science*
HA	*Human All Too Human*
TI	*Twilight of the Idols*
WP	*The Will to Power*
Z	*Thus Spoke Zarathustra*

Multiple numbers refer to levels in the work, for example, "GM II.12" refers to *Genealogy of Morals*, second essay, section 12; "Z IV.19.ix" refers to *Thus Spoke Zarathustra*, fourth part, chapter 19 ("The Drunken Song"), section 9; "TI VII.1" refers to *Twilight of the Idols*, chapter 7 ("The 'Improvers' of Mankind"), section 1.

1. WP 205, 221, 252, 343, 351, 390, 397, 400, 786, 897; GS 130; BG&E 46; GM II.7; TI V.4; AC 7, and many other places in Nietzsche's writings.

2. This connection has been noted by John Wilcox in *Truth and Value in Nietzsche* (Ann Arbor, Mich.: University of Michigan Press, 1974), p. 198, and Ivan Soll in "Nietzsche on Cruelty, Asceticism, and the Failure of Hedonism," in *Nietzsche, Genealogy, and Morality*, ed. Richard Schacht (Berkeley: University of California Press, 1994), pp. 170–171.

3. In some places Nietzsche describes the will to power as a thing's tendency to increase its power (AC 6; WP 660, 663, 675). In other places he describes it as the tendency to use or expend power (BG&E 13; WP 619, 650).

4. BG&E 13; WP 619, 688.

5. WP 477, 478, 551, 666, 670; TI VI.3; GS 127. Also see Walter Kaufmann, *Nietzsche*, 3d ed. (Princeton: Princeton University Press, 1968), pp. 262–269.

6. According to Danto, Nietzsche holds that

> [T]he world . . . is not the kind of thing of which it logically makes sense to say either that it is worth little, or that it has such and such a higher value. Values have no more application to the world than weights do to numbers. . . . Strictly, it follows that the world has no value from the fact that there is nothing in it which might sensibly be supposed to have value. (Arthur C. Danto, *Nietzsche as Philosopher* [New York: Macmillan, 1965], pp. 32–33)

7. Danto, *Nietasche as Philosopher*, p. 32. This is Danto's translation of a passage from *Aus dem Nachlaß der Achtziger Jahre* (which contains much of the same material as *The Will to Power*), in *Nietzsches Werke in Drei Bänden*, ed. Karl Schlechta (Munich: Carl Hanser Verlag, 1958), p. 678. Richard Schacht criticizes Danto's interpretation in "Nietzsche and Nihilism," in *Nietzsche: A Collection of Critical Essays*, ed. Robert Solomon (New York: Anchor Books, 1973), pp. 58–82.

8. WP 4, 20, 275; GS 5.

9. Nietzsche was an early proponent of the "error theory" of morality defended more recently by J. L. Mackie in *Ethics: Inventing Right and Wrong* (New York: Penguin, 1977) and "The Refutation of Morals," *Australasian Journal of Philosophy and Psychology* 24 (1946): 77–90. Nietzsche's version of the error theory differs from Mackie's in several important respects. First, Nietzsche dislikes morality and urges the "higher types" of people to dispense with it altogether. Mackie "likes" morality and thinks that we must "invent" it. Second, Nietzsche uses the term "morality" in a more narrow sense than Mackie.

10. "Let us therefore limit ourselves to the purification of our opinions and valuations and the *creation of our own new tables of what is good*, and let us stop brooding

about the 'moral value of our actions'" (GS 335; see also WP 258, 290, 373, 391, 462, 583.B, 710, 1006; EH II.10).

11. If I am correct in what I have said about Nietzsche's distinction between moral and non-moral values, then Nietzsche's views are similar to those G. E. M. Anscombe attributes to Aristotle. According to Anscombe, the concepts of moral duty (obligation) and moral praiseworthiness and blameworthiness are mostly a product of the Judeo-Christian tradition; they played little or no role in Aristotle's moral philosophy. See Anscombe, "Modern Moral Philosophy," in *Ethics*, ed. Judith Thomson and Gerald Dworkin (New York: Harper & Row, 1968), pp. 186–187, 191, 196. Alan Gibbard also uses the word "morality" in a very narrow sense, much as Nietzsche does. According to Gibbard, normative codes that do not contain norms for guilt and anger are not moral codes. Gibbard takes it to be a consequence of his position that many societies do not have moral codes. See, Gibbard, *Wise Choices and Apt Feelings* (Cambridge: Harvard University Press, 1990), pp. 51–52, 298–300.

12. GS 250; Z I.6; GM III.16; WP 233–235; HA I.107.

13. GM II.11.

14. The German word *schlecht*, which Kaufmann translates as "bad," also means "poor," "lousy," and "inferior." *Schlecht* does not necessarily carry any connotations of guilt, blameworthiness, or condemnation. This word can be applied to animals and inanimate objects as well as people. However, the word *böse* ("evil"), at least in its primary sense, is a term of condemnation which implies guilt and blameworthiness.

15. WP 874; Z IV.3.i.

16. TI V.2.

17. Cf. Aristotle, *Nicomachean Ethics* 1119b15–20. "And the appetitive element of a self-controlled man must be in harmony with the guidance of reason. For the aim of both his appetite and his reason is to do what is noble. The appetite of a self-controlled man is directed at the right objects, in the right way, and at the right time. . . ." Martin Ostwald translation (Indianapolis: Bobbs Merrill, 1962).

18. WP 289, 319; TI VI.2; GS 3.

19. WP 384.

20. See 4.III.2 for a discussion of sublimation.

21. Nietzsche never explains exactly what he means by "energy" or "force." Clearly he means something more than just physical energy.

22. WP 995.

23. AC 24, 38; TI V.4; WP 37, 215.

24. A person who accepts other people's values has no motivation to create new ones. In order to do this a person must first become dissatisfied with the values which he has learned from others (see WP 32; Z III.12.xxvi).

25. TI IX.11.

26. Z III.12.xxiii, IV.11; WP 1051.

27. Z I.7, I.10, III.2, III.11.ii, III.12.xiii, IV.11, IV.17.i; GM I.10.

28. WP 699.

29. Z I.7, III.2.

30. See GM I.10 and many other places in Nietzsche's writings.

31. Max Scheler, *Ressentiment*, trans. by William Holdheim (New York: Schocken Books, 1972), pp. 39–40. The "root" meaning of the French word *ressentiment* is "re-feeling" or "feeling again."

32. Scheler, *Ressentiment*, pp. 45–46. Dostoyevsky's "underground man" is a perfect example of this kind of impotent hostility. The underground man is constantly humiliated and insulted by his associates. His inability to avenge himself causes him to "relive" the feelings of hatred and revenge to which these injuries gave rise. He is often gripped by feelings of hatred and revenge while reflecting on past events.

33. Scheler discusses the connection between *ressentiment* and the lack of self-respect at some length; see *Ressentiment*, pp. 46–56.

34. GS 341; Z III.2, III.13.ii, III.16. Zarathustra has great difficulty passing the test of eternal recurrence. He is perfectly pleased with his own life. However, he is greatly distressed by the thought that "the small man recurs eternally" (Z III.13.ii).

35. Z Prol. 4, I.22.i; and GS 3.

36. Z Prol. 4.

37. Z II.1.

38. Z II.3; see also Z III.12.iv.

39. Ostwald translation.

40. Z I.22.i.

41. Z Prol. 1; TI IX.44; WP 935. For an excellent discussion of Nietzsche's views about generosity see Lester Hunt, *Nietzsche and the Origin of Virtue* (London: Routledge, 1991), chapter 6.

42. George Morgan, *What Nietzsche Means* (Cambridge: Harvard University Press, 1941), p. 139. This passage was translated by Morgan from Nietzsche's *Nachgelassene Werke*, vol. 10, p. 309, in *Nietzsche's Werke: Groß-Oktav Ausgabe* (Leipzig: Alfred Kröner, 1894).

43. Cf. Perry, *General Theory of Value*:

Is a thing valuable because it is valued? . . . Or, is a thing valued because it is valuable? (p. 4)

Perry endorses the view that things are valuable because they are valued. In the passages quoted here Nietzsche defends a view similar to Perry's.

44. See TI IX.24; WP 298, 808; and Morgan, *What Nietzsche Means*, p. 207.

45. The German word *Vergeistigung* is translated as "spiritualization." A less elegant, but perhaps more accurate, translation would be "mentalization." For the German word *Geist* has a somewhat broader meaning than the English word "spirit." It also means "mind." The activities that Nietzsche mentions in connection with spiritualization—love (TI V.3), art (WP 800), and philosophy (GM III.9, WP 978)—could all be considered "mental" or "spiritual" activities.

46. See Alexander Nehamas, *Nietzsche: Life as Literature* (Cambridge, Mass.: Harvard University Press, 1985), p. 167, and J. P. Stern, *A Study of Nietzsche* (Cambridge: Cambridge University Press, 1979), pp. 120–121.

47. Nietzsche seems to think that a superior person could not be moved to help others out of pity. I think that we should question this. I see no reason to suppose that pity is as debilitating as Nietzsche thinks. It is not clear why an *Übermensch* could not be moved by pity.

48. See Scheler, *Ressentiment*, chapter 3, "Christian Morality and *Ressentiment.*"

49. Thomas Hurka, *Perfectionism* (Oxford: Oxford University Press, 1993).

50. Hurka, *Perfectionism*, p. 171.

51. Hurka, *Perfectionism*, p. 75.

52. Wilcox, *Truth and Value in Nietzsche*, p. 198.

Chapter 5. Human Purpose and Human Nature: Aristotelian Theories of Value

1. On one reading, Sartre's claim that "existence precedes essence" means that human beings have no purpose or function apart from their own goals and reasons for wanting to live; our only purposes are those that we freely choose for ourselves. See Sartre's "Existentialism," in *Existentialism and Human Emotions*, trans. Bernard Frechtman (New York: Philosophical Library, 1957).

2. P. T. Geach, "Good and Evil," in *Theories of Ethics*, ed. Philippa Foot (Oxford: Oxford University Press, 1968), p. 64.

3. Geach, "Good and Evil," p. 64.

4. Geach, "Good and Evil," p. 65.

5. Geach, "Good and Evil," pp. 65–66.

6. Geach, "Good and Evil," pp. 68–69. Cf. Charles Pigden, "Geach on 'Good'," *Philosophical Quarterly* 40 (1990): 129–154. According to Pigden, Geach holds the following:

m is a good X = df. m is, or does, to a high or satisfactory degree what X's are supposed, or required, to be or do. (p. 134)

7. For reasons that needn't concern us here, Geach thinks that we should dispense with the notion of right and wrong actions and instead speak only of good and bad human actions.

8. Geach, "Good and Evil," p. 69.

9. Here, I am assuming that Geach holds that if there are any things whose purpose or proper functioning is inconsistent with the purpose or proper functioning of human beings, then the purpose or function of those things is less important or less valuable than that of human beings.

10. Often children are conceived unintentionally by parents who do not want to have children. Further, even if both parents wanted to conceive a child, they may not have had the same reasons for wanting to do so. P1 needs to be revised in order to speak intelligibly to these cases.

11. This is an analogue of a standard objection to the divine-command theory (DCT). Roughly, DCT says that an act is morally obligatory (wrong) if, and only if,

God commands (forbids) it. The objection in question is that the DCT implies that if God does not exist (or if God does not command or forbid anything), then every act is permissible.

12. This is an analogue of another standard objection to the DCT, namely, that if God commanded us to act cruelly, we would have a moral obligation to act cruelly.

13. Robert M. Adams modifies the divine command theory along similar lines in his paper "A Modified Divine Command Theory of Ethical Wrongness," in *The Virtue of Faith* (Oxford: Oxford University Press, 1987), pp. 97–127. According to Adams, an act is morally wrong if, and only if, it is contrary to the commands of a *loving* God.

14. P2b is an analogue of the version of the divine command theory presented by Robert Adams in "Divine Command Metaethics Modified Again," in Adams's *The Virtue of Faith* (Oxford: Oxford University Press, 1987), pp. 128–143. P3 could be modified along the lines of P2b, but I won't bother to do so here. The differences between P2b and analogous versions of P3 are not significant for the present discussion.

15. Cf. C.D.C. Reeve, *Practices of Reason: Aristotle's Nicomachean Ethics* (Oxford: Oxford University Press, 1992), p. 115, and Richard Kraut, *Aristotle on the Human Good* (Princeton: Princeton University Press, 1989), p. 1.

16. The relevant passage reads as follows:

> For the present we define as "self-sufficient" that which taken by itself makes life something desirable and deficient in nothing. It is *eudaimonia*, in our opinion, which fits this description. Moreover, happiness is of all things the one most desirable, and it is not counted as one good thing among many others. But if it were counted as one among many others, it is obvious that the addition of even the least of the goods would make it more desirable; for the addition would produce an extra amount of good, and the greater amount of good is always more desirable than the lesser. (*Nicomachean Ethics* 1097b [Ostwald translation])

It is a matter of great controversy among Aristotle scholars whether this passage commits Aristotle to the view that *eudaimonia* is an inclusive good.

17. Aristotle's theory may be a plausible analysis of pleasures derived from enjoyable actions, but it does not seem plausible as an account of pleasures involving pleasant sensations, e.g., pleasures derived from such things as sunbathing, eating, and being massaged.

18. Cf. *Nicomachean Ethics*, 1175a (Ostwald translation):

> We need not discuss for the present the question whether we choose life for the sake of pleasure or pleasure for the sake of life. For the two are obviously interdependent and cannot be separated: there is no pleasure without activity, and every activity is completed by pleasure.

19. In *The Eudemian Ethics* (1220a1–10) Aristotle says that *eudaimonia* includes both practical and theoretical excellence.

20. Among those who take this position are J. L. Ackrill, "Aristotle on *Eudaimonia*," in *Essays on Aristotle's Ethics*, ed. Amelie Rorty (Berkeley: University of California Press, 1980), pp. 15–33; Jennifer Whiting, "Human Nature and Intellectualism in Aristotle," *Archive für Geschichte der Philosophie* 68 (1986): 70–95; and Timothy Roche, "*Ergon* and *Eudaimonia* in *Nicomachean Ethics* I," *Journal of the History of Philosophy* 26 (April 1988): 175–194.

21. Among those who accept this interpretation are Kraut, *Aristotle on the Human Good*; H. F. R. Hardie, "The Final Good in Aristotle's *Ethics*," in *Aristotle: A Collection of Critical Essays*, ed. J. M. E. Moravcsik (Notre Dame, Ind.: University of Notre Dame Press, 1968), pp. 297–322; and John Cooper, *Reason and Human Good in Aristotle* (Cambridge: Harvard University Press, 1975). Cooper has subsequently repudiated his "intellectualist" reading of Aristotle; see Cooper, "Contemplation and Happiness: A Reconsideration," *Synthese* 72 (1987): 187–216.

22. See chapter 1 of Kraut, *Aristotle on the Human Good*.

23. Cf. *Nicomachean Ethics* 1098a (Ostwald translation): "We reach the conclusion that the good of man is an activity of the soul in conformity with excellence or virtue, and if there are several virtues, in conformity with the best and most complete."

24. Sarah Broadie questions whether we should attribute premise b to Aristotle. She claims that, while Aristotle says that reason *(nous)* is the best element in us, it is unclear that he means only theoretical (as opposed to practical) reason.

> Again, what is the best element in us? Aristotle here calls it 'nous', but there is practical as well as theoretical *nous*, and in Book VI (1139a5–15) he presented these as distinct elements in the rational soul. So is *nous* here only theoretical, or is it practical too? The latter, I think. . . . (Broadie, *Ethics with Aristotle*, p. 415)

25. The statement that *theoria* is always pursued as an end, never as a means, seems false, inasmuch as *theoria* is sometimes pursued for the sake of relaxation or for the sake of worldly fortune and honor.

26. Cf. Hurka, *Perfectionism*, p. 11. Hurka attributes this criticism to Bernard Williams in *Morality* (New York: Harper & Row, 1972), p. 64, and Kai Nielsen in "Alienation and Self-Realization," *Philosophy* 48 (1973): 23–24.

27. Hurka, *Perfectionism*, p. 11. Hurka attributes this idea to Robert Nozick, *Philosophical Explanations* (Cambridge: Harvard University Press, 1981), pp. 515–517.

28. Hurka, *Perfectionism*, p. 13. Hurka also attributes this view to Marx.

29. Cf. Kraut, *Aristotle on the Human Good*, p. 313. Aristotle accepts the following: (1) *theoria* is the only activity of the gods, and (2) humans are the only rational beings other than the gods. Given (1) and (2), A1, A2, and A3 each imply that *theoria* is *not* constitutive of human *eudaimonia*. On these assumptions, A1 implies that *praxis* is at least partly constitutive of human *eudaimonia* and A2 and A3 strongly lend themselves to this view.

30. This is a very dubious interpretation of Aristotle. Aristotle does not hold that the Prime Mover created the universe.

31. Kraut, *Aristotle on the Human Good*, p. 317.

32. This interpretation is defended by Jennifer Whiting, "Aristotle's Function Argument: A Defense," *Ancient Philosophy* 8 (1988): 37–38, and Reeve, *Practices of Reason*, pp. 125–126.

33. Unlike some commentators (see previous note), Hurka does not attribute this view to Aristotle.

34. Hurka, *Perfectionism*, p. 46.

35. Hurka, *Perfectionism*, p. 39.

36. Hurka, *Perfectionism*, p. 22.

37. Ibid.

38. Being a Caucasian (European) human being includes being a human being. Hurka would not take it to be absurd to say that I should fulfill my essence as a Caucasian human being, because this would involve fulfilling my essence as a *human being*. But I take it that we could both agree that the development of those features of myself that are essential to my being a Caucasian but not essential to my being human, e.g., my being particularly liable to sunburn, is not constitutive of a good life.

39. Hurka, *Perfectionism*, p. 31.

40. Ibid.

41. See Hurka, *Perfectionism*, chapter 7 ("The Well-Rounded Life"), and his paper "The Well Rounded Life," *The Journal of Philosophy* 84 (1987): 707–726. The importance of developing a wide range of abilities is an important theme in Marx's writing about the human good and human fulfillment. In a well-known passage from *The German Ideology* in which he gives one of his few descriptions of unalienated work, Marx is at pains to stress that people will engage in many different kinds of activities that employ a wide range of their abilities (*The German Ideology*, trans. Lawrence and Wishart [New York: International Publishers, 1970], p. 53.) One of Marx's central criticisms of capitalism and the minute division of labor that it promotes is that they result in a "one-sided" or incomplete development of human potential: see *Capital*, trans. Samuel Moore and Edward Aveling (New York: International Publishers, 1967), pp. 349, 361, 645.

Interlude 1

1. Moore, *Principia Ethica*, pp. 83–84.

2. Cf. Sidgwick, *The Methods of Ethics*:

Since it is implied in the very notion of Truth that it is essentially the same for all minds, the denial by another of a proposition that I have affirmed has a tendency to impair my confidence in its validity. . . . the absence of such disagreement must remain an indispensable negative condition of the certainty of our beliefs. For if I find any of my judgments, intuitive or inferential, in direct conflict with a judgment of some other mind, there must be error somewhere: and I have no more reason to suspect error in the other mind than in my own. (pp. 341–342)

Chapter 6. The Concept of Value: A Pragmatic Approach

1. Moore, *Ethics*, p. 24.

2. Moore, *Ethics*, p. 68. See also Moore, *Principia Ethica*, pp. 93, 95, and 187, and "A Reply to My Critics," in *The Philosophy of G. E. Moore*, ed. P. A. Schilpp (La Salle, Ill.: Open Court, 1968), p. 600. Chisholm attributes a similar view to Brentano and seems to accept such a definition himself; see *Brentano and Intrinsic Value*, pp. 18, 61; see also Chisholm's "Intrinsic Value," in *Values and Morals*, ed. A. I. Goldman and J. Kim (Dordrecht: Reidel, 1978), pp. 121–122, and "On the Logic of 'Intrinsically Better'" (with Ernest Sosa), *American Philosophical Quarterly* 3 (1966): 1.

3. This is one of the main theses of Christine Korsgaard's "Two Distinctions in Goodness," *The Philosophical Review* 92 (1983): 169–195. This is an excellent paper to which I am very much indebted. Almost everything that I say in this section is consistent with Korsgaard's view. She makes additional distinctions that I do not develop here. According to Korsgaard, things that are good as ends can be either conditionally good or unconditionally good (she claims that this distinction can be found in Kant). Things that are conditionally good are good and make the world a better place but only if certain conditions hold. Things that are unconditionally good are good and make the world a better place regardless of what other conditions hold. According to Kant, happiness is only conditionally good. Happiness is good on the condition that the person who possesses it is morally good and thus worthy of being happy. Kant thinks that a "good will" is the only thing that is unconditionally good (*Grounding for the Metaphysics of Morals*, pp. 393–397 [Prussian Academy page numbers]).

4. For extensive support of the latter claim see Chisholm's discussion of the "defeat" of value in "The Defeat of Good and Evil," pp. 53–68, and *Brentano and Intrinsic Value*.

5. NIV2 is very similar to Korsgaard's notion of being "objectively good." Note the following passage from Korsgaard:

> "objectively good" is a judgment applying to real particulars: this woman's knowledge, this man's happiness, and so on. To say of a thing that it is good objectively is not to say that it is the type of thing that is usually good (a good kind of thing like knowledge or happiness) but that it contributes to the actual goodness of the world: here and now the world is a better place for this. ("Two Distinctions in Goodness," p. 179; see also p. 169)

Korsgaard seems to agree with me that whether or not something has value as an end is determined by its contribution to the value of the world. She speaks in terms of things which "make the world a better place." Non-instrumentally good things, in my sense, might be instances of things that are either conditionally or unconditionally good in Korsgaard's sense (see note 3). A particular occurrence of a state of affairs that is "conditionally good" might contribute to the value of the universe because those conditions that are necessary for it to be good as an end are, in fact, met. For example, a particular instance of the state of affairs someone being happy might contribute to the value of the universe because the condition of its being good as an end (that the happiness is "deserved") is met.

6. Chisholm's criticisms are directed at Zimmerman's "Evaluatively Incomplete States of Affairs," *Philosophical Studies* 43 (1983): 211–224.

7. Chisholm, *Brentano and Intrinsic Value*, pp. 81–82.

8. Kant agrees. He claims that the happiness of those who are morally good (and thus deserve to be happy) is unconditionally good; see *Grounding for the Metaphysics of Morals*, pp. 393–397 (Prussian Academy page numbers). See also W. D. Ross, *The Right and the Good*, pp. 135 ff., and Korsgaard, "Two Distinctions in Goodness," p. 193.

9. Cf. Blackburn, *Essays in Quasi-Realism*, pp. 6, 150–151. Blackburn claims that if our notion of morality commits us to an error theory, we would be well advised to cease using moral norms and adopt an alternative normative system whose use does not involve systematic error.

10. Most of the major figures in the history of Western moral philosophy accept something much stronger than this; most would take "x is better than y" to entail "other things being equal, it is correct *for anyone* (any human being/any rational being) to prefer x to y."

11. For more on this see Carson, "Relativism and Nihilism," *Philosophia* 15 (1985): 1–23, and chapter 3 of *The Status of Morality*.

12. See Bertrand Russell, "A Reply to My Critics," in *The Philosophy of Bertrand Russell*, ed. P. A. Schilpp (La Salle, Ill.: Open Court, 1944), p. 724.

13. Lemos, *Intrinsic Value*, pp. 6–15.

14. Note the following passage from Sidgwick's *The Methods of Ethics*:

> Here we are met by the suggestion that the judgments or propositions which we commonly call moral—in the narrow sense—really affirm no more than the existence of a specific emotion in the mind of the person who utters them; that when I say 'Truth ought to be spoken' or 'Truthspeaking is right,' I mean no more than that the idea of truthspeaking excites in my mind a feeling of approbation or satisfaction. . . . If I say that 'the air is sweet,' or 'the food disagreeable,' it would not be exactly true to say that I mean no more than I like the one or dislike the other; but if my statement is challenged, I shall probably content myself with affirming the existence of such feelings in my own mind. But there appears to me to be a fundamental difference between this case and that of moral feelings. The peculiar emotion of moral approbation is, in my experience, inseparably bound up with the conviction, implicit or explicit, that the conduct approved is 'really' right, i.e., that it cannot without error be disapproved by any other mind. (pp. 26–27)

15. W. D. Ross, *The Foundations of Ethics* (Oxford: Clarendon Press, 1939), pp. 40–41.

16. Kraut, "Desire and the Human Good," p. 45.

17. In *The Definition of Good* (New York: Macmillan, 1947), A. C. Ewing defines "good" as "what ought to be the object of a pro-attitude" (pp. 148–149). He goes on to define "morally ought" as follows:

'A morally ought to do this' means (1) it would be fitting for A to do this and (2) if he does not do it it is fitting that he should be an object of disapproval, or perhaps simply (2) without (1). (p. 168)

18. See J. O. Urmson, *The Emotive Theory of Ethics* (Oxford: Oxford University Press, 1968), pp. 58–59:

'This is good' is more like 'it is correct (in a sense of 'correct' which is opposed to 'mistaken') to approve of this' . . . 'good' seems to resemble 'correctly to be approved of.'

19. Brandt, *Ethical Theory*, p. 159.
20. Christine Korsgaard, *The Sources of Normativity* (Cambridge: Cambridge University Press, 1996), pp. 8–9.
21. Korsgaard, *The Sources of Normativity* p. 114. See also her "Two Distinctions in Goodness," p. 169.
22. Brentano, *The Origin of Our Knowledge of Right and Wrong*, p. 18. The German word that Chisholm and Schneewind translate as "correct" is *richtig*.
23. Brentano, *The Origin of Our Knowledge of Right and Wrong*, p. 74.
24. Brentano, *The Origin of Our Knowledge of Right and Wrong*, p. 26. Also note the following passages:

And when we call certain objects good and bad we are merely saying that whoever loves the former and hates the latter has taken the right stand. (Brentano, *The Foundation and Construction of Ethics*, p. 131)

Accordingly, everything that can be thought about belongs in one of two classes — either the class of things for which love is appropriate, or the class of things for which hate is appropriate. Whatever falls into the first class we call good, and whatever falls into the second we call bad. (Brentano, *The True and the Evident*, pp. 21–22)

Brentano uses the words *Lieben* and *Hassen* interchangeably with *Gefallen* and *Missfallen* — "*Lieben oder hassen oder (wie man ebenso richtig ausdrucken könnte) ein Gefallen oder Missfallen*" (*The Origin of Our Knowledge of Right and Wrong*, p. 16). The German word *Gefallen* can be translated as "pleasure," "preference," "choice," or "favor." *Gefallen* with an object is a matter both of how one feels about it or is disposed to feel about it and of how one is disposed to act with respect to it; one is disposed to feel pleased with it and to prefer its existence or occurrence to its non-existence or non-occurrence all other things being equal. Brentano distinguishes between choice and preference. A person can have preferences concerning things that are not a matter of choice for him. For example, someone may have a preference that the sun rise in the morning (*The Origin of Our Knowledge of Right and Wrong*, pp. 150–151, and

Foundation and Construction of Ethics, p. 200). However, we can still say that a person's preferences are ultimately determined by facts about how he would choose in various *hypothetical* situations. For example, to say that someone prefers that the sun rise rather than not is to say that he would choose to have it rise if it were within his power to decide. The analysis of love and hatred (*Gefallen* and *Missfallen*) in terms of both feelings and action tendencies is supported by Brentano's analysis of "better" as that which it is correct to prefer (*vorziehen*) and the passages in *Psychology from an Empirical Standpoint*, trans. Antos Rancurello, D. B. Terrell, and Linda McAlister (New York: Humanities Press, 1973), in which he says that the phenomena of love and hatred include both feeling and will (pp. 246, 251).

For further defenses of this view see C. D. Broad, "Some Reflections on Moral Sense Theories in Ethics," in *Broad's Critical Essays in Moral Philosophy*, ed. David Cheney (New York: Humanities, 1971), esp. p. 194; and Broad's *Five Types of Ethical Theory*, p. 283. See also chapter 1 of Carson, *The Status of Morality*.

25. Brentano, *The Origin of Our Knowledge of Right and Wrong*, p. 74.

26. Carl Wellman, "Emotivism and Ethical Objectivity," in *Readings in Ethical Theory*, 2d. ed., ed. John Hospers and Wilfrid Sellars (Englewood Cliffs, N.J.: Prentice-Hall, 1970), p. 286.

27. Julia Annas defends this reading of Aristotle in *The Morality of Happiness* (Oxford: Oxford University Press, 1993), p. 36.

28. Aristotle, *Nicomachean Ethics*, trans. Terence Irwin (Indianapolis: Hackett, 1985).

29. Hume and Firth use the ideal observer theory as a theory about the meaning of normative concepts. Others who defend the ideal observer theory do not accept it as a theory of meaning, but only as a standard of truth or correctness for moral judgments.

30. In the *Treatise of Human Nature*, 2d ed. (Oxford: Oxford University Press, 1978), Hume says that when we call someone virtuous or vicious, we simply mean that the contemplation of his character (from an impartial perspective) causes one to feel approbation or disapprobation (pp. 469, 471–472). In the *Enquiry Concerning the Principles of Morals*, 2d ed. (Oxford: Oxford University Press, 1972), Hume defines virtue to be "Whatever mental action or *quality* gives to a spectator the pleasing sentiment of approbation; and vice the contrary" (p. 289). He goes on to add that the spectator must have a full knowledge of all the relevant facts and circumstances (p. 290).

31. Roderick Firth, "Ethical Absolutism and the Ideal Observer," in *Morality and the Good Life*, ed. Thomas Carson and Paul Moser (New York: Oxford University Press, 1997), pp. 40–60.

32. For a detailed examination of Firth's theory see chapter 2 of Carson, *The Status of Morality*. See also Richard Brandt's article "Ideal Observer" in the *Encyclopedia of Ethics*, ed. Lawrence Becker and Charlotte Becker (New York: Garland, 1992), for discussion and additional references.

33. Firth, "Ethical Absolutism and the Ideal Observer," pp. 47–48.

34. Ibid.

35. Firth, "Ethical Absolutism and the Ideal Observer," p. 47.

36. Firth, "Ethical Absolutism and the Ideal Observer," pp. 47–48. See Wolfgang Köhler, *The Place of Value in a World of Fact* (New York: Liveright, 1938).

37. Here, Firth might protest that I and those who give similar reports have misdescribed our experiences and have failed to notice or attend to genuine features of our own experiences. This is *possible*. But, in order to support this claim, Firth needs to give a clearer description of the experiences he has in mind.

38. For more on the possibility of disagreement between Firthian ideal observers, see chapter 2 of Carson, *The Status of Morality*, Charles Taliaferro, "Relativizing the Ideal Observer Theory," *Philosophy and Phenomenological Research* 49 (1988): 123–138, and Carson, "Could Ideal Observers Disagree? A Reply to Taliaferro," *Philosophy and Phenomenological Research* 50 (1989): 115–124.

39. Gibbard, *Wise Choices, Apt Feelings*, p. 42.

40. Gibbard writes the following:

A final loose end: Carson and Railton both want to know what I'd say about intrinsic value. I'll be discussing this elsewhere at length, but briefly: good means desirable. Something is intrinsically good if an intrinsic desire for it is warranted. This, of course, needs refinement. ("Reply to Blackburn, Carson, Hill and Railton," in a symposium on his book *Wise Choices, Apt Feelings*, in *Philosophy and Phenomenological Research* 42 (1992): 980)

41. Gibbard, *Wise Choices, Apt Feelings*, p. 31.

42. Cf. Carson, *The Status of Morality*, p. 79, and Carson, "Could Ideal Observers Disagree? A Reply to Taliaferro," p. 123.

43. R. M. Hare, "Some Confusions about Subjectivity," in *Essays in Ethical Theory* (Oxford: Oxford University Press, 1989), p. 18.

44. "A *Reductio ad Absurdum* of Descriptivism," in Hare, *Essays in Ethical Theory*, p. 120.

45. Foot's theory is perhaps the most well-known theory of this kind. I discuss her theory and other "mixed" theories in 6.VIII.

46. Cf. Hare, "Ethics and Ontology," in *Essays in Ethical Theory*, p. 96.

47. My discussion of disagreement owes a great deal to R. M. Hare. See Hare's *The Language of Morals* (Oxford: Oxford University Press, 1952), pp. 148–149 and "How to Decide Moral Questions Rationally," pp. 99–112, and "A *Reductio ad Absurdum* of Descriptivism," pp. 113–130, both included in his *Essays in Ethical Theory*.

48. Cf. Hare, "A *Reductio ad Absurdum* of Descriptivism," in *Essays in Ethical Theory*, p. 130.

49. My readers are English speakers who are familiar with the Western philosophical tradition. But what about non-English speakers who are not familiar with the Western tradition? The first two pragmatic criteria still apply to them. All human beings have reasons to employ normative concepts that can guide practice and allow them to make sense of disagreements about first-order questions of value. It's not so clear that everyone has reasons to employ normative concepts that are part of the Western tradition.

There is some presumption in favor of employing normative concepts that are intelligible within one's own native language and ethical/philosophical tradition. We all need to be able to discuss normative questions with members of our own communities. However, many educated people throughout the world are (non-native) English speakers who are familiar with the Western tradition. Non-English speakers who are unfamiliar with the Western philosophical tradition can profit by talking about normative questions with *them*. Thus, many non-English speakers who are unfamiliar with the Western tradition also have reasons to employ normative concepts that will enable them to address normative issues discussed in English and the Western tradition. The same sort of thing holds for those of us who are native English speakers and/or familiar with the Western tradition. Other things equal, normative concepts that enable us to engage in normative discussions about issues that are discussed in other languages and traditions are preferable to concepts that do not permit this.

50. Locke may be the clearest example of a pure reductivist descriptivist in the history of philosophy. Note the following passage:

> Things are good or evil, only in reference to pleasure or pain. That we call *good*, which is apt to cause or increase pleasure, or diminish pain in us; or else to procure, or preserve us the possession of any other good, or absence of any evil. And on the contrary we name that *evil*, which is apt to produce or increase any pain, or diminish any pleasure in us; or else to procure us any evil, or deprive us of any good. (John Locke, *Essay Concerning Human Understanding*, Book II, Chapter XX, paragraph 2; from *British Moralists 1650–1800*, ed. D. D. Raphael [Oxford: Oxford University Press, 1969])

51. Ewing writes, "Certain characteristics are such that the fitting response to whatever possesses them is a pro-attitude, and that is all there is to it" (*The Definition of Good*, p. 172). Note the following passage from C. D. Broad:

> The fundamental fact seems to me to be that rightness is a relational characteristic, and not a pure quality. When I say that *x* is right I am saying something about its relations to certain other terms. Rightness is a species of fittingness or appropriateness, and a term which is 'fitting' must be fitting *to* something. The above, I believe, is a true statement about rightness, but it is not a definition of it. For, so far as I can see, rightness is quite a unique kind of appropriateness, just as red is a quite unique kind of colour. ("Analysis of Some Ethical Concepts," in *Broad's Critical Essays in Moral Philosophy* [London: Allen & Unwin, 1971], p. 76)

See also Brentano, *The Origin of Our Knowledge of Right and Wrong*, pp. 22–24, 84, 114, 147.

52. Such a view is defended by W. H. F. Barnes, "A Suggestion About Value," in *Readings in Ethical Theory*, 2d ed., ed. Hospers and Sellars, p. 241.

53. Stevenson says that an ethical disagreement consists in a disagreement "in interest" or a disagreement "in attitude," "The Emotive Meaning of Ethical Terms,"

in *Readings in Ethical Theory*, 2d ed., ed. Hospers and Sellars, p. 263. See also Stevenson's *Ethics and Language* (New Haven: Yale University Press, 1944), pp. 3–4).

54. A. J. Ayer, *Language, Truth and Logic* (New York: Dover, 1952), p. 108.

55. Stevenson, *Ethics and Language*, pp. 21–24, and "The Emotive Meaning of Ethical Terms," p. 262.

56. Cf. Vincent Tomas, "Ethical Disagreement and the Emotive Theory of Values," *Mind* 60 (1950): 215, and Brandt's *Ethical Theory*, p. 226.

57. Tomas, "Ethical Disagreement and the Emotive Theory of Values," p. 226.

58. Hare, *The Language of Morals*, pp. 175–179.

59. R. M. Hare, *Freedom and Reason* (Oxford: Oxford University Press, 1963), p. 11.

60. See Hare, *Freedom and Reason*, pp. 168, 176.

61. Hare, *Moral Thinking*, p. 55.

62. Hare, *Moral Thinking*, pp. 60–61.

63. Hare, *Moral Thinking*, p. 56.

64. The *Language of Morals* is the only one of his three major books in which Hare discusses the concept of value at any length. His later books say very little about the concepts of good and bad. Hare's index to *Moral Thinking* doesn't contain a single entry under "good," "bad," or "value." Hare introduced the concept of overridingness into his analysis of meaning in *Freedom and Reason*. I conjecture that when Hare modified his theory by introducing the concept of overridingness he didn't pay much attention to the implications of this change for the concepts of good and bad.

65. Sincerely prescribing that x be chosen over y doesn't entail that one thinks it correct to prefer x to y. An immoralist (someone whose attitudes and preferences are self-consciously opposed to those he believes to be moral/correct) might sincerely prescribe actions contrary to the preferences he takes to be correct. I won't bother to defend this point in any greater detail here, since if I am mistaken about this matter (and sincerely prescribing that X be chosen over Y commits one to saying that it is correct to prefer X to Y), then Hare's theory is consistent with my theory of meaning—his theory implies that saying that something is good implies that it is correct to prefer it. For an elaboration of the objection that prescriptivism cannot allow for the logical possibility of amoralism or immoralism, see Carson, *The Status of Morality*, pp. 18–21, and David Brink, *Moral Realism and the Foundations of Ethics* (Cambridge: Cambridge University Press, 1989), pp. 46–50, 59–60.

66. Hare's theory is widely criticized on the grounds that it denies the existence of moral weakness. According to Hare, accepting a moral judgment entails assenting to a prescription. For example, accepting the moral judgment that killing is wrong entails assenting to the prescription "don't kill." Hare says that in order for one to be said to "assent to" a prescription (or an overriding prescription) it is necessary that one follow it whenever possible (*Freedom and Reason*, p. 79, and *Moral Thinking*, pp. 57–58). According to Hare, if a person fails to do something that he professes to believe he ought to do, then it follows that either he was unable to do it or that he didn't really believe that he ought to do it. This is tantamount to a denial of the existence of moral weakness in the ordinary sense. Hare defends his view of moral weakness at length in all of his major works (*Language of Morals*, pp. 166–170, *Freedom*

and Reason, chapter 5, and *Moral Thinking,* pp. 57–60). Although Hare's discussion of moral weakness merits careful study, in the end he does not give us adequate reasons for denying what seems to be one of the most obvious features of the moral life. I have discussed this issue elsewhere and will not pursue it further here (Carson, "Hare's Defense of Utilitarianism," *Philosophical Studies* 50 (1986): 97–115, especially 108–109). Even if we reject Hare's views on moral weakness, modified versions of prescriptivism which incorporate alternative accounts of what it is to accept a prescription might still be acceptable.

67. See Bernard Williams, *Ethics and the Limits of Philosophy* (Cambridge: Harvard University Press, 1985).

68. See Philippa Foot, "Moral Beliefs," in *Theories of Ethics,* ed. Foot (Oxford: Oxford University Press, 1968), pp. 83–100.

69. Foot, "Moral Beliefs," p. 91.

70. See "Moral Arguments," in Foot's *Virtues and Vices* (Berkeley: University of California Press, 1978), p. 100.

Chapter 7. Moral/Axiological Realism

1. Cf. Michael Devitt, *Realism and Truth,* 2d ed. (Blackwell, 1991), p. 13.

2. Michael Dummett, *Truth and Other Enigmas* (Cambridge: Harvard University Press, 1978), p. 146. Also see his definition in "Realism," *Synthese* 52 (1982):

[S]tatements in the given class relate to some reality that exists independently of our knowledge of it, in such a way that reality renders each statement in the class determinately true or false, again independently of whether we know, or are even able to discover, its truth value. (p. 55)

3. Brink, *Moral Realism and the Foundation of Ethics,* p. 16. Brink notes that this definition has the unfortunate consequence of making psychological realism incoherent, because psychological states are surely mind-dependent. But this is not an objection to defining moral/axiological realism in terms of mind-independent facts.

4. Putnam, *Reason, Turth, and History,* pp. 61–62.

5. Robert Arrington, *Rationalism, Realism, and Relativism* (Ithaca, N.Y.: Cornell University Press, 1989), p. 179.

6. R.M. Hare, "Ontology in Ethics," in *Essays in Ethical Theory,* p. 84.

7. Brink, *Moral Realism and the Foundations of Ethics,* p. 17; see also p. 7. Cf. Brandt, *Ethical Theory,* p. 153.

8. Mark Platts, "Moral Reality and the End of Desire," in *Reference, Truth, and Meaning,* ed. Mark Platts (London: Routledge & Kegan Paul, 1981), p. 69.

9. Richard Boyd, "How to Be a Moral Realist," in *Essays on Moral Realism,* ed. Geoffrey Sayre-McCord (Ithaca, N.Y.: Cornell University Press, 1988), p. 182.

10. Brink, *Moral Realism and the Foundations of Ethics,* pp. 130–143. See John Heil, "Recent Work on Realism and Anti-Realism," *Philosophical Books* 30 (1989):

65–73, for criticisms of the view that realism is compatible with a coherence theory of truth.

11. Cf. Putnam, *Reason, Truth, and History*, p. 55.

12. For a powerful and suggestive defense of agnosticism about metaphysical or ontological realism that has helped to form my own views about axiological realism, see chapter 1 of Paul Moser's *Philosophy after Objectivity* (Oxford: Oxford University Press, 1993).

13. Realists and non-realists will, of course, give a very different account of this. Realists will say that the fact that something is non-instrumentally good *gives one reasons* to choose or prefer it, reasons independent of one's actual desires or the desires one would have were one rational. A non-realist defender of the rational-desire-satisfaction theory would say that something's being non-instrumentally good *consists in* its being rational to choose or prefer it.

14. Warnock gives a forceful statement of this argument in *Contemporary Moral Philosophy* (New York: St. Martin's, 1969), pp. 15–16.

15. Ewing, *The Definition of the Good*, p. 172.

16. Broad, "Analysis of Some Ethical Concepts," p. 76.

17. Ross, *The Foundations of Ethics*, p. 146. Brentano also seems to take goodness to be a non-natural relational quality. He claims that the correctness of love and hatred for certain things is self-evident; love and hatred can be experienced as "being correct." This makes sense only if we suppose that correctness is a relational property capable of being directly intuited. (See Brentano, *The Origin of Our Knowledge of Right and Wrong*, pp. 22–24, 84, 114, 147.)

18. See Frankena, "The Naturalistic Fallacy," *Mind* 48 (1939): 464–477.

19. Moore, *Principia Ethica*, p. 6.

20. Moore, *Principia Ethica*, p. 8.

21. Moore, *Principia Ethica*, p. 15.

22. Moore, *Principia Ethica*, p. 16.

23. Hilary Putnam, "The Meaning of Meaning," in Putman's *Mind, Language, and Reality*, Philosophical Papers, vol. 2 (Cambridge: Cambridge University Press, 1975), pp. 215–271.

24. Nicholas Sturgeon, "Moral Explanations," in *Essays on Moral Realism*, ed. Geoffrey Sayre-McCord (Ithaca, N.Y.: Cornell University Press), p. 239.

25. Brink, *Moral Realism and the Foundations of Ethics*, pp. 157, 177.

26. Brink, *Moral Realism and the Foundations of Ethics*, p. 166.

27. Boyd, "How to Be a Moral Realist," p. 199.

28. Gilbert Harman, *The Nature of Morality* (Oxford: Oxford University Press, 1977).

29. Harman, *The Nature of Morality*, p. 6.

30. Sturgeon, "Moral Explanations," p. 249.

31. Sturgeon, "Moral Explanations," p. 246.

32. On this point, see Ian Kershaw, *Hitler (1889–1936): Hubris* (New York: Norton, 1998).

33. Charles Silbermann contends that the particularly virulent form of anti-negro (anti-African) racism which developed in the United States was the result of an attempt

to make the institution of slavery consistent with the moral principles asserting the right of all "men" to liberty. Other societies did not have comparable beliefs about the right to liberty and did not need to deny the humanity of people in order to justify enslaving them. See Silbermann, *The Crisis in Black and White* (New York: Vintage Books, 1964).

34. Sturgeon, "Moral Explanations," p. 249.

35. Sturgeon, "Moral Explanations," p. 250.

36. Sturgeon, "Moral Explanations," pp. 250–251. Brink endorses the same argument in *Moral Realism and the Foundation of Ethics*, pp. 190–191.

37. Sturgeon, "Moral Explanations," p. 237.

38. Ibid. Cf. Boyd, "How to Be a Moral Realist," pp. 182, 222.

39. Harman himself is unclear on this point. On p. 7 of *The Nature of Morality* he says that moral facts (and alleged observations of moral facts) are "completely irrelevant" to explanation. On p. 6 he says that we don't "need" moral facts to explain our experience (observations). Sturgeon answers the objection that Harman states on p. 7 of *The Nature of Morality*, but he does not answer the objection that Harman states on p. 6. Cf. Geoffrey Sayre-McCord, "Moral Theory and Explanatory Impotence," in *Essays on Moral Realism*, ed. Sayre-McCord (Ithaca, N.Y.: Cornell University Press, 1988), pp. 272–273.

40. Cf. Sayre-McCord, "Moral Theory and Explanatory Impotence," pp. 272–273. Harman claims that supervenient moral properties are mere epiphenomena from an explanatory point of view, in "Moral Explanations of Natural Facts—Can Moral Claims Be Tested against Moral Reality?" *Southern Journal of Philosophy* (Supplement) 24 (1986): 63.

41. David Copp, "Explanation and Justification in Ethics," *Ethics* 100 (1990): 237–258.

42. Brink, *Moral Realism and the Foundations of Ethics*, p. 46.

43. Brink, *Moral Realism and the Foundations of Ethics*, pp. 46–47.

44. Brink, *Moral Realism and the Foundations of Ethics*, pp. 47–48. For internalist defenses of the appeal to inverted-commas use of language see Stevenson, *Ethics and Language*, pp. 16–17, and Hare *The Language of Morals*, pp. 124–126 and 163–165, and *Freedom and Reason*, pp. 189–191.

45. I have previously defended these views along very similar lines myself. In *The Status of Morality* I gave very similar arguments to show that emotivism and prescriptivism (both internalist theories) make amoralism and immoralism conceptually impossible (see pp. 16–21). I also discuss and reject the internalist's reply that all apparent cases of amoralism and immoralism involve the inverted-commas use of moral concepts (see pp. 18–19).

46. Brink, *Moral Realism and the Foundations of Ethics*, pp. 29–31.

47. Brink, *Moral Realism and the Foundations of Ethics*, p. 30.

48. I defended just such a theory in *The Status of Morality*, chapter 2.

49. Brink, *Moral Realism and the Foundations of Ethics*, p. 31.

50. Hume was an earlier proponent of the view that moral properties are secondary properties. In *A Treatise of Human Nature* Hume says that when we call someone virtu-

ous or vicious, we simply mean that the contemplation of her character (from an impartial perspective) causes one to feel approbation or disapprobation (pp. 469, 471–472). In *Enquiry Concerning the Principles of Morals*, Hume defines virtue to be "Whatever mental action or quality gives to a spectator the pleasing sentiment of approbation; and vice the contrary" (p. 289). He goes on to add that the spectator must have a full knowledge of all the relevant facts and circumstances (p. 290). Platts acknowledges that his views bear a strong resemblance to Hume's. But Platts claims that Hume is not a realist because he doesn't think that secondary properties such as color and virtue and vice exist outside the mind. See Platts, *Moral Realities*, p. 116. McDowell is also at pains to stress that he believes that secondary qualities exist outside the mind and are not merely subjective; see John McDowell, "Values and Secondary Qualities," in *Essays on Moral Realism*, ed. Geoffrey Sayre-McCord (Ithaca, N.Y.: Cornell University Press, 1988), pp. 170–171.

For my own part, I am not so sure that we should classify the views of Platts and McDowell as genuine versions of AR. I take realism to be the view that moral and normative properties exist independently of the actual or possible experiences, beliefs, or attitudes of human beings. The views of Platts and McDowell do not count as realist theories in this sense. Their account of realism leads to the implausible consequence that Firth's version of the ideal-observer theory is a realist theory. I am not alone in questioning whether the view that moral properties are secondary properties is a version of realism. See Christopher Hookaway, "Two Conceptions of Moral Realism," *Proceedings of the Aristotelian Society* (Supplement) 60 (1986): 188–205.

51. Platts, *Moral Realities* (London: Routledge & Kegan Paul, 1991), pp. 98–99.

52. Platts, *Moral Realities*, p. 101.

53. Jonathan Dancy also faults the view that moral properties are secondary properties on phenomenological grounds; see Dancy, *Moral Reasons* (Oxford: Blackwell, 1993), pp. 159–162.

54. Cf. Blackburn, *Essays in Quasi-Realism*, p. 160.

55. McDowell, "Values and Secondary Qualities," pp. 166–180, and "Non-Cognitivism and Rule Following," in *Wittgenstein: To Follow a Rule*, ed. Steven Holtzman and Christopher Leich (London: Routledge & Kegan Paul, 1981), pp. 141–162.

56. McDowell, "Values and Secondary Qualities," pp. 175–177.

57. Mark Platts, "Moral Reality," in *Essays on Moral Realism*, ed. Geoffrey Sayre-McCord (Ithaca, N.Y.: Cornell University Press, 1988), p. 283.

58. S. L. Hurley, *Natural Reasons* (Oxford: Oxford University Press, 1989), pp. 292–293.

59. Platts, "Moral Reality," p. 285.

60. Platts, "Moral Reality," pp. 282–283, and "Moral Reality and the End of Desire," p. 69.

61. Hurley, *Natural Reasons*, pp. 292–293.

62. This is something that Copp denies. Copp says that we can use normative terms to pick out complex facts that may have explanatory significance, without endorsing the standards from which the concepts derive. See Copp, "Explanation and Justification in Ethics," pp. 237–258.

63. Platts, "Moral Reality and the End of Desire," pp. 80–81.

64. McDowell, "Non-Cognitivism and Rule Following," pp. 144–147.

65. Platts, "Moral Reality and the End of Desire," pp. 69–70.

66. Simon Blackburn has argued that realists cannot account for the supervenience of moral properties on natural properties. See Blackburn, "Moral Realism" and "Supervenience Revisited," in *Essays in Quasi-Realism*, and chapter 6 of *Spreading the Word: Groundings in the Philosophy of Language* (Oxford: Oxford University Press, 1984). A recent series of papers by Terrance Horgan and Mark Timmons is also very noteworthy. See their "New Wave Moral Realism Meets Moral Twin Earth," *Journal of Philosophical Research* 16 (1991): 447–465; "Troubles on Moral Twin Earth: Moral Queerness Revived," *Synthese* 92 (1992): 221–260; and "Troubles for New Wave Moral Semantics: The 'Open Question Argument' Revived," *Philosophical Papers* 21 (1992): 153–175. Horgan and Timmons only purport to show that the kind of "synthetic naturalism" defended by Cornell realists is untenable. They do not claim to have refuted all versions of realism.

Interlude 2

1. Korsgaard, *The Sources of Normativity*, p. 242. Her characterization of Kant's view is puzzling in that she characterizes herself both as a Kantian and as a realist.

2. Kant, *Grounding for the Metaphysics of Morals*, p. 427, and *The Metaphysics of Morals*, trans. Mary Gregor (Cambridge: Cambridge University Press, 1991), pp. 381–382, 385 (Prussian Academy page numbers).

3. In "Theory and Practice" Kant defines happiness as the attainment of the sum of our ends ("Theory and Practice," in *Perpetual Peace and Other Essays*, trans. Ted Humphrey [Indianapolis: Hackett, 1983], pp. 282–283). In *Grounding for the Metaphysics of Morals*, Kant defines happiness as "the sum of the satisfactions of all inclinations," p. 399. He gives a somewhat different definition in *The Metaphysics of Morals*. There he defines happiness as satisfaction or contentment with one's state or situation, p. 387 (Prussian Academy page numbers).

4. Kant, *Grounding for the Metaphysics of Morals*, pp. 428–429. See Korsgaard, *Creating the Kingdom of Ends* (Cambridge: Cambridge University Press, 1996), pp. 120–121.

5. Kant, *Grounding for the Metaphysics of Morals*, p. 393.

6. Kant, *Grounding for the Metaphysics of Morals*, p. 431; *The Metaphysics of Morals*, pp. 380–381, 385; and *The Critique of Practical Reason*, trans. Lewis Beck (Indianapolis: Bobbs-Merrill, 1956), pp. 61–63. (Page numbers for *The Critique of Practical Reason* refer to the Beck translation.) See also Korsgaard, *Creating the Kingdom of Ends*, pp. 120–131, and Victoria Wike, *Kant on Happiness* (Albany: SUNY Press, 1994), pp. 68–69.

7. Note also that if Kant holds that objective ends are good independently of being the object of rational desires, then it is doubtful that he is a non-realist.

8. Korsgaard, *Creating the Kingdom of Ends*, p. 122.

9. Korsgaard, *Creating the Kingdom of Ends*, pp. 261–262.

Chapter 8. The Concept of Rationality as a Basis for Normative Theories

1. Gert defines rationality and irrationality in terms of "lists" of goods and evils:

> People act irrationally when they act in ways that they know (justifiably believe), or should know, will significantly increase the probability that they, or those for whom they are concerned, will suffer any of the items on the following list: death, pain (including mental suffering), disability, loss of freedom, or loss of pleasure, and they do not have an adequate reason for so acting. A reason for acting is a conscious belief that one's action (or the rule or policy that requires the action) will significantly increase the probability that either someone will avoid suffering any of the items on the previous list or they will gain greater ability, freedom, or pleasure. (Bernard Gert, "Rationality and Lists," *Ethics* 100 [1990]: 280)

The things that make for irrational acts, e.g., death and pain, are all evils (bads); the things which make for rational actions, e.g., freedom and pleasure, are all goods (pp. 281, 283, 285). Therefore, Gert's theory defines acting rationally in terms of choosing what is good and avoiding what is bad.

2. See Rawls, *A Theory of Justice*, pp. 143, 401; Firth, "Ethical Absolutism and the Ideal Observer"; Gauthier, *Morals By Agreement*, chapter 1; Brandt, *A Theory of the Good and the Right*, p. 112; Hare, *Moral Thinking*, pp. 214–17. My characterization of Rawls applies to his views in *A Theory of Justice*, not to his more recent views in *Political Liberalism*. Even if it is conceivable that a version of normative non-realism is independent of a theory of rationality, all the prominent non-realist normative theories are based on theories of rationality.

3. However, a realist need not endorse a theory of rationality like Gert's. Believing in the existence of independent moral facts does not commit one to the view that rationality needs to be defined in terms of those independent moral facts. A non-realist could endorse a full-information theory of rationality similar to Brandt's. Harry Gensler and Peter Railton are both moral realists who endorse full-information theories of rationality. See Harry Gensler, *Formal Ethics* (London: Routledge, 1996), and Peter Railton, "Facts and Values," *Philosophical Topics* 14 (1986): 5–31, and "Moral Realism," *Philosophical Review* 95 (1986): 163–207.

4. See Rawls, *A Theory of Justice*, pp. 155–157. To follow a maximin strategy is to act so as to minimize the badness of the worst possible outcome. From the standpoint of those in the original position, the worst possible outcome is that of being a member of the least well-off group in society. To follow a maximin strategy in the original position is to choose principles whose implementation makes the position of the least advantaged members of the society as good or better than the implementation of any alternative set of principles.

5. Rawls's arguments for thinking that it would be rational for people in the original position to adopt a maximin strategy have been widely criticized; see, for example, Brian Barry, *The Liberal Theory of Justice* (Oxford: Oxford University Press, 1973), chapter 9; Thomas Nagel, "Rawls on Justice," in *Reading Rawls*, ed. Norman Daniels

(New York: Basic Books, 1976), pp. 11–12; and R. M. Hare, "Rawls' Theory of Justice," in *Reading Rawls*, pp. 102–107.

6. Brandt, *A Theory of the Good and the Right*, p. 10. Brandt does not propose his theory as an analysis of the meaning of "rational." Rather, he suggests that we replace talk of rationality with his talk about desires and actions that withstand suitable reflection on full information.

7. Richard Brandt, "The Concept of Rational Action," *Social Theory and Practice* 9 (1983): 161.

8. On some of the problems, see Allan Gibbard, "A Noncognitivistic Analysis of Rationality in Action," *Social Theory and Practice* 9 (1983): 204–205; and Robert Audi, "Rationality and Valuation," in *Rationality In Action*, ed. Paul Moser (Cambridge: Cambridge University Press, 1990), pp. 429–430.

9. I develop this in greater detail in *The Status of Morality*, pp. 66–67 and 178–179. For some alternative accounts that also dispense with Brandt's notion of cognitive psychotherapy, see Stephen Darwall, *Impartial Reason* (Ithaca, N.Y.: Cornell University Press, 1983), chapter 8, and Richard Foley, *The Theory of Epistemic Rationality* (Cambridge: Harvard University Press, 1987), chapter 1.

10. For a more detailed discussion of empathy and knowing what it would be like to be in another person's position, see Carson, *The Status of Morality*, pp. 58–66.

11. This example and the solution are derived from Mark Overvold. "Self-Interest, Self-Sacrifice, and the Satisfaction of Desires," Ph.D. dissertation, University of Michigan, 1976, pp. 135–138. Overvold presents this objection as an objection to the (ideal) desire-satisfaction theory of welfare. I have modified the objection to make it an objection to the full-information theory of rationality.

12. J. David Velleman, "Brandt's Definition of 'Good'," *Philosophical Review* 97 (1988): 365.

13. Velleman, "Brandt's Definition of 'Good'," pp. 365–366.

14. Velleman, "Brandt's Definition of 'Good'," pp. 367–368.

15. Velleman, "Brandt's Definition of 'Good'," pp. 369–370.

16. Connie Rosati, "Persons, Perspectives, and Full Information Accounts of the Good," *Ethics* 105 (1995): 296–325.

17. Rosati, "Persons, Perspectives, and Full Information Accounts of the Good," p. 309.

18. See Railton, "Facts and Values," p. 22.

19. Rosati, "Persons, Perspectives, and Full Information Accounts of the Good," pp. 310–311.

20. This calls to mind an unintended irony in Firth's description of the ideal observer. Firth says that an ideal observer is omniscient, but a "normal" person (human being) "in other respects." By person Firth means "human being."

[O]ur conception of the personality of an ideal observer has not yet undergone the refining processes which have enabled theologians, apparently with clear conscience, to employ the term "person" in exceedingly abstract ways. Most of us, indeed, can be said to have a conception of an ideal observer only in the sense that the characteristics of such a person are implicit in the procedures by which we compare and evaluate moral judges, and it seems doubtful, therefore, that an ideal observer can be said to lack any of the determinable properties of human beings." (p. 58)

In his arguments to show that ideal observers would all agree in their "ethically significant reactions" to at least some moral issues, Firth appeals to general features of human psychology and thus presupposes that an ideal observer must be a human being. (See Firth, "A Reply to Professor Brandt," *Philosophy and Phenomenological Research* 15 [1955]: 415–416.)

21. Don Loeb, "Full Information Theories of the Good," *Social Theory and Practice* 21 (1995): 19–20.

22. Cf. Railton, "Facts and Values":

The proposal I would make, then, is the following: an individual's good consists in what he would want himself to want, or pursue, were he to contemplate his present situation from a standpoint fully and vividly informed about himself and his circumstances, and entirely free of cognitive error or lapses of instrumental rationality. (p. 16)

23. Rosati herself acknowledges this in "Persons, Perspectives, and Full Information Accounts of the Good," p. 325.

24. Crispin Wright, *Truth and Objectivity* (Cambridge: Harvard University Press, 1992), p. 48.

25. Crispin Wright, "Realism: The Contemporary Debate—W(h)ither Now?" in *Reality, Representation, and Projection*, ed. J. Haldane and C. Wright (Cambridge: Cambridge University Press, 1993), p. 67. Also see Wright's *Realism, Meaning, and Truth*, 2d ed. (Oxford: Blackwell, 1993), pp. 414–415.

26. Richard Brandt defends this view in "The Definition of an 'Ideal Observer' in Ethics," *Philosophy and Phenomenological Research* 15 (1954): 407–413.

27. Roderick Firth raises this objection in "A Reply to Professor Brandt," pp. 414–421.

28. Cf. Wright, *Truth and Objectivity*, p. 45.

29. Rosati, "Persons, Perspectives, and Full Information Accounts of the Good," pp. 312–313.

30. Velleman, "Brandt's Definition of 'Good'," p. 360.

31. Rosati, "Persons, Perspectives, and Full Information Accounts of the Good," p. 312, and "Naturalism, Normativity, and the Open Question Argument," *Nous* 29 (1995): 62.

32. Connie Rosati, "Naturalism, Normativity, and the Open Question Argument," p. 62.

33. See Adams's "Divine Command Metaethics Modified Again." Adams writes:

My new divine command theory of the nature of ethical wrongness, then, is that ethical wrongness *is* (i.e., is identical with) the property of being contrary to the commands of a loving God. I regard this as a metaphysically necessary, but not an analytic or a priori truth. (p. 139)

If there is no loving God, then . . . ethical wrongness is the property with which it is identified by the best remaining alternative theory. (p. 141)

34. See Adams, "A Modified Divine Command Theory," pp. 114–116.

35. Adams agrees that different possible loving Gods could have very different preferences. See "Moral Arguments for Theistic Belief," in Adams's *The Virtue of Faith*, pp. 148–149. It might make sense to restrict 2 by saying that the correctness of our preferences is determined by the preferences of those possible loving omniscient creators of the universe *who would have chosen to create this universe and human beings*. This restriction would reduce, but not eliminate, conflicts between the preferences of the possible Gods in question.

36. It is likely that God has preferences about many things that I have never imagined or thought about. Presumably, God doesn't fault me for not having preferences about these matters unless God also faults me for not having thought about them. But, God may still prefer that *if* I consider the matters in question, I have certain preferences about them. God might prefer that I be *disposed* to have particular preferences about certain matters if I consider them. Thus, it seems likely that there are many cases in which God doesn't prefer that I have an actual preference between X and not-X, but still prefers that if I consider or reflect on X and not-X, then I should prefer X to not-X (or vice versa).

37. Since he holds that standards of good and bad are independent of God's will, Adams can say that God commands us to do certain acts because they are good or good for us. This kind of answer to the Euthyphro objection is not open to those who (like me) would try to use God's will as the basis for a complete normative theory.

38. *Nichomachean Ethics* 1155b28–1156a5 (Ostwald translation).

39. David Hamlyn, "The Phenomena of Love and Hate," in *Eros, Agape, and Philia*, ed. Alan Soble (New York: Paragon House, 1989), p. 224.

40. Gabriele Taylor, "Love," *Proceedings of the Aristotelian Society* 86 (1975–76): 153–154.

41. Sidgwick, *The Methods of Ethics*, p. 244.

42. Robert Brown, *Analyzing Love* (Cambridge: Cambridge University Press, 1987), p. 30; see also Alan Soble, *The Structure of Love* (New Haven: Yale University Press, 1990), pp. 257–258.

43. John McTaggart Ellis McTaggart, *The Nature of Existence*, vol. 2 (Cambridge: Cambridge University Press, 1927), p. 148.

44. McTaggart, *The Nature of Existence*, vol. 2, p. 150.

45. See Brown *Analyzing Love*, p. 215, and Soble, *The Structure of Love*, pp. 4–9. Soble takes himself to be analyzing the concept of *eros*; he allows that there is an alternative concept of love, *agape*, to which this claim does not apply.

46. Anders Nygren, *Agape and Eros*, trans. Philip Watson (Philadelphia: Westminster Press, 1953), p. 78.

47. Gene Outka, *Agape: An Ethical Analysis* (New Haven: Yale University Press, 1972), p. 260.

48. This sort of possibility is discussed by Philo in Hume's *Dialogues Concerning Natural Religion* (New York: Hafner, 1948), Part V, p. 41.

49. John Hick, *Evil and the God of Love*, rev. ed. (New York: Harper & Row, 1978).

50. Some theists attempt to answer the problem of evil by denying that God is omnipotent. See J. S. Mill, *Theism* (Indianapolis: Bobbs-Merrill, 1957), pp. 34, 43; David R. Griffin, *God, Power, and Evil: A Process Theodicy* (Philadelphia: Westminster, 1976); and Alfred North Whitehead, *Process and Reality* (New York: Macmillan, 1929), Part 5, chapter 2.

51. Mackie, *Ethics*, p. 48. Mackie concludes:

> I concede that if the requisite theological doctrine could be defended, a kind of objective ethical presciptivity could be introduced. Since I think that theism cannot be defended, I do not regard this as any threat to my argument. . . . Those who wish to keep theism as a live option can read the arguments . . . hypothetically, as a discussion of what we can make of morality without recourse to God. . . . (p. 48)

Later on, Mackie characterizes this kind of theistic ethical theory as "no more than a bare theoretical possibility" (p. 232).

52. I don't know enough about Islam to speak to the issue of the Islamic conception of God.

53. This objection was noted by Francis Hutcheson. Hutcheson writes:

> Human laws may be called *good*, because of their conformity to the divine. But to call the laws of the supreme Deity *good*, or *holy*, or *just*, if all goodness, holiness, and justice be constituted by *laws*, or the *will* of a *superior* any way revealed, must be an insignificant tautology, amounting to no more than this, 'that God *wills* what he *wills*. Or that his *will* is comfortable to his *will*.' (*An Inquiry Concerning the Origin of Our Ideas of Virtue or Moral Good*, Section VII.V. Included in *Divine Commands and Morality: Historical and Contemporary Readings*, ed. Janine Idziak [New York: Edward Mellon Press, 1979])

54. Some philosophers would object to my using the word "God" to refer to an imperfect being who is not omnipotent or who suffers from weakness of will. Rather than argue about the meaning of the word "God," let me simply stipulate that I am using the term in a broader and looser sense than some philosophers. (The reader may wish to substitute the word "deity" for "God" in certain places.) I believe that most English

speakers use the word "God" in this broader way. (For more on this, see the next paragraph.)

55. Metaethical relativism denies that ethical judgments are objectively true or false. It claims that conflicting ethical judgments can be equally correct or equally valid. Metaethical relativists hold that the truth or correctness of moral judgments is relative to different individuals or different societies. What is true for one individual (society) may not be true for others. Cf. William Frankena, *Ethics*, 2d ed. (Englewood Cliffs, N.J.: Prentice-Hall, 1973), p. 109; Richard Brandt, "Ethical Relativism," in *The Encyclopedia of Philosophy*, vol. 3, ed. Paul Edwards (New York: Macmillan, 1967), pp. 75–78; and Gilbert Harman, "What Is Moral Relativism?" in *Values and Morals*, ed. A. I. Goldman and J. Kim (Dordrecht: Reidel, 1978), pp. 143–161.

56. Gauthier, *Morals by Agreement*, pp. 49–59.

57. It is debatable whether the moral standards stated in the scriptures should be taken to be *ultimate* or *basic* moral principles. (The scriptures leave open many philosophical questions about ultimate standards of right and wrong.)

58. Here I am assuming that the pleasantness or unpleasantness of an experience is simply a function of its immediate introspectable qualities (or one's preferences with respect to those qualities).

59. Hick, *Evil and the Good of Love*, chapters 15 and 16.

60. Many other philosophers, including Moore, Ross, and Chisholm, also defend this kind of pluralism about what things are good and bad. Cf. Kraut, "Desire and the Human Good," p. 39, and Griffin, *Well-Being*, pp. 31–34, 65–68.

61. Some moral theories based on theories of rationality make impartiality a necessary condition for being rational. My formulation of COR leaves open the question of whether being impartial is necessary for being rational (this is not a question to which I am prepared to defend an answer). If being impartial is not necessary for being rational, then cases in which people are partial to their own self-interests will often be cases in which the rational preferences of different people conflict. Consider the following example. S_1 is the child of very rich parents. S_2 is the child of very poor parents. If being impartial is not necessary for being rational, then the canons of rationality underdetermine one's preferences about inheritance tax laws. Being as rational as it is possible for one to be is consistent with being either for or against raising inheritance taxes. Given this, it is possible that both: (i) COR implies that it is correct for S_1 to be opposed to laws that raise inheritance taxes, and (ii) COR implies that it is correct for S_2 to favor those same laws.

62. Whether or not the present view commits us to extreme metaethical relativism depends on whether or not COR implies that it would be correct for different people to have conflicting preferences about every possible matter. If, for any preference that it is correct for someone to have, there is another person who is such that it is not correct for him to have that preference, then the present view commits us to extreme metaethical relativism. I'm not sure whether or not COR has this consequence. This is an important question, but one I won't try to answer here. The answer, I suspect, depends on such things as whether canons of rationality permit malicious preferences and whether they require (or should require) impartiality.

63. This kind of case strongly inclines me to prefer the welfarist to the non-welfarist version of the desire-satisfaction theory. It seems correct to say that the goodness or badness of *my life* depends on what it is correct or rational for *me* to want for myself.

64. At this point, I'm only entitled to draw this conclusion about the *non-welfarist version* of the rational-desire-satisfaction theory of value (when it is combined with the ideal-observer version of the divine-preference theory of rationality). But the following paragraph gives reasons for thinking that the welfarist version of this theory also commits us to some kind of relativism.

Bibliography

Ackrill, J. L. "Aristotle on *Eudaimonia*." In *Essays on Aristotle's Ethics*, edited by Amelie Rorty, pp. 15–33. Berkeley: University of California Press, 1980.

Adams, Robert. "Divine Command Metaethics Modified Again." In *The Virtue of Faith*, pp. 128–143. Oxford: Oxford University Press, 1987.

———. "A Modified Divine Command Theory of Ethical Wrongness." In *The Virtue of Faith*, pp. 97–127. Oxford: Oxford University Press, 1987.

———. "Moral Arguments for Theistic Belief." In *The Virtue of Faith*, pp. 144–163. Oxford: Oxford University Press, 1987.

Alston, William. "Pleasure." In *The Encyclopedia of Philosophy*, edited by Paul Edwards, vol. 6, pp. 341–347. New York: Macmillan, 1967.

Annas, Julia. *The Morality of Happiness*. Oxford: Oxford University Press, 1993.

Anscombe, G. E. M. "Modern Moral Philosophy." In *Ethics*, edited by Judith Thomson and Gerald Dworkin, pp. 186–210. New York: Harper & Row, 1968.

Arrington, Robert. *Rationalism, Realism, and Relativism*. Ithaca, N.Y.: Cornell University Press, 1989.

Aristotle. *The Eudemian Ethics*. In *The Complete Works of Aristotle*, edited by Jonathan Barnes. Princeton: Princton University Press, 1984.

———. *The Metaphysics*. In *The Complete Works of Aristotle*, edited by Jonathan Barnes. Princeton: Princeton University Press, 1984.

———. *Nicomachean Ethics*. Translated by Martin Ostwald. Indianapolis: Bobbs-Merrill, 1962.

———. *Nicomachean Ethics*. Translated by Terence Irwin. Indianapolis: Hackett, 1985.

Audi, Robert. "Rationality and Valuation." In *Rationality In Action*, edited by Paul Moser, pp. 416–446. Cambridge: Cambridge University Press, 1990.

Ayer, A. J. *Language, Truth, and Logic*. 2d ed. New York: Dover, 1952.

Barnes, W. H. F. "A Suggestion about Value." In *Readings in Ethical Theory*, edited by John Hospers and Wilfred Sellars, 2d. ed., p. 241. Englewood Cliffs, N.J.: Prentice-Hall, 1970.

Barry, Brian. *The Liberal Theory of Justice*. Oxford: Oxford University Press, 1973.

Bentham, Jeremy. *Principles of Morals and Legislation*. New York: Hafner, 1948.

Berger, Fred. *Happiness, Justice, and Freedom*. Berkeley: University of California Press, 1984.

Blackburn, Simon. *Essays in Quasi-Realism*. Oxford: Oxford University Press, 1993.

———. *Spreading the Word: Groundings in the Philosophy of Language*. Oxford: Oxford University Press, 1984.

Bond, E.J. *Reason and Value*. Cambridge: Cambridge University Press, 1983.

Boyd, Richard. "How to Be a Moral Realist." In *Essays on Moral Realism*, edited by Geoffrey Sayre-McCord, pp. 181–228. Ithaca, N.Y.: Cornell University Press, 1988.

Bradley, F.H. *Ethical Studies*. 2d ed. Oxford: Oxford University Press, 1927.

Brandt, Richard. "The Concept of Rational Action." *Social Theory and Practice* 9 (1983): 143–164.

———. "The Definition of an 'Ideal Observer' in Ethics." *Philosophy and Phenomenological Research* 15 (1954): 407–413.

———. "Ethical Relativism." In *The Encyclopedia of Philosophy*, edited by Paul Edwards, Vol. 3, pp. 75–78. New York: Macmillan, 1967.

———. *Ethical Theory*. Englewood Cliffs, N.J.: Prentice-Hall, 1959.

———. "Fairness to Happiness." *Social Theory and Practice* 15 (1989): 33–58.

———. *Hopi Ethics*. Chicago: University of Chicago Press, 1954.

———. "Ideal Observer." In *Encyclopedia of Ethics*, edited by Lawrence Becker and Charlotte Becker. New York: Garland, 1992.

———. *Morality, Utilitarianism, and Rights*. Cambridge: Cambridge University Press, 1992.

———. "Overvold on Self-Interest and Self-Sacrifice." In *Rationality, Morality, and Self-Interest: Essays Honoring Mark Carl Overvold*, edited by John Heil, pp. 221–232. Lanham, Md.: Rowman Littlefield, 1993.

———. "Rationality, Egoism, and Morality." *Journal of Philosophy* 69 (1972): 681–697.

———. *A Theory of the Good and the Right*. Oxford: Oxford University Press, 1979.

———. "Two Concepts of Utility." In *The Limits of Utilitarianism*, edited by Harlan Miller and William Williams, pp. 169–185. Minneapolis: University of Minnesota Press, 1982.

Brentano, Franz. *The Foundation and Construction of Ethics*. Translated by Elizabeth Schneewind. New York: Humanities Press, 1973.

———. *The Origin of Our Knowledge of Right and Wrong*. Translated by Roderick Chisholm and Elizabeth Schneewind. New York: Humanities Press, 1969.

———. *Psychology from an Empirical Standpoint*. Translated by Antos Rancurello, D.B. Terrell, and Linda McAlister. New York: Humanities Press, 1973.

———. *The True and the Evident*. Translated by Roderick Chisholm, Ilse Politzer, and Kurt Fischer. New York: Humanities Press, 1966.

Brink, David. *Moral Realism and the Foundations of Ethics.* Cambridge: Cambridge University Press, 1989.

Broad, C. D. "Analysis of Some Ethical Concepts." In *Broad's Critical Essays in Moral Philosophy*, pp. 63–81. London: Allen & Unwin, 1971.

———. *Five Types of Ethical Theory.* London: Routledge & Kegan Paul, 1930.

———. "Some Reflections on Moral Sense Theories in Ethics." In *Broad's Critical Essays in Moral Philosophy*, pp. 188–222. New York: Humanities Press, 1971.

Broadie, Sarah. *Ethics with Aristotle.* Oxford: Oxford University Press, 1991.

Brown, Robert. *Analyzing Love.* Cambridge: Cambridge University Press, 1987.

Burge, Tyler. "Individuation and Causation in Psychology." *Pacific Philosophical Quarterly* 70 (1989): 303–322.

Camus, Albert. *The Myth of Sisyphus.* Translated by J. O'Brien. New York: Albert Knopf, 1955.

Carson, Thomas. "Could Ideal Observers Disagree? A Reply to Taliaferro." *Philosophy and Phenomenological Research* 50 (1989): 115–124.

———. "The Desire-Satisfaction Theory of Welfare: Overvold's Critique and Reformulation." In *Rationality, Morality, and Self-Interest: Essays Honoring Mark Carl Overvold*, edited by John Heil, pp. 233–246. Lanham, Md.: Rowman Littlefield, 1993.

———. "Happiness, Contentment, and the Good Life." *Pacific Philosophical Quarterly* 62 (1981): 378–392.

———. "Hare's Defense of Utilitarianism." *Philosophical Studies* 50 (1986): 97–115.

———. "Relativism and Nihilism." *Philosophia* 15 (1985): 1–23.

———. *The Status of Morality.* Dordrecht: Reidel, 1984.

———. "The Übermensch and Nietzsche's Theory of Value." *International Studies in Philosophy* 13 (1981): 9–30.

Chisholm, Roderick. *Brentano and Intrinsic Value.* Cambridge: Cambridge University Press, 1986.

———. "The Defeat of Good and Evil." In *The Problem of Evil*, edited by Marilyn Adams and Robert Adams, pp. 53–68. Oxford: Oxford University Press, 1990.

———. "Intrinsic Value." In *Values and Morals*, edited by A. I. Goldman and J. Kim, pp. 121–130. Dordrecht: Reidel, 1978.

Chisholm, Roderick, and Ernest Sosa. "On the Logic of 'Intrinsically Better.'" *American Philosophical Quarterly* 3 (1966): 244–249.

Cooper, John. "Contemplation and Happiness: A Reconsideration." *Synthese* 72 (1987): 187–216.

———. *Reason and Human Good in Aristotle.* Cambridge: Harvard University Press, 1975.

Copp, David. "Explanation and Justification in Ethics." *Ethics* 100 (1990): 237–258.

Cowan, J. L. *Pleasure and Pain.* New York: St. Martin's Press, 1968.

Dancy, Jonathan. *Moral Reasons.* Oxford: Blackwell, 1993.

Danto, Arthur C. *Nietzsche as Philosopher.* New York: Macmillan, 1965.

D'Arms, Justin, and Daniel Jacobson. "Expressivism, Morality, and Emotions." *Ethics* 104 (1994): 739–763.

Darwall, Stephen. *Impartial Reason.* Ithaca, N.Y.: Cornell University Press, 1983.

Devitt, Michael. *Realism and Truth.* 2d ed. Oxford: Blackwell, 1991.

Donner, Wendy. *The Liberal Self.* Ithaca, N.Y.: Cornell University Press, 1991.

Dummett, Michael. "Realism." *Synthese* 52 (1982): 55–112.

———. *Truth and Other Enigmas.* Cambridge: Harvard University Press, 1978.

Duncker, Karl. "Pleasure, Emotion, and Striving." *Philosophy and Phenomenological Research* 1 (1940): 391–430.

Dworkin, Ronald. *Taking Rights Seriously.* Cambridge: Harvard University Press, 1977.

Edwards, Rem. *Pleasures and Pains.* Ithaca, N.Y.: Cornell University Press, 1979.

Epicurus. "Letter to Menoeceus." In *Letters, Principal Doctrines, and Vatican Sayings,* translated by Russell Geer. Indianapolis: Bobbs-Merrill, 1964.

Ewing, A. C. *The Definition of the Good.* New York: Macmillan, 1947.

Feldman, Fred. *Confrontations With the Reaper.* Oxford: Oxford University Press, 1992.

———. *Introductory Ethics.* Englewood Cliffs, N.J.: Prentice-Hall, 1978.

Firth, Roderick. "Ethical Absolutism and the Ideal Observer." In *Morality and the Good Life,* edited by Thomas Carson and Paul Moser, pp. 40–60. New York: Oxford University Press, 1997.

———. "A Reply to Professor Brandt." *Philosophy and Phenomenological Research* 15 (1955): 414–421.

Fodor, Jerold. *Representations.* Cambridge: MIT Press, 1981.

Foley, Richard. *The Theory of Epistemic Rationality.* Cambridge: Harvard University Press, 1987.

Foot, Philippa. "Moral Beliefs." In *Theories of Ethics,* ed. Foot, pp. 83–100. Oxford: Oxford University Press, 1968.

———. *Virtues and Vices.* Berkeley: University of California Press, 1978.

Frankena, William. *Ethics.* 2d ed. Englewood Cliffs, N.J.: Prentice-Hall, 1973.

———. "The Naturalistic Fallacy." *Mind* 48 (1939): 464–477.

Fuchs, Alan. "Posthumous Satisfactions and the Concept of Individual Welfare." In *Rationality, Morality, and Self-Interest: Essays Honoring Mark Carl Overvold,* edited by John Heil, pp. 215–220. Lanham, Md.: Rowman Littlefield, 1993.

Gauthier, David. *Morals by Agreement.* Oxford: Oxford University Press, 1986.

Geach, P.T. "Good and Evil." In *Theories of Ethics,* edited by Philippa Foot, pp. 64–73. Oxford: Oxford University Press, 1968.

Gensler, Harry. *Formal Ethics.* London: Routledge, 1996.

Gert, Bernard. "Rationality and Lists." *Ethics* 100 (1990): 279–300.

Gibbard, Allan. "A Noncognitivistic Analysis of Rationality in Action." *Social Theory and Practice* 9 (1983): 199–222.

———. "Reply to Blackburn, Carson, Hill, and Railton." *Philosophy and Phenomenological Research* 42 (1992): 969–980.

———. *Wise Choices, Apt Feelings.* Cambridge: Harvard University Press, 1990.

Griffin, David R. *God, Power, and Evil: A Process Theodicy.* Philadelphia: Westminster Press, 1976.

Griffin, James. *Well-Being.* Oxford: Oxford University Press, 1986.

Grim, Patrick. "There Is No Set of All Truths." *Analysis* 44 (1984): 206–208.

Hamlyn, David. "The Phenomena of Love and Hate." In *Eros, Agape, and Philia*, edited by Alan Soble, pp. 218–234. New York: Paragon House, 1989.

Hardie, H. F. R. "The Final Good in Aristotle's *Ethics*." In *Aristotle: A Collection of Critical Essays*, edited by J. M. E. Moravcsik, pp. 297–322. Notre Dame, Ind.: University of Notre Dame Press, 1968.

Hare, R. M. *Essays in Ethical Theory*. Oxford: Oxford University Press, 1989.

———. *Freedom and Reason*. Oxford: Oxford University Press, 1963.

———. *The Language of Morals*. Oxford: Oxford University Press, 1952.

———. *Moral Thinking*. Oxford: Oxford University Press, 1981.

———. "Rawls' Theory of Justice." In *Reading Rawls*, edited by Norman Daniels, pp. 81–107. New York: Basic Books, 1976.

Harman, Gilbert. "Moral Explanations of Natural Facts—Can Moral Claims Be Tested against Moral Reality?" *Southern Journal of Philosophy* (Supplement) 24 (1986): 57–68.

———. *The Nature of Morality*. Oxford: Oxford University Press, 1977.

———. "What is Moral Relativism?" In *Values and Morals*, edited by A. I. Goldman and J. Kim, pp. 143–161. Dordrecht: Reidel, 1978.

Harsanyi, John. *Essays on Ethics, Social Behavior, and Scientific Explanation*. Dordrecht: Reidel, 1976.

Heil, John. "Recent Work on Realism and Anti-Realism." *Philosophical Books* 30 (1989): 65–73.

———, ed. *Rationality, Morality, and Self-Interest: Essays Honoring Mark Carl Overvold*. Lanham, Md.: Rowman Littlefield, 1993.

Hick, John. *Evil and the God of Love*. Revised ed. New York: Harper & Row, 1978.

Hookaway, Christopher. "Two Conceptions of Moral Realism." *Proceedings of the Aristotelian Society* (Supplement) 60 (1986): 188–205.

Hooker, Brad. "A Breakthrough in the Desire Theory of Welfare." In *Rationality, Morality, and Self-Interest: Essays Honoring Mark Carl Overvold*, edited by John Heil, pp. 205–214. Lanham, Md.: Rowman Littlefield, 1993.

Horgan, Terrance, and Mark Timmons. "New Wave Moral Realism Meets Moral Twin Earth." *Journal of Philosophical Research* 16 (1991): 447–465.

———. "Troubles for New Wave Moral Semantics: The 'Open Question Argument' Revived." *Philosophical Papers* 21 (1992): 153–175.

———. "Troubles on Moral Twin Earth: Moral Queerness Revived." *Synthese* 92 (1992): 221–260.

Hume, David. *Dialogues Concerning Natural Religion*. New York: Hafner, 1948.

———. *An Enquiry Concerning the Principles of Morals*. 2d ed. Oxford: Oxford University Press, 1972.

———. *A Treatise of Human Nature*. 2d ed. Oxford: Oxford University Press, 1978.

Hunt, Lester. *Nietzsche and the Origin of Virtue*. London: Routledge, 1991.

Hurka, Thomas. *Perfectionism*. Oxford: Oxford University Press, 1993.

———. "The Well-Rounded Life." *The Journal of Philosophy* 84 (1987): 707–726.

Hurley, S. L. *Natural Reasons*. Oxford: Oxford University Press, 1989.

Idziak, Janine, ed. *Divine Commands and Morality: Historical and Contemporary Readings*. New York: Edward Mellon Press, 1979.

Jones, Hardy. "Mill's Argument for the Principle of Utility." *Philosophy and Phenomenological Research* 38 (1978): 338–354.

Kant, Immanuel. *The Critique of Practical Reason*. Translated by Lewis White Beck. Indianapolis: Bobbs-Merrill, 1956.

———. *Grounding for the Metaphysics of Morals*. Translated by James Ellington. 3d ed. Indianapolis: Hackett, 1993.

———. *The Metaphysics of Morals*. Translated by Mary Gregor. Cambridge: Cambridge University Press, 1991.

———. "Theory and Practice." In *Perpetual Peace and Other Essays*, translated by Ted Humphrey, pp. 61–92. Indianapolis: Hackett, 1983.

Kaufmann, Walter. *Nietzsche*. 3d ed. Princeton: Princeton University Press, 1968.

Kavka, Greg. *Hobbesian Moral and Political Theory*. Princeton: Princeton University Press, 1986.

Kershaw, Ian. *Hitler (1889–1936): Hubris*. New York: Norton, 1998.

Köhler, Wolfgang. *The Place of Value in a World of Fact*. New York: Liveright, 1938.

Korsgaard, Christine. *Creating the Kingdom of Ends*. Cambridge: Cambridge University Press, 1996.

———. *The Sources of Normativity*. Cambridge: Cambridge University Press, 1996.

———. "Two Distinctions in Goodness." *Philosophical Review* 92 (1983): 169–195.

Kraut, Richard. *Aristotle on the Human Good*. Princeton: Princeton University Press, 1989.

———. "Desire and the Human Good." *Proceedings and Addresses of the American Philosophical Association* 68 (1994): 39–54.

Kretzmann, Norman. "Desire as Proof of Desirability." In *Mill's Utilitarianism*, edited by James Smith and Ernest Sosa, pp. 110–116. Belmont, Calif.: Wadsworth, 1969.

Lemos, Noah. *Intrinsic Value*. Cambridge: Cambridge University Press, 1994.

Locke, John. *Essay Concerning Human Understanding* (selections). In *British Moralists 1650–1800*, edited by D. D. Raphael. Oxford: Oxford University Press, 1969.

Loeb, Don. "Full Information Theories of the Good." *Social Theory and Practice* 21 (1995): 1–30.

Lovibond, Sabina. *Realism and Imagination in Ethics*. Minneapolis: University of Minnesota Press, 1983.

Mackie, J. L. *Ethics*. Middlesex, England: Penguin, 1978.

———. "The Refutation of Morals." *Australasian Journal of Philosophy and Psychology* 24 (1946): 77–90.

Marshall, John. "The Proof of Utility and Equity in Mill's *Utilitarianism*." *Canadian Journal of Philosophy* 3 (1973): 13–26.

Marx, Karl. *Capital*. Translated by Samuel Moore and Edward Aveling. New York: International Publishers, 1967.

———. *The German Ideology*. Translated by Lawrence and Wishart. New York: International Publishers, 1970.

McDowell, John. "Non-Cognitivism and Rule Following." In *Wittgenstein: To Follow a Rule*, edited by Steven Holtzman and Christopher Leich, pp. 141–162. London: Routledge & Kegan Paul, 1981.

———. "Values and Secondary Qualities." In *Essays on Moral Realism*, edited by Geoffrey Sayre-McCord, pp. 166–180. Ithaca, N.Y.: Cornell University Press, 1988.

McFall, Lynne. *Happiness*. New York: Peter Lang, 1988.

McTaggart, John McTaggart Ellis. *The Nature of Existence*. Cambridge: Cambridge University Press, 1927.

Mill, J. S. *Examination of Sir William Hamilton's Philosophy*. In *Collected Works*, vol. 9. Toronto: University of Toronto Press, 1979.

———. "Letter to Henry Jones." In *Collected Works*, vol. 16. Toronto: University of Toronto Press, 1972.

———. "Remarks on Bentham's Philosophy." In *Collected Works*, vol. 10. Toronto: University of Toronto Press, 1969.

———. *System of Logic*. In *Collected Works*, vol. 7–8. Toronto: University of Toronto Press, 1973.

———. *Theism*. Indianapolis: Bobbs-Merrill, 1957.

———. *Utilitarianism*. Indianapolis: Hackett, 1979.

Moore, G. E. *Ethics*. Oxford: Oxford University Press, 1965.

———. *Principia Ethica*. Cambridge: Cambridge University Press, 1903.

———. "A Reply to My Critics." In *The Philosophy of G. E. Moore*, edited by P. A. Schilpp, pp. 535–677. La Salle, Ill.: Open Court, 1968.

Morgan, George. *What Nietzsche Means*. Cambridge: Harvard University Press, 1941.

Moser, Paul. *Philosophy after Objectivity*. Oxford: Oxford University Press, 1993.

Nagel, Thomas. "Rawls on Justice." In *Reading Rawls*, edited by Norman Daniels, pp. 1–15. New York: Basic Books, 1976.

Nehamas, Alexander. *Nietzsche: Life as Literature*. Cambridge: Harvard University Press, 1985.

Nielsen, Kai. "Alienation and Self-Realization." *Philosophy* 48 (1973): 21–33.

Nietzsche, Friedrich. *The Anti-Christ*. In *Twilight of the Idols and the Anti-Christ*, translated by R. J. Hollingdale. Middlesex, England: Penguin, 1968.

———. *Beyond Good and Evil*. Translated by Walter Kaufmann. New York: Vintage Books, 1966.

———. *Daybreak*. Translated by R. J. Hollingdale. Cambridge: Cambridge University Press, 1982.

———. *Ecce Homo*. In *On the Genealogy of Morals and Ecce Homo*, translated by Walter Kaufmann. New York: Vintage Books, 1967.

———. *Gay Science*. Translated by Walter Kaufmann. New York: Vintage Books, 1974.

———. *Human, All-Too-Human*. Translated by R. J. Hollingdale. Cambridge: Cambridge University Press, 1986.

———. *Nietzsches Werke in Drei Bänden*. Edited by Karl Schlechta. Munich: Carl Hanser Verlag, 1958.

———. *On the Genealogy of Morals*. In *On the Genealogy of Morals and Ecce Homo*, translated by Walter Kaufmann. New York: Vintage Books, 1967.

———. *Thus Spoke Zarathustra*. In *The Portable Nietzsche*, translated by Walter Kaufmann. New York: Viking Press, 1968.

———. *Twilight of the Idols*. In *The Portable Nietzsche*, translated by Walter Kaufmann. New York: Viking Press, 1968.

———. *The Will To Power*. Translated by Walter Kaufmann and R. J. Hollingdale. New York: Vintage Books, 1968.

Nozick, Robert. *Anarchy, State, and Utopia*. New York: Basic Books, 1974.

———. *Philosophical Explanations*. Cambridge: Harvard University Press, 1981.

Nygren, Anders. *Agagpe and Eros*. Tranlated by Philip Watson. Philadelphia: Westminster Press, 1953.

Outka, Gene. *Agape: An Ethical Analysis*. New Haven: Yale University Press, 1972.

Overvold, Mark. "Morality, Self-Interest, and Reasons for Being Moral." *Philosophy and Phenomenological Research* 44 (1984): 493–507.

———. "Self-Interest and Getting What You Want." In *The Limits of Utilitarianism*, edited by Harlan Miller and William Williams, pp. 186–194. Minneapolis: University of Minnesota Press, 1982.

———. "Self-Interest and the Concept of Self-Sacrifice." *Canadian Journal of Philosophy* 10 (1980): 105–118.

———. "Self-Interest, Self-Sacrifice, and the Satisfaction of Desires," Ph.D. dissertation, University of Michigan, 1976.

Parfit, Derek. *Reasons and Persons*. Oxford: Oxford University Press, 1984.

Paul, Ellen Frankel, Fred Miller Jr., and Jeffrey Paul, eds. *The Good Life and the Human Good*. Cambridge: Cambridge University Press, 1992.

Perry, R.B. *General Theory of Value*. Cambridge: Harvard University Press, 1926.

Pigden, Charles. "Geach on 'Good'." *Philosophical Quarterly* 40 (1990): 129–154.

Plato. *Euthyphro*. Translated by G.M.A. Grube. In *The Trial and Death of Socrates*, edited by G.M.A. Grube. Indianapolis: Hackett, 1975.

———. *Philebus*. Translated by R. Hackforth. In *The Collected Dialogues of Plato*, edited by Edith Hamilton and Huntington Cairns. Princeton: Princeton University Press, 1969.

Platts, Mark. *Moral Realities*. London: Routledge & Kegan Paul, 1991.

———. "Moral Reality." In *Essays on Moral Realism*, edited by Geoffrey Sayre-McCord, pp. 282–300. Ithaca, N.Y.: Cornell University Press, 1988.

———. "Moral Reality and the End of Desire." In *Reference, Truth, and Meaning*, edited by Mark Platts, pp. 69–82. London: Routledge & Kegan Paul, 1981.

———. *Ways of Meaning*. London: Routledge & Kegan Paul, 1979.

Putnam, Hilary. *Mind, Language, and Reality*. Philosophical Papers, vol. 2. Cambridge: Cambridge University Press, 1975.

———. *Reason, Truth, and History*. New York: Cambridge University Press, 1981.

Quinton, Anthony. *Utilitarian Ethics*. New York: Saint Martin's Press, 1973.

Railton, Peter. "Facts and Values." *Philosophical Topics* 14 (1986): 5–31.

———. "Moral Realism." *Philosophical Review* 95 (1986): 163–207.

Raphael, D.D. "Mill's Proof of the Principle of Utility." *Utilitas* 6 (1994): 55–65.

Rashdall, Hastings. *Theory of Good and Evil*. Oxford: Clarendon Press, 1928.

Rawls, John. *A Theory of Justice.* Cambridge: Harvard University Press, 1971.

Reeve, C. D. C. *Practices of Reason: Aristotle's Nicomachean Ethics.* Oxford: Oxford University Press, 1992.

Roche, Timothy. "*Ergon* and *Eudaimonia* in *Nicomachean Ethics* I." *Journal of the History of Philosophy* 26 (1988): 175–194.

Rodzinski, Witold. *A History of China.* Oxford: Pergamon Press, 1979.

Rosati, Connie. "Naturalism, Normativity, and the Open Question Argument." *Nous* 29 (1995): 46–70.

———. "Persons, Perspectives, and Full Information Accounts of the Good." *Ethics* 105 (1995): 296–325.

Ross, W. D. *The Foundations of Ethics.* Oxford: Clarendon Press, 1939.

———. *The Right and the Good.* Oxford: Clarendon Press, 1930.

Russell, Bertrand. "A Reply to My Critics." In *The Philosophy of Bertrand Russell*, edited by P. A. Schlipp, pp. 681–741. La Salle, Ill.: Open Court, 1944.

Ryle, Gilbert. *The Concept of Mind.* New York: Barnes & Noble, 1969.

———. "Pleasure." In *Moral Concepts*, edited by Joel Feinberg, pp. 19–28. Oxford: Oxford University Press, 1970.

Sartre, J. P. "Existentialism." In *Existentialism and Human Emotions*, translated by Bernard Frechtman. New York: Philosophical Library, 1957.

Sayre-McCord, Geoffrey, ed. *Essays on Moral Realism.* Ithaca, N.Y.: Cornell University Press, 1988.

Schacht, Richard. "Nietzsche and Nihilism." In *Nietzsche: A Collection of Critical Essays*, edited by Robert Solomon, pp. 58–82. New York: Anchor Books, 1973.

Scheler, Max. *Ressentiment.* Translated by William Holdheim. New York: Schocken Books, 1972.

Schneewind, J. B. *Sidgwick's Ethics and Victorian Moral Philosophy.* Oxford: Oxford University Press, 1977.

Schopenhauer, Arthur. *Essays and Aphorisms.* Tranlated by R. J. Hollingdale. New York: Penguin, 1970.

———. *The World as Will and Representation.* Translated by E. F. J. Payne. New York: Dover, 1966.

Schwartz, Thomas. "Human Welfare: What It Is Not." In *The Limits of Utilitarianism*, edited by Harlan Miller and William Williams, pp. 195–206. Minneapolis: University of Minnesota Press, 1982.

———. "Von Wright's Theory of Human Welfare: A Critique." In *The Philosophy of Georg Henrick Von Wright*, edited by P. A. Schilpp and L. E. Hahn, pp. 217–232. La Salle, Ill.: Open Court, 1990.

Seth, James. "Is Pleasure the Summum Bonum?" *International Journal of Ethics* 6 (1896): 409–424.

Sidgwick, Henry. *The Methods of Ethics.* 7th ed. New York: Dover, 1966.

———. *Miscellaneous Essays and Addresses.* London: Macmillan, 1904.

———. *Philosophy, Its Scope and Relations.* London: Macmillan, 1902.

Silber, John. "The Moral Good and the Natural Good in Kant's Ethics." *Review of Metaphysics* 36 (1982): 397–437.

Silbermann, Charles. *The Crisis in Black and White*. New York: Vintage Books, 1964.

Skorupski, John. *John Stuart Mill*. London: Routledge, 1989.

Slote, Michael. *Goods and Virtues*. Oxford: Oxford University Press, 1983.

Smart, J. J. C., and Bernard Williams. *Utilitarianism For and Against*. Cambridge: Cambridge University Press, 1973.

Sobel, David. "Full Information Theories of the Good." *Ethics* 104 (1994): 784–810.

Soble, Alan. *The Structure of Love*. New Haven: Yale University Press, 1990.

Soll, Ivan. "Nietzsche on Cruelty, Asceticism, and the Failure of Hedonism." In *Nietzsche, Genealogy, and Morality*, edited by Richard Schacht, pp. 168–192. Berkeley: University of California Press, 1994.

Spinoza, Benedict. *Ethics*. Translated by William White and Amelia Hutchinson Stirling. New York: Hafner, 1949.

Stalnacker, Robert. "On What's in the Head." *Philosophical Perspectives* 3 (1989): 287–316.

Stern, J. P. *A Study of Nietzsche*. Cambridge: Cambridge University Press, 1979.

Stevenson, Charles L. "The Emotive Meaning of Ethical Terms." In *Readings in Ethical Theory*, edited by John Hospers and Wilfrid Sellars, 2d ed., pp. 254–266. Englewood Cliffs, N.J.: Prentice-Hall, 1970.

———. *Ethics and Language*. New Haven: Yale University Press, 1944.

Sturgeon, Nicholas. "Moral Explanations." In *Essays on Moral Realism*, edited by Geoffrey Sayre-McCord, pp. 229–255. Ithaca, N.Y.: Cornell University Press, 1988.

Taliaferro, Charles. "Relativizing the Ideal Observer Theory." *Philosophy and Phenomenological Research* 49 (1988): 123–138.

Taylor, Charles. *Philosophical Arguments*. Cambridge: Harvard University Press, 1995.

Taylor, Gabriele. "Love." *Proceedings of the Aristotelian Society* 86 (1975–76): 153–54.

Taylor, Paul. "Social Science and Ethical Relativism." In *Ethical Relativism*, edited by John Ladd, pp. 95–107. Belmont, Calif.: Wadsworth, 1973.

Tomas, Vincent. "Ethical Disagreements and the Emotive Theory of Values." *Mind* 60 (1951): 205–222.

Urmson, J. O. *The Emotive Theory of Ethics*. Oxford: Oxford University Press, 1968.

Velleman, J. David. "Brandt's Definition of 'Good'." *Philosophical Review* 97 (1988): 353–372.

———. "Well-Being and Time." *Pacific Philosophical Quarterly* 72 (1991): 48–77.

Von Wright, Georg H. "A Reply to My Critics." In *The Philosophy of Georg Henrick Von Wright*, edited by P. A. Schilpp and L. E. Hahn, pp. 731–887. La Salle, Ill.: Open Court, 1990.

———. *The Varieties of Goodness*. London: Routledge, 1963.

Warnock, G. J. *Contemporary Moral Philosophy*. New York: St. Martin's Press, 1969.

———. *The Object of Morality*. London: Methuen, 1971.

Wellman, Carl. "Emotivism and Ethical Objectivity." In *Readings in Ethical Theory*, edited by John Hospers and Wilfrid Sellars, 2d ed., pp. 276–287. Englewood Cliffs, N.J.: Prentice-Hall, 1970.

West, Henry. "Mill's 'Proof' of Utility." In *The Limits of Utilitarianism*, edited by Harlan Miller and William Williams, pp. 23–34. Minneapolis: University of Minnesota Press, 1982.

Whitehead, Alfred North. *Process and Reality*. New York: Macmillan, 1929.

Whiting, Jennifer. "Aristotle's Function Argument: A Defense." *Ancient Philosophy* 8 (1988).

———. "Human Nature and Intellectualism in Aristotle." *Archive für Geschichte der Philosophie* 68 (1986): 70–95.

Wike, Victoria. *Kant on Happiness*. Albany: SUNY Press, 1994.

Wilcox, John. *Truth and Value in Nietzsche*. Ann Arbor: University of Michigan Press, 1974.

Williams, Bernard. *Ethics and the Limits of Philosophy*. Cambridge: Harvard University Press, 1985.

———. *Morality*. New York: Harper & Row, 1972.

Wright, Crispin. *Realism, Meaning and Truth*. 2d ed. Oxford: Blackwell, 1993.

———. "Realism: The Contemporary Debate—W(h)ither Now?" In *Reality, Representation, and Projection*, edited by J. Haldane and C. Wright, pp. 63–84. Cambridge: Cambridge University Press, 1993.

———. *Truth and Objectivity*. Cambridge: Harvard University Press, 1992.

Zimmerman, Michael. "Evaluatively Incomplete States of Affairs." *Philosophical Studies* 43 (1983): 211–224.

Index

Ackrill, J. L., 289n20
Adams, Robert
    on divine command theory, 241–242,
        246, 248, 288nn13, 14, 306n35
Alston, William, 13
amoralism, 203–204, 297n65
Annas, Julia, 294n27
Anscombe, G. E. M., 285n11
Appiah, A. K., 171
Aristotle, 111, 172
    on contemplation (*theoria*), 137–140
    on function of human beings,
        134–135, 140–144
    on good life (*eudaimonia*), 133–144
    on meaning of "good", 161–162
    on *philia*, 246
    on pleasure, 136
    on virtue (excellence), 135–136
Arrington, Robert, 183, 185
Audi, Robert, 304n8
Averroes, 171
Ayer, A. J., 174–175

Barnes, W. H. F., 296n52
Barry, Brian, 303n5
Bentham, Jeremy, 275n6
Berger, Fred, 270n11

Berkley, George, 182
Blackburn, Simon, 216, 282n27, 292n9,
    301n54, 302n66
Bond, E. J., 83–84
Boyd, Richard, 184–185, 192–194, 300n38
Bradley, F. H., 269n10
Brandt, Richard, 66, 72, 74–75, 160,
    219–220, 269nn4, 5, 270n16,
    280n13, 281n20, 305n26, 308n55
    on cognitive psychotherapy, 222–223
    objections to the desire-satisfaction
        theory, 84–87
    on rationality, 222–223
Brentano, Franz, 56, 62–63, 160–162,
    280n8, 293n24, 296n51, 299n17
Brink, David, 182, 184–185, 192–194,
    203–205, 300n36
Broad, C. D., 173, 190–191, 277n25,
    294n24
Broadie, Sarah, 278n31, 289n24
Brown, Robert, 246
Burge, Tyler, 276n20

Camus, Albert, 278n31
Chisholm, Roderick, 62–63, 157–158,
    291n4, 308n60
Cooper, John, 289n21

323

Parfit, Derek, 74–75, 280n9
Perry, Ralph Barton, 279n6, 280n8,
     281n21, 282n25, 286n43
Pigden, Charles, 287n6
Plato, 38
Platts, Mark, 184, 223, 301n50
     on moral realism, 205–212
pleasure (and pain)
     Aristotle on, 136
     behavioristic (adverbial) theory, 14–15
     felt quality theory, 13–14
     motivational theory, 13–15, 44–45, 61
     Sidgwick's definition of, 26–28
prescriptivism, 177–178
Putnam, Hilary, 56, 66, 182–183, 193,
     276n15

Quine, Willard van Orman, 165
Quinton, Anthony, 269n10

Railton, Peter, 194, 230, 303n5, 305n22
Raphael, D. D., 270n16
rationality, 219–268
     divine-preference theory of, 239–262
     full-information theory of, 220–230
     informed preference theory of,
          230–239
     and ordinary language, 221–222
     and realism, 219–221
Rawls, John, 69, 219–220
realism (metaphysical), 182–183
realism (moral, axiological), 55–56, 152,
     181–214
     British, 205–212
     Cornell, 192–205
     definition of, 183–187
     and desire-satisfaction theory, 66–67,
          82, 84, 92, 94
     and divine purpose, 133, 243, 245
     and meaning of "good," 159–160, 169
     non-naturalist, 187–192
     and rationality, 219–221
realism (scientific), 199–201
relativism, moral axiological

and desire-satisfaction theory, 93–94,
     256–266
     vs. irrationalism, 264–265
Reeve, C. D. C., 288n15
Roche, Timothy, 289n20
Rodzinski, Witold, 273n40
Rosati, Connie, 305n23
     objections to full-information theory
          of rationality/value, 228–229, 231,
          236–238
Ross, W. D., 71, 160, 190–191, 277n28,
     292n8, 308n60
Russell, Bertrand, 160
Ryle, Gilbert, 14–15

Sartre, J. P., 287n1
Sayre-McCord, Geoffrey, 300n40
Schacht, Richard, 284n2
Scheler, Max
     on *ressentiment*, 108, 287n48
Schneewind, Jerome, 273n31, 274n45
Schopenhauer, Arthur, 277n30
Schwatz, Thomas, 280n16
Seth, James, 273n39
Sidgwick, Henry, 172, 275n7, 278n34
     arguments for hedonism, 26–35
     on disagreement, 290n2
     on love, 246
     on meaning of "good," 160
     on pleasure, 26–28
Silbermann, Charles, 299n33
Skorupki, John, 276n21
slavery (moral explanations of), 194–195
Slote, Michael, 61–66, 73, 87
Smart, J. J. C., 57–58, 274n4, 276n12
Socrates, 38
Soll, Ivan, 284n2
Sosa, Ernest, 291n2
Spencer, Herbert, 27
Spinoza, Benedict, 69
Stalnacker, Robert, 276n20
Stern, J. P., 286n46
Stevenson, Charles, 174–175, 300n44
Sturgeon, Nicholas, 192–198